Digital Government Models for Resilient Public Management

Rafael Ignacio Pérez-Uribe
https://orcid.org/0000-0001-9924-6657
Investproject VR, Colombia

Ivan Rodrigo Vargas Ramírez
https://orcid.org/0000-0001-9037-0571
Investproject VR, Colombia

María Teresa Ramírez-Garzón
https://orcid.org/0000-0002-6319-3386
Investproject VR, Colombia

Luz Janeth Lozano-Correa
Santo Tomas University, Colombia

IGI Global
Scientific Publishing
Publishing Tomorrow's Research Today

VP of Publishing Ethics & Research Integrity Melissa Wagner
Director of Acquisitions Mikaela Felty
Director of Book Development Jocelynn Hessler
Production Manager Mike Brehm
Cover Design Jose Rosado

Published in the United States of America by
IGI Global Scientific Publishing
701 East Chocolate Avenue
Hershey, PA, 17033, USA
Tel: 717-533-8845 | Fax: 717-533-7115
Website: https://www.igi-global.com E-mail: cust@igi-global.com

Library of Congress Cataloging-in-Publication Data

Names: Pérez Uribe, Rafael Ignacio editor | Vargas-Ramírez, Ivan Rodrigo, 1984- editor | Ramírez Garzón, María Teresa editor | Lozano-Correa, Luz, 1968- editor
Title: Digital government models for resilient public management / Rafael Ignacio Pérez-Uribe, Ivan Rodrigo Vargas-Ramírez, María Teresa Ramírez-Garzón, Luz Janeth Lozano-Correa.
Description: Hershey : IGI Global Scientific Publishing, 2027. | Includes bibliographical references and index. | Summary: "This book analyzes how governments around the world can anticipate, design, and manage public policies in a context of accelerating change, uncertainty, and global interdependence. It examines the maturity of AI in government and the evolution of cloud and intelligent automation"-- Provided by publisher.
Identifiers: LCCN 2026014707 (print) | LCCN 2026014708 (ebook) | ISBN 9798337397658 hardcover | ISBN 9798337397665 paperback | ISBN 9798337397672 ebook
Subjects: LCSH: Internet in public administration--Law and legislation | Public administration--Data processing--Law and legislation | Artificial intelligence--Law and legislation | Big data--Law and legislation | Sustainable development--Government policy--Law and legislation | LCGFT: Law materials
Classification: LCC K564.C6 D555 2027 (print) | LCC K564.C6 (ebook)
LC record available at https://lccn.loc.gov/2026014707
LC ebook record available at https://lccn.loc.gov/2026014708

British Cataloguing in Publication Data
A Cataloguing in Publication record for this book is available from the British Library.

Editorial Advisory Board

Sandra Bibiana Clavijo Olmos, *EAN University, Colombia*
Selvakumar P., *Nehru Institute of Technology, India*
Varanasi Rahul, *Jain (Deemed to be) University, India*
Rajveer Samuel Rawlin, *Christ (Deemed to be) University, India*
Sapna Sharma, *Thapar Institute of Engineering and Technology, India*
Doni Sugianto Sihotang, *Universitas Negeri Jakarta, Indonesia*
Rubee Singh, *GLA University, India*
Muhammad Usman Tariq, *Abu Dhabi University, India*
Venelin Terziev, *Black Sea Institute, Bulgaria*
Alberto Castro Valencia, *Instituto Tecnológico José Mario Molina Pasquel y Henríquez, Mexico*
Iván Vargas-Ramírez, *Invesproject, Colombia*
Srinivasan Vasan, *Graphic Era University, India*
Amit Verma, *Kalicharan PG College Lucknow, India*
Muhammed Ali Yetgin, *Karabük University, Turkey*
Novy Setia Yunas, *University of Brawijaya, Indonesia*

Table of Contents

Detailed Table of Contents

This chapter examines the governance challenges of platform-based digital states and proposes a Public Value-Centric Platform Governance (PVCPG) framework to enhance resilience and democratic accountability. As governments transition from traditional e-government models to integrated digital ecosystems, risks related to algorithmic opacity, data concentration, and institutional fragility increase. Drawing from digital government studies, public administration theory, and resilience scholarship, this chapter synthesizes interdisciplinary insights to develop a normative governance model. The PVCPG framework consists of three interdependent pillars: Resilience-by-Design Architecture, Stewardship-Oriented Data Governance, and Institutionalized Public Value Feedback Loops. The chapter provides policymakers and public managers with structured principles for designing digital infrastructures that balance innovation, efficiency, accountability, and equity in dynamic and crisis-prone environments.

As states adopt platform-based models of public governance, understanding how institutional capabilities and governance arrangements translate into societal value has become a central concern for public administration research. No quantitative

and provides strategic recommendations for modernizing public management in an uncertain future.

This chapter explores issues in Cambodia's fragmented e-services and proposes frameworks for resilient, trusted digital governance. It argues that resilient public service ecosystems rely on digital government as a governance change framework and filling governance gaps. Using insights from complex systems, digital governance, AI in public administration, and trust, it presents a six-block framework. The chapter also builds a Cambodia-focused framework based on five core capability areas: digital infrastructure and platforms, interoperability and data stewardship, anticipatory capacity, ethical AI governance, and trust-building networks. The five core capability areas are complemented by five primary enablers: leadership, legal frameworks, sustainable financing, digital skills, and standards and interoperability. The policy road map includes these capabilities in five pillars. In the Global South, it provides an ethical, feasible digital governance model that focuses on public value and enhances digital governance.

This chapter analyses how public libraries in Latin America can serve as digital governance infrastructures oriented towards creating public value and resilient public management. The central argument is that the digital transformation of libraries should not be limited to the incorporation of online technologies, platforms, or services, but should be evaluated for its capacity to expand effective access, strengthen citizens' capacities, promote institutional trust, and reduce territorial gaps. The chapter proposes the Digital Governance and Public Value Creation Model for Public Libraries, structured into six dimensions: digital governance, technological infrastructure, digital inclusion, public value, organisational capacities, and territorial

Preface

INTRODUCTION

The digital transformation of the public sector has evolved from a mere technological aspiration into a structural prerequisite for institutional resilience. In a world defined by uncertainty, complexity, and rapid change, governments face the challenge of maintaining their operational capacity while simultaneously reconfiguring their management models, information systems, and modes of engagement with citizens. This book, *"Digital Government Models for Resilient Public Management"*, emerges precisely at this pivotal juncture—where technological innovation meets governance, and where evidence-based insights form the foundation for smarter, more inclusive, and sustainable public policy decisions.

This work proposes a conceptual and operational framework for understanding how digital government models can bolster institutional resilience—not only in the face of external crises (such as health, economic, climate, or social emergencies) but also against internal pressures like organizational fragmentation, technological obsolescence, talent turnover, and the rising demand for quality public services. Adopting a multidimensional approach, the book integrates elements of strategy, data, interoperability, artificial intelligence, organizational design, and knowledge management, offering a systemic perspective that transcends the traditional, purely instrumental view of digitalization.

This research-based book is addressed to those who lead, study, or support transformation processes within the public sector: executives, policymakers, academics, consultants, researchers, and professionals committed to building more adaptive institutions. Its purpose is twofold: to provide rigorous, actionable models that guide decision-making in real-world contexts, and to foster critical reflection on the role of digital government in building societies that are more equitable, transparent, and resilient.

Within these pages, readers will find not only concepts and analytical frameworks but also an invitation to rethink public management through the lens of resilience—defined as the capacity to anticipate, absorb, adapt, and transform. For true digital transformation lies not in the mere adoption of technology, but in redesigning the very ways in which institutions learn, collaborate, and create public and private values. May this book contribute to strengthening the global conversation on the future of digital government and to inspiring those who work every day to build institutions that are more robust, humane, and prepared for the challenges of the 21st century.

ORGANIZATION OF THE BOOK

Chapter 1: Platform Governance and Data-Driven Public Value: Architecting Digital States for Resilience

This chapter examines the governance challenges of platform-based digital states and proposes a Public Value-Centric Platform Governance (PVCPG) framework to enhance resilience and democratic accountability. As governments transition from traditional e-government models to integrated digital ecosystems, risks related to algorithmic opacity, data concentration, and institutional fragility increase. Drawing from digital government studies, public administration theory, and resilience scholarship, this chapter synthesizes interdisciplinary insights to develop a normative governance model. The PVCPG framework consists of three interdependent pillars: Resilience-by-Design Architecture, Stewardship-Oriented Data Governance, and Institutionalized Public Value Feedback Loops. The chapter provides policymakers and public managers with structured principles for designing digital infrastructures that balance innovation, efficiency, accountability, and equity in dynamic and crisis-prone environments.

Chapter 2: Creating Digital Public Value in Platform States; The Influence of Public Digital Capability, Data Governance, and Platform Governance

As states adopt platform-based models of public governance, understanding how institutional capabilities and governance arrangements translate into societal value has become a central concern for public administration research. No quantitative model had jointly tested how public digital capability, data governance, and platform governance interact to shape digital platform use and digital public value creation in emerging economies such as Morocco. This chapter develops and empirically validates an integrative tripartite structural model grounded in Public Value Theory,

New Public Management, and Sociotechnical Theory, using PLS-SEM on a sample of 350 Moroccan public employees, civil servants, and citizens. All seven hypotheses were confirmed at p < 0.001: public digital capability and platform governance emerged as the strongest direct determinants of platform use, which fully mediates digital public value creation. The chapter offers theoretical and managerial insights for decision-makers engaged in digital transformation in emerging platform states.

Chapter 3: Algorithmic Public Management for Democratic Resilience-AI-Driven Futures in Government Decision-Making

As societies become more divided, misinformation, complex governance, and a lack of public trust in governance increase. Technology that applies AI in governance has both positive and negative aspects. This chapter examines how algorithmic technology can strengthen democracy by enhancing the forecasting of policies, allocation of resources, management of crises, and public engagement. It examines new approaches in countries such as Estonia and Singapore, where digital public management technology has large and positive innovations. However, it also examines critical issues such as bias in algorithms, lack of transparency, lack of accountability, and threats to people's freedoms. It proposes a set of guidelines for applying AI in public management responsibly, with democratic control, explainability, and public engagement in designing the technology. Ultimately, applying AI in governance should increase trust in governance institutions while safeguarding basic freedoms to ensure a bright future for democracy.

Chapter 4: Behavioural Game Theory in Managerial Decision-Making: Why Real Executives Deviate from Nash Equilibrium

The chapter presents a systematic review of the literature on behavioural game theory to investigate the reasons for managers making decisions that are often at variance with those predicted by the Nash equilibrium. The classical game theory builds upon assumptions that players are fully rational, have complete information and definite preferences. Behavioural game theory combines the psychological and the behavioural aspects of these models, thereby dropping the requirement of perfect rationality. The review shows that managers are constrained by bounded rationality, limited information processing and time pressure, and are constrained to rely on heuristics and intuitive judgment instead of equilibrium-based optimization. The aim of this chapter is not to use Nash equilibrium to predict executive behaviour, but to focus on it as a theoretical benchmark, and to highlight the value of integrating behaviour into strategic theory and practice.

Chapter 5: Anticipatory Governance in the Digital Age: Building Resilient Public Institutions for Uncertain Futures

This chapter examines the emerging concept of anticipatory governance as a transformative approach to public management in the digital age. As governments face increasing uncertainty driven by technological disruption, climate risks, global health crises, and geopolitical instability, traditional reactive governance models are proving insufficient. The chapter explores how anticipatory governance integrates strategic foresight, digital intelligence, resilience theory, and public value principles to strengthen the capacity of public institutions to anticipate and manage complex future challenges. It proposes a Digital Anticipatory Governance Framework (DAGF) that combines foresight infrastructure, data-driven intelligence systems, adaptive policy mechanisms, collaborative governance networks, and ethical safeguards. The chapter also discusses global practices, institutional implications, and the risks associated with algorithmic governance and digital divides.

Chapter 6: Anticipatory Governance Strategic Foresight and Government Preparedness for Emerging Risks: A Forward-Looking Analytical Framework for Managing Uncertainty and Complexity

This chapter analyses anticipatory governance as a public policy approach to strengthen state capacity in addressing emerging risks under conditions of high uncertainty. Drawing on a theoretical, comparative, and applied review, it examines how strategic foresight can be systematically integrated into the policy cycle, including formulation, implementation, and evaluation. The analysis identifies institutional mechanisms aimed at reducing systemic vulnerabilities in key domains such as public health, cybersecurity, energy transition, and artificial intelligence. It argues that effective anticipation depends less on precise forecasting and more on adaptive decision-making architectures, inter-institutional coordination, and continuous learning processes. The chapter also compares international experiences from Finland, Singapore, United Kingdom, the European Union, and the United States to extract lessons on analytical capacity, political leadership, regulatory quality, and democratic legitimacy.

Chapter 7: Digital Financial Inclusion as Anticipatory Governance: Public Value, Resilience, and Equity

Governments now rely on digital finance to deliver welfare, raise revenue, and move money at a speed and scale beyond the reach of older administrative systems.

This chapter treats such systems as a mode of anticipatory governance rather than as technical plumbing. By allowing states to act earlier, faster, and across whole populations, they redistribute risk, alter who becomes visible to the state, and determine who is left out. Drawing together public value theory, scholarship on anticipatory and robust governance, and critical work on datafication, the chapter assembles an integrated lens that reads digital financial infrastructure as a governance choice rather than a neutral upgrade. That lens is then tested against four well-documented cases: Brazil's Pix, Kenya's M-Pesa, India's Aadhaar-enabled benefit transfers and Unified Payments Interface, and Nigeria's 2023 currency redesign. Considered together, the cases demonstrate that one class of technology can either generate or erode public value, according to how authentication, redress, and accountability are designed.

Chapter 8: Digital Transformation and Social Policy Effectiveness in Digital Government: Institutional Perspectives from Bulgaria

This chapter examines digital government's role in enhancing social policy effectiveness by focusing on Bulgaria's social assistance system. Integrating theoretical and empirical analysis, the study explores how technologies like artificial intelligence, big data, and blockchain improve governance and service delivery. Using a systemic approach, the research demonstrates that digital transformation strengthens coordination and accessibility to foster resilient and inclusive welfare systems. Despite progress, the digital divide and limited administrative capacity remain barriers. The study conceptualizes social effectiveness within digital welfare and provides strategic recommendations for modernizing public management in an uncertain future.

Chapter 9: From E-Services to Anticipatory Governance: Cambodia's Digital Government Pathways for Resilient, Trustworthy, and AI-Enabled Public Management

This chapter explores issues in Cambodia's fragmented e-services and proposes frameworks for resilient, trusted digital governance. It argues that resilient public service ecosystems rely on digital government as a governance change framework and filling governance gaps. Using insights from complex systems, digital governance, AI in public administration, and trust, it presents a six-block framework. The chapter also builds a Cambodia-focused framework based on five core capability areas: digital infrastructure and platforms, interoperability and data stewardship, anticipatory capacity, ethical AI governance, and trust-building networks. The five core capability areas are complemented by five primary enablers: leadership, legal frameworks, sustainable financing, digital skills, and standards and interoperability. The policy road map includes these capabilities in five pillars. In the Global South, it provides an ethical, feasible digital governance model that focuses on public value and enhances digital governance.

Chapter 10: Digital Governance in Latin American Public Libraries Public Value and Resilient Management

This chapter analyses how public libraries in Latin America can serve as digital governance infrastructures oriented towards creating public value and resilient public management. The central argument is that the digital transformation of libraries should not be limited to the incorporation of online technologies, platforms, or services, but should be evaluated for its capacity to expand effective access, strengthen citizens' capacities, promote institutional trust, and reduce territorial gaps. The chapter proposes the Digital Governance and Public Value Creation Model for Public Libraries, structured into six dimensions: digital governance, technological infrastructure, digital inclusion, public value, organisational capacities, and territorial resilience. The model shows how libraries can mediate between the digital state and citizens through access, training, guidance, participation and territorial adaptation.

IN CONCLUSION

Ultimately, the discussion converges on a fundamental idea: digital transformation is now a structural requirement for national governments and private organizations to navigate contemporary complexity and sustain their capacity for action. It is not merely a matter of adopting technologies, but of redesigning management models to strengthen institutional resilience in both the public and private sectors. The book proposes a systemic vision in which digitalization, interoperability, data, and artificial intelligence are integrated with strategy, governance, and organizational learning. Ultimately, the work invites us to rethink digital government to build public and private institutions that are more adaptive, transparent, and capable of generating sustainable value amidst rapid change.

Rafael Ignacio Pérez-Uribe
Investproject VR, Colombia

Ivan Rodrigo Vargas-Ramírez
Investproject VR, Colombia

María Teresa Ramírez-Garzón

Investproject VR, Colombia

Luz Janeth Lozano-Correa
Santo Tomas University, Colombia

Acknowledgment

First, as an act of humility and contrition, we would like first to express our sentiment of gratitude to the Creator. We are truly grateful for yet another opportunity to learn, to write, to evaluate, to revise and to share and disseminate knowledge. In this case, about Digital Government Models for Resilient Public Management.

Secondly, it is our honour and our privilege to share "the stage" with colleagues from different countries and cultures. It will always be an enrichening experience to read and evaluate their works.

A very loud and special THANK YOU for our panel of peer reviewers, who so selflessly have taken time out of their busy schedules to revise every chapter of this book. They are the cornerstone of this project and without their invaluable collaboration this book would have never seen the light of day.

Last, but not least, we strongly hope this book will contribute to the academic and organizational world to develop different types of approaches, methodologies, strategies, and management techniques to face the phenomenon of "Digital Government Models for Resilient Public Management" from different points of view and different contexts.

Chapter 1

Platform Governance and Data-Driven Public Value:
Architecting Digital States for Resilience

Anang Sugeng Cahyono
http://orcid.org/0000-0003-0355-9419
Universitas Tulungagung, Indonesia

ABSTRACT

This chapter examines the governance challenges of platform-based digital states and proposes a Public Value-Centric Platform Governance (PVCPG) framework to enhance resilience and democratic accountability. As governments transition from traditional e-government models to integrated digital ecosystems, risks related to algorithmic opacity, data concentration, and institutional fragility increase. Drawing from digital government studies, public administration theory, and resilience scholarship, this chapter synthesizes interdisciplinary insights to develop a normative governance model. The PVCPG framework consists of three interdependent pillars: Resilience-by-Design Architecture, Stewardship-Oriented Data Governance, and Institutionalized Public Value Feedback Loops. The chapter provides policymakers and public managers with structured principles for designing digital infrastructures that balance innovation, efficiency, accountability, and equity in dynamic and crisis-prone environments.

INTRODUCTION

The digital transformation of government signifies a major paradigm shift in public administration since the New Public Management reforms of the late 20th

DOI: 10.4018/979-8-3373-9765-8.ch001

century (Jovanovic et al., 2021; Yabe et al., 2022). What commenced as isolated e-government initiatives digitizing current services and forms has progressed into a significant transformation: the advent of the Digital State (Nagaraj, 2024; Rozgonyi, 2023). This new paradigm conceptualizes government not solely as a service provider with digital interfaces, but as an integrated, platform-based ecosystem where data functions as a strategic public asset, decisions are progressively guided by algorithms, and citizen-state interactions are redefined as ongoing, personalized engagements (Esposito & Tufo, 2024; Han & Xie, 2025).

The COVID-19 pandemic acted as a significant evaluation of global digital government infrastructures, exposing both their capabilities and vulnerabilities (Lu et al., 2023; Van Der Heide, 2025). Countries with developed digital ecosystems could swiftly implement contact-tracing applications, digital vaccine passports, and emergency aid distribution systems (Anubi & Konstantinou, 2020; Cristofari & Gerbaudo, 2025). Nonetheless, these systems revealed considerable vulnerabilities: algorithmic biases that marginalized certain populations, centralized data repositories that attracted cyber-attacks, and opaque decision-making processes that undermined public trust (Dincă et al., 2025; Mersico et al., 2025). This experience elucidates the primary thesis of this chapter: In the age of the Digital State, resilience in public management is inherently connected to the structure and governance of its essential digital platforms (Kud, 2021; Wang et al., 2025a).

Resilience must be integrated into the socio-technical framework of the state, rather than being viewed merely as strong physical infrastructure or bureaucratic contingency plans (Buttow & Weerts, 2022; Luna et al., 2015). This chapter explores a critical inquiry for scholars and practitioners in public administration: How can we deliberately design and govern state-level digital platforms to ensure they are intrinsically resilient to shocks and crises while being constitutionally aimed at producing equitable, democratic public value? The objective of this chapter is to transcend techno-utopian narratives and critical dystopian perspectives by proposing a constructive and principled framework for action. This objective is grounded in prior discussions on platform governance and public value in digital transformation contexts (Vestues et al., 2021).

This chapter articulates the Public Value-Centric Platform Governance (PVCPG) Framework, contending that realizing the dual aims of resilience and public value necessitates a conscious transition from perceiving platforms as mere Information Technology (IT) projects to recognizing them as fundamental institutions of contemporary governance. This perspective builds upon prior discussions in the literature that emphasize the evolving role of digital platforms and public value in governance contexts (Buyannemekh et al., 2024; Egala et al., 2025). It further aligns with arguments highlighting the need to integrate technical capabilities with public ethics in digital transformation (McCarthy et al., 2023). Accordingly, this framework offers a guide for policymakers, chief information officers, and public managers engaged in the design or oversight of significant digital public infrastructure initiatives, extending prior governance approaches (Calzati & Van Loenen, 2023).

BACKGROUND

The Evolution of Digital Government: From E-Government to Platform-Based Governance

The evolution of digital government has traversed multiple distinct phases, each signifying a fundamental transformation in the comprehension and application of technology within the public sector (Hein et al., 2019; Korotun & Veretin, 2025). The preliminary stage, commonly referred to as e-government, concentrated mainly on the digital transformation of existing governmental services and procedures (Tang et al., 2025; Y. Wang et al., 2024). This methodology regarded technology as a means to automate administrative functions and enhance operational efficiency, with success evaluated through metrics like transaction completion rates and cost-per-transaction savings (Davies et al., 2023; Nicoli & Paltrinieri, 2019).

The subsequent phase, transformational government, acknowledged that technology could facilitate significant alterations in governmental operations and citizen interactions (Sukma & Yamnill, 2025). This phase highlighted service integration, citizen-focused design, and organizational reconfiguration to utilize digital capabilities (Dmitrieva et al., 2022). The transformational approach transcended simple automation to examine how digital technologies could redefine the relationship between the state and its citizens, promoting enhanced transparency and participation (Lewerenz et al., 2025; Walravens & Ballon, 2013).

The present phase, referred to in this chapter as platform-based governance or the Digital State, signifies a substantial advancement in both aspiration and intricacy (Profiroiu et al., 2023). This paradigm is inspired by the platform ecosystems that have revolutionized the private sector, exemplified by Amazon, Google, and Airbnb. In the public sector, platform-based governance entails the establishment of integrated digital ecosystems that facilitate interaction, value exchange, and co-creation of services among various stakeholders, including government agencies, citizens, businesses, and civil society organizations (Andreoni & Roberts, 2022). This approach redefines the essential structure of government instead of simply digitizing current services.

Platform Governance: Theoretical Foundations and Public Sector Implications

The notion of platform governance arises from the examination of digital platforms in the private sector, denoting the regulations, technical standards, and institutional frameworks that influence interactions within platform ecosystems (Chowdhury, 2022). Platform governance includes the technical framework that facilitates specific behaviors while limiting others, as well as the formal and informal regulations that oversee participation, data sharing, and value allocation.

In the public sector, platform governance exhibits unique characteristics and requirements. In contrast to commercial platforms that focus on maximizing shareholder value or market supremacy, public platforms must reconcile various, occasionally conflicting, objectives: efficiency and equity, innovation and stability, transparency and privacy, agility and accountability (Wang et al., 2025b). The administration of public platforms must consequently integrate democratic oversight, public accountability measures, and safeguards for fundamental rights that are less emphasized in commercial environments.

Recent academic research has started to investigate the elements that define public value in digital governance. Expanding upon Mark Moore's (1995) seminal research, modern scholars contend that digital government initiatives ought to be assessed not solely on technical efficacy or financial savings, but also on their impact on wider societal outcomes: promoting democratic engagement, mitigating inequality, cultivating public trust, and enhancing social cohesion (Sadhu, 2025). This broadened understanding of public value necessitates novel metrics and evaluative frameworks capable of encompassing the multifaceted effects of digital platforms.

Resilience Theory and its Application to Digital Governance

Resilience has become a pivotal concept in various fields, including ecology, engineering, organizational studies, and public administration. Resilience, in its most comprehensive definition, denotes the ability of a system to endure shocks and stresses while preserving its fundamental functions, structures, and identity (MacArthur et al., 2022). Advanced concepts like adaptive resilience and antifragility highlight the capacity not only to recover from disruptions but also to learn, adapt, and enhance in response to challenges (Kausche & Weiss, 2024).

In the context of digital governance, resilience assumes distinct dimensions. Technical resilience denotes the ability of digital systems to maintain functionality in the face of hardware malfunctions, software errors, cyber intrusions, or increased demand. Organizational resilience refers to the capacity of government agencies to sustain service delivery and decision-making functions amid crises. Democratic resilience involves safeguarding fundamental rights and democratic processes in digital contexts, especially during emergencies when extraordinary measures may be enacted (Ooijen et al., 2019).

The COVID-19 pandemic underscored the significance of resilience in digital governance, exposing both strengths and weaknesses. Countries possessing advanced digital infrastructures exhibited enhanced technical and organizational resilience, facilitating remote work, digital service provision, and data-informed decision-making. The pandemic revealed substantial challenges to democratic resilience, such as the swift implementation of surveillance technologies lacking proper oversight, algorithmic systems that intensified pre-existing inequalities, and digital divides that marginalized vulnerable populations from critical services. (Calzati & Van Loenen, 2025).

The Data Governance Imperative in Digital States

Data has become the fundamental resource of the Digital State, facilitating predictive analytics, personalized services, evidence-based policymaking, and algorithmic decision-making. The governance of resource data has thus emerged as a significant issue for public administrators and policymakers (Chen et al., 2021).

Conventional methods of data governance in the public sector have frequently prioritized control, security, and compliance. Although these factors are significant, modern challenges necessitate a more sophisticated strategy that reconciles various priorities: promoting innovation while safeguarding privacy, facilitating data sharing while maintaining security, and utilizing data for public advantage while mitigating harm (Lee et al., 2024). The balancing act is especially intricate in federated systems, where data must traverse jurisdictional boundaries while adhering to various legal frameworks and cultural norms.

Innovative concepts like data stewardship provide a promising framework for governance of public sector data. In contrast to ownership models that emphasize control and asset models that prioritize economic value extraction, stewardship highlights responsibility, care, and fiduciary duty (Idzi & Gomes, 2022). In this framework, the state functions not as an owner of citizen data, but as a steward responsible for managing this resource for the public benefit. This change in viewpoint significantly affects the design and implementation of data governance frameworks.

MAIN FOCUS OF THE CHAPTER

Methodology

This chapter utilizes a qualitative, conceptual research design that emphasizes theory synthesis and the development of normative frameworks. The methodology comprises three interrelated phases, each intended to enhance the insights derived from the preceding phase while ensuring analytical precision and practical applicability.

Phase One: Systematic Literature Synthesis

The initial phase entails a thorough and methodical examination of academic literature across four principal domains pertinent to the research inquiries:

1. Digital Government and E-Governance Literature: This review examines evolutionary models of digital governance, critical analyses of phantomization in the public sector, and empirical investigations into the results of digital transformation initiatives. Special emphasis is placed on literature analysing the governance challenges unique to public sector platforms.
2. Platform Studies and Digital Infrastructure Literature: This review, informed by platform studies, analyses the technical architectures, business models, and governance mechanisms of digital platforms, particularly focusing on their application in public sector contexts.
3. Public Administration and Public Value Theory: This component integrates foundational and contemporary research on public value creation, focusing on the impact of digital technologies on the processes and outcomes of public value generation.
4. Resilience Theory Across Disciplines: This review encompasses literature from ecology, engineering, organizational studies, and public administration to cultivate a comprehensive understanding of resilience relevant to digital governance contexts.

    The synthesis process utilized a thematic analysis method, identifying convergent themes, theoretical deficiencies, and foundational principles that guide the development of the PVCPG framework. This phase encompassed roughly 200 peer-reviewed articles, books, and policy documents published from 1995 to 2023, chosen for their pertinence to the primary research questions and their impact within their respective domains.

Phase Two: Critical Comparative Case Analysis

The second phase entails a critical examination of chosen international case studies and cautionary examples to anchor theoretical arguments in empirical reality. Cases were chosen based on their pertinence to particular facets of platform governance, geographic diversity, and the accessibility of high-quality documentation in English. The examination centres on:

1. Estonia's Digital Resilience Ecosystem: Analysing the technical framework of the X-Road data exchange layer, the oversight of the data embassy initiative, and the organizational structures that facilitate digital continuity amid disruptions.
2. Denmark's Interoperability Governance: Examining the compulsory interoperability standards, the administration of the digital identity system (MitID), and the institutional frameworks for inter-agency collaboration in digital service provision.
3. Singapore's Smart Nation Initiative: Examining the comprehensive governance framework, the equilibrium between innovation and regulation in AI implementation, and the methods for public participation in digital strategy formulation.
4. Comparative Lessons from Implementation Challenges: Analysing instances where digital government initiatives faced substantial challenges, including algorithmic bias in welfare fraud detection systems and deficiencies in integrated crisis response platforms.

The case analysis aims not to deliver exhaustive case studies, but to employ empirical examples that demonstrate the practical ramifications, achievements, and shortcomings of various governance options. This method facilitates the creation of a framework that is both theoretically robust and empirically substantiated.

Phase Three: Normative Framework Development

The third phase, informed by the insights from Phases One and Two, entails the development of the Public Value-Centric Platform Governance (PVCPG) Framework. This is a prescriptive, normative framework designed for policymakers, chief information officers, and public managers engaged in digital transformation initiatives.

The framework development process employs an iterative design methodology, wherein each component is evaluated for theoretical consistency and practical viability. The framework synthesizes insights from various disciplines while concentrating on the distinct challenges and necessities of public sector platform governance. The outcome is a systematic model featuring distinct pillars, principles, and suggested governance tools that respond to the primary research inquiries while offering practical guidance for practitioners.

The Public Value-Centric Platform Governance (PVCPG) framework

This chapter's primary contribution is the formulation and detailed explanation of the PVCPG Framework. This integrative model asserts that resilient Digital States must be established on three interdependent, mutually reinforcing pillars, each addressing distinct yet interconnected aspects of platform governance.

Pillar One: Resilience-by-Design Architecture

The first pillar pertains to the technical and structural underpinnings of digital platforms, contending that resilience must not be an afterthought or supplementary feature; it must be inherently integrated from the initial design phase through intentional architectural decisions.

Technical Architecture Principles

1. Interoperability Through Open Standards: Platform architectures must emphasize interoperability by adopting open technical standards and application programming interfaces (APIs). This strategy mitigates vendor lock-in, fosters ecosystem expansion via third-party innovation, and allows for seamless degradation during partial system failures. The European Union's "Once-Only" principle requires that citizens and businesses submit standard information to public administrations only once, illustrating this approach on a large scale (Zhalgas, 2025).
2. Modularity and Loose Coupling: Platform components must be constructed as distinct modules with clearly defined interfaces, allowing for the updating, replacement, or removal of individual components without resulting in systemic failure. This architectural pattern, commonly referred to as "loose coupling," improves adaptability and mitigates systemic risk. Estonia's X-Road system exemplifies this methodology, featuring independent data services that can be integrated into intricate workflows while preserving separation of concerns (Janssen et al., 2017).
3. Federated or Decentralized Architectures: Instead of establishing monolithic, centralized data repositories, resilient platforms should prefer federated or decentralized architectures that allow data to remain under the control of originating agencies or individuals. This method mitigates the "honey pot" phenomenon that renders centralized systems appealing targets for cyber-attacks, while con-

currently adhering to the principles of data minimization and purpose limitation outlined in contemporary privacy frameworks such as the GDPR.

4. Security and Privacy by Design: Security and privacy safeguards must be integrated as fundamental design principles rather than incorporated as ancillary features. This encompasses principles such as data minimization, end-to-end encryption for sensitive data transmissions, and the adoption of zero-trust architectures that authenticate each request as if it originates from an unsecured network.

Governance Principles for Technical Architecture

1. Public Oversight of Critical Digital Infrastructure: The administration of public digital platforms must incorporate mechanisms for democratic oversight, especially for systems that influence or determine decisions impacting citizen rights or resource distribution. This may encompass legislative examination of algorithmic systems, mandates for independent audits, and obligations for transparency concerning system functionalities and constraints.
2. Strategic Vendor Management: To mitigate detrimental dependencies on individual vendors, platform governance must incorporate strategies for managing vendor relationships, including stipulations for software escrow agreements (where source code is held in trust), right-to-audit provisions, and competitive procurement procedures for significant system components.
3. Public Sector Digital Capability: Ensuring sufficient digital competence within the public sector is crucial for the effective management of digital platforms. This encompasses technical proficiency to function as an informed client in procurement activities, architectural supervision to guarantee conformity with public values, and operational capability to sustain systems during vendor transitions or market exits.

Table 1. Resilience-by-Design Architecture Principles and Implementation Mechanisms

Principle	Technical Implementation	Governance Mechanism
Interoperability	Open APIs, Standard Data Formats	Mandatory Interoperability Standards, Compliance Certification
Modularity	Microservices Architecture, Containerization	Component Independence Requirements, Interface Specifications
Decentralization	Federated Identity, Distributed Ledgers	Data Sovereignty Policies, Cross-Jurisdictional Agreements
Security & Privacy	Encryption, Zero-Trust Architecture	Security-by-Design Mandates, Privacy Impact Assessments

Source: Developed by the authors based on literature synthesis

Pillar Two: Stewardship-Oriented Data Governance

The second pillar redefines the state's engagement with data, advocating a transition from viewing data as a "state-owned asset" or "economic commodity" to perceiving it as a "common-pool resource managed for the public good." This conceptual transformation significantly affects the design and implementation of data governance frameworks.

Operationalizing Data Stewardship

1. Sectoral Data Trusts: Data trusts are proposed as institutional arrangements, inspired by legal trust structures in other domains, wherein independent trustees manage data with fiduciary obligations to act in the best interests of specified beneficiary communities. In the public sector, sectoral data trusts could oversee sensitive information in domains such as healthcare, education, or social services, ensuring that data utilization aligns with public interest goals while safeguarding individual rights. The Open Data Institute in the UK has developed data trust prototypes that may guide public sector applications (Törnberg, 2023).
2. Mandatory Algorithmic Impact Assessments: Analogous to environmental impact assessments for significant projects, algorithmic impact assessments (AIAs) would be mandated prior to the implementation of algorithmic decision-making systems in the public sector. These evaluations would assess potential effects on equity, privacy, transparency, and democratic accountability, with public disclosure of results for systems that substantially influence citizen rights. The Government of Canada's Directive on Automated Decision-Making exemplifies this innovative approach (Dunleavy & Margetts, 2023).

3. Public Transparency Registers: To mitigate opacity in public sector data practices, transparency registers would record the data collected, the algorithms employed, the purposes served, and the governance safeguards implemented. These registers would function as public accountability instruments, facilitating scrutiny by civil society, researchers, and impacted communities. The European Union's proposed Artificial Intelligence Act incorporates aspects of this methodology by mandating stipulations for high-risk AI systems within the public sector (Valle-Cruz & García-Contreras, 2023).
4. Independent Ethical Review Boards: In sensitive public sector applications of data and algorithms, such as predictive policing, social benefit eligibility assessments, or risk evaluations in child protective services, independent ethical review boards could offer oversight akin to that of institutional review boards in human subject's research. These boards would assess proposals based on ethical frameworks that weigh potential benefits against risks to rights and values.

Balancing Innovation and Protection

The stewardship model explicitly acknowledges and aims to reconcile two occasionally conflicting imperatives: promoting innovation via data utilization and safeguarding fundamental rights through data governance. This equilibrium is attained not via a uniform strategy, but through tailored governance predicated on:

1. Risk-Based Tiers: Distinguishing governance requirements according to data sensitivity and the potential consequences of its utilization, imposing more rigorous standards for high-risk applications.
2. Purpose-Based Limitations: Limiting data utilization to designated purposes with explicit justifications for public benefit, instead of permitting unrestricted repurposing.
3. Proportionality Assessments: Mandating that data collection and utilization be commensurate with the public benefit pursued, favouring less intrusive methods whenever feasible.

The stewardship-oriented data governance model is illustrated in Figure 1, which depicts Public Stewardship as the central normative anchor surrounded by four interdependent governance mechanisms: Data Trusts, Impact Assessments, Transparency Registers, and Ethical Review Boards.

Figure 1. Stewardship-oriented data governance framework

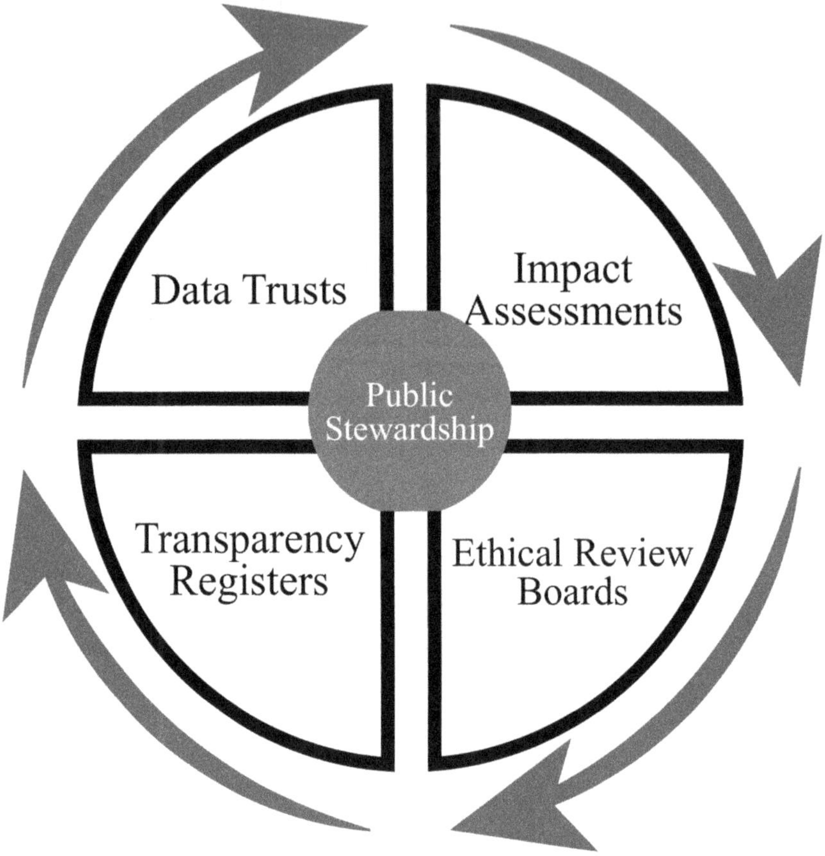

Source: Developed by the authors based on literature synthesis

Pillar Three: Institutionalized Public Value Feedback Loops

The third pillar guarantees that digital platforms stay true to their fundamental objective: the generation of public value. It emphasizes the establishment of formal mechanisms for democratic engagement, value assessment, and adaptive learning, which are incorporated into the continuous operations of digital platforms.

Mechanisms for Co-Creation and Continuous Alignment

1. Participatory Design Processes: Instead of relying solely on technical or bureaucratic processes for platform design, resilient digital governance employs participatory design methods that involve a variety of stakeholders, including

citizens, civil society organizations, frontline workers, and impacted communities throughout the design and development lifecycle. This approach acknowledges that individuals impacted by systems should participate in their design, especially for platforms that facilitate access to public services or resources. Techniques like citizen assemblies, design charrettes, and participatory budgeting for digital initiatives can formalize this input.

2. Real-Time Public Value Dashboards: Advancing beyond conventional performance metrics cantered on efficiency and uptime, public value dashboards would monitor multidimensional outcomes associated with the creation of public value. These may encompass:
    1. Equity Metrics: Distribution of benefits across demographic groups, accessibility for persons with disabilities, reduction of digital divides
    2. Trust Metrics: Citizen confidence in digital systems, perceptions of fairness and transparency
    3. Democratic Metrics: Opportunities for participation through digital channels, transparency of algorithmic decision-making
    4. Sustainability Metrics: Environmental impacts of digital systems, alignment with sustainable development goals
3. Adaptive Governance Processes: The PVCPG Framework acknowledges the evolution of public values and the unintended consequences of digital systems by integrating mechanisms for ongoing adaptation. This encompasses routine evaluation periods wherein platform performance metrics guide policy and design modifications, termination clauses for systems that do not exhibit public benefit, and experimental governance strategies that facilitate secure testing of innovations with suitable protections.

The Feedback Loop Architecture

The institutionalization of public value feedback functions through an ongoing cycle of assessment, contemplation, and modification:

1. Value Articulation: Democratic processes (both representative and participatory) define what constitutes public value in specific contexts.
2. Value Encoding: These value definitions are translated into technical requirements and performance metrics embedded in platform design.
3. Value Measurement: Platforms generate data on their performance against these value-based metrics.
4. Value Reflection: This performance data informs public deliberation and decision-making about platform governance.
5. Value Adaptation: Governance decisions lead to adjustments in platform design or operation.

This feedback loop establishes a "cybernetic" framework for platform governance, wherein the system's functions yield the necessary data for its own development, directed by democratically established value priorities.

Applying the PVCPG Framework: Comparative Case Analysis

This section utilizes the three pillars of the PVCPG Framework to analyse specific international instances of digital government innovation.

Estonia Through the PVCPG Lens

The digital governance framework of Estonia presents a notable example for analysing resilience-by-design architecture. The X-Road data exchange layer of the country exemplifies multiple principles from Pillar One: its decentralized architecture (data is retained by service providers instead of being centralized), its interoperability via standardized APIs, and its security-by-design methodology, which includes end-to-end encryption. Estonia's data embassy initiative creating secure data backups in allied nations embodies a novel strategy for continuity planning that adheres to resilience principles.

Nonetheless, implementing the complete PVCPG Framework uncovers opportunities for improvement. Although Estonia demonstrates exceptional technical resilience and efficiency, concerns have emerged regarding the extent to which its systems effectively integrate the stewardship principles of Pillar Two, especially in relation to algorithmic transparency and the ethical governance of emerging technologies such as artificial intelligence. Likewise, although Estonia has established digital participation channels, enhancing the public value feedback loops outlined in Pillar Three could fortify the democratic aspects of its digital ecosystem.

Denmark's Interoperability Governance

Denmark's strategy for digital governance prioritizes compulsory interoperability standards and a comprehensive governmental framework. This closely corresponds with Pillar One's focus on interoperability and modularity. The Danish Basic Data Program, which creates authoritative registers for essential reference data (individuals, corporations, addresses, etc.), exemplifies a governance strategy that harmonizes efficiency with oversight.

Viewed through the PVCPG framework, Denmark's model exhibits strengths in establishing cohesive architectural governance; however, it could enhance its approach by placing greater emphasis on the stewardship principles of Pillar Two, especially concerning data usage restrictions and algorithmic accountability. The

Danish Model for Responsible AI in the Public Sector signifies progress, yet its application across all agencies is still ongoing.

Singapore's Smart Nation Initiative

Singapore exemplifies comprehensive digital governance characterized by robust central coordination. The nation's focus on digital inclusion and skills enhancement corresponds with the creation of public value, while its regulatory sandbox methodology for innovation reconciles experimentation with supervision. The Personal Data Protection Act of Singapore encompasses provisions that surpass those of numerous other jurisdictions in acknowledging data stewardship principles.

Utilizing the PVCPG Framework, Singapore's strategy exhibits strengths in synchronized execution and innovative governance. Nonetheless, inquiries persist regarding the implementation of Pillar Three's participatory design principles within a political framework characterized by constrained competitive democracy. The framework indicates that, even in these contexts, mechanisms for public value feedback and adaptive governance can be established, albeit in different institutional forms compared to more pluralistic systems.

Addressing Implementation Challenges and Trade-Offs

The execution of the PVCPG framework encounters numerous substantial challenges that require recognition and resolution.

Technical and Organizational Complexity

Executing resilience-by-design architecture necessitates technical proficiency and organizational maturity, which may be deficient in numerous public sector environments. This challenge can be mitigated through incremental implementation, capacity-building initiatives, and strategic collaborations with academic institutions and ethical technology providers.

Democratic Trade-Offs

Certain principles of the framework may seem to contradict conventional democratic values or procedures. Participatory design processes may impede decision-making, whereas transparency mandates may hinder international data sharing for security reasons. These trade-offs necessitate meticulous consideration and context-dependent equilibrium rather than universal mandates.

Resource Constraints

Numerous public agencies, especially in developing nations or resource-limited jurisdictions, encounter substantial limitations in funding, expertise, and infrastructure. The framework must be adaptable to various resource contexts, with recommendations scalable according to capacity and risk.

Cross-Jurisdictional Coordination

Digital platforms frequently traverse jurisdictional boundaries, resulting in difficulties for cohesive governance. The framework's principles of interoperability and federated architecture establish a basis for cross-jurisdictional coordination; however, supplementary institutional mechanisms, such as mutual recognition agreements or joint governance bodies, may be required.

The Role of Adaptive Governance in Dynamic Environments

An essential understanding derived from the application of the PVCPG Framework is that robust digital governance necessitates adaptive capacity, which encompasses the ability to learn, modify, and progress in reaction to evolving circumstances, emerging technologies, and fluctuating public values. The institutionalization of this adaptive capacity is facilitated by the feedback loops of Pillar Three, while also relying on the development of specific organizational and cultural traits.

1. Experimental Mindset: Willingness to test innovative approaches through controlled experiments with appropriate safeguards
2. Learning Orientation: Systematic collection and analysis of performance data, including unexpected outcomes and failures
3. Collaborative Capacity: Ability to work across organizational boundaries and with diverse stakeholders
4. Tolerance for Ambiguity: Comfort with uncertainty and complexity in rapidly evolving technological landscapes

These traits are not inherently prevalent in conventional bureaucratic organizations, indicating that the adoption of the PVCPG Framework may necessitate concurrent changes in organizational culture and competencies.

Table 2. Implementation challenges and mitigation strategies for the PVCPG framework

Challenge Category	Specific Challenges	Potential Mitigation Strategies
Technical Complexity	Legacy system integration, Skill gaps	Phased modernization, Public-private-academic partnerships, Digital competency frameworks
Democratic Trade-offs	Participation vs. efficiency, Transparency vs. security	Context-specific balancing, Tiered approaches, Deliberative processes for difficult trade-offs
Resource Constraints	Limited funding, Infrastructure gaps	Open-source solutions, Shared service models, Progressive implementation based on risk assessment
Cross-Jurisdictional Issues	Conflicting regulations, Governance fragmentation	Mutual recognition agreements, Joint governance bodies, Reference architectures for federation

Source: Developed by the authors based on literature synthesis

SOLUTIONS AND RECOMMENDATIONS

For Policymakers and Public Leaders

The PVCPG Framework provides distinct implications and recommendations for individuals tasked with digital government strategy and policy.

1. Adopt a Public Value-Centric Approach to Digital Investment: Instead of assessing digital initiatives solely based on cost efficiency or technical efficacy, create evaluation frameworks that measure their contributions to public value aspects such as equity, trust, democratic engagement, and resilience. This may necessitate the development of new metrics, data collection methodologies, and reporting standards for digital initiatives.
2. Establish Stewardship as the Foundation for Data Governance: Transition from compliance-oriented strategies to data governance by embracing stewardship principles. This entails formulating sector-specific data trust frameworks, enforcing algorithmic impact assessment mandates, and establishing independent oversight systems for high-risk data applications.
3. Institutionalize Participatory Design and Adaptive Governance: Establish enduring frameworks and mechanisms for citizen and stakeholder involvement in digital governance, encompassing participatory design panels, digital citizen assemblies, and systematic review cycles for significant digital systems. Guarantee that these engagement mechanisms encompass diverse representation, especially from marginalized communities significantly impacted by digital exclusion.

4. Develop Cross-Boundary Governance Mechanisms: For digital platforms that traverse jurisdictional boundaries (local, regional, or international), implement formal governance structures that facilitate coordinated decision-making while honouring diverse legal frameworks and value priorities. This may encompass joint governance boards, mutual recognition agreements, or federated identity and data-sharing frameworks.

For Public Administrators and Digital Service Teams

The framework proposes various pragmatic strategies for individuals tasked with the implementation and operation of digital platforms.

1. Embed Resilience in Technical Architecture: Emphasize architectural attributes including interoperability, modularity, and decentralization in system design. Embrace open standards and APIs to avert vendor lock-in and facilitate eco-system development. Integrate security and privacy safeguards as fundamental design criteria instead of supplementary features.
2. Implement Ethical Governance Practices: Establish and execute ethical review procedures for algorithmic systems, especially those impacting rights or resource distribution. Establish transparency mechanisms that elucidate system operations to impacted stakeholders. Create mechanisms for addressing citizen grievances and inquiries regarding automated decisions.
3. Build Public Value Measurement into Operations: Design and execute public value dashboards that monitor results extending beyond technical performance. Utilize this data to facilitate ongoing enhancement and to exhibit accountability to the public. Ensure that measurement frameworks encompass distributional effects across various demographic groups.
4. Cultivate Adaptive Capacity: Promote organizational cultures that prioritize learning, experimentation, and collaboration. Establish procedures for the systematic evaluation and modification of digital systems in accordance with performance metrics and evolving requirements. Establish connections with varied stakeholders to guide system design and development.

For Researchers and Scholars

The PVCPG Framework delineates multiple promising directions for future research:

1. Empirical Validation: Evaluate the framework's assertions via comparative case studies, longitudinal analyses of digital government initiatives, and experimental investigations of various governance strategies.
2. Measurement Development: Formulate and authenticate metrics for the diverse dimensions of public value in digital governance, specifically concerning equity, trust, and the quality of democracy.
3. Institutional Design: Investigate the institutional frameworks that optimally facilitate public value-oriented platform governance, encompassing a comparative analysis of various models for data trusts, algorithmic oversight entities, and participatory design methodologies.
4. Cross-Cultural Adaptation: Examine the applicability of the framework's principles across various political, cultural, and administrative contexts, focusing specifically on implementations in the Global South and within non-democratic political systems.
5. Emerging Technology Integration: Examine the applicability of the framework to governance issues arising from emerging technologies, including artificial intelligence, blockchain, quantum computing, and the metaverse, within public sector contexts.

FUTURE RESEARCH DIRECTIONS

The evolution of the Digital State is expected to accelerate with the rapid advancement of emerging technologies such as artificial intelligence, blockchain, and the Internet of Things (IoT). These technologies will further transform platform governance by enabling more autonomous decision-making systems, real-time data integration, and predictive public service delivery. As a result, future digital governance models must address not only efficiency and innovation, but also the increasing complexity of ethical, legal, and societal implications.

From the perspective of the PVCPG framework, its long-term viability depends on the ability of institutions to operationalize its three core pillars in dynamic and resource-constrained environments. While resilience-by-design architecture can be technically implemented, challenges remain in ensuring interoperability across jurisdictions, maintaining cybersecurity resilience, and managing legacy system integration. Similarly, stewardship-oriented data governance will face increasing pressure as data volumes grow and cross-border data flows become more complex, requiring adaptive regulatory mechanisms and international cooperation.

Another critical trend is the growing importance of participatory and inclusive governance in digital ecosystems. Future digital platforms will need to embed more advanced mechanisms for citizen engagement, transparency, and algorithmic accountability. The institutionalization of public value feedback loops will become essential to maintain public trust, particularly in contexts where algorithmic decision-making directly affects citizens' rights and access to services.

Implementation challenges will also persist, particularly in developing countries where limitations in digital infrastructure, human capital, and financial resources may hinder the adoption of comprehensive platform governance frameworks. Therefore, scalable and context-sensitive adaptations of the PVCPG framework are necessary to ensure its applicability across diverse governance settings.

Future research should focus on empirically validating the PVCPG framework through comparative case studies and quantitative analysis. Additionally, there is a need to develop standardized metrics for measuring public value in digital governance, particularly in terms of equity, trust, and democratic participation. Further studies may also explore the integration of emerging technologies within the framework and examine how different political and cultural contexts influence its implementation.

Overall, the future of platform governance in the Digital State will be shaped by the ability to balance technological innovation with ethical responsibility, institutional capacity, and democratic values.

CONCLUSION

The shift from traditional governance to the Digital State signifies one of the most profound changes in public administration since the advent of the modern bureaucratic state. This transformation presents unparalleled opportunities to improve service delivery, stimulate innovation, and involve citizens in novel manners. Nevertheless, it also presents significant new risks: the possible deterioration of democratic accountability, the exacerbation of existing inequalities, the emergence of new susceptibilities to disruption, and the replacement of public values by technical or commercial priorities.

This chapter contends that these risks are not unavoidable outcomes of digital transformation, but rather results of governance decisions. By implementing a public value-oriented strategy for platform governance that deliberately prioritizes resilience, manages data as a public trust, and formalizes democratic feedback mechanisms, we can leverage the capabilities of digital technologies while protecting and potentially augmenting the democratic attributes of the state.

The Public Value-Centric Platform Governance (PVCPG) Framework established in this chapter offers a blueprint for this initiative. The three pillars Resilience-by-Design Architecture, Stewardship-Oriented Data Governance, and Institutionalized Public Value Feedback Loops provide a holistic strategy for addressing the intricate issues of digital statecraft. Although implementation will differ across various contexts and encounter considerable challenges, the framework offers a collection of principles and mechanisms to assist policymakers, public administrators, and civil society in managing this transformation.

The paramount evaluation of digital governance will hinge not on the complexity of its technology or the efficacy of its operations, but rather on its role in fostering more just, equitable, resilient, and democratic societies. By prioritizing public value creation in platform governance, we can guarantee that the Digital State functions not only as a more efficient administrator but also as a more adept steward of the public good in an increasingly digital and uncertain environment.

REFERENCES

Andreoni, A., & Roberts, S. (2022). Governing digital platform power for industrial development: Towards an entrepreneurial-regulatory state. *Cambridge Journal of Economics*, *46*(6), 1431–1454. Advance online publication. DOI: 10.1093/cje/beac055

Anubi, O., & Konstantinou, C. (2020). Enhanced resilient state estimation using data-driven auxiliary models. *IEEE Transactions on Industrial Informatics*, *16*(1), 639–647. DOI: 10.1109/TII.2019.2924246

Buttow, C. V., & Weerts, S. (2022). Public sector information in the European Union policy: The misbalance between economy and individuals. *Big Data & Society*, *9*(2), 20539517221124587. Advance online publication. DOI: 10.1177/20539517221124587

Buyannemekh, B., Picazo-Vela, S., Luna, D., & Luna-Reyes, L. (2024). Understanding value of digital service delivery by governments in Mexico. *Government Information Quarterly*, *41*(2), 101936. DOI: 10.1016/j.giq.2024.101936

Calzati, S., & Van Loenen, B. (2023). A fourth way to the digital transformation: The data republic as a fair data ecosystem. *Data & Policy*, *5*, e21. Advance online publication. DOI: 10.1017/dap.2023.18

Calzati, S., & Van Loenen, B. (2025). The Data Republic: Fostering a sustainable, inclusive and resilient digital transformation for the European Union. *Frontiers in Political Science*, *7*, 1670152. Advance online publication. DOI: 10.3389/fpos.2025.1670152

Chen, L., Tong, T., Tang, S., & Han, N. (2021). Governance and Design of Digital Platforms: A Review and Future Research Directions on a Meta-Organization. *Journal of Management*, *48*(1), 147–184. DOI: 10.1177/01492063211045023

Chowdhury, R. H. (2022). *Digital government initiatives and national resilience: How digital governance frameworks were transformed post-COVID to maintain national services*. World Journal of Advanced Engineering Technology and Sciences., DOI: 10.30574/wjaets.2022.7.1.0098

Cristofari, G., & Gerbaudo, P. (2025). Towards an empowered 'Platform State'. *In Proceedings of Digital Government Research*. DOI: 10.59490/dgo.2025.958

Davies, P., Fritzsche, A., Parry, G., & Wood, Z. (2023). Data, resilience, and identity in the digital age. *Strategic Change*, *32*(6), 169–174. Advance online publication. DOI: 10.1002/jsc.2560

Dincă, G., Bărbu ă, M., & Dincă, D. (2025). Crisis as a Catalyst: Difference-in-Differences Evidence on Digital Public Service Transformation in the European Union. *Administrative Sciences.* Advance online publication. DOI: 10.3390/admsci15100393

Dmitrieva, N., Minchenko, O., & Rylskikh, E. (2022). Digital platforms as a regulator and the regulated subject, or how platforms change the system of public administration. *Public Administration Issues.* DOI: 10.17323/1999-5431-2022-0-2-60-84

Dunleavy, P., & Margetts, H. (2023). Data science, artificial intelligence and the third wave of digital era governance. *Public Policy and Administration, 40*(2), 185–214. DOI: 10.1177/09520767231198737

Egala, S., Alhassan, A.-H. S., & Boakye, J. A. (2025). Unleashing public sector innovation. *In Proceedings of Digital Government Research.* DOI: 10.59490/dgo.2025.976

Esposito, P., & Tufo, M. (2024). How to Retrace Public Value Creation in the Era of Digital and Sustainable Transformation? Insights from a Recovery Plan. *Journal of Comprehensive Social Science Research.* DOI: 10.33790/jcssr1100107

Han, Y., & Xie, L. (2025). Sustainable Governance of Digital Platform Ecosystem: A life cycle perspective through multiple governance parties. *Sustainability (Basel), 17*(8), 3628. Advance online publication. DOI: 10.3390/su17083628

Hein, A., Schreieck, M., Riasanow, T., Setzke, D. S., Wiesche, M., Böhm, M., & Krcmar, H. (2019). Digital platform ecosystems. *Electronic Markets, 30*(1), 87–98. DOI: 10.1007/s12525-019-00377-4

Idzi, F., & Gomes, R. (2022). *Digital governance: government strategies that impact public services.* Global Public Policy and Governance., DOI: 10.1007/s43508-022-00055-w

Janssen, M., Konopnicki, D., Snowdon, J., & Ojo, A. (2017). Driving public sector innovation using big and open linked data (BOLD). *Information Systems Frontiers, 19*(2), 189–195. DOI: 10.1007/s10796-017-9746-2

Jovanovic, M., Sjodin, D., & Parida, V. (2021). Co-evolution of platform architecture, platform services, and platform governance: Expanding the platform value of industrial digital platforms. *ArXiv*, abs/2102.04862. DOI: 10.1016/j.technovation.2020.102218

Kausche, K., & Weiss, M. (2024). Platform power and regulatory capture in digital governance. *Business and Politics.* Advance online publication. DOI: 10.1017/bap.2024.33

Korotun, O., & Veretin, L. (2025). *Theoretical and methodological principles of state regulation of the digitalization of consumer market infrastructure in the context of sustainable development.* Market Infrastructure., DOI: 10.32782/infrastruct85-2

Kud, A. (2021). Decentralized Information Platforms in Public Governance: Reconstruction of the Modern Democracy or Comfort Blinding. *International Journal of Public Administration, 46*(3), 195–221. DOI: 10.1080/01900692.2021.1993905

Lee, J.-Y., Kim, B., & Yoon, S.-H. (2024). A conceptual digital policy framework via mixed-methods approach: Navigating public value for value-driven digital transformation. *Government Information Quarterly, 41*(3), 101961. DOI: 10.1016/j.giq.2024.101961

Lewerenz, S., Moen, A., & Martins, H. (2025). Public value and digital health: The example of guiding values in the national digital health strategy of France. *International Journal of Medical Informatics, 196*, 105794. DOI: 10.1016/j.ijmedinf.2025.105794 PMID: 39862565

Lu, P., Zhou, L., & Fan, X. (2023). Platform governance and sociological participation. *The Journal of Chinese Sociology, 10*(1), 3. Advance online publication. DOI: 10.1186/s40711-023-00181-w PMID: 36909780

Luna, D., Duarte-Valle, A., Picazo-Vela, S., & Luna-Reyes, L. (2015). Digital governance and public value creation at the state level. *Information Polity, 20*(2,3), 167–182. DOI: 10.3233/IP-150360

MacArthur, B., Dorobantu, C., & Margetts, H. (2022). Resilient government requires data science reform. *Nature Human Behaviour, 6*(8), 1035–1037. DOI: 10.1038/s41562-022-01423-6 PMID: 35941235

McCarthy, S., Rowan, W., Mahony, C., & Vergne, A. (2023). The dark side of digitalization and social media platform governance: A citizen engagement study. *Internet Research, 33*(6), 2172–2204. DOI: 10.1108/INTR-03-2022-0142

Mersico, L., Aureli, S., & Foschi, E. (2025). *Exploring the role of digital platforms in promoting value co-creation: evidence from the Italian municipal solid waste management system.* Sustainability Accounting, Management and Policy Journal., DOI: 10.1108/SAMPJ-03-2024-0317

Nagaraj, A. (2024). A mapping lens for estimating data value. *Special Issue 4: Democratizing Data.* DOI: 10.1162/99608f92.82f0de5a

Nicoli, M., & Paltrinieri, L. (2019). Platform cooperatives. *The South Atlantic Quarterly, 118*(4), 801–819. Advance online publication. DOI: 10.1215/00382876-7825624

Ooijen, C., Ubaldi, B., & Welby, B. (2019). A data-driven public sector. *OECD Working Papers on Public Governance*. DOI: 10.1787/19934351

Profiroiu, C., Negoi ă, C. I., & Costea, A. V. (2023). Digitalization of public administration in EU member states in times of crisis: The contributions of the national recovery and resilience plans. *International Review of Administrative Sciences, 90*(2), 336–352. DOI: 10.1177/00208523231177554

Rozgonyi, K. (2023). Accountability and platforms' governance: The case of online prominence of public service media content. *Internet Policy Review, 12*(4). Advance online publication. DOI: 10.14763/2023.4.1723

Sadhu, S. K. (2025). Data protection as a public good: leveraging ai/ml for scalable digital resilience. *Journal of Computer Science and Technology Studies*. DOI: 10.32996/jcsts.2025.7.131

Sukma, N., & Yamnill, S. (2025). A new public management model for open data collaboration in sustainable digital insurance ecosystems. *Frontiers in Political Science, 7*, 1598403. Advance online publication. DOI: 10.3389/fpos.2025.1598403

Tang, X., Zena, K., & Fillip. (2025). Communication pathways in multilevel governance: A review of digital innovation and public value. *Review of Communication Research*. DOI: 10.52152/RCR.V13.S9

Törnberg, P. (2023). How platforms govern: Social regulation in digital capitalism. *Big Data & Society, 10*(1), 20539517231153808. Advance online publication. DOI: 10.1177/20539517231153808

Valle-Cruz, D., & García-Contreras, R. (2023). Towards AI-driven transformation and smart data management: Emerging technological change in the public sector value chain. *Public Policy and Administration, 40*(2), 254–275. DOI: 10.1177/09520767231188401

Van Der Heide, J. (2025). *Data driven & high tech (KB-38) : Digital transformation of the agro-food and life sciences towards a sustainable*. Resilient And Equitable Future State., DOI: 10.18174/693994

Vestues, K., Mikalsen, M., & Monteiro, E. (2021). Using digital platforms to promote a service-oriented logic in public sector organizations. *A case studies*. 1–10. DOI: 10.24251/HICSS.2021.269

Walravens, N., & Ballon, P. (2013). Platform business models for smart cities: From control and value to governance and public value. *IEEE Communications Magazine, 51*(6), 72–79. DOI: 10.1109/MCOM.2013.6525598

Wang, J., Zhou, X., Ma, Y., & Choi, Y. (2025, May 20). Yunning, & Choi, Y. (2025a). Public data elements and enterprise digital transformation: A quasi-natural experiment based on open government data platforms for sustainable urban planning. *Sustainability (Basel), 17*(10), 4676. Advance online publication. DOI: 10.3390/su17104676

Wang, X., Lei, M., Wang, D., & Cao, J. (2025b). Research on dynamic incentive mechanism for co-creation of value in innovation-oriented platform ecosystem considering supervision. *Symmetry, 17*(11), 1884. Advance online publication. DOI: 10.3390/sym17111884

Wang, Y., Wang, J., Gao, F., & Song, J. (2024). Unveiling value patterns via deep reinforcement learning in heterogeneous data analytics. *Patterns (New York, N.Y.), 5*(5), 100965. Advance online publication. DOI: 10.1016/j.patter.2024.100965 PMID: 38800362

Yabe, T., Rao, P., Ukkusuri, S., & Cutter, S. (2022). Toward data-driven, dynamical complex systems approaches to disaster resilience. *In Proceedings of the National Academy of Sciences of the United States of America,* 119. DOI: 10.1073/pnas.2111997119

Zhalgas, Y. (2025). State creative procurement in the digital age: challenges of transparency and public trust. *Человек и Культура*. DOI: 10.25136/2409-8744.2025.5.75808

KEY TERMS AND DEFINITIONS

Adaptive Governance: An approach to governance that emphasizes learning, experimentation, and flexibility in response to changing conditions, complex challenges, and evolving public values, particularly important in dynamic technological environments.

Algorithmic Impact Assessment: A systematic evaluation process conducted before deploying algorithmic decision-making systems in the public sector to identify potential impacts on equity, privacy, transparency, and democratic accountability.

Data Stewardship: A governance model that treats data as a common-pool resource held in trust for the public, emphasizing fiduciary responsibilities, ethical management, and accountability for data use outcomes rather than ownership or control.

Digital State: A governance paradigm in which state functions and citizen interactions are primarily mediated through integrated digital platforms and ecosystems, moving beyond mere digitization of existing services to fundamentally reimagining the architecture of government.

Interoperability: The capacity of different information systems, devices, or applications to connect and exchange data in a coordinated manner, enabling seamless interaction across organizational and technical boundaries while preserving the autonomy of individual components.

Platform Governance: The rules, technical standards, and institutional arrangements that shape interactions within digital platform ecosystems, encompassing both the architecture that enables certain behaviors and the formal and informal regulations that govern participation and value distribution.

Public Value-Centric Platform Governance (PVCPG): A framework for designing and governing digital platforms in the public sector that prioritizes the creation of public value through three interdependent pillars: resilience-by-design architecture, stewardship-oriented data governance, and institutionalized public value feedback loops.

Public Value Feedback Loops: Institutionalized mechanisms for continuous democratic input, value measurement, and adaptive learning that are integrated into the operations of digital platforms to ensure alignment with evolving public values.

Resilience-by-Design: An approach to system architecture that embeds capacities for continuity, adaptability, and learning from the initial design phase, ensuring that systems can withstand shocks and stresses while maintaining essential functions.

Socio-Technical Systems: Integrated systems comprising both social elements (people, organizations, norms) and technical elements (technologies, infrastructure, data), recognizing that these dimensions are interdependent and must be designed and governed together.

Chapter 2
Creating Digital Public Value in Platform States:
The Influence of Public Digital Capability, Data Governance, and Platform Governance

Abdallah Ousri
http://orcid.org/0009-0008-0883-1622
Ecole Nationale de Commerce et de Gestion BENI-MELLAL, Morocco

Youssef Jouali
http://orcid.org/0009-0001-0351-8978
Ecole Nationale de Commerce et de Gestion BENI-MELLAL, Morocco

Ismail El Bazi
http://orcid.org/0000-0002-8511-8651
Ecole Nationale de Commerce et de Gestion BENI-MELLAL, Morocco

Soufiane Ghyati
http://orcid.org/0009-0008-7988-9434
Ecole Nationale de Commerce et de Gestion BENI-MELLA, Morocco

ABSTRACT

As states adopt platform-based models of public governance, understanding how institutional capabilities and governance arrangements translate into societal value has become a central concern for public administration research. No quantitative model had jointly tested how public digital capability, data governance, and platform governance interact to shape digital platform use and digital public value creation in emerging economies such as Morocco. This chapter develops and empirically

DOI: 10.4018/979-8-3373-9765-8.ch002

validates an integrative tripartite structural model grounded in Public Value Theory, New Public Management, and Sociotechnical Theory, using PLS-SEM on a sample of 350 Moroccan public employees, civil servants, and citizens. All seven hypotheses were confirmed at p < 0.001: public digital capability and platform governance emerged as the strongest direct determinants of platform use, which fully mediates digital public value creation. The chapter offers theoretical and managerial insights for decision-makers engaged in digital transformation in emerging platform states.

INTRODUCTION

The contemporary state is undergoing a profound institutional transformation, driven by what public administration scholars describe as a second public digital revolution (Haug et al., 2024). Far from a simple digitization of paper-based procedures, the deployment of disruptive technologies from predictive artificial intelligence and sovereign cloud infrastructures to decentralized data ecosystems is rewriting the underlying logic of public service delivery (Dunleavy & Margetts, 2023). This shift marks a transition away from the classic, siloed, top-down bureaucratic model toward a networked and interconnected framework theorized as the "platform state" (Lee et al., 2024). Within this framework, public authority no longer acts as the sole producer of services; it becomes a macro-infrastructure architect that orchestrates and regulates an ecosystem in which ministries, local governments, firms, and citizen-users co-create value (Esposito, 2024).

This transition is no longer reserved for hyper-developed economies. It is actively redefining the development agendas of emerging countries, which view digital platforms as a leapfrogging mechanism for public-sector modernization (Díaz-Arancibia et al., 2024). Morocco is an emblematic case through its national strategy, *Maroc Digital* (Belhaj & Boulahoual, 2024). By channeling public investment into national digital infrastructures, interoperable e-government portals, and unified socio-economic registries, the country offers a relevant empirical laboratory of an emerging platform state seeking to reconcile technical efficiency, territorial inclusion, and institutional legitimacy.

Beneath the promises of seamless automation, however, the operationalization of the platform state reveals persistent democratic frictions and managerial challenges. Recent scholarship cautions against a blind reliance on algorithmic rationality, highlighting the widening of the digital divide, opacity in automated decisions, and a loss of civic control over centralized data architectures (Grimmelikhuijsen, 2023). These concerns revive a fundamental question: what is the ultimate purpose of digital transformation, and who benefits from it? Herein lies the enduring relevance of Public Value Theory (Moore, 1995), which holds that public institutions must be assessed not by internal productivity alone but by their capacity to generate societal outcomes such as trust, equity of access, transparency, and social justice.

In a platformized ecosystem, this value takes on a sociotechnical nature. Public platforms, when underpinned by ethical standards and inclusive governance, can act as catalysts for digital public value through user-centric co-creation (Lee et al., 2024). Conversely, weak institutional safeguards or a mismatch between new tools and legacy administrative cultures can trigger "public disvalue," where digital tools exacerbate exclusion or alienate the citizen-user (Cordella et al., 2024). Untangling these dynamics requires a pluralistic lens that combines Public Value Theory to assess democratic outcomes, New Public Management to evaluate efficiency, and Sociotechnical Theory to capture the alignment between technological artifacts and human structures (Iden & Bygstad, 2024).

This intersection reveals a major gap. Despite the growth of digital-governance research, existing studies approach the dimensions of the platform state in a fragmented manner, and the field remains concentrated in a few Western institutions without an integrated explanatory framework (Lin & Yaakop, 2024). Some inquiries focus exclusively on technical infrastructure, while others analyze data governance or collaborative arrangements in isolation. While prior work has examined public digital capability, data governance, and public platform governance separately, no quantitative model has jointly tested how these institutional dimensions interact within a single framework to determine platform use and, ultimately, the creation of digital public value, leaving international benchmarks and mature platform states largely absent from the discussion.

This chapter addresses that gap. It develops and empirically tests an integrative model in which public digital capability, data governance, and public platform governance influence the use of public digital platforms, which in turn drives digital public value. Using partial least squares structural equation modeling (PLS-SEM) on 350 respondents from the Moroccan public sector and citizen users, the study pursues three objectives: to consolidate a fragmented literature into a single tripartite framework; to quantify the direct and mediated effects linking institutional resources to public value; and to derive actionable guidance for emerging platform states. The remainder of the chapter reviews the background literature, presents the theoretical framework and hypotheses, details the methodology, reports the results, and discusses their theoretical and managerial implications.

BACKGROUND

A digital state systematically integrates digital technologies, data infrastructures, and algorithmic systems into its governance and service-delivery functions, transforming its administrative capacities and its interactions with citizens (Zhao et al., 2023). The platform state extends this idea: it is a model of public action in which the state operates as an open digital infrastructure, providing data, standards, and interfaces that enable third parties to co-create services and public value (Hein et al., 2023). Platform governance, in turn, refers to the mechanisms, rules, and institutional arrangements through which platforms organize interactions among actors, control access, and regulate data within digital ecosystems (Doshi & Schmidt, 2024).

The Platform State as a Structural Transformation of Public Action

The literature converges on the idea that the platform state represents a profound shift in the role of the state, from a direct provider of services to an orchestrator of data-based digital ecosystems (Addo, 2022). In this view, the *Government as a Platform* (GaaP) model is not a mere technological innovation but a new organizational and economic paradigm of public action (Brown et al., 2017). This transformation redefines the state as a facilitator of public-value creation, requiring strong orchestration capabilities to align actors and resources within complex ecosystems (Cordella & Paletti, 2019). Public digital infrastructures thereby function as strategic collective goods that reshape the mechanisms of public-value production (Türk, 2020), embedding public administration in ecosystem-based logics where innovation relies on the integration of technologies, institutions, and actors (Caron, 2021).

Data as a Strategic Resource and the Foundation of Public Value

A second stream highlights data as the strategic resource at the core of state digital transformation. Public data becomes a central infrastructure of public action, redefining decision-making and value creation (Mericskay, 2021), while platforms organize the circulation and valorization of data, generating network effects but also tensions between cooperation and competition (Marty, 2020). Open data emerges as a driver of public-value co-creation, though its impact depends on institutional, technical, and organizational conditions (Toots et al., 2017). This perspective is reinforced by approaches that conceptualize data as digital commons requiring appropriate governance to ensure equitable, public-oriented value (Gil, 2023). Data thus lies at the heart of both value-creation dynamics and the broader challenges of regulation and digital sovereignty (Abbas et al., 2024).

Platform Governance and Issues of Regulation and Sovereignty

A third group of studies emphasize platform governance, based on the rules, norms, and regulatory mechanisms that organize interactions among actors and control access to digital resources (Lanna, 2025). This governance operates within a reconfiguration of power relations, where large platforms increasingly capture value and exert influence over states (Boullier, 2022), raising critical issues of digital sovereignty and prompting strategies to regulate data use and strengthen technological autonomy (Tonon, 2020). Platform governance must also arbitrate tensions between market logic, public interest, and state regulation in a context of progressive privatization of certain public functions (Doré, 2023), while introducing new forms of data-based governmentality in which control, surveillance, and value extraction become intertwined (Arsène et al., 2021).

Digital Transformation, Ecosystems, and Public Value Creation

Finally, several studies frame the digital transformation of the public sector as a systemic process based on interactions among actors, technologies, and institutions (Hietala & Päivärinta, 2025), which follows no universal model but depends on context-specific strategic choices (Jacob et al., 2022). Public value is increasingly conceptualized as a co-creation process in which administrations act as orchestrators rather than sole producers of value (Virtanen & Harri, 2023). This dynamic depends on the quality of digital public services delivered to citizens (Asmawanti-S et al., 2025) and reflects a more experiential understanding of public value centered on users' experiences (Francis-Auton et al., 2024). It also raises issues of regulation and trust, where regulatory technologies (RegTech) enhance transparency and compliance (Bolton & Mintrom, 2023), even as public–private interactions in sensitive sectors generate risks of commodification (Gross & Geiger, 2023). Overall, the literature identifies three dynamics shaping public value in the digital era: an ecosystemic logic based on platforms, a co-productive logic centered on citizen participation, and a data-driven governance logic integrating advanced technologies (Chandrasekhar, 2025).

The Platform State and Digital Public Value Creation: Foundations and Modernization

Analyzing the platform state requires re-evaluating the foundational paradigms of public administration. The New Public Management framework formalized by Hood (1991) emphasizing efficiency, disaggregation, and competitive mechanisms remains an essential reference but demands a conceptual update: public efficiency is no longer measured solely by internal cost reduction but by the capacity of infrastructures to coordinate hybrid ecosystems while addressing cybersecurity and institutional resilience (Wirtz et al., 2022). Similarly, Public Value Theory (Moore, 1995) must be reassessed in the age of algorithmic governance. Public value now encompasses "digital public value," defined as a state's capacity to guarantee transparency, algorithmic equity, and technological sovereignty for its citizens (Janssen et al., 2020). This modernization bridges classic conceptual frameworks and contemporary approaches that measure platform performance through cross-cutting impact indicators. Table 1 synthesizes representative studies at this intersection.

Table 1. Comparative literature review on the platform state, data governance, and digital public value creation

Authors & Year	Focus / context	Main findings
Brown et al. (2017)	Government as a Platform (GaaP) as an economic and organizational model.	GaaP is a transformative model, not merely a technical infrastructure; the authors propose a Platform Assessment Framework (PAF).
Cordella & Paletti (2019)	Conditions under which the platform state creates public value.	Value emerges only when orchestration mechanisms effectively coordinate actors and resources.
Türk (2020)	The digital platform state.	The state becomes a producer and organizer of value through digital technologies.
Tonon (2020)	GovTech and digital sovereignty.	GovTech redefines state digital sovereignty through data governance and regulation.
Boullier (2022)	Impact of platforms on territories and sovereignty.	Platforms deterritorialize public action and centralize the value generated from data.
Jacob et al. (2022)	Challenges of public-sector digital transformation.	Transformation relies on the reorganization of public data and strategic governmental choices.
Caron (2021)	Digital transformation ecosystem of public administration.	Digital transformation depends on a complex ecosystem of actors and technologies.
Frucquet & Carassus (2023)	Public-value co-creation in digital territories.	Digital public-value creation depends on cooperation among territorial actors.
Yukhno (2024)	Big-data governance and the unified "digital state."	A unified, big-data-centered ecosystem is needed to move from e-government to digital government and raise public value.
Danneels & Viaene (2025)	Capabilities needed to build a successful GaaP.	Three interlinked capabilities asset management, architecture, and orchestration are essential to engage a platform ecosystem.
Belhaj & Boulahoual (2024)	Data governance and public-value creation in Morocco.	Data governance is a central lever for public-value creation in the Moroccan administration.

Source: compiled by the authors.

MAIN FOCUS OF THE CHAPTER

Tripartite Theoretical Framework and Complementary Theories

The proposed five-construct model is grounded in three complementary perspectives that justify its structural relationships. First, treating *public digital capability* as a key antecedent draws on the Resource-Based View: an administration's digital capability is not a mere collection of IT tools but an internal strategic resource valuable, rare, and difficult to imitate that combines technical infrastructure, managerial skills, and organizational routines to deploy agile services and orchestrate application ecosystems. Second, understanding *data governance* and *public platform governance* falls within Institutional Theory, which analyzes how coercive, normative, and mimetic pressures shape digital regulation. Data governance is not merely a technical constraint but an institutional structure for organizing trustworthy data (Janssen et al., 2020), and administrations legitimize platform use by adopting governance standards and cybersecurity protocols that meet citizens' expectations for protection (Wirtz et al., 2022).

Third, introducing the mediating variable *public digital platform use* mobilizes technology-acceptance models, notably the Technology Acceptance Model and its extension, UTAUT (Venkatesh & Bala, 2008). Whereas classic sociotechnical theory (Trist, 1981) focused on the joint optimization of social and technical systems, TAM/UTAUT adds behavioral rigor by showing that the impact of digital capabilities on public value is mediated by the perceived usefulness and ease of use of platforms. Without continuous and effective use, even sophisticated infrastructures remain empty shells. This framework also addresses a persistent tension between a techno-optimistic stream, anchored in New Public Management, which sees digital transformation as a linear and positive process (Vial, 2019), and a critical stream that warns against public-disvalue creation and the loss of democratic oversight. The present study connects these perspectives by statistically testing whether data governance and platform governance are the conditions under which platform use generates sustainable digital public value.

Research Hypotheses

H1: Public digital capability positively influences the use of public digital platforms.

Public digital capability comprises the technological resources, interoperable infrastructures, and organizational competencies that enable administrations to support digital transformation (Ly et al., 2026). From a New Public Management perspective, digital technologies are a lever for administrative efficiency (Hood,

1991), and sociotechnical theory stresses that infrastructure quality conditions effective adoption (Trist, 1981). The digital maturity of administrations significantly enhances the adoption of governmental platforms (Mergel et al., 2019).

H2: Data governance positively influences the use of public digital platforms.

Data governance refers to the mechanisms ensuring data quality, security, confidentiality, and sharing within public environments (Janssen et al., 2020). Trust in data management is a major determinant of platform use (Attard et al., 2016), and transparent, secure data enhances the legitimacy of public action and citizens' trust (Twizeyimana & Andersson, 2019). Data-protection policies directly influence the acceptance of digital technologies in the public sector (Alqahtani et al., 2025).

H3: Public platform governance positively influences the use of public digital platforms.

Platform governance denotes the coordination mechanisms, institutional rules, and standards that regulate public platforms. Within the platform state, administrations orchestrate interactions among public and private stakeholders (Villodre, 2025), and clear governance, interoperable standards, and open APIs strengthen platform use (Jonathan et al., 2024). Collaborative governance models significantly improve platform effectiveness and adoption (Cao, 2024).

H4: The use of public digital platforms positively influences digital public value.

Platform use is a central mechanism for creating public value in digital states. According to Public Value Theory (Moore, 1995), public action aims to generate collective benefits such as service quality, transparency, inclusion, and trust. Digital platforms improve accessibility, reduce administrative costs, and enhance participation; the greater the use, the higher the digital public value generated (Wirtz et al., 2021).

H5: Platform use mediates the relationship between public digital capability and digital public value.

Technological resources do not automatically generate value; their impact depends on effective appropriation and use (Weigl et al., 2024). Digital capability generates value only when platforms are effectively used (Lee et al., 2024), so platform use acts as a mediating mechanism a logic strongly supported in public-sector transformation research (Rukanova et al., 2023).

H6: Platform use mediates the relationship between data governance and digital public value.

Data governance improves the quality, reliability, and security of information on public platforms (Begany Grace & Gil-Garcia, 2024), yet these mechanisms generate value only when platforms are effectively used. Data governance facilitates use by strengthening digital trust and service quality, which subsequently leads to value creation (Attard et al., 2015).

H7: Platform use mediates the relationship between public platform governance and digital public value.

Platform governance structures interactions among stakeholders through rules, standards, and coordination (Sung & Lee, 2024), but these arrangements generate value only when platforms are effectively used (Chen et al., 2022). Platform use is therefore the primary channel through which governance contributes to digital public value (Porcher et al., 2024).

Figure 1. Conceptual model

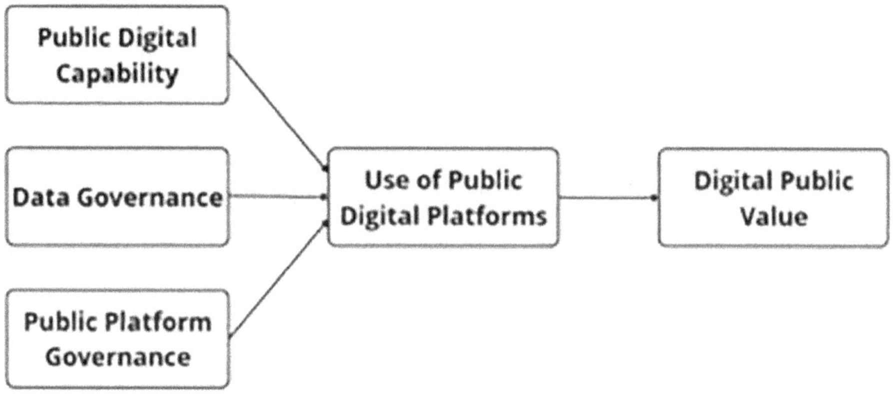

Source: developed by the authors.

Research Methodology

Research Design

The study adopts a quantitative, explanatory, and cross-sectional design and tests its hypotheses using partial least squares structural equation modeling (PLS-SEM). PLS-SEM is appropriate here for three reasons: the model is relatively complex, combining five latent constructs with mediation effects; the research goal is predictive and theory-building rather than confirmatory of an established theory; and the variance-based estimator is robust to non-normal survey data and moderate sample sizes (Hair et al., 2022). Estimation was carried out in SmartPLS 4 following the standard two-stage procedure: assessment of the measurement model, then assessment of the structural model (Hair et al., 2022).

Population and Sampling

The target population comprises the actors of Morocco's public digital ecosystem: public officials involved in digital services, private-sector partners who interact with public transactional platforms, and citizen users of e-government services. In the absence of an exhaustive national register of public-platform users, a non-probability convenience sampling technique was used an accepted practice in e-government research where complete sampling frames are unavailable (Twizeyimana & Andersson, 2019). To limit selection bias, the questionnaire was distributed through a multi-channel strategy spanning professional networks, targeted mailing lists within public administrations, and alumni networks. Data were collected over four months (February–May 2026). Of 480 questionnaires administered electronically, 350 valid responses were retained after removing incomplete records and unqualified profiles, an effective response rate of 72.9%. This sample size exceeds the thresholds recommended for stable PLS-SEM estimation with mediation (Hair et al., 2022). The four-month collection window also spanned distinct phases of the annual administrative calendar, which helped avoid concentrating responses within a single, potentially atypical period of platform activity.

Respondent Profile

The final sample reflects the dual sociotechnical nature of public digital governance. It combines internal actors public administrators, digital-service directors, and middle managers within ministries and agencies with external actors, including private-sector professionals whose activities depend on public transactional platforms (e-procurement, digital tax and customs interfaces) and citizen users with verified experience of national e-government services. The detailed composition is reported in Table 2. This mixed profile was a deliberate design choice: because platform governance and data governance affect internal administrators and external users differently, capturing both perspectives within the same sample allows the model to reflect the two-sided nature of platform-state interactions rather than only the supply side of public digital services.

Measures

The instrument operationalizes five reflective constructs: public digital capability (CNP, four items), data governance (GD, five items), public platform governance (GPP, four items), use of public digital platforms (UPNP, four items), and digital public value (VPN, five items). Items were adapted from validated scales in the public-management and government-information literature and contextualized to the Moroccan public sector; each was measured on a five-point Likert scale. The full list of items and their sources is presented in Table 3. Content and face validity were established through a two-stage pre-test: an expert panel of four academics specializing in public management and information systems reviewed the wording and item alignment, and a pilot study (N = 35) confirmed internal consistency, with Cronbach's alpha and composite reliability above the 0.70 threshold (Kline, 2023). Minor wording adjustments identified by the expert panel were incorporated before the pilot, and the pilot itself led to no further item deletions, indicating that the adapted scales transferred adequately to the Moroccan public-sector context without requiring further modification.

Analytical Strategy

The measurement model was assessed for indicator reliability (outer loadings $\geq$ 0.708), internal consistency (Cronbach's alpha, ρ_A, and $\rho\_C \geq 0.70$), convergent validity (average variance extracted ≥ 0.50), and discriminant validity using the heterotrait–monotrait ratio (HTMT < 0.85) (Hair et al., 2022). Indicator collinearity was screened through variance inflation factors (VIF). The structural model was then evaluated by estimating path coefficients and their significance through bootstrapping with 5,000 subsamples, together with the coefficient of determination (R^2), effect size (f^2), and the standardized root mean square residual (SRMR) as an approximate fit index. Mediation (H5–H7) was tested through the significance of bootstrapped indirect effects rather than the causal-steps approach, as recommended for variance-based models (Sarstedt et al., 2020). This approach is preferable to the traditional causal-steps procedure because it directly tests the significance of the indirect path itself rather than inferring mediation from a sequence of separate significance tests, and it does not require the direct effect to be significant on its own for mediation to be established.

Common Method Bias

Because all constructs rely on self-reported data from a single informant at one point in time, common method bias was addressed through both procedural and statistical remedies. Procedurally, predictor and outcome scales were visually separated, and respondents were assured of anonymity and the absence of "right or wrong" answers to reduce social-desirability pressure. Statistically, Harman's single-factor test showed that the first unrotated factor accounted for 36.4% of the variance, below the 50% ceiling, indicating that common method bias does not threaten the results (Podsakoff et al., 2003). Nonetheless, as a single-source, single-wave design, the study cannot fully eliminate the possibility that some portion of the observed associations reflects respondents' general tendency toward consistency between their attitudes and their self-reported behavior, a limitation partially addressed by the procedural remedies described above but not eliminated by them.

Ethical Considerations

The protocol complied with international research ethics and Moroccan data-protection law. Participants provided electronic informed consent before accessing the survey, participation was voluntary and revocable, and in line with Law No. 09-08 and GDPR benchmarks all data were anonymized at the source, stored securely, and processed in aggregate form to preclude re-identification. No individually identifying information was retained after data cleaning, and access to the raw dataset was restricted to the research team throughout the analysis.

RESULTS

Descriptive Statistics of the Sample (N = 350)

The sample comprises 350 respondents recruited through an online questionnaire distributed among civil servants, administrative managers, and citizens who actively use public digital platforms in Morocco, exceeding the minimum of 300 observations recommended for PLS-SEM with multiple latent variables and mediation (Hair et al., 2022). Men form a slight majority (63.7%), broadly mirroring the gender structure of Category A civil-service corps in Morocco. The age distribution concentrates in the 35–44 bracket (42.6%), and the sample is highly qualified, with more than half holding a master's degree. Institutionally, it spans public agencies (34.0%), central administration (29.7%), local authorities (19.1%), and private-sector users (17.1%); over 73% of respondents use public platforms at least several times a week, reflecting the accelerating digitalization of public services under the Maroc Digital strategy (Belhaj & Boulahoual, 2024). Table 2 details the sociodemographic profile.

Table 2. Sociodemographic and professional characteristics of the sample (N = 350)

Sociodemographic Dimension	Category	Count (n)	Percentage (%)
Gender	Male	223	63.7
	Female	127	36.3
	Total	350	100.0

continued on following page

Table 2. Continued

Sociodemographic Dimension	Category	Count (n)	Percentage (%)
Age Group	Under 25	19	5.4
	25 – 34	88	25.1
	35 – 44	149	42.6
	45 – 54	73	20.9
	55 and over	21	6.0
	Total	350	100.0
Educational Level	High school diploma or below	24	6.9
	Bachelor's degree (Bac+3)	97	27.7
	Master's degree (Bac+5)	185	52.9
	Doctorate (PhD)	44	12.6
	Total	350	100.0
Employment Sector	Central government administration	104	29.7
	Local and regional authorities	67	19.1
	Public institutions and agencies	119	34.0
	Private sector (users of public services)	60	17.1
	Total	350	100.0
Frequency of Use of Public Digital Platforms	Never	12	3.4
	Rarely (less than once a month)	27	7.7
	Occasionally (1–3 times a month)	54	15.4
	Regularly (1–3 times a week)	145	41.4
	Daily	112	32.0
	Total	350	100.0

Source: compiled by the authors.

Evaluation of the Measurement Model

Table 3 presents the measurement instrument item codes, descriptions, and the sources that informed their operationalization. All items were adapted from validated scales in the government-information and public-management literature.

Table 3. Measurement instrument: items, constructs, and sources

Variable	Item Code	Item Description	Key References
Public Digital Capability (CNP)	**CNP1**	Public administrations have adequate digital infrastructure to support digital public services.	Haug, Dan, & Mergel (2024)
	CNP2	Public institutions effectively integrate interoperable digital systems.	
	CNP3	Public organizations have sufficient digital skills to manage digital transformation.	
	CNP4	Digital technologies improve the operational efficiency of public administrations.	
Data Governance (GD)	**GD1**	Public administrations ensure high standards of data security and privacy.	Janssen et al. (2020)
	GD2	Public data management practices are transparent and trustworthy.	
	GD3	Public institutions effectively share and coordinate digital data across departments.	
	GD4	Data governance mechanisms improve the quality and reliability of digital public services.	
	GD5	Data governance policies ensure ethical, compliant, and responsible use of public data.	
Public Platform Governance (GPP)	**GPP1**	Public digital platforms operate according to clear governance rules and standards.	Janowski, Estevez, & Baguma (2018); Haug, Dan, & Mergel (2024)
	GPP2	Coordination among stakeholders within public digital platforms is effective.	
	GPP3	Public digital platforms facilitate collaboration between public and private actors.	
	GPP4	Interoperability standards improve the functioning of public digital platforms.	
Use of Public Digital Platforms (UPNP)	**UPNP1**	Citizens frequently use public digital platforms to access public services.	Sung & Lee (2024); Haug, Dan, & Mergel (2024)
	UPNP2	Public digital platforms simplify interactions between citizens and public administrations.	
	UPNP3	Public digital platforms are easy to use and accessible.	
	UPNP4	Public administrations increasingly rely on digital platforms to deliver services.	

continued on following page

Table 3. Continued

Variable	Item Code	Item Description	Key References
Digital Public Value (VPN)	VPN1	Public digital platforms improve the quality of public services.	Luna et al. (2024); Sung & Lee (2024)
	VPN2	Digital public services strengthen transparency and citizens' trust.	
	VPN3	Public digital platforms promote greater citizen participation.	
	VPN4	Digital transformation creates collective benefits for society.	
	VPN5	Public digital platforms improve accessibility, inclusion, and equity in access to public services.	

Source: compiled by the authors.

Table 4. Internal consistency, reliability, and convergent validity of the constructs

	Cronbach's Alpha (α)	Composite Reliability (ρ_A)	Composite Reliability (ρ_C)	Average Variance Extracted (AVE)
CNP	0.892	0.896	0.925	0.754
GD	0.918	0.936	0.938	0.752
GPP	0.892	0.893	0.925	0.755
UPNP	0.878	0.881	0.916	0.732
VPN	0.930	0.932	0.947	0.782

Source: compiled by the authors.

Internal consistency and convergent validity were assessed using Cronbach's alpha (α), ρ_A, composite reliability (ρ_C), and average variance extracted (AVE). As shown in Table 4, all indicators exceed the recommended thresholds: alpha ranges from 0.878 (UPNP) to 0.930 (VPN), composite reliability from 0.916 to 0.947, and AVE from 0.732 (UPNP) to 0.782 (VPN), comfortably above the 0.50 benchmark (Fornell & Larcker, 1981; Hair et al., 2022). These results confirm satisfactory reliability and convergent validity for all five constructs.

Table 5. Discriminant validity heterotrait-monotrait ratio (HTMT)

	CNP	GD	GPP	UPNP
CNP				
GD	0.084			
GPP	0.049	0.062		
UPNP	0.368	0.238	0.391	
VPN	0.167	0.136	0.188	0.524

Source: compiled by the authors.

Discriminant validity was assessed with the HTMT ratio (Henseler et al., 2015). Under the conservative 0.85 threshold (Hair et al., 2022), all values are acceptable, ranging from 0.049 (CNP–GPP) to 0.524 (UPNP–VPN). The highest value, between platform use and public value, reflects a theoretically expected relationship yet remains well below the critical boundary, confirming that each construct captures a distinct domain.

Table 6. Outer loadings of measurement items

Item	CNP	GD	GPP	UPNP	VPN
CNP1	0.864				
CNP2	0.882				
CNP3	0.876				
CNP4	0.852				
GD1		0.856			
GD2		0.883			
GD3		0.867			
GD4		0.872			
GD5		0.856			
GPP1			0.886		
GPP2			0.876		
GPP3			0.852		
GPP4			0.862		
UPNP1				0.878	
UPNP2				0.844	
UPNP3				0.838	
UPNP4				0.862	
VPN1					0.879

continued on following page

Table 6. Continued

Item	CNP	GD	GPP	UPNP	VPN
VPN2					0.883
VPN3					0.869
VPN4					0.901
VPN5					0.889

Source: compiled by the authors.

All outer loadings surpass the 0.708 threshold (Hair et al., 2022), ranging from 0.838 (UPNP3) to 0.901 (VPN4). No item removal is warranted, reinforcing the robustness of the measurement model alongside the reliability and validity evidence above.

Table 7. Variance inflation factors (VIF) collinearity assessment

Item	VIF
CNP1	2.233
CNP2	2.491
CNP3	2.625
CNP4	2.242
GD1	2.670
GD2	2.694
GD3	2.392
GD4	2.872
GD5	2.750
GPP1	2.620
GPP2	2.437
GPP3	2.230
GPP4	2.323
UPNP1	2.439
UPNP2	2.176
UPNP3	2.047
UPNP4	2.196
VPN1	2.828
VPN2	3.047
VPN3	2.746

continued on following page

Table 7. Continued

Item	VIF
VPN4	3.392
VPN5	3.302

Source: compiled by the authors.

Indicator collinearity was screened using the VIF. As shown in Table 7, all values fall between 2.047 (UPNP3) and 3.392 (VPN4), well below the critical threshold of 5.0 and mostly under the more stringent 3.3 benchmark (Kock, 2015). This confirms the absence of problematic multicollinearity and ensures unbiased path estimates.

Structural Model and Hypothesis Testing

Table 8. Structural model results direct and mediation effects (bootstrapping, n = 5,000)

Hyp.	Relation	β (O)	Mean (M)	STDEV	T-Stat	p-value	Decision
H1	CNP → UPNP	0.335	0.338	0.042	8.014	0.000	Validated
H2	GD → UPNP	0.229	0.232	0.045	5.054	0.000	Validated
H3	GPP → UPNP	0.323	0.324	0.044	7.337	0.000	Validated
H4	UPNP → VPN	0.477	0.479	0.042	11.335	0.000	Validated
H5	CNP → UPNP → VPN	0.160	0.162	0.024	6.540	0.000	Validated
H6	GD → UPNP → VPN	0.109	0.111	0.024	4.491	0.000	Validated
H7	GPP → UPNP → VPN	0.154	0.155	0.025	6.219	0.000	Validated

Source: compiled by the authors.

The structural model was evaluated through bootstrapping with 5,000 subsamples to test the seven hypotheses. All path coefficients are significant at $p < 0.001$, providing robust support for the model. Among direct effects, public digital capability (CNP → UPNP: $\beta = 0.335$, $t = 8.014$), data governance (GD → UPNP: $\beta = 0.229$, $t = 5.054$), and public platform governance (GPP → UPNP: $\beta = 0.323$, $t = 7.337$) each significantly increase platform use, confirming H1–H3. Platform use, in turn, exerts the strongest direct effect on digital public value (UPNP → VPN: $\beta = 0.477$, $t = 11.335$), supporting H4 and establishing use as a substantive driver of collective value (Moore, 1995).

Mediation Analysis

The three indirect effects confirm that institutional resources are converted into public value through platform use. The mediated paths from capability (H5: β = 0.160, t = 6.540), data governance (H6: β = 0.109, t = 4.491), and platform governance (H7: β = 0.154, t = 6.219) are all positive and significant. These results establish that public value does not emerge spontaneously from digital resources but depends on patterns of use embedded in governance frameworks (Weigl et al., 2024).

Table 9. Structural model assessment results

Construct/Relationship	Indicator	Value	Interpretation
Public Digital Platform Usage (UPNP)	Adjusted R^2	0.266	Weak to Moderate Explanatory Power
Digital Public Value (VPN)	Adjusted R^2	0.225	Weak Explanatory Power
Public Digital Capability (CNP) → UPNP	f^2	0.154	Moderate Effect
Data Governance (GD) → UPNP	f^2	0.071	Small Effect
Public Platform Governance (GPP) → UPNP	f^2	0.143	Small to Moderate Effect
UPNP → VPN	f^2	0.295	Moderate Effect
Estimated Model	SRMR	0.041	Excellent Model Fit

Source: compiled by the authors.

The exogenous constructs explain 26.6% of the variance in platform use and 22.5% of the variance in digital public value (adjusted R^2 = 0.266 and 0.225), a weak-to-moderate explanatory power that remains acceptable for behavioral phenomena in public administration (Hair et al., 2022). Effect sizes indicate a moderate contribution of capability (f^2 = 0.154) and platform governance (f^2 = 0.143) to platform use, a smaller contribution of data governance (f^2 = 0.071), and a moderate effect of use on public value (f^2 = 0.295). The model produced an SRMR of 0.041, well below the 0.08 threshold, indicating an excellent fit (Henseler et al., 2015). Overall, the model demonstrates satisfactory explanatory power, meaningful effect sizes, and a strong fit.

Figure 2. Extract from SmartPLS output

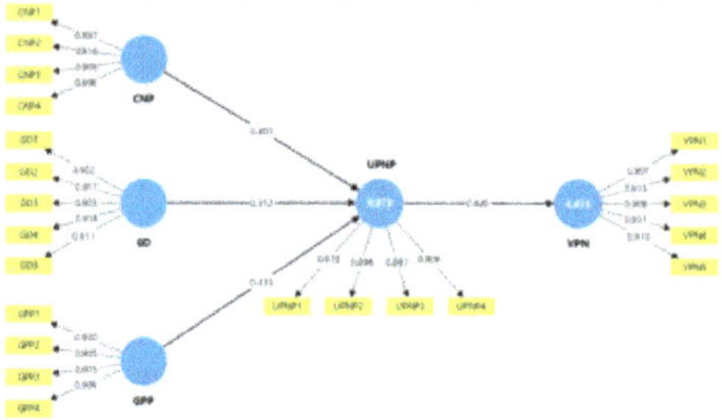

Source: SmartPLS 4 software output.

SOLUTIONS AND RECOMMENDATIONS

By mobilizing Public Value Theory, New Public Management, and Sociotechnical Theory simultaneously, this study does more than confirm a model: it enriches the debate on the governance and performance of public digital platforms. All seven hypotheses were supported at high significance ($p < 0.001$), and the magnitude of each coefficient is discussed below.

Public Digital Capability: a Necessary Yet Insufficient Driver of Platform Adoption

H1 is confirmed ($\beta = 0.335$), yet the coefficient is more moderate than infrastructure-centric accounts would predict, suggesting that digital endowment does not mechanically translate into use. The mediation result (H5: $\beta = 0.160$) reinforces this reading: the value generated by capability passes largely through how platforms are appropriated by users (Weigl et al., 2024). In the Moroccan context, where infrastructural investment often outpaces organizational adaptation, this gap between endowment and appropriation is especially salient (Belhaj & Boulahoual, 2024). Capability thus remains foundational, but its value is realized only when paired with training, accessibility, and responsive service design (Mergel et al., 2019). Beyond its statistical significance, however, the practical weight of this pathway warrants a cautious reading: a standardized beta coefficient of 0.335 means that even substantial gains in perceived digital capability translate into a comparatively modest shift in platform use, and the cross-sectional design cannot rule out the reverse possibility that respondents who already use platforms frequently subsequently rate institutional capability more favorably.

Data Governance: Building Institutional Trust as a Precondition for Value Creation

The direct effect of data governance (H2: β = 0.229) and its mediated contribution (H6: β = 0.109) confirm that trust in public data management underpins platform adoption. The modest direct coefficient suggests that data governance operates primarily as an enabling condition: it lowers barriers and strengthens perceived reliability, which then catalyzes use and value (Attard et al., 2016). Where algorithmic surveillance and data commercialization are growing concerns (Arsène et al., 2021), the quality of data governance becomes a decisive differentiator between administrations that generate trust and those that struggle to legitimize their digital agendas (Abbas et al., 2024). Beyond statistical significance, the comparatively modest size of this coefficient relative to platform governance (β = 0.229 vs. 0.323) suggests that data governance functions as a threshold condition rather than a differentiating driver: once a baseline of perceived data security is met, further gains in governance quality yield diminishing returns on use, a pattern that self-reported, single-time-point data cannot fully disentangle from reverse causation.

Platform Governance: the Central Institutional Architecture of the Digital State

The effect of platform governance on use (H3: β = 0.323) and its indirect contribution (H7: β = 0.154) establish it as the most structurally influential antecedent. This aligns with the Government-as-a-Platform literature: value emerges only when orchestration mechanisms effectively coordinate actors and resources (Cordella & Paletti, 2019). Interoperability standards, open APIs, coordination rules, and accountability mechanisms stimulate use and, through it, collective benefits underscoring that the platform state is as much a governance challenge as a technological one. Even so, an f^2 of 0.143 indicates that platform governance alone leaves most of the variance in use unexplained, a reminder that governance quality is a necessary rather than sufficient condition and that its practical influence should not be overstated relative to its statistical significance.

Platform Use as the Nexus Between Institutional Resources and Public Value

The effect of use on public value (H4: β = 0.477) is the strongest direct coefficient in the model, confirming that effective use is a proximate predictor of digital public value. Widely adopted platforms improve accessibility, reduce costs, and deepen participation. Interpreted through Moore's (1995) framework, this suggests that platforms have become a foremost mechanism through which states generate collective goods, so strategies that broaden and deepen use digital-literacy programs, inclusive interfaces, and mobile accessibility carry a high return in public value. Yet statistical significance should not be conflated with explanatory completeness: use accounts for less than a quarter of the variance in digital public value, implying that roughly three-quarters of what citizens and administrators experience as public value is shaped by factors external to the model street-level implementation quality, interpersonal service interactions, and broader institutional trust among them.

Mediation Effects: Platform Use as a Transformative Mechanism

The three mediation effects jointly confirm a sociotechnical postulate: institutional resources generate value not by themselves but through their social appropriation (Trist, 1981). Taken together, the three indirect effects converge on a single explanatory channel the everyday use of public digital platforms through which capability, data governance, and platform governance each translate into value (Begany Grace & Gil-Garcia, 2024). It is worth noting, however, that these indirect effects represent only a fraction of the corresponding total effects, indicating partial rather than full mediation: institutional resources retain a residual influence on digital public value that operates outside platform use, plausibly through channels such as institutional legitimacy or perceived procedural fairness that this model does not directly capture.

Illustrative Evidence From Mature and Emerging Platform States

The magnitude and configuration of these effects resonate with the trajectory of platform states widely regarded as international benchmarks. Estonia offers a particularly instructive illustration of how the three institutional dimensions tested in this model jointly translate into digital public value (Espinosa & Pino, 2025). Its X-Road data-exchange layer functions less as a technical pipe than as a governance infrastructure: it enforces interoperability standards, access rules, and audit trails across hundreds of public and private organizations and underpins more than three thousand digital services, illustrating the type of platform-governance architecture that the present model identifies as the strongest driver of platform use (H3: $\beta = 0.323$). Estonia's data-governance regime, built on the once-only principle and strict citizen control over personal data, performs the same trust-building function attributed here to data governance (H2), while two decades of sustained investment in digital skills and institutional capability illustrate the capability-to-use pathway captured by H1 and its mediated counterpart, H5. Read against this benchmark, Morocco's more moderate explained variance (adjusted R^2 of 0.266 for platform use and 0.225 for digital public value) should not be read as a methodological shortcoming but as a realistic signature of a platform state still consolidating institutional foundations that took more mature digital governments over two decades to align.

A cautionary counterpoint, illustrating the boundary conditions of the present findings, comes from South Korea, whose otherwise advanced and internationally recognized e-government infrastructure has nonetheless struggled to translate capability and governance investment into uniform platform use among vulnerable citizens, including older adults, rural residents, and lower-income groups, revealing a persistent digital divide despite high aggregate adoption (Sung & Lee, 2024). This experience underscores a boundary condition of the present model: the positive path from capability and governance to use, confirmed here at the aggregate level, need not hold uniformly across sub-populations, and Morocco's own digital-inclusion strategy should anticipate similarly uneven adoption across age, income, and geographic strata rather than assuming that institutional investment alone will translate into homogeneous platform use. For Morocco, whose Maroc Digital strategy channels substantial public investment into national digital infrastructures, both benchmarks carry a shared lesson: the Estonian trajectory shows the long-run payoff of sequencing governance ahead of infrastructure, while the Korean experience warns that aggregate adoption figures can mask persistent gaps among rural, older, or lower-income users that a purely infrastructure-led strategy would not detect.

Theoretical and Managerial Implications

Theoretically, the study provides empirical validation of an integrative tripartite framework Public Value Theory, New Public Management, and Sociotechnical Theory rarely tested quantitatively in prior work, and it clarifies that the link between institutional resources and public value is mediated by patterns of use and conditioned by governance quality (Weigl et al., 2024).

This theoretical synthesis also clarifies how the three complementary perspectives introduced earlier operate together rather than in parallel. The Resource-Based View explains why public digital capability alone yields only a moderate effect (H1: $\beta = 0.335$): capability is a necessary strategic resource, but, consistent with resource-based logic, it generates a public-value advantage only when combined with complementary organizational routines rather than treated as a standalone asset. Institutional Theory clarifies why data governance and platform governance operate as legitimacy-conferring mechanisms rather than pure efficiency levers: their comparatively strong association with use (H2, H3) reflects the coercive and normative pressures that push administrations to adopt visible governance standards even before efficiency gains materialize. Finally, technology-acceptance logic (TAM/

UTAUT) explains the mediating role of platform use (H4–H7): institutional resources are necessary conditions, but digital public value materializes only through the behavioral layer of perceived usefulness and ease of use that TAM/UTAUT places at the center of technology adoption. Read together, the tripartite framework advanced in the introduction and the constructs' theoretical foundations converge on a single conclusion: platform states are simultaneously resource-based, institutional, and behavioral phenomena, and none of the three lenses is sufficient on its own.

Managerially, three recommendations follow. First, infrastructure investment should be paired with user-adoption programs, since capability without use fails to create value (Mergel et al., 2019). Second, data governance should be treated as a strategic priority: transparent policies and robust privacy guarantees are value-creation levers, not merely legal obligations (Janssen et al., 2020). Third, platform-governance architecture interoperability, coordination rules, and open APIs emerges as the single most powerful lever for maximizing digital public value. These recommendations carry particular weight in Morocco, where modernization programs still face governance and accessibility challenges (Belhaj & Boulahoual, 2024).

These implications extend beyond the Moroccan case. For emerging platform states across the Middle East and North Africa, Sub-Saharan Africa, and South and Southeast Asia that share comparable constraints fragmented legacy infrastructures, uneven digital literacy, and nascent data-protection regimes the same sequencing logic applies: governance architecture should precede or accompany, rather than trail, infrastructure investment. Regional digital-transformation strategies could operationalize this lesson by conditioning platform-infrastructure financing on the prior adoption of interoperability standards and data-governance frameworks, rather than treating governance as a downstream implementation detail. More broadly, because platform use consistently mediates the effect of all three institutional antecedents, emerging platform states should track adoption and usage indicators not merely infrastructure-deployment metrics as the primary performance benchmark for digital-government programs, a recommendation consistent with the experience of more mature platform states such as Estonia, where usage-centered governance rather than infrastructure spending alone sustained digital public value over time.

FUTURE RESEARCH DIRECTIONS

Several limitations temper these findings and open avenues for future inquiry. The cross-sectional design and reliance on self-reported data limit causal inference and may introduce common method bias (Podsakoff et al., 2003); longitudinal panel designs would allow scholars to track how governance capacity translates into value over time and to identify sequencing effects between capability building and institutional maturation. The reliance on non-probability convenience sampling compounds this limitation: because respondents were reached through professional networks, administrative mailing lists, and alumni contacts, the sample likely over-represents digitally literate, urban, and professionally connected respondents relative to the broader population of public-service users, including rural citizens, older users, and those with intermittent platform access. This skew plausibly inflates both the reported frequency of platform use and the favorability of governance perceptions, and it constrains the external validity of the path coefficients beyond digitally engaged segments of the population; future studies should pursue stratified or quota-based probability sampling, or triangulate self-reported measures with platform usage logs, to verify whether the relationships identified here hold among less digitally engaged citizens. The focus on a single emerging economy, while offering contextual depth, constrains generalizability and calls for multi-country comparative studies testing whether the relative weight of the three institutional dimensions varies across administrative cultures and regulatory environments; benchmarking Morocco's coefficients against mature platform states such as Estonia would help determine whether the moderate effect sizes observed here reflect a universal early-stage pattern of platform-state development or context-specific institutional frictions particular to the Moroccan administrative culture. The model also does not capture the potential "public disvalue" of platformized governance digital exclusion, algorithmic opacity, or the erosion of democratic accountability; future work should integrate such indicators to measure the net societal impact of platformization rather than its benefits alone. Data security and privacy constitute a related blind spot: although the data-governance construct captures perceived security and compliance, the model does not measure actual breach incidence, algorithmic data-sharing risks, or citizens' evolving privacy expectations as platforms accumulate increasingly sensitive personal data; future research combining survey-based governance perceptions with technical security audits and privacy-impact assessments would provide a more complete picture of the trade-off between platform efficiency and citizen data protection. In addition, the growing concentration of public digital infrastructures in the hands of large technology firms raises unresolved questions of digital sovereignty and long-term administrative autonomy (Boullier, 2022). Finally, the expanding role of artificial intelligence in automating public services raises new questions of trust, explainability, and citizen agency: as administrations delegate more decisions to automated systems, future models should incorporate perceived algorithmic fairness and explainability as antecedents of trust, alongside the governance and capability dimensions already tested here. Extending the model to sub-national governments where capacity is often weaker and digital divides more pronounced would further show how platform states can be built inclusively from the ground up, rather than reproducing at the local level the same uneven adoption patterns observed among vulnerable citizens in more digitally mature contexts.

CONCLUSION

This study investigated the determinants of digital public value creation in emerging platform states, applying PLS-SEM to 350 respondents from Moroccan public administrations and citizen users. Integrating Public Value Theory, New Public Management, and Sociotechnical Theory, it shows that public digital capability, data governance, and platform governance each exert significant positive effects on the use of public digital platforms, which in turn is the principal generative mechanism of digital public value. All seven hypotheses were supported. The most notable finding is that platform use consistently mediates the relationship between the three institutional antecedents and public value. Platform governance emerges as the strongest composite driver ($\beta = 0.323$ direct; $\beta = 0.154$ indirect), closely followed by digital capability ($\beta = 0.335$ direct; $\beta = 0.160$ indirect). The practical message is clear: the platform state is fundamentally a governance challenge, not merely a technological one. Without coherent institutional architectures interoperability standards, coordination rules, and accountability mechanisms even the most sophisticated infrastructures fail to generate sustained public value. For Morocco and for emerging platform states more broadly, investment strategies should prioritize the alignment of governance frameworks with platform design rather than infrastructure deployment alone. Benchmarked against more mature digital governments such as Estonia, Morocco's trajectory appears to be an early but coherent stage of the same institutional pathway, provided that governance architecture, and not infrastructure spending alone, remains the organizing principle of the country's digital-transformation agenda in the years ahead. These conclusions should nonetheless be read alongside the study's main limitations, foremost among them the cross-sectional, convenience-sampled design and the fact that the data-governance construct captures citizens' perceptions of data security and privacy rather than measured breach incidence or technical audit outcomes; as platforms accumulate increasingly sensitive personal data, this remains an important boundary of what the present findings can support and a priority for future research.

REFERENCES

Abbas, A. E., Van Velzen, T., Ofe, H., Van De Kaa, G., Zuiderwijk, A., & De Reuver, M. (2024). Beyond control over data: Conceptualizing data sovereignty from a social contract perspective. *Electronic Markets*, *34*(1), 20. DOI: 10.1007/s12525-024-00695-2

Addo, A. (2022). Orchestrating a digital platform ecosystem to address societal challenges: A robust action perspective. *Journal of Information Technology*, *37*(4), 359–386. DOI: 10.1177/02683962221088333

Alqahtani, A., Yan, J., Vlahu-Gjorgievska, E., & Cao, C. (2025). *Factors influencing citizens' adoption of AI-enabled public services in Saudi Arabia: The role of cybersecurity, privacy, and trust.* DOI: 10.1145/3785153

Arsène, S., Mabi, C., & Carey-Libbrecht, L. (2021). Public action through the lens of digital governmentality. *Reseaux (London)*, *225*(1), 9–22. DOI: 10.3917/res.225.0009

Asmawanti-S, D., Afiah, N. N., Ritchi, H., & Suharman, H. (2025). Literature review of government digital services based on public value theory and citizen perspectives. *Cogent Business & Management*, *12*(1), 2518494. DOI: 10.1080/23311975.2025.2518494

Attard, J., Orlandi, F., & Auer, S. (2016). Data driven governments: Creating value through open government data. In *Transactions on Large-Scale Data- and Knowledge-Centered Systems XXVII* (Vol. 9860, pp. 84-110). DOI: 10.1007/978-3-662-53416-8_6

Attard, J., Orlandi, F., Scerri, S., & Auer, S. (2015). A systematic review of open government data initiatives. *Government Information Quarterly*, *32*(4), 399–418. DOI: 10.1016/j.giq.2015.07.006

Begany Grace, M., & Gil-Garcia, J. R. (2024). Open government data initiatives as agents of digital transformation in the public sector: Exploring the extent of use among early adopters. *Government Information Quarterly*, *41*(3), 101955. Advance online publication. DOI: 10.1016/j.giq.2024.101955

Belhaj, Y., & Boulahoual, A. (2024). La gouvernance des données au service de la création de valeur publique: Cas du Maroc. *American Scientific Journal*, *3*(23), 635–654. DOI: 10.5281/zenodo.11122145

Bolton, M., & Mintrom, M. (2023). RegTech and creating public value: Opportunities and challenges. *Policy Design and Practice*, *6*(3), 266–282. DOI: 10.1080/25741292.2023.2213059

Boullier, D. (2022). *Puissance des plateformes numériques, territoires et souverainetés* (2e éd.) [Research paper]. Sciences Po, Centre d'Études Européennes et de Politique Comparée.

Brown, A., Fishenden, J., Thompson, M., & Venters, W. (2017). Appraising the impact and role of platform models and Government as a Platform (GaaP) in UK Government public service reform: Towards a Platform Assessment Framework (PAF). *Government Information Quarterly*, *34*(2), 167–182. Advance online publication. DOI: 10.1016/j.giq.2017.03.003

Cao, J. (2024). The role of digital governance in improving government transparency and citizen engagement. *Applied Mathematics and Nonlinear Sciences*, *9*(1), 20243368. Advance online publication. DOI: 10.2478/amns-2024-3368

Caron, D. J. (2021). *Écosystème de la transformation de l'administration publique vers le numérique*. Presses de l'Université du Québec. https://www.puq.ca/catalogue/livres/ecosysteme-transformation-administration-publique-vers-numerique-3906.html

Chandrasekhar, R. (2025). *Sustainable open data ecosystems through data quality, governance, and infrastructure: Unlocking social, political and economic value.* https://hal.science/hal-05328147v1

Chen, L., Yi, J., Li, S., & Tong, T. W. (2022). Platform governance design in platform ecosystems: Implications for complementors' multihoming decision. *Journal of Management*, *48*(3), 630–656. DOI: 10.1177/0149206320988337

Cordella, A., Gualdi, F., & Van de Laar, M. (2024). Digital skills within the public sector: A missing link to achieve the Sustainable Development Goals (SDGs). *Information Polity*, *29*(1), 13–33. Advance online publication. DOI: 10.3233/IP-230008

Cordella, A., & Paletti, A. (2019). Government as a platform, orchestration, and public value creation: The Italian case. *Government Information Quarterly*, *36*(4), 101409. DOI: 10.1016/j.giq.2019.101409

Danneels, L., & Viaene, S. (2025). Organizational capabilities for Government as a Platform: The case of engaging the labour market ecosystem. *Information Polity*, *30*(3), 180–200. Advance online publication. DOI: 10.1177/15701255251349949

Díaz-Arancibia, J., Hochstetter-Diez, J., Bustamante-Mora, A., Sepúlveda-Cuevas, S., Albayay, I., & Arango-López, J. (2024). Navigating digital transformation and technology adoption: A literature review from small and medium-sized enterprises in developing countries. *Sustainability (Basel)*, *16*(14), 5946. DOI: 10.3390/su16145946

Doré, G. (2023). La privatisation numérique: Déstabilisation et réinvention du service public [Compte rendu]. *RECMA, 370-371*(4), 133–134. DOI: 10.3917/recma.370.0134

Doshi, A. R., & Schmidt, W. (2024). Soft governance across digital platforms using transparency. *Strategy Science, 9*(2), 185–204. DOI: 10.1287/stsc.2023.0006

Dunleavy, P., & Margetts, H. (2023). Data science, artificial intelligence and the third wave of digital era governance. *Public Policy and Administration*. Advance online publication. DOI: 10.1177/09520767231198737

Espinosa, V. I., & Pino, A. (2025). E-Government as a development strategy: The case of Estonia. *International Journal of Public Administration, 48*(2), 86–99. DOI: 10.1080/01900692.2024.2316128

Esposito, F. M. (2024). Platforming public administration: An empirical analysis on the institutionalization of digital technologies. *Tecnoscienza — Italian Journal of Science &. Technology Studies, 15*(1), 39–59. DOI: 10.6092/issn.2038-3460/18779

Fornell, C., & Larcker, D. F. (1981). Evaluating structural equation models with unobservable variables and measurement error. *JMR, Journal of Marketing Research, 18*(1), 39–50. DOI: 10.1177/002224378101800104

Francis-Auton, E., Cheek, C., Austin, E., Ransolin, N., Richardson, L., Safi, M., Hayba, N., Testa, L., Harrison, R., Braithwaite, J., & Clay-Williams, R. (2024). Exploring and understanding the 'experience' in experience-based codesign: A state-of-the-art review. *International Journal of Qualitative Methods, 23*, 16094069241235563. Advance online publication. DOI: 10.1177/16094069241235563

Frucquet, P., & Carassus, D. (2023). *Territoires numériques: Comment favoriser la (co-)création de valeur publique?* https://univ-pau.hal.science/hal-04362404

Gil, L. R. A. (2023). *La gouvernance des données en tant que « biens communs »: étude juridico-stratégique pour une valorisation publique des données informationnelles [Thèse de doctorat].* https://theses.hal.science/tel-04042474

Grimmelikhuijsen, S. (2023). Explaining why the computer says no: Algorithmic transparency affects the perceived trustworthiness of automated decision-making. *Public Administration Review, 83*(2), 241–262. DOI: 10.1111/puar.13483

Gross, N., & Geiger, S. (2023). Choreographing for public value in digital health? *Big Data & Society, 10*(2), 20539517231220622. Advance online publication. DOI: 10.1177/20539517231220622

Hair, J. F., Hult, G. T. M., Ringle, C. M., & Sarstedt, M. (2022). *A primer on partial least squares structural equation modeling (PLS-SEM)* (3rd ed.). Sage.

Haug, N., Dan, S., & Mergel, I. (2024). Digitally-induced change in the public sector: A systematic review and research agenda. *Public Management Review*, *26*(7), 1963–1987. DOI: 10.1080/14719037.2023.2234917

Hein, A., Engert, M., Ryu, S., Schaffer, N., Hermes, S., & Krcmar, H. (2023). Building open government data platform ecosystems: A dynamic development approach that engages users from the start. *Government Information Quarterly*, *40*(4), 101878. DOI: 10.1016/j.giq.2023.101878

Henseler, J., Ringle, C. M., & Sarstedt, M. (2015). A new criterion for assessing discriminant validity in variance-based structural equation modeling. *Journal of the Academy of Marketing Science*, *43*(1), 115–135. DOI: 10.1007/s11747-014-0403-8

Hietala, H., & Päivärinta, T. (2025). Governing collective ambidexterity: Antecedents, mechanisms, and outcomes in digital service ecosystems. *Government Information Quarterly*, *42*(1), 102001. DOI: 10.1016/j.giq.2024.102001

Hood, C. (1991). A public management for all seasons? *Public Administration*, *69*(1), 3–19. DOI: 10.1111/j.1467-9299.1991.tb00779.x

Iden, J., & Bygstad, B. (2024). Managing digital transformation with sociotechnical systems theory. *European Journal of Information Systems*, *33*(6), 789–807. DOI: 10.1080/0960085X.2024.2347950

Jacob, S., Defacqz, S., & Agossou, N. (2022). *Promesses et défis de la transformation numérique du secteur public.* Chaire de recherche sur l'administration numérique, Université Laval.

Janowski, T., Estevez, E., & Baguma, R. (2018). Platform governance for sustainable development: Reshaping citizen-administration relationships in the digital age. *Government Information Quarterly*, *35*(4, Suppl.), S1–S16. DOI: 10.1016/j.giq.2018.09.002

Janssen, M., Brous, P., Estevez, E., Barbosa, L. S., & Janowski, T. (2020). Data governance: Organizing data for trustworthy Artificial Intelligence. *Government Information Quarterly*, *37*(3), 101493. DOI: 10.1016/j.giq.2020.101493

Jonathan, G. M., Perjons, E., & Rusu, L. (2024). Digital transformation-driven decentralisation of public governance. *Procedia Computer Science*, *239*, 1220–1229. DOI: 10.1016/j.procs.2024.06.290

Kline, R. B. (2023). *Principles and practice of structural equation modeling* (5th ed.). Guilford Press.

Kock, N. (2015). Common method bias in PLS-SEM: A full collinearity assessment approach. *International Journal of e-Collaboration, 11*(4), 1–10. DOI: 10.4018/ijec.2015100101

Lanna, M. (2025). Plateformes et gouvernance des données. *RPN, 1*(1). Advance online publication. DOI: 10.62688/RPN20259194

Lee, J.-Y., Kim, B., & Yoon, S.-H. (2024). A conceptual digital policy framework via mixed-methods approach: Navigating public value for value-driven digital transformation. *Government Information Quarterly, 41*(3), 101961. DOI: 10.1016/j.giq.2024.101961

Lin, Z., & Yaakop, M. R. (2024). Research on digital governance based on Web of Science - A bibliometric analysis. *Frontiers in Political Science, 6*, 1403404. DOI: 10.3389/fpos.2024.1403404

Luna, D. E., Picazo-Vela, S., Battulga, B., & Luna-Reyes, L. F. (2024). Creating public value through digital service delivery from a citizen's perspective. *Government Information Quarterly, 41*(2), 101928. DOI: 10.1016/j.giq.2024.101928

Ly, B., Ly, R., & Ma, S. (2026). Digital transformation and flexibility in public services: Knowledge, culture and digital infrastructures. *Journal of Innovation & Knowledge, 13*, 100947. DOI: 10.1016/j.jik.2026.100947

Marty, F. (2020). Accès aux données, coopétition intra-plateforme et concurrence inter-plateformes numériques. *Revue d'Economie Industrielle, 169*, 221–246. DOI: 10.4000/rei.8967

Mergel, I., Edelmann, N., & Haug, N. (2019). Defining digital transformation: Results from expert interviews. *Government Information Quarterly, 36*(4), 101385. DOI: 10.1016/j.giq.2019.06.002

Mericskay, B. (2021). Les effets de l'open data et du big data dans la fabrique des cartes de l'action publique. In Les cartes de l'action publique (pp. 107-128). DOI: 10.4000/books.septentrion.127177

Moore, M. H. (1995). *Creating public value: Strategic management in government.* Harvard University Press.

Podsakoff, P. M., MacKenzie, S. B., Lee, J.-Y., & Podsakoff, N. P. (2003). Common method biases in behavioral research: A critical review of the literature and recommended remedies. *The Journal of Applied Psychology, 88*(5), 879–903. DOI: 10.1037/0021-9010.88.5.879 PMID: 14516251

Porcher, S., Cristofini, O., Gimenez, J., & Beuve, J. (2024). Transformation digitale des services publics locaux et valeur publique: Une étude de cas sur la santé et la formation professionnelle en France. *Gestion et management public, 12*(3), 31-47. DOI: 10.3917/gmp.123.0031

Rukanova, B., Van Engelenburg, S., Ubacht, J., Tan, Y.-H., Geurts, M., Sies, M., Molenhuis, M., Slegt, M., & Van Dijk, D. (2023). Public value creation through voluntary business to government information sharing enabled by digital infrastructure innovations. *Government Information Quarterly, 40*(2), 101786. DOI: 10.1016/j.giq.2022.101786

Sarstedt, M., Hair, J. F.Jr, Nitzl, C., Ringle, C. M., & Howard, M. C. (2020). Beyond a tandem analysis of SEM and PROCESS: Use of PLS-SEM for mediation analyses! *International Journal of Market Research, 62*(3), 288–299. DOI: 10.1177/1470785320915686

Sung, W., & Lee, J. (2024). A longitudinal study on the diffusion and the divide in the use of e-government services among vulnerable citizens in Korea. *Government Information Quarterly, 41*(2), 101938. Advance online publication. DOI: 10.1016/j.giq.2024.101938

Tonon, C. (2020). La GovTech, nouvelle frontière de la souveraineté numérique. *Institut français des relations internationales (IFRI).* https://www.ifri.org/sites/default/files/migrated_files/documents/atoms/files/tonon_govtech_nov2020.pdf

Toots, M., McBride, K., Kalvet, T., & Krimmer, R. (2017). Open data as enabler of public service co-creation: Exploring the drivers and barriers. In 2017 Conference for E-Democracy and Open Government (CeDEM) (pp. 102-112). DOI: 10.1109/CeDEM.2017.12

Trist, E. (1981). *The evolution of socio-technical systems: A conceptual framework and an action research program* (Occasional Paper No. 2). Ontario Quality of Working Life Centre.

Türk, P. (2020). L'État plateforme numérique. *Revue du droit public, 2020*(5), 1189-1212. https://droit.cairn.info/article/RDP_095_1189

Twizeyimana, J. D., & Andersson, A. (2019). The public value of E-Government — A literature review. *Government Information Quarterly*, *36*(2), 167–178. DOI: 10.1016/j.giq.2019.01.001

Venkatesh, V., & Bala, H. (2008). Technology Acceptance Model 3 and a research agenda on interventions. *Decision Sciences*, *39*(2), 273–315. DOI: 10.1111/j.1540-5915.2008.00192.x

Vial, G. (2019). Understanding digital transformation: A review and a research agenda. *The Journal of Strategic Information Systems*, *28*(2), 118–144. DOI: 10.1016/j.jsis.2019.01.003

Villodre, J. (2025). A three-model approach to understand social media-mediated transparency in public administrations. *International Review of Administrative Sciences*, *91*(1), 111–129. DOI: 10.1177/00208523241261896

Virtanen, P., & Harri, J. (2023). Public value creation mechanisms in the context of public service logic: An integrated conceptual framework. *International Journal of Public Administration*. Advance online publication. DOI: 10.1080/14719037.2023.2268111

Weigl, L., Roth, T., Amard, A., & Zavolokina, L. (2024). When public values and user-centricity in e-government collide — A systematic review. *Government Information Quarterly*, *41*(3), 101956. DOI: 10.1016/j.giq.2024.101956

Wirtz, B. W., Langer, P. F., & Schmidt, F. W. (2021). Digital government: Business model development for public value creation - A dynamic capabilities based framework. *Public Administration Quarterly*, *45*(3), 232–255. DOI: 10.37808/paq.45.3.2

Wirtz, B. W., Weyerer, J. C., & Kehl, I. (2022). Governance of artificial intelligence: A risk and guideline-based integrative framework. *Government Information Quarterly*, *39*(4), 101685. DOI: 10.1016/j.giq.2022.101685

Yukhno, A. (2024). Digital transformation: Exploring big data governance in public administration. *Public Organization Review*, *24*(1), 335–349. DOI: 10.1007/s11115-022-00694-x

Zhao, B., Cheng, S., Schiff, K. J., & Kim, Y. (2023). Digital transparency and citizen participation: Evidence from the online crowdsourcing platform of the City of Sacramento. *Government Information Quarterly*, *40*(4), 101868. DOI: 10.1016/j.giq.2023.101868

KEY TERMS AND DEFINITIONS

Data Governance: The set of institutional mechanisms, rules, and practices that ensure the quality, security, transparency, and ethical use of data within public digital systems.

Data Sovereignty: The capacity of a state to control the storage, processing, and circulation of public data within its jurisdiction, particularly when digital infrastructures depend on foreign or private technology providers.

Digital Divide: The unequal access to, and capacity to benefit from, digital public platforms across citizens differentiated by age, income, geographic location, or digital literacy, which can limit the realization of digital public value even where institutional capability and governance are strong.

Digital Public Value: The collective societal benefits, such as transparency, trust, inclusion, and service quality, generated when public administrations use digital technologies and platforms to serve citizens.

New Public Management (NPM): A reform doctrine in public administration that emphasizes market-oriented efficiency, performance measurement, and the disaggregation of bureaucratic structures.

Partial Least Squares Structural Equation Modeling (PLS-SEM): A variance-based statistical technique used to estimate complex models of relationships among multiple latent constructs from survey data.

Platform State: A model of public governance in which the state acts as an open digital infrastructure, providing data, standards, and interfaces that allow third parties to co-create public services and value.

Public Digital Capability: The combination of technological infrastructure, organizational competencies, and digital skills that enable a public administration to design, deploy, and sustain digital public services.

Public Platform Governance: The coordination mechanisms, institutional rules, and interoperability standards that regulate interactions among public and private stakeholders within a public digital ecosystem.

Public Value Theory: A normative framework holding that the performance of public institutions should be assessed by the societal outcomes they generate rather than by internal efficiency alone.

Sociotechnical Theory: A theoretical perspective stating that the performance of technological systems depends on the joint optimization of technical and social subsystems rather than on technology alone.

Use of Public Digital Platforms: The extent to which civil servants, administrators, and citizens actively and routinely engage with governmental digital platforms to access or deliver public services.

Chapter 3

Algorithmic Public Management for Democratic Resilience-AI-Driven Futures in Government Decision-Making

Muhammad Usman Tariq
http://orcid.org/0000-0002-7605-3040
Abu Dhabi University, UAE & University College Cork, Ireland

ABSTRACT

As societies become more divided, misinformation, complex governance, and a lack of public trust in governance increase. Technology that applies AI in governance has both positive and negative aspects. This chapter examines how algorithmic technology can strengthen democracy by enhancing the forecasting of policies, allocation of resources, management of crises, and public engagement. It examines new approaches in countries such as Estonia and Singapore, where digital public management technology has large and positive innovations. However, it also examines critical issues such as bias in algorithms, lack of transparency, lack of accountability, and threats to people's freedoms. It proposes a set of guidelines for applying AI in public management responsibly, with democratic control, explainability, and public engagement in designing the technology. Ultimately, applying AI in governance should increase trust in governance institutions while safeguarding basic freedoms to ensure a bright future for democracy.

DOI: 10.4018/979-8-3373-9765-8.ch003

INTRODUCTION

Public administration has undergone significant changes in the last 20 years because of technology. Initially, the aim was to make record-keeping easier and to develop government websites. However, it is currently going beyond that. Governments use computer systems and algorithms to make decisions. Computer systems assist in predicting job losses, planning healthcare, identifying tax fraud and controlling traffic. This is not only an aspect of using new technology but also of decision-making in governments. In the past, the aim was to make services easier and work faster (Masoudi, 2025). Currently, algorithms influence decisions, deciding which cases to prioritize first, and even making decisions automatically that were previously made by humans. Technology not only assists the government but also influences its operations. The application of algorithms in the government has increased for several reasons.

Currently, more data are available on social services, economic activities, environmental monitoring, and citizen interactions. Traditional methods of dealing with government work cannot process all data quickly and effectively. Citizens also want the same fast and efficient services they receive from the private sector. In sectors such as social welfare and public health, algorithms can identify patterns that humans are unaware of. In times of major crises, such as pandemics or natural disasters, algorithms assist governments in making decisions instantly.

However, this change is not only about efficiency. This is changing the way public administration operates. In the past, the government made decisions based on clear rules, hierarchy, and human judgment. These decisions were visible and challenging. The algorithms are different. These are based on numbers, risks, and past outcomes. Decisions are made by models that consider previous outcomes (He et al., 2025). This makes decisions appear more technical and less human-like. Although this could make decisions less discriminatory in some instances, it is unclear how clear and fair the decision-making process is in practice. If a person's benefits are determined by a risk score or if police allocations are determined by predicting crime, it is difficult to explain, in simple terms, why. This causes difficulty in following past rules regarding explaining decisions and ensuring fairness. The shift from digital government to algorithmic governance represents a significant transition.

Public management has oscillated among various approaches to managing things, such as hierarchical models, market-oriented reforms, organizational networks, and collaboration. Algorithmic governance corresponds to these approaches. It assists in making things more efficient and effective but also makes the public sector more dependent on technology and data. It is becoming increasingly difficult to determine who is responsible for the problem. Democracy requires clarity on these matters, and the public sector is subject to public law. In this case, the importance of resilience in democracy cannot be overstated. Democracies face many challenges, including misinformation, division, unequal money distribution, and environmental problems (Aragani et al., 2025). Algorithms can increase resilience by assisting governments in planning and acting quickly. The predictive capabilities of algorithms can indicate how policies affect people, allowing governments to act before problems worsen. Data analysis can assist in efforts to reduce unfairness and prevent large-scale risks.

However, resilience is not simply about using appropriate tools. It also involves maintaining people's trust and including them in the process of implementation. If algorithms make people feel left out or treated unfairly, they could undermine the resilience they are trying to build. This chapter examines the impact of algorithmic systems on the nature of government and how democratic principles are not undermined in the process. It does not merely examine technology or rules (Androutsopoulou et al., 2025). To understand the impact of algorithms on public management, it is necessary to examine how institutions are structured, the laws that regulate them, how institutions function, and how individuals experience these systems in practice. Mechanisms are also required to discuss how these systems affect and shape them in the future. Mechanisms are also required to discuss how these systems affect and shape them in the future. While algorithms can be employed in ways that are open, responsible, and participatory, helping to build trust and facilitate greater flexibility in government, they also have the potential to lead to greater unfairness and erode public trust in government if they are not sufficiently monitored. The question is not whether governments will employ AI but how they can do so in ways that will help rather than harm the underpinnings of democracy.

BACKGROUND

Algorithmic public management results from the intersection of public management, data science, and institutional functioning. Essentially, it is the application of algorithmic systems, particularly artificial intelligence and machine learning, to the way governments formulate policies, allocate resources, and regulate and measure their performance. Unlike previous transformations that only expedited paperwork or used computers to perform simple tasks, algorithmic public management alters decision-making. It is more than just technology and impacts decision-making in the government. Algorithms are not only used to store and retrieve information; they also sort, forecast, prioritize, and recommend. This shapes what happens and the outcomes achieved (Kim, 2026). The application of algorithmic public management includes, but is not limited to, the application of data to forecast needs in social services, automatically determining eligibility for benefits, determining risk in regulatory inspections, smart infrastructure management, and performance dashboards to inform decision-making by leaders. Thus, APM is not merely a more effective use of technology but a radical shift in how power, decision-making, and responsibility are exercised in government. People working with data, analysts, and technology vendors have a say in decision-making, along with other regular employees of the government. Decisions are partially encoded in models that are difficult for non-technical personnel to interpret. Consequently, the impact of APM trickles down into how organizations function, what professionals consider to be the right thing, and how different groups within the government function.

To determine whether this is helpful or a hindrance to the government, it might be useful to apply the theory of public value may be applied. Public value extends beyond the goal of making things more efficient and aims to achieve better societal outcomes. Digital technology can add value by making services more accessible, reducing the workload for people interacting with the government, and assisting in making policies more responsive to people's needs. For instance, the use of real-time data can help identify where services are needed and direct resources to those areas. Open data platforms can make governments more transparent and enable more public innovation. However, public value is not automatically added by simply applying technology; it requires a design that is beneficial to all, fair outcomes, and opportunities for participation. Digital transformation, when performed with public value in mind, involves making decisions about how things are designed and governed (Moon et al., 2025).

Decisions regarding data collection, rules for algorithms, and models demonstrate what matters. The public value approach provides clear guidelines for rapid transformations that are taking place. The concept of democratic resilience is another piece of this puzzle. Democratic resilience refers to the capacity of institutions to cope with shocks, adjust to new circumstances, and maintain public trust even during difficult times.

When we become too reliant on the results of algorithms, it is easy to feel that we know what we are doing, and decisions are made by experts rather than through democratic deliberation. However, when we openly discuss uncertainty, citizens can make informed decisions regarding the vaccine. When governments are open about the benefits and limitations of AI tools, they help build a culture in which everyone shares responsibility rather than simply trusting technology (Badawy, 2025). Anticipation is not only about technology; it also involves politics and ethics. Identifying the risks to focus on, the signs to look for, and what to do about them can reveal what society values. Anticipatory governance must strike a balance between data analysis and conversations that involve different experiences. Otherwise, it may privilege expert knowledge over the many ways in which people live and experience the world. Public problems such as climate change, urban inequality, and migration are complex. They have many interrelated variables and unpredictable results. What happens in one place may have unforeseen effects elsewhere in the world. Although algorithms can be used to understand some of these relationships, they cannot eliminate all uncertainties. Another crucial aspect of complexity is the influence of society on data.

Data are not simply an objective reflection of the world; they are socially produced. Official records reflect some aspects of behavior but not others. Past biases can be embedded in data, which then affect the algorithm outputs. It is crucial to acknowledge this fact to ensure fair governance. This implies that data quality needs to be enhanced and that the data needs to be representative and less biased. This also implies that outcomes must be checked periodically to detect unjust outcomes. A democracy can endure only if we correct our mistakes. Fixed models that do not seek feedback can increase rather than reduce inequality (Kim, 2026). Complexity and foresight indicate the need to be humble, flexible, and forward-looking. These concepts influence the application of algorithms in public management, not as a necessity to automate but as a body of choices based on values. As governments address these challenges, they have two primary responsibilities.

On the one hand, they must leverage technology to address large challenges that cannot be addressed through traditional governance. However, they must maintain the democratic principles that underpin public governance. Incorporating AI into governance can yield positive and negative outcomes. This can enable more informed and timely responses to data. However, it can also lead to a concentration of power, lack of transparency in decision-making, and diminished opportunities for people to contest or challenge decisions (Anand & Wan Mohamed, 2025). The key lies in the design of institutions, which include standards for transparency, opportunities for participation, legal frameworks and ethics. Ultimately, having good ideas is significant because it has implications for policymaking.

If algorithmic public management is simply a technical solution, the conversation may be limited to purchasing solutions and increasing efficiency. However, if it is considered a major shift in the way the government is conducted, more fundamental questions arise: Who determines what is of value to the public? How are trade-offs made? What are the appropriate rules for machine-made decisions? These questions require conversations that span multiple disciplines and ongoing reflection (Masoudi, 2025). The future of democratic governance in the age of AI will be less about how intelligent machines are and more about how wisely they are integrated into our systems.

The Architecture of AI-Driven Decision-Making in Government

The use of AI in government decision-making is based on factors that may not be visible to the public but are important for making decisions. At the bottom of this is the data infrastructure, which refers to the systems that collect, store, link, protect, and use information across various government departments. Without good data flowing smoothly, even the best AI systems cannot function effectively. Therefore, the beginning of AI use in the government is not the technology itself but the quality and ability of government records to share information with each other.

Governments that have developed safe ways to identify people, linked record systems, and databases that can work together are better at using AI practically. These systems allow agencies to link data from different areas, such as job records with education or health information with population data, while ensuring people's privacy and security. If data are divided among different departments, the use of AI is limited and ineffective. Digital state capacity also encompasses the people and entities required to oversee technological systems. Experts such as data scientists, policy analysts, cybersecurity experts, and lawyers need to collaborate within the government. However, if they have strong in-house expertise, they will retain control and ensure that the technology aligns with public values and adheres to the democratic principles. Once data systems are established, predictive analytics becomes an important component of AI decision-making. The outcome relies on the quality and fairness of the data used to train models. If past data are unfair, they may be replicated in new models, and the problem may worsen. Therefore, the use of predictive analytics requires careful checks to ensure that the models are fair and effective. It is easy to track the origin of the data and the models used to verify and challenge outcomes. Moreover, human involvement is required for these methods. Predictions should assist people in making decisions rather than replacing them. Automated decision systems represent further development of AI because they make decisions. Table 1 summarizes the key components of AI-driven decision-making systems in the government.

Table 1. Architecture of AI-Driven Decision-Making in Government

Component	Description	Function in Governance	Key Risks
Data Infrastructure	Systems for collecting, linking, and managing public data	Enables integration across departments and supports decision-making	Data bias, privacy breaches, fragmentation
Predictive Analytics	Models that identify patterns and forecast outcomes	Supports policy planning, risk detection, and resource allocation	Bias amplification, lack of transparency
Automated Decision Systems	AI systems that execute decisions without direct human input	Improves speed, consistency, and scalability of public services	Lack of explainability, reduced accountability

continued on following page

Table 1. Continued

Component	Description	Function in Governance	Key Risks
Scenario Modelling & Foresight	Simulation tools for predicting future outcomes	Supports long-term planning and adaptive governance	Model assumptions bias, over-reliance on projections
Human Oversight Systems	Mechanisms for monitoring and intervening in AI processes	Ensures ethical use and accountability	Oversight fatigue, limited technical capacity

Source. Own elaboration

Whereas predictive analytics provides recommendations, automated systems can act (He et al., 2025). For instance, in social welfare, AI systems can determine whether a person is eligible for assistance and automatically grant or deny the benefits. In taxation, AI systems can identify questionable tax returns and scrutinize them. In law enforcement, AI systems can determine where to deploy police patrols based on crime patterns. In healthcare, AI systems can assist in determining who requires special care (Tariq, 2024). The key advantage of automated systems is that they can process many cases quickly, saving time and money. The use of the same rules helps ensure consistency in decisions and prevents discrimination. However, there are some disadvantages. When decisions are made without much human oversight, people may not understand or question the outcomes. Errors may occur in the data or code, which can quickly impact many cases. Additionally, these systems tend to rely on complex models that are difficult to comprehend. Ensuring that people can explain, appeal, and make correct decisions is important for ensuring fairness.

Automation in the welfare area would be quicker but might fail to acknowledge that some people do not fit into these brackets. Police predictive systems might also apply to the deployment of police, which might resemble the old ways of doing things. Automated systems may work effectively in taxation but must offer a balance between efficiency, fairness, and transparency (Kim, 2026). Although AI can help healthcare professionals make decisions, it should not replace human decision-making. In all these sectors, a combination of AI and human decision-making is critical to ensure fair and effective governance. In addition to practical applications, AI assists in planning and thinking about the future. Scenario modeling applies data to simulate possible futures based on specific assumptions. Such models can include demographics, the economy, the environment, and policy adjustments. Governments can identify trade-offs and possible issues by examining different futures. For example, climate models can forecast the long-term impact of road construction, and economic models can approximate the impact of alterations in laws. AI adds value to such models by helping identify trends and adapt to new data. Foresight models are particularly useful in complex and uncertain situations (Tariq, 2024).

Conventional planning usually involves simple predictions in straight lines that do not consider changes. AI models can process large amounts of information and modify predictions as new information emerges (Al Mokdad, 2025). This is useful for enabling leaders to modify their plans based on emerging events. However, these models have some assumptions upon which they are found, which affect their results. The choice of variables to focus on and the extent of emphasis indicate the values of the people. Thus, the application of foresight models requires an appropriate transfer of assumptions and constraints to the new context. The way AI makes decisions is composed of several pieces: the data that support it, the models that interpret it, the systems that enable actions to be automated, and the tools that assist in future planning. These pieces work together, and each depends on the other (Badawy, 2025).

Quality data lead to better predictions, which in turn lead to automated actions. These automated actions generate new data that are fed back into the models, forming a continually improving cycle. However, this cycle requires solid guidelines to ensure that everything is protected from the beginning. Privacy, security against cyberattacks, and ethics must be included in every aspect. The organization of institutions is important for the interaction of these components.

It is necessary to determine accountability when things go wrong. When automated systems fail or cause problems, there must be a system that identifies who is at fault. The algorithms should have internal and external controls to ensure that they perform as expected. Experts from different disciplines, such as law, ethics, and social sciences, are important for developing better systems. Public participation is also important for gaining trust in the system. When people are informed about how AI is used and can share their views, they feel more included and trust it (Qadri, 2025). It is essential to note that AI does not obviate the need for political choices. The most effective AI systems operate under parameters determined by politicians. Policy considerations help to define eligibility, risk, and resource allocation criteria. Artificial intelligence machines can help make decisions within given parameters; however, they cannot specify what these parameters should be. This plays an important role in preventing the idea that technology can replace democracy itself. The AI framework in the government is designed to facilitate responsible decision-making (Tariq, 2024).

As governments turn to AI, maintaining harmony among the various components of the system is becoming increasingly crucial. The lack of a plan to implement AI may lead to disorganized systems. An integrated approach that incorporates data systems, analytical power, and an ethical framework provides a firm basis. The need to invest in training and learning will allow public servants to apply AI selectively and not merely follow it (Nascimento et al., 2025). Finally, the structure of AI in the government is not merely a technological issue. It shows what the government is concerned with and how it plans to utilize its resources. Such choices regarding whether to share data, the extent of automation, and who is responsible for it, reveal how governments balance speed and fairness, innovation, and responsibility. The success of AI in government has more to do with the fairness and inclusiveness of the systems in which it operates than with the power of computers.

Opportunities: Strengthening Democratic Resilience through AI

Artificial intelligence can strengthen democracies if it is developed and used in a manner that considers people's concerns. If used properly, artificial intelligence will enable governments to anticipate problems before they become too serious, respond to emergencies better, prevent corruption, ensure that public services are more equal, and make decisions based on up-to-date information (Kim, 2026). Democracies are currently dealing with rapidly changing events that impact people all over the world. Economic crises can simultaneously affect several countries, diseases can spread rapidly, natural disasters can intensify, and misinformation can spread faster than ever before. To address these issues, governments must act quickly, think ahead, and adapt to what is happening and how it can change. Artificial intelligence can help them with all of this and make public institutions seem more trustworthy. One of the most useful applications of AI is in early warning systems, which can identify potential threats before they develop into serious issues.

Governments gather significant amounts of information about individuals and the environment. If this information is effectively analyzed, it can indicate when a negative event is about to occur. For example, in the health industry, an unusual number of hospital visits or purchases of specific drugs may exceed the normal level. In finance, abnormal expenditure patterns may indicate a threat or fraud. Sensors and AI applications can also be employed in environmental research to detect circumstances that may cause natural disasters, such as floods or wildfires. Early warning systems help ensure that strong democracies remain strong because the cost of responding to crises is minimized. These systems allow governments to bring together resources, communicate risks to the population, and prepare to avoid escalating problems in the future. Moreover, rapid government response and willingness to respond can increase citizens' confidence in the government. However, these systems should be open and simple in design. The conclusions made by AI algorithms should be explainable, and a system to prevent errors or inequitable results must be established. When these systems are used appropriately, they allow governments to react to uncertainty without inspiring fear or concentrating excessive power in a single location.

In addition to early warnings, AI assists in responding to crises and developing policies that adapt to new information (Masoudi, 2025). In emergency situations, AI can help combine different types of information, such as satellite photos, social media, phone calls, and sensors, to provide information about what is happening and where the greatest need is located. This technology can make decisions quickly and allocate resources where they are most needed. In difficult situations, in which things are constantly changing, AI can continue to update its suggestions, allowing governments to be flexible and learn as they go. This flexibility is part of what makes good governance possible in challenging situations.

Moreover, AI can help solve long-term problems, such as economic problems, new immigrants in a country and climate change. These problems require flexible policies that can be changed as new information becomes available. AI technology can analyze how policies work and identify areas where things are not going as expected. Rather than waiting for lengthy reports or set evaluations, governments can receive almost real-time information. This rapid learning ability allows governments to make changes before the problems escalate. This is crucial for maintaining public trust in a democracy because it indicates that the government is willing to improve and become better. AI can also be used to prevent corruption by increasing transparency (Badawy, 2025). It can also reveal covert relationships among people who are perceived to receive government contracts. Transparency tools not only track bad behavior but also prevent it from occurring. When leaders and businesses know that their actions are under observation, they are less likely to behave inappropriately. Access to information on government spending and projects is also beneficial. This allows journalists, organizations, and citizens to use AI to analyze complex information that would otherwise be difficult to comprehend. This allows more people to monitor how government funds are spent on public health. By making it easier to hold leaders accountable, these tools promote the checks and balances of democracy. AI can help democracies become fairer and better at providing services.

Public systems often do not function in the same manner, have slow processes, and do not satisfy specific requirements. Using these data, AI can identify areas where people are not receiving adequate support and tailor support accordingly (He et al., 2025). When services are provided consistently and transparently, people perceive the system as being fair. Automated systems can help decrease waiting times, and some systems can help people track the status of their applications. Fairness also involves planning and preparation. It is necessary to test AI systems to ensure that they do not lead to unfairness or worsen the situation for certain people. It is important to involve people affected by these systems in their designs. When AI systems are designed to involve different communities, there is a greater chance that they will address real needs and help make society more inclusive. Evidence-based and real-time policy analyses are major areas for improvement. Typically, policy analysis occurs after a policy has been implemented, and sometimes after several months or even years. Although these analyses are useful, they may be too late to implement the changes. If environmental policies do not work as intended, AI can analyze various solutions to determine what might work better. Real-time evaluations allow public institutions to learn more effectively (Tariq, 2024).

Instead of adhering to outdated policies, leaders can now make superior decisions based on actual data that inspire confidence and demonstrate that goals are being achieved. This assists in creating trust and demonstrates that the goals are being achieved. When evaluation results are made public, the government becomes more accountable (Kim, 2026). Citizens can understand the decision-making processes and whether the right objectives are being achieved. Visual tools that help people understand data in simple ways also assist citizens in better understanding complex issues and having more informed discussions on them. Constant reviews also help policies improve over time. However, achieving these benefits requires the appropriate use of AI by the government.

However, technology alone is insufficient. There must be a clear framework regarding ethics, adequate safeguards for data, and the ability to appeal to decisions if necessary. Educating both public servants and the public about how AI works enables better utilization of AI technology. Clarifying what AI does or does not increases trust. When people understand that AI is checked and adheres to democratic principles, they are more likely to accept it as part of their governance (Moon et al., 2025). Finally, AI supports democracy by empowering the people. Democracies work well in the sense that they can foresee issues, address them successfully, be honest, provide equal services, and learn from experience. AI can assist in all these aspects. The problem faced by leaders is that they need to utilize this help in a manner that is open, accountable, and involves people. If performed properly, AI can be a good ally for democratic governance, strengthening rather than weakening its foundations.

Risks and Democratic Vulnerabilities

The application of artificial intelligence in government decision-making is associated with large risks that, if not managed well, may weaken democracy rather than strengthen it. While artificial intelligence systems are efficient and can make predictions, they also have new weaknesses (Liu & Li, 2025). These weaknesses are not only associated with errors but also with issues such as bias, lack of transparency, concentration of power in the hands of a few, insufficient accountability, and the way people view things. Democracy requires efficient administration, fairness, transparency, and trust. When artificial intelligence systems interact with these factors, they demonstrate weaknesses that may cause people to gradually lose their trust in the government. One of the biggest risks is the bias and unfairness of algorithms.

Algorithms are often viewed as unbiased because they are based on mathematics.

However, algorithms are trained on past data, which may include unfairness, prejudice, and biases. For instance, if past policing data are biased against certain communities, new algorithms trained on these data could be biased in the same way. In addition, if past data show that certain communities have it tougher to get employment or loans, algorithms could ensure that these communities remain disadvantaged. Bias could occur at many different points, including data selection, deciding which variables to focus on, determining goals, and interpreting outcomes. Even seemingly neutral things could be associated with things that are protected, which could result in unfair outcomes without anyone intending to be unfair (Badawy, 2025). Those who are discriminated against may not know enough to establish that discrimination has occurred. Otherwise, unfair patterns may become a regular part of government businesses.

Another major problem with AI is that it is difficult to comprehend. The functioning of advanced AI, such as deep learning, is a complex system that is difficult to comprehend. Even the creators of such systems may not understand why they make certain decisions. This is a major problem for the government. A democratic government requires people to explain why they make decisions that impact their lives. If AI is used instead, people may not understand the rationale behind the decisions. For instance, if a welfare benefits application is rejected by an algorithm or a tax audit is conducted by an automated system, people may not understand the reasons. This ambiguity makes it difficult for government representatives to verify and comprehend the systems. Members of parliament, judges, and regulators may lack the expertise to investigate such models. Practical reasoning in proprietary software bases can be difficult to perceive or access because of laws that protect intellectual property. Table 2 outlines the major risks associated with algorithmic public management and the corresponding governance mechanisms required to mitigate these risks and protect these democratic values.

Table 2. Key Risks of Algorithmic Public Management and Governance Responses

Risk Category	Description	Democratic Implication	Governance Response
Algorithmic Bias	AI systems reflect historical inequalities in data	Reinforces discrimination and inequality	Bias audits, inclusive data design, fairness testing
Lack of Transparency	Complex models are difficult to interpret	Weakens accountability and public trust	Explainable AI, transparency requirements, algorithm registries
Concentration of Power	Reliance on large tech firms and data control	Shifts power away from democratic institutions	Public procurement reform, open standards, public sector capacity building

continued on following page

Table 2. Continued

Risk Category	Description	Democratic Implication	Governance Response
Accountability Gaps	Unclear responsibility for automated decisions	Weakens legal and ethical responsibility	Clear accountability frameworks, audit trails, human oversight
Loss of Public Trust	Citizens perceive AI as unfair or opaque	Reduces legitimacy of public institutions	Public engagement, communication, participatory governance

Source. Own Elaboration

The development of AI requires large amounts of data and powerful computing capabilities. Big-tech firms possess the information, resources, and capabilities to utilize AI effectively in their operations. Governments tend to collaborate with these companies to create and run AI systems. This can encourage innovation, although it alters power dynamics (Carrillo, 2026). When governments become overly reliant on a select group of companies, the problem of freedom and power mobility emerges. These companies may set rules, determine how technology should work, and influence policies because of their control over critical tools and platforms. Digital power gaps also exist in society today.

Not everyone has equal skills or technological abilities. Those without a good level of digital skills and access to the Internet would face challenges in engaging with automated systems or challenging decisions made by AI when such decisions are unfair. Conversely, the more one has, that is, large corporations or wealthy groups, the more data and analysis they can utilize and the more power they can gain. This can lead to a situation in which people who are better at using technology have more power than those who are more democratic in their approach. Another significant issue is the lack of human responsibility (Gomes & Cardoso, 2025). It is difficult to assign responsibility when systems are automated. If the result is harmful or incorrect, it is difficult to assign responsibility to the programmer, source of the data, official who authorizes the system, or the organization that uses it. This could create a problem in which no one accepts the total responsibility. In the traditional form of government, officials are held accountable and removed when they commit mistakes. In AI systems, the decision-making process appears to be a function of the machine itself, and people feel that the result is merely the product of a neutral process. This could lower the amount of ethical thinking in such agencies.

When government officials become overly reliant on the outputs of algorithms, they may feel less accountable for their actions. The power of computers may become too large, and people may overly rely on their suggestions. Although automation may eliminate some inconsistencies and unfairness, it should not eliminate people's responsibilities. It is important to keep people in charge and to maintain clear lines of responsibility. A lack of trust is one of the most significant risks associated with the application of AI in the public sector. Trust is a crucial component of a democracy. This enables people to comply with laws, participate in public activities and submit to institutions. The use of AI in decision-making can be a point of concern, especially when individuals are convinced that AI is unclear and unjustifiable. Algorithms are more likely to raise concerns among people if they report being erroneous or unfair, although such incidents are rare. If citizens develop the notion that AI systems are too complicated to be managed and comprehended, they can view the government as remote and dominated by professionals alone. Lack of trust is both an emotional and behavioral issue. A lack of trust in AI might make citizens less willing to provide their personal information, which is essential for a successful decision-making process. They can also disagree with decisions that they interpret as being unfair. Extreme cases of lack of trust may result in the view that institutions are not legitimate (Masoudi, 2025). To solve this issue, governments should clarify how AI systems work, what regulations are in place, and how citizens can object to their decisions and actions. None of these risks are independent.

A lack of knowledge regarding the functioning of AI may conceal injustice. The fact that a small number of corporations have too much data can result in excessively acquired power and a sense of irresponsibility. In the absence of accountability, trust can degrade. An all-encompassing approach to risk mitigation needs to consider the way AI is being developed, as well as the infrastructure that supports it. It is important to check whether AI is biased, make AI explainable, restructure the way the government purchases AI, and introduce a set of rules regarding accountability. Additionally, public institutions must promote critical thinking, ethical discourse, and new technologies. The key takeaway is that AI does not work independently but reflects the values and infrastructure surrounding it. New technology threatens democracy as the rules that protect it fall behind its development. Trust must be gained through openness and receptivity. Only by addressing these issues can democracies use AI to their advantage without losing the value of their inception.

MAIN FOCUS OF THE CHAPTER

Governance Models for Responsible Algorithmic Public Management

To successfully apply algorithms in public systems, governments must be structured to view artificial intelligence as an effective but not infallible tool in a democracy. The question is not whether governments will embrace AI but how to manage it, who will have authority, and ensure that AI serves their values, as stipulated in their laws. Good governance encompasses designing systems, the ethics upon which the system is founded, the rules governing the system, monitoring the system, and the participation of citizens. These factors combine to form a system that ensures AI supports a robust democracy. An important aspect of dealing with this situation is deciding between two different models: human-in-the-loop and human-on-loop. In the human-in-the-loop model, humans make the final decision, even when AI provides recommendations. This ensures that humans remain in control, which is important in areas such as justice, immigration, and welfare, where errors can cause significant harm. It also enables human understanding and ethical considerations. The disadvantage is that it may become cumbersome if humans are too busy or if the process is merely going through the motions. The human-on-the-loop approach allows AI to act quickly, such as detecting fraud or controlling traffic flows (Romanishyn et al., 2025).

However, some people monitor the system and intervene if problems occur. This means that individuals monitoring the system must have the ability to question the AI system, halt it if necessary, and make corrections. Without proper oversight, AI systems can make decisions that no one can verify. The choice of model is not purely a technological concern. Ethical guidelines assist in the use of AI in public systems. Figure 1 presents an integrated conceptual framework that synthesizes the key arguments of this study.

Figure 1. Conceptual Framework of Algorithmic Public Management and Democratic Resilience

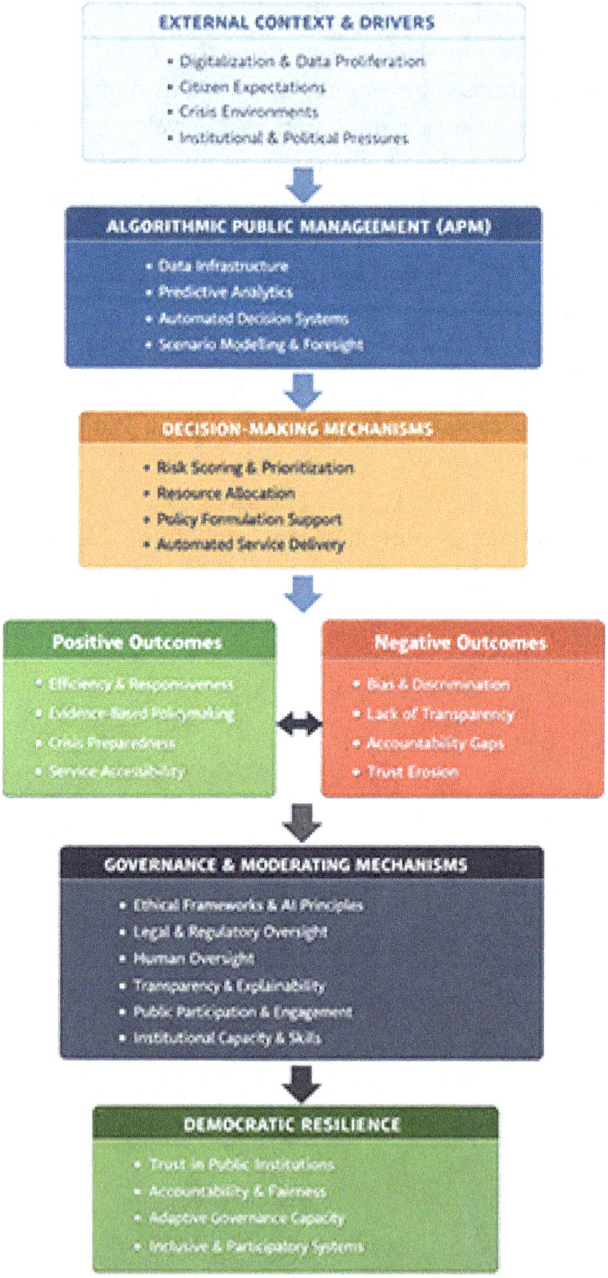

Source. Own elaboration

The guidelines are based on ethics, such as fairness, transparency, responsibility, safety of private information, and ensuring that no one is discriminated against. Most public institutions have developed ethical guidelines that must be checked before using AI. The charts include testing for bias, documenting the source of the data and assumptions made by the model, and how errors can be corrected in the future. Ethics guidelines also assist in ensuring that AI is used in a manner that corresponds to its purpose and does not interfere with people's rights. The importance of ethical guidelines extends to both their content and implementation processes (Kim, 2026). Ensuring that ethical guidelines are implemented early in the development process brings together people from different fields, such as technology, law, and policy. This collaboration assists in the development of systems that do not consider the larger implications for society. However, guidelines that cannot be enforced are ineffective. Guidelines should become standards and be part of how things are purchased and how well the systems work. This is because they might only be promised without any changes. At the regional and national levels, governments are enacting laws to responsibly control AI.

It also emphasizes the importance of maintaining records so that decisions can be traced back later. At the national level, many governments are working on plans to ensure the appropriate use of AI in healthcare. These plans often include regulations and support for innovation so that the public sector can lead the responsible use of new technology. However, because regulations differ from country to country, sharing data and ensuring that companies follow the rules may be difficult (Badawy, 2025). More global studies are required. Although the regulations differ, they all have the same goal of ensuring that AI systems operate within the laws that support a democracy. Effective oversight and audit mechanisms are key to ensuring that rules are implemented in a real way.

Independent entities, data protection authorities, and ombudsmen can monitor whether AI systems operate under these rules. An audit conducted internally by a company or expert examines the origin of the data, the efficiency of the system, and the sharing of the output. Monitoring the system over time helps identify problems as they occur. Maintaining a record of decision-making helps examine past decisions and contest them if necessary. Good oversight requires technical expertise and independence from the government. The bodies that monitor these systems should have sufficient resources and authority to examine the complex systems (Zhu, 2026). Collaboration between different agencies may be helpful if AI is applied in several sectors. Democracy requires checks from above and below. If people affected by AI systems are involved in shaping the system, the outcomes are likely to include diverse views. Public participation may include public meetings, workshops with interested groups, and public forums where leaders can explain their plans and receive feedback.

Comparative Case Studies

Some governments employ predictive models to forecast the impact of policies on the economy, enhance procurement processes, and allocate funds based on performance. However, there are challenges. It is essential to ensure the security of personal information in such cases. Citizens trust public services when digital ID systems are optional, transparent, and overseen (Masoudi, 2025). Citizens become resistant when digital ID systems are rushed or not clearly understood. In general, when comparing various countries, it becomes apparent that the effectiveness of algorithmic systems is directly related to the maturity of governance.

Effective systems include rules, checks, experts from various sectors, and feedback. Less mature systems may employ cutting-edge technologies without sufficient regulation, leading to a divide between the intended and implemented. The most important takeaway is that effective technology is insufficient (He et al., 2025). The effective use of AI in public management requires it to be coupled with legal safeguards, ethical considerations, and participation. Countries that view algorithmic systems as part of an evolving process rather than a technological upgrade are better equipped to handle these shifts.

Designing Democratic-by-Design Algorithmic Systems

In this regard, transparency and explainability are essential considerations. Democracy depends on citizens' ability to understand how decisions that affect them are made. In the case of algorithmic systems, this means providing clear and understandable explanations of why the system exists, where the data originate, how decisions are made, and what the system cannot do. Transparency operates in various ways. Governments must provide clear explanations of why they are using a system and what they are trying to accomplish (Masoudi, 2025). Citizens must also receive clear explanations of how the system impacts them, particularly in matters that are significant, such as receiving benefits or being sued by the government. Fairness is not merely a technical issue; it also involves judgments about what is acceptable regarding trade-offs. Engaging a broad set of people in determining fairness ensures that these criteria are consistent with societal values and not merely optimized for efficiency.

Another method for increasing openness and accountability is the establishment of public algorithm registries. By maintaining records of the algorithms used in public services, the government can demonstrate transparency. Public algorithm registries contain information such as the purpose of the system, the government department it falls under, the data it uses, the risks associated with the system, and how it is monitored. Making this information available to the public helps researchers, the media, and citizens monitor the use of these systems. It also encourages them to be more careful and open, helping create a culture of responsible and reflective governance. Open data and public engagement are also beneficial.

When governments make data that do not contain personal information available, it becomes easier for people to analyze and use it to make improvements in the field. People and technological communities can build tools, identify areas where data are missing, and provide ideas on how to make improvements. Events such as hackathons, public conversations, and co-designing with others make people feel that they are part of the development of new technology. This not only improves the systems but also helps build trust by showing that they are not developed in a top-down manner. In other words, democratic-by-design approaches view technology as part of the nation's values and rules rather than as a tool used separately (Moon et al., 2025). Governments can develop AI systems that reflect democratic values by incorporating transparency, fairness, public engagement, and rights protection into the design process. This proactive approach to technology can turn the potential weaknesses of algorithm use into an opportunity to develop more responsible and trustworthy systems.

Strategic Framework for AI-Driven Democratic Governance

A good plan for using AI in a democratic way requires several important elements: skills, tools, ethics, rules, and public engagement. This can help technology become a positive force for democracy rather than a negative one. The first important element is the development of skills and knowledge in public groups. Using AI effectively requires more than simply having good tools (Panda et al., 2025). It requires public groups with trained staff, people with different areas of knowledge, and the right processes to deal with complex systems that combine technology and society to achieve this. The second part ensures that digital systems are robust and safe. To operate AI, it is necessary to have strong systems that are safe from attacks, equipment failures, or other interruptions that could stop or slow down AI. Thus, different parts of the government can easily share information to make predictions, perform tasks, and plan. Keeping data safe and private is also important.

Having a way to deal with data helps systems run well, reduces errors, and increases trust. Being prepared for interruptions, such as natural disasters or failures, is important to ensure that systems continue to function even when things go wrong. The third part is to ensure that AI use is fair and that there are ways to make people accountable for their actions. Governments should consider the use of AI with guidelines that ensure fairness, prevent bias, and respect people's rights. There should be constant checks to ensure that there is no unfairness, ways to identify and correct unfairness if it occurs, and ways to ensure that people are involved in decision-making processes (Kim, 2026). Ensuring that processes are transparent and understandable is helpful for government workers and citizens. Having groups that monitor AI use is helpful for ensuring that AI use is fair, and guidelines are helpful for ensuring that daily processes are fair. Using ethics for AI management ensures that AI use is fair and that AI is treated fairly. Fourth, rules that can change as technology changes.

Old rules may not be suitable for the new uses of AI. A good way to handle this is to have rules that look at risks, check new technologies frequently, and update laws and processes, if necessary. Rules should allow innovation but also protect basic rights. Methods for quickly checking new uses, providing exceptions under controlled conditions, and establishing time limits for experiments will help to ensure control. The fifth part is to allow people to participate in the use of AI. Democracy implies that people must be involved in creating, using, and checking AI systems. People's meetings, working groups, and data tools will allow people to have a say, identify risks, and check results. People will learn how AI affects decisions, and governments will gain different views that may help identify problems before they become major issues (Masoudi, 2025). Putting all these parts of a plan together gives us a plan for using AI in a way that strengthens democracy, rather than weakening it. Having the right skills means having the right people and systems. Having good digital systems means having systems that function well. Ethical controls mean having systems that align well with the values of the people. Having flexible controls means having systems that can keep pace with new developments. Having people involved means having fair and accountable systems.

SOLUTIONS AND RECOMMENDATIONS

The new form that the government might take could be that of an algorithmic state, in which data-driven systems are used to manage many aspects of government, such as the distribution of benefits, police operations, and law enforcement. In such a system, government decisions are made more intelligently, quickly, and accurately using live data and artificial intelligence. Such a system can identify patterns that humans cannot see, making the government more efficient and equitable. However, it can also make citizens feel disconnected from the process of government decision-making. The real question is whether the government should be by the people or for the people alone. In contrast, participatory digital democracy views AI not as a replacement for human decision-making but as a tool that will help people make better decisions. Digital democracy may enable many people to contribute their opinions on issues such as how money should be spent or which policies to support (Azhar, 2026). Moreover, AI can be used to organize opinions, show the benefits and drawbacks of decisions, and predict possible outcomes in the future. This will enable people to participate in the government. However, not everyone may have equal opportunities to use digital democracy, and there may be inequalities in the use of AI.

Therefore, digital democracy must be transparent and accountable to avoid increasing inequalities. Another factor that may change is how leaders make decisions. Politicians use data to predict problems, such as climate change, health problems, and economic problems, and they prepare for these problems in advance. They may also use virtual environments to test and predict the outcomes of their decisions. However, politicians may rely too much on data, which may mean that the data dictate everything. This may mean that politicians do not make decisions based on their values but only on the data.

Problems may arise if the government becomes more complex, as people may believe that they cannot understand or influence it. This may cause people to distrust the government, resulting in anger. Another factor is that AI systems may be based on the biases of their creators. These systems may support unfair practices because they may be based on speed rather than fairness. Too much reliance may be placed on experts in the government, but this may mean that people are not given the space to question what they are doing. To create a strong democracy in the age of AI, we must strike a balance between new technologies and fairness (Singh et al., 2025). Governments must be able to regulate and understand new technologies. In addition, the public must be educated about the effects of AI on decision-making. There must also be an opportunity for the public to have a say in technology use. The rules and laws must also keep up with new technologies and not lag. The future of democracy lies in our engagement with the public, promotion of discussions, and sharing of power.

CONCLUSION

As we continue to discuss artificial intelligence, it is more important than ever to change our thinking. Instead of viewing it as a tool to replace human work and decisions, we should view it as a means of improving performance (Yannis and Gerasimos, 2026). While automation replaces people with machines, augmentation works with machines. Augmentation involves exploring methods to improve learning, thinking, and access to information. The way we discuss artificial intelligence can shape our expectations, design, regulation, and culture. Making democratic strength the foundation for AI use provides a forward direction.

Being strong democratically is not just about coping with unexpected events such as changes in technology, financial issues, or international pressures. It is about being able to change while maintaining important values such as fairness, participation, equality, and the rule of law. New challenges will emerge with AI, such as cybersecurity, fake news, decisions that are too complex to understand, and too much power given to technology. A strong democracy prepares for these challenges in advance and develops defenses before problems arise (He et al., 2025).

Governments need to understand many things, including computer science, economics, political thought, social sciences, and ethics. It is important to allow room for new ideas, but it is equally important to set boundaries to ensure that these ideas are not misused for unfair control. Government spending can be used to ensure that artificial intelligence systems are transparent, fair, and protect personal information (Masoudi, 2025). Additionally, more funding needs to be allocated to research on public goods. Schools and research centers need to be funded to investigate how society is being impacted by artificial intelligence, develop open-source technology, and train more experts who are aware of technology and democracy.

REFERENCES

Al Mokdad, A. (2025). Inclusive and intelligent governance: Enabling sustainability through policy and technology. In *Social system reforms to achieve global sustainability* (pp. 173–238). IGI Global. DOI: 10.4018/979-8-3373-1280-4.ch008

Anand, S., & Wan Mohamed, W. M. (2025). AI as an autonomous decision-maker in governance: A new era of policy formulation. In *The power of agentic AI: Redefining human life and decision-making in Industry 6.0* (pp. 81–96). Springer Nature Switzerland. DOI: 10.1007/978-3-031-89424-4_6

Androutsopoulou, M., Carayannis, E. G., Askounis, D., & Zotas, N. (2025). Leveraging AI for enhanced e-government: Optimizing the use of open governmental data. *Journal of the Knowledge Economy*, *16*(3), 12998–13033. DOI: 10.1007/s13132-024-02317-w

Aragani, V. M., Anumolu, V. R., & Selvakumar, P. (2025). Democratization in the age of algorithms: Navigating opportunities and challenges. In *Democracy and democratization in the age of AI* (pp. 39–56). IGI Global. DOI: 10.4018/979-8-3693-8749-8.ch003

Azhar, A. (2026). AI in government: Future trends and recommendations. In *Artificial intelligence and government: Examining the roles and uses of AI in enhancing government operations* (pp. 367–393). Springer Nature Switzerland. DOI: 10.1007/978-3-032-12344-2_16

Badawy, W. (2025). Algorithmic sovereignty and democratic resilience: Rethinking AI governance in the age of generative AI. *AI and Ethics*, *5*(5), 4855–4862. DOI: 10.1007/s43681-025-00739-z

Carrillo, F. (2026). Artificial intelligence and big data in global politics: How AI and ML influence power, governance, and democracy. In *International relations, misinformation and polarization* (pp. 1–11).

Gomes, P. M., & Cardoso, T. (2025). AI-driven transformation in public governance. In *Public governance practices in the age of AI* (pp. 81–108). IGI Global. DOI: 10.4018/979-8-3693-9286-7.ch005

He, J., He, Y., Hu, J., & Guo, Y. (2025). Intelligent governance: The AI-driven new paradigm of governmental adaptive governance. *Journal of US-China Public Administration*, *22*(1), 1–27.

Kim, E. (2026). Institutionalizing predictive AI in public administration: Algorithmic governance and the case of a wildfire forecasting system. *Policy and Internet, 18*(1), e70029. DOI: 10.1002/poi3.70029

Liu, C., & Li, Y. (2025). Research on AI-driven public policy decision support systems. In *Proceedings of the 2025 2nd International Conference on Digital Economy and Computer Science* (pp. 777–781). DOI: 10.1145/3785706.3785827

Masoudi, M. (2025). Algorithmic governance, data-driven decision making, and the transformation of democratic accountability in contemporary states. *Advanced Journal of Management. Humanity and Social Science*, *2*(1), 10–22.

Moon, M. J., Lee, S., Park, S., & Park, I. (2025). The dawn of disruptive technology-driven future government. *Futures for the Public Sector, 141.*

Nascimento, P. V. M., de Siqueira, P. B. B., Chrispim, N., Chaves, R. M., Barbosa, C. E., & de Souza, J. M. (2025). The future of AI in government services and global risks: Insights from design fictions. *European Journal of Futures Research, 13*(1), 9. DOI: 10.1186/s40309-025-00253-9

Panda, M., Hossain, M. M., Puri, R., & Ahmad, A. (2025). Artificial intelligence in action: Shaping the future of public sector. *Digital Policy. Regulation & Governance, 27*(6), 668–686. DOI: 10.1108/DPRG-10-2024-0272

Qadri, S. (2025). Artificial intelligence and public administration: Actors, governance, and policies. *Social Science Review Archives*, *3*(4), 3200–3212.

Romanishyn, A., Malytska, O., & Goncharuk, V. (2025). AI-driven disinformation: Policy recommendations for democratic resilience. *Frontiers in Artificial Intelligence, 8*, 1569115. DOI: 10.3389/frai.2025.1569115 PMID: 40821951

Singh, B., Jain, A., Wongmahesak, K., & Chandra, S. (2025). Reimagining democracy in the digital era: Transformative role of artificial intelligence in modern governance. In *Democracy and democratization in the age of AI* (pp. 1–18). IGI Global. DOI: 10.4018/979-8-3693-8749-8.ch001

Tariq, M. U. (2024). Metaverse in business and commerce. In Kumar, J., Arora, M., & Erkol Bayram, G. (Eds.), *Exploring the use of metaverse in business and education* (pp. 47–72). IGI Global., DOI: 10.4018/979-8-3693-5868-9.ch004

Tariq, M. U. (2024). Leveraging artificial intelligence for a sustainable and climate-neutral economy in Asia. In Ordóñez de Pablos, P., Almunawar, M., & Anshari, M. (Eds.), *Strengthening sustainable digitalization of Asian economy and society* (pp. 1–21). IGI Global., DOI: 10.4018/979-8-3693-1942-0.ch001

Tariq, M. U. (2024). Integrating ESG Principles Into Corporate Governance for Sustainable Ecosystem Services. In Castanho, R. (Ed.), *ESG and Ecosystem Services for Sustainability* (pp. 89–118). IGI Global., DOI: 10.4018/979-8-3693-3771-4.ch004

Yannis, C., & Gerasimos, K. (2026). Rule-based AI systems for public governance: A framework for smarter, transparent, and citizen-centered governance. In *Artificial intelligence and government: Examining the roles and uses of AI in enhancing government operations* (pp. 59–87). DOI: 10.1007/978-3-032-12344-2_4

Zhu, X. (2026). Public administration with, of, and through AI: Toward a new paradigm in the era of intelligence. *Journal of Chinese Governance*, *11*(1), 30–57. DOI: 10.1080/23812346.2025.2578589

KEY TERMS AND DEFINITIONS

Algorithmic Accountability: Responsibility mechanisms for automated governmental decisions

Algorithmic Public Management: Use of AI in government decision-making

Democratic Resilience: Institutions withstand shocks while protecting rights

Chapter 4
Behavioural Game Theory in Managerial Decision-Making:
Why Real Executives Deviate From Nash Equilibrium

Rhea Manocha
http://orcid.org/0009-0006-7416-7024
Christ University, India

Rajveer S. Rawlin
http://orcid.org/0000-0003-4359-3363
Christ University, India

Divyaani Somani
Christ University, India

Ram Dhawan
Christ University, India

Aflah Shadil
Christ University, India

ABSTRACT

The chapter presents a systematic review of the literature on behavioural game theory to investigate the reasons for managers making decisions that are often at variance with those predicted by the Nash equilibrium. The classical game theory builds upon assumptions that players are fully rational, have complete information and definite preferences. Behavioural game theory combines the psychological and

DOI: 10.4018/979-8-3373-9765-8.ch004

the behavioural aspects of these models, thereby dropping the requirement of perfect rationality. The review shows that managers are constrained by bounded rationality, limited information processing and time pressure, and are constrained to rely on heuristics and intuitive judgment instead of an equilibrium-based optimization. The aim of this chapter is not to use Nash equilibrium to predict executive behaviour, but to focus on it as a theoretical benchmark, and to highlight the value of integrating behaviour into strategic theory and practice.

INTRODUCTION

Despite being widely used in economics and strategic management, BGT in managerial decision-making is very popular because it elucidates why real-life executives do not behave in the way classical game theory predicts, particularly in terms of the Nash equilibrium. The traditional game theory offers a formal structure to study the strategic interaction of rational decision-makers. It assumes that people could compute optimal strategies, have constant preferences, and are fully informed. Under these assumptions, equilibria (such as the Nash equilibrium) are the solutions in which no player wants to change his adopted strategy unilaterally. These models are mathematically neat and conceptually plausible but have come under growing doubt as applied to real managerial situations.

In real-life business situations, managers do not make decisions in optimal conditions as described in classical game theory. Managerial decision-making is made under uncertainty, time constraints, information gap and complex constraints within the organization. Executives are held to account for their performance in the short term, as well as in the long term, and for their reactions to competition, within the context of their internal stakeholders, which include their employees, boards, and investors. In addition, the human decision maker is influenced by psychological factors, emotions, prior experience, and social factors that would not be captured by traditional models affecting strategic decision-making. Managers, as rational actors, therefore, are more likely to use disequilibrium strategies, even if, optimally, they should not.

This theoretical–observational gap is filled by behavioural game theory. It assumes less than perfect rationality, drawing on ideas and evidence from psychology, behavioural economics, and experimental work, and integrates them into conventional game-theoretic models. Managers rarely make decisions based on computing equilibrium strategies but instead use rules of thumb, heuristics, intuition, and previous experience-based judgment. These reduced-form decision-making functions are efficient and useful but can give systematically different results than predictions based on Nash equilibrium.

An important area of behavioural game theory has been the identification of cognitive mistakes that affect the decisions of managers. Executives breach the perception of risks, competitor action assessment, and prediction of market results through biases including overconfidence, anchoring, availability bias and confirmation bias. Similarly, loss aversion and reference dependence influence risk-taking behaviour, and managers are more risk averse with the prospect of losses than similar gains, often resulting in a conservative approach or delayed market entry.

Besides the individual psychology, behavioural game theory incorporates social preferences and relational aspects. Real executives have concerns about the fairness, the reputation, the reciprocity, and the long-term relationship, as opposed to the classical model of purely self-interested agents. These social and reputational factors emerge regularly in a series of interactions, and the logic of trust and retaliation and cooperation is more powerful than the logic of one-shot equilibrium.

Moreover, behavioural game theory deals with learning and adaptation in the long term. Executives refine their strategies through experience, peer monitoring of behaviour and incremental learning. It is explained that markets are prone to failure of coordination, slow convergence and cycles of competitive behaviour using reinforcement learning and belief-based learning models.

This chapter discusses with the help of these theoretical developments the importance of behavioural game theory in the explanation of systematic deviations in managerial decisions from the Nash equilibrium. It is argued that classical equilibrium principles are not really valid predictors of executive behaviour, but rather serve as reference points, the deviations from which can be measured. It covers how cognitive biases, loss aversion, social preferences and learning mechanisms affect strategic decisions in key domains of managerial activity such as pricing, market entry, mergers and acquisitions, bargaining and strategic alliances.

It also emphasises the role of organizational factors in the managers' behaviour. Incentives, performance measures, corporate culture, and corporate politics plus individual biases all influence strategic decisions. Managers may be driven to safer or more justifiable actions or strategies in the short term, driven by short-term performance pressures, considerations of their careers, or demands from their shareholders, despite the fact that equilibrium actions or strategies may be better over the longer term.

This chapter fills a gap between normative game models and descriptive managerial behaviour and so contributes to the field of strategic management and decision-making in general. It provides a more practical way of thoughtfully assessing how executives think and behave in situations with strategic implications and brings to attention the importance of incorporating behavioural knowledge into the process of managerial preparation, strategic planning, and organizational design.

BACKGROUND

In this chapter, the conceptual framework that is developed brings together the thematic findings, explaining the systematic deviations in managerial decision making from the Nash equilibrium. The framework is designed to show a multi-layered view of how cognitive limitations, behavioural drivers, social factors, organisational factors and learning mechanisms interact to influence strategic outcomes. Non-equilibrium behaviours are not considered as exceptions, but rather as strategic responses that are reasonable and predictable.

Framework Structure and Explanation

Layer 1: Foundational Cognitive Constraints

The basic cognitive prerequisites for managers' operations are at the bottom of the structure. These include bounded rationality, incomplete information and time pressure, and strategic uncertainty. These constraints preclude comprehensive participation in equilibrium optimization and reduce managers' capacity for higher-order thinking about competitive beliefs and actions, resulting in suboptimal understanding when making strategic decisions.

Layer 2: Behavioural and Psychological Drivers

Behavioural and psychological factors build on cognitive constraints and affect the way that managers process information and evaluate strategic options. Cognitive biases (such as overconfidence, anchoring, and availability bias) influence the formation of beliefs, and systematic risk preferences are influenced by loss aversion and reference dependence. Fear, pride, anger, and regret are emotional factors that create additional perception distortions. Combined, they systematically influence judgments and shift decision-making from equilibrium predictions.

Layer 3: Social and Relational Factors

The social and relational issues related to strategic interaction are then added in the framework. Managers may assess the results of their work in terms of fairness, trust, and reputation, especially when working repeatedly in the same work environment, which can result in social preferences that affect the value of the payoff and can thereby foster cooperation, punishment, or retaliation over time.

Layer 4: Organizational and Institutional Moderators

Organizational and institutional context (incentive structure, performance evaluation, and career concerns), affecting strategic feasibility and choice, is further shaping strategic decision-making. All of these can make it easier to choose strategies that have a short-term effect on the system instead of optimal ones (that aim for equilibrium) and consequently strengthen non-equilibrium behavior as a rational organizational response.

Layer 5: Learning and Adaptation Processes

Managers do not jump straight to equilibrium; rather, they behave differently over time, learning to do so. Strategic adjustment occurs through reinforcement learning, belief updating, and trial and error processes, which are based on previous results and observation of competitors' actions. These learning dynamics provide some intuitive understanding of how delayed convergence, cyclic competition, and continuous coordination failure are characteristics of real markets.

Layer 6: Strategic Outcomes

All the above combine to result in overall strategic consequences such as non-Nash equilibria, escalation, price competition, delayed or failed cooperation, and sub-optimal entry, pricing, and bargaining decisions. The framework illustrates how such outcomes are the result of a combination and interaction of cognitive, behavioural, social, and organizational mechanisms (Table 1).

Table 1. Conceptual framework table: Behavioural layers leading to non-Nash strategic outcomes

Conceptual Framework: Behavioral Layers Leading to Non-Nash Strategic Outcomes	
Layer / Stage	**Key Elements**
Layer 1: Foundational Cognitive Constraints	Bounded Rationality, Limited Information, Strategic Uncertainty
Layer 2: Behavioural and Psychological Drivers	Cognitive Biases, Loss Aversion, Emotions
Layer 3: Social and Relational Factors	Fairness, Reciprocity, Reputation
Layer 4: Organizational and Institutional Moderators	Incentives, Performance Evaluation, Career Pressure

continued on following page

Table 1. Continued

Conceptual Framework: Behavioral Layers Leading to Non-Nash Strategic Outcomes	
Layer 5: Learning and Adaptation Processes	Reinforcement Learning, Belief Updating
Layer 6: Strategic Outcomes	Persistent Non-Nash Behaviour, Coordination Failures, Escalation

Source: Authors' compilation based on thematic synthesis

Research Gaps

Despite the extensive literature search about behavioural game theory, there are still several gaps that can be seen.

First, many current studies are based on laboratory experiments and/or simplified strategic environments that limit the external validity of the results for real-life executive and organizational decision-making environments.

Second, the literature is quite focused on developed economies with little regard towards underdeveloped economies and emerging markets with varied institutional environments. The possible cross-cultural and cross-regulatory differences in managerial cognition, social preferences, and risk behaviour indicate the necessity of cross-country and comparative research.

Third, although there was a good body of knowledge on behavioural biases and learning dynamics, the interaction of cognitive, emotional, social, and organizational factors in one analytical framework was not very well researched. Many studies studied the mechanisms separately instead of the effect of the interaction of the mechanisms on strategic behaviour.

Fourth, digital transformation and technology is underutilized. There is an important opportunity for further research in this area, given the interaction between man-made behavioral biases and algorithmic decision-making, AI-driven tactics, and platform-based competition.

Lastly, lack of attention to practical interventions. There are only a few studies that focused on aspects of organizational design, incentive systems, governance, and debiasing strategies that would help reduce systematic deviation from equilibrium and enhance the quality of managerial decisions.

MAIN FOCUS OF THE CHAPTER

Methodology

To investigate the deviations from the Nash equilibrium in managerial decision-making, this study used a Systematic Literature Review (SLR) methodology to analyze the role of behavioural game theory in explaining deviations from the Nash equilibrium in managerial decision-making. To ensure that the synthesis of existing research is both transparent, rigorous, and reliable, this method was selected, in line with research review methodology used in management and economic literature.

The names of data sources are displayed on the left. The data sources are shown on the left.

To get a wide spectrum of peer-reviewed studies, a comprehensive literature search was carried out in academic databases such as Google Scholar, Web of Science, JSTOR and ScienceDirect. The articles sought included a mix of terms, including "behavioral game theory," "managerial decision-making," "bounded rationality," "Nash equilibrium," "cognitive biases," and "strategic interaction."

The inclusion and exclusion criteria are defined as follows. Inclusion and Exclusion Criteria:

For this review, studies examined aspects of behavior in games, strategic decision-making in management or organizational settings, and theoretical, experimental, or empirical analyses of deviations from outcomes of Nash equilibria. This research excluded those articles that were purely mathematical with no behavioural or managerial application and those opinion pieces that did not come from peer reviews.

Screening and Selection Process

The primary search resulted in a number of articles, which were carefully explored at the title and abstract level, eliminating duplicate and irrelevant studies. A full-text screening was then performed to check eligibility by inclusion criteria. This multi-stage screening process resulted in more than 85 articles being relevant for the final analysis. Documentation of the selection process was done using the PRISMA framework, which has been used to assure systematic filtering and transparency.

Data extraction and synthesis

Information from selected studies was obtained with the aid of the reference management software Zotero. Studies were not summarized on an individual basis, but results were aggregated by themes to uncover patterns of behaviour. To understand

and segregate the articles, eight themes were identified. This themed synthesis was used to develop a conceptual framework and research gaps for future exploration.

Prisma Methodology

We adopted the PRISMA 2020 (Preferred Reporting Items for Systematic Reviews and Meta-Analyses) framework to systematically search, screen, and synthesize the literature regarding behavioural game theory in managerial decision-making and, specifically, to provide an explanation for why real executives often fall short of what the Nash equilibrium predicts. The review is structured and is based on articles in the peer-reviewed journal literature from the Zotero reference library (table 2).

Identification

During the identification phase, 100 scholarly articles related to game theory and behavioural decision-making were identified and added to Zotero's reference library. The articles were from quality academic databases such as Google Scholar, Web of Science, JSTOR, and ScienceDirect to cover the complete spectrum of disciplines: economics, management, and behavioural sciences.

Records retrieved by the database search and citation computer system: n = 100

Screening

A total of 100 records were abstracted and screened at the title and abstract level for relevance to the research aim of understanding the deviation from the Nash equilibrium using the methodology of behavioural game theory in managerial decision contexts. The screening was done on game theory, topics concerning behavioural strategic interaction, and topics concerning conceptual, experimental, or empirical relevance to the topic. Articles that were purely mathematical or axiomatic and did not contain any behavioural interpretations, articles not related to business management and strategic decision-making, and articles that were editorial notes, articles of commentary, or articles that were not scholarly in nature were excluded.

Excluded at screening: n = 15; Full text assessed: n = 85

Eligibility

Of the 85 articles that contained full text, only those that had a good depth of theory, were behaviourally relevant and could be directly applied to the topic of managerial/executive decision-making were assessed for eligibility. Additionally, evaluation was carried out on the clarity of concepts, methodological rigor, and contribution to the understanding of deviations from the rational choice or equilibrium assumption. In addition, the eligibility criteria specified a clear connection to managerial or strategic decision-making contexts and specified the need for a discussion of deviation from an equilibrium solution or rational choice modelling.

Exclusions: full-text articles (n = 23); studies that met the eligibility criteria (n = 62).

Included Studies

There is a total of 62 peer-reviewed studies that are included in the final synthesis. These included behavioural and experimental game theory research, empirical research with decision-makers, managers, and/or strategic agents, and conceptual frameworks that combined behavioural economics with strategic management. The literature provided in this appendix is unanimous about the deviations of managerial decisions from the Nash equilibrium predictions because of cognitive constraints, behavioural biases, social preferences, and organizational constraints.

Thematic Synthesis of Inclusive Studies

Thematic analysis was undertaken on the final 62 papers to uncover the recurring explanations for non-equilibrium behaviour that focused on behaviour. The literature was not summarised but synthesized by identifying key conceptual themes. The analysis was then broken down into eight key themes, as detailed in the next section. The thematic findings section was based on these themes, including bounded rationality, cognitive biases, social preferences, learning and adaptation, and others.

Table 2. PRISMA flow summary of the systematic literature review

Stage	Action	Count
Identification	Records identified through database searching	n = 100
Screening	Records screened (title & abstract)	n = 100
	Records excluded at screening stage	n = 15
	Records retained for full-text assessment	n = 85
Eligibility	Full-text articles assessed for eligibility	n = 85
	Full-text articles excluded	n = 23
Included	Studies included in qualitative synthesis	n = 62

Source: Authors' compilation

Thematic Findings

Thematic Overview

This section summarizes the literature on the application of behavioural game theory to managerial decision-making in a thematic summary. It is not a summary of individual research but a review of the results of the peer-reviewed theoretical, experimental, and applied studies that are able to identify common behavioural mechanisms that explain why real executives do not behave in line with Nash equilibrium. The themes identified indicate that there are regularities in different strategic settings such as pricing, negotiating, bargaining, entering the market, and repeated competition. All these themes show that the departure from equilibrium is not a coincidence but the natural consequence of cognitive limitations, behavioural biases, social preferences, learning mechanisms, and organizational constraints.

Theme 1: Strategic Reasoning and Bounded Rationality

The theory of bounded rationality is used as the underlying premise to explain deviations from the Nash equilibrium in managerial decision making. The rationality of decision makers is assumed to be unlimited, and they can calculate the best strategies in classical game theory (Wang et al., 2025a; Petracca & Grayot, 2023a).

A critique of this assumption comes from behavioural game theory, which focuses on the constraints that managers face in terms of information, cognition, and time (Cai et al., 2025; Chang, 2025). It has been shown in a large volume of experiments and applications that managers use heuristics, rules of thumb, and simplified decision rules instead of equilibrium optimization in complicated strategic games. These heuristic strategies require fewer cognitive resources and will result in systematic deviation from Nash equilibrium in the games of pricing, bargaining, and market entry (Xiao et al., 2024). In organizations, the hierarchical structure, the information asymmetry, and delegation of decision-making further reinforce the concept of bounded rationality (Dusi, 2024; Botzen et al., 2025). The complexity of the real world is then a natural response to the non-equilibrium results and not a lack of strategic intelligence on the part of managers because they are more interested in getting things done and moving them forward quickly and in ways that make sense internally than in achieving theoretical optimality (Khalil 2022).

Theme 2: Strategic Misperception and Cognitive Biases

Cognitive biases can play a major role in the development of managers' beliefs and strategic decisions in competitive settings. Some systematic biases lead managers to misinterpret information and to misestimate competitor reactions: overconfidence, anchoring, availability bias, and confirmation bias (Thiedmann et al., 2025). Excessive optimism on the part of managers leads them to overestimate a competitor's response and to offer products at excessive prices, engaging in early entry and escalation patterns that are out of equilibrium with projections of competitors' reaction (Kole et al., 2025; Chattopadhyay et al., 2022; Máté et al., 2025).

The tendency to ignore updates to beliefs is known as the anchoring effect, and the tendency of decision makers to pay attention to salient or recent experiences rather than probabilistic information is referred to as the availability bias (Sumar & Martin, 2024; Oren, 2022). These biases have consistently been found in empirical studies to result in ongoing non-equilibrium conditions, for example, price wars and coordination failures (Li & Cheung, 2019). Behavioural game theory is thus able to reframe strategic misperception as a legitimate element of managerial thought, instead of a random mistake (Li & Cheung, 2019).

Theme 3: Loss Aversion, Risk Preferences, and Reference Dependence

Allegretta et al. (2025) and Duan & Guo (2025) have already discussed the most important behavioural processes that prevent the Nash equilibrium in a risky strategic environment: loss aversion and reference dependence. Behavioural game theory is based on the concept of prospect theory, in which managers not only are considering outcomes but also have a reference point, and losses have a greater effect than gains with the same value (Oren, 2022; Botzen et al., 2025).

The literature suggests that managers with a loss aversion tendency are hesitant to follow equilibrium strategies that are viewed as risky and tend to price conservatively, enter the market slowly, invest less, and exhibit high risk aversion. Managers, on the other hand, have the potential to act risk-seeking and strategically escalatory differently from equilibrium predictions when outcomes are less than reference points (Aumann, 2023). They lead to unequal risk attitudes and to the fact that equilibrium is not reached in many situations of high stakes strategic contests. The behavioural game theory thus offers a more satisfactory account of risk-taking under strategy than do classical models (Torres-Vila, 2024).

Theme 4: Social Preferences, Reputation Concerns, and Fairness

In behavioural game theory, it is recognized that the manager's decision-making process considers social preferences, such as fairness, reciprocity, trust, and reputation, which are not necessarily self-interested. Both relational and moral dimensions of strategic interaction are often considered by managers, in addition to material incentives, as confirmed by both experimental and empirical studies (Tan, 2025; Keskin, 2025; Luque-Cerpa & Gutiérrez-Naranjo, 2025). Even if it is not the most advantageous strategy for the manager, they will not pursue those tactics that they consider unfair or exploitative (Matusitz, 2009; Ushakov et al., 2024). The motives of reputation also play a part in the game for repeated games in order to create cooperation, punish lack of cooperation, maintain cooperation over the long term (Hédoin, 2015; Nie et al., 2025). Such social incentives result in recurring deviations from the equilibrium solutions, particularly in negotiations, alliances and long-term competition between partners (Linsbichler, 2023). The importance of relational capital in the managerial strategy has been emphasized by behavioural game theory (Allegretta et al., 2025).

Theme 5: Adaptation, Dynamic Strategic Interaction, and Learning

Behavioural game theory emphasizes that managers don't necessarily choose equilibrium strategies straight off the bat. On the contrary, strategic behaviour is learned, adjusted, and modified in a relatively long process (Sorin, 2023; Duan & Guo, 2025). Learning models such as reinforcement learning and belief-based learning (Thiedmann et al., 2025) are used to explain delayed convergence, cyclical behaviour, and lack of coordination. When managers shift strategies in response to results, rather than the grounds for an equilibrium, they result in path-dependent strategies (Lawyer et al., 2024; McColl-Kennedy et al., 2025). This dynamic approach is counter to the assumptions of the Nash equilibrium and better captures the managerial decisions in repeated interaction in a real-world context (Akçay, 2020; Petracca & Grayot, 2023b).

Theme 6: Organizational Constraints and Institutional Pressures

Decision-making by managers is interwoven in organizational and institutional frameworks. Strategic decisions are influenced by behavioural biases through incentive systems, performance appraisal systems, corporate culture, and governance structures (Ahmed et al., 2016; Shen et al., 2007). In fact, managers are often influenced by short-term performance objectives, career concerns, and shareholders' expectations to pursue strategies that are defensible and/or politically correct but not necessarily equilibrium-optimal (Deuerlein et al., 2023; Fares et al., 2025). The forces of these organizations complement the deviation from the Nash equilibrium by limiting strategic flexibility. Following Hédoin (2015) and Deuerlein et al. (2023), in a behavioural game theory perspective the non-equilibrium behaviour is not seen as irrational, but rather a rational response to institutional constraints.

Theme 7: Formation of Beliefs, Higher-Order Reasoning, and Strategic Uncertainty

There is strategic uncertainty and poor reasoning abilities at higher levels of cognition that severely inhibit equilibrium play. The assumption of classical models, in which rationality is a given, is supported by behavioural research that shows that recursive belief formation for Nash equilibrium is difficult for managers (Deuerlein et al., 2023; Petracca & Grayot, 2023b). In contrast, managers typically employ first-order reasoning or make "simplified" strategic adjustments, resulting in miscoordination and asymmetric strategic adjustments (Petracca & Grayot, 2023a; Wang et al., 2025b).

Narratives, analogies, and industry practices rather than formal equilibrium logic (Oren, 2022; Chang et al., 2025) are what shape beliefs. Behavioral game theory thus offers a new definition of the deviation from equilibrium because of limited beliefs instead of irrationality and envisions expectation management as a prime strategic capability (Keskin, 2025; Davis, 2024).

Theme 8: Emotional and Affective Motivators of Strategic Choice

Recent research on behaviour in game theory has focused on the role of emotions in strategic behaviour. Emotions, particularly fear, anger, pride, and regret, also influence risk perception (Botzen et al., 2025; Rao, 2024) and belief updating (Botzen et al., 2025) as well as strategic persistence (Rao, 2024). Loss of fear or blame can lead to riskier strategies for balancing risk and reward, and anger and competitive pride can result in escalation beyond rational considerations of payoff (Allegretta et al., 2025; Zhang et al., 2026).

Another restriction in strategic experimentation is the fear of regrets (Sun & Parilina, 2025). Recurring managerial encounters are critical in creating and maintaining non-equilibrium behaviour in these encounters, highlighting the importance of emotional processes in strategic decision-making (Pignot et al., 2025; Orlob, 1992).

SOLUTIONS AND RECOMMENDATIONS

Based on our findings, it is very clear that classical economic models based on game theory, such as the Nash equilibrium, fail to predict managerial behaviour accurately, as they ignore human cognitive behaviour, social aspects, emotional drivers, and organizational limits. In the real world, managers need to act rapidly and prioritize practical decision-making in complex and changing institutional dynamics over mathematical model recommendations. To bridge this gap, organizations need to fine-tune their decision-making prowess, incentive mechanisms, and strategic planning processes. Based on our findings, we propose the following specific recommendations:

Limiting the Effects of Bounded Rationality and Heuristic Traps

Managers often face very tight constraints regarding time, information, and cognitive bandwidth. This makes them rely on heuristics and basic rules of thumb. While these decisions may save cognitive resources, they lead to profound deviations from optimal outcomes in several key areas, such as pricing, bargaining, and market entry. Organizational hierarchies and information asymmetries further increase these cognitive limitations. The following recommendations may be considered:

Implementation of Quick and Prudent Decision Frameworks:

Instead of expecting managers to follow complex equilibrium calculations, standardized decision trees tailored to complicated strategic games can be designed and implemented. Standardized protocols can help reduce cognitive pressure while preventing ad-hoc rule-of-thumb errors.

Reduction of Information Channels for Strategic Tasks:

Reduction in organizational hierarchies and information asymmetries during important decision-making processes must be implemented. Authority must be delegated with clear, simplified decision parameters that allow managers to act quickly and effectively while optimising strategic priorities.

Establishment of Strategic Audit Protocols:

Implementation of periodic reviews for pricing and entry decisions can ensure that operational speed and internal alignment of goals and objectives do not entirely eliminate strategic rigor from key operations.

Reducing Cognitive Biases & Strategic Misperception

Systematic biases such as overconfidence, anchoring, availability bias, and confirmation bias often cause managers to misinterpret data and misjudge competitor intentions. Excessively misguided optimism often leads to premature decisions resulting in failed market entry, needless price wars, overpricing, and irrational escalation patterns. Furthermore, managers frequently anchor on initially observed values or overemphasize recent experiences over statistical probabilities. This results in ongoing non-equilibrium conditions and coordination failures. Specific suggestions to avoid this include:

Conducting "Red Teaming" and Pre-Mortem Exercises:

Requiring dedicated teams to analyze and simulate countermoves of competitors before finalizing early market entry or major pricing changes. This directly questions managerial overconfidence and excessive exuberance over competitor reactions.

Establishing Probabilistic Decision Anchors:

Removing the bias from strategic reviews by forcing decision-makers to consider quantitative probabilistic information rather than relying on recently available or highly salient events, thereby minimizing availability bias.

Formalizing Belief-Updating Milestones:

Introducing structured stage-gate processes where strategic plans must be updated against objective market data. This helps prevent managers from ignoring crucial updates, thereby reducing anchoring and confirmation bias.

Managing Reference Points, Loss Aversion, and Risk Profiles

Managers tend to evaluate strategic outcomes relative to key reference points rather than absolute gains generated. As more often than not, losses appear larger than equivalent gains, loss-averse managers often act very conservatively. This makes them enter markets slowly, underinvest more often, and adopt defensive pricing strategies. Conversely, when outcomes lag their reference points, managers switch to over-aggressive strategies that significantly escalate risk, producing destabilizing risk asymmetries. To avoid this, the following suggestions are recommended:

Resetting Organizational Benchmarks:

Key managerial benchmark metrics must be routinely calibrated. If targets are set unrealistically high, managers operating "in the loss zone" will engage in dangerous, risk-seeking escalation practises as they seek to catch up to performance metrics.

Decoupling Loss Framing from Performance Evaluation:

Strategic investments must be structured properly. Early-stage losses must be framed as non-punitive experimental costs. This prevents loss-averse managers from delaying required investments and important market-entry strategies from being undertaken.

Implementing Dynamic Risk-Capping Mechanisms:

Establishing checks and balances in the form of hard stop-loss policies for key strategic initiatives in the event of failure is essential. This will halt any escalatory, risk-seeking behavior from being undertaken by managers when performance falls below desired benchmarks.

Social Preferences, Reputation Concerns, and Fairness

Managerial decisions are heavily governed by non-self-interested motives. These include fairness, trust, reciprocity, and reputation concerns. Managers often reject tactics they view as unfair or exploitative, even when such tactics yield significantly higher short-term material payoffs. In repeated interactions, concerns for reputation often foster long-term cooperation and stability in alliances, highlighting the need for relational capital. A few points to be noted in this regard:

Incorporating Fairness Rules into Negotiation Strategy:

Establishing clear metrics of mutual gain first becomes important. Only after this can negotiations, joint ventures, and alliance terms be discussed and structured. Care must be taken to avoid aggressive, exploitative terms that trigger moral backlashes or retaliatory measures from partners.

Protecting Relational Capital as a Strategic Asset:

Managers must recognize that maintaining corporate reputation and trust generate higher returns in repeated games that happen over a longer time frame than short-term optimization-based solutions. Hence, it is important to formally account for partner well-being while evaluating strategic alliances.

Deploying Reputation-Based Partner Enforcement:

In the long term, reciprocity, viewed as cooperative behavior, is often rewarded in the context of inter-firm competition and bargaining. Clear, predictable mechanisms exist to punish uncooperative behavior. Not understanding this could prove extremely costly at several levels of decision-making.

Structuring Dynamic Strategic Interaction and Learning

Strategic behavior tends to evolve over time and is very rarely optimal at the start. It evolves dynamically over time through reinforcement learning practices, ingrained belief systems, and learning through trial-and-error mechanisms. This iterative process often generates path-dependent strategies, delayed acceptances, cyclical patterns, and coordination bottlenecks in repeated real-world interactions. Specific suggestions to arrive at optimal strategies faster include:

Implementing Simulation-Based Learning Programs:

Using strategic flight simulators and dynamic business games helps managers experience reinforcement and belief-based learning in controlled environments. This helps in testing and developing strategies before deploying them in a real-world market environment.

Auditing Path-Dependent Strategies:

Establishing routine strategy reviews is essential to verify that ongoing initiatives reflect current competitive realities. This helps avoid outdated feedback loops or historical inertia in decision-making.

Design Modular, Adaptable Strategic Plans:

Managers often adjust strategies based on operational outcomes rather than static equilibrium calculations. This makes it mandatory to build flexible pivot points directly into long-term strategic roadmaps.

Realigning Organizational & Institutional Frameworks

Managerial behavior is often confined to institutional frameworks, governance structures, performance appraisal systems, and corporate cultures. To justify short-term performance targets, career risk, and shareholder expectations, managers often choose politically defensible, risk-averse, or consensus-driven strategies rather than optimal competitive moves. Non-equilibrium behavior is often a rational outcome stemming from these internal institutional pressures. To avoid these traps, managers can consider the following:

Aligning Executive Incentives with Long-Term Strategy:

Reducing the pressure of short-term quarterly goals by restructuring incentive and performance appraisal systems is essential to developing a long-term strategic focus. This will help managers to better position their organizations in highly competitive environments.

Protecting Defensive Risk-Taking:

Governance mechanisms must be introduced that prevent executives from being penalised for taking well-designed, calculated strategic moves that fail due to unexpected market shifts.

Streamlining Governance for Agility:

In a dynamically evolving competitive landscape, managers must not be bogged down by bureaucracy when responding to competitor strategy shifts. This can be achieved by removing institutional bottlenecks that limit strategic flexibility.

Managing Strategic Uncertainty & Higher-Order Beliefs

Managers often struggle with complex, higher-order recursive reasoning when seeking to understand competitors' motives. They mostly focus on first-order reasoning, simplified adjustments, industry practices, historical analogies, and corporate narratives. This creates discrepancies that lead to asymmetric adjustments, miscoordination, and strategic uncertainty in rapidly evolving competitive markets. Ways to overcome this include:

Developing Active Expectation Management:

Using core strategic capabilities in shaping market expectations, industry narratives, and competitors' beliefs is very important. Strategic intent must be communicated clearly to guide competitor assumptions and minimize miscoordination.

Standardizing Higher-Order Competitor Analysis:

Structured competitor-profiling protocols must be used to understand and model the strategy and tactics of competitors, rather than simply making assumptions about their actions. Specifically, historical analogies, organizational narratives, and executive team preferences of competitors must be monitored before key decisions are made.

Simplifying Internal Strategic Narratives:

Overly complex, theoretical strategic plans must be replaced with clear, concrete analogies and actionable playbooks that operational managers can easily relate to and execute.

Managing Emotional & Affective Motivators

Strategic decision-making is highly impacted by emotional drivers. These include fear, anger, pride, competitive jealousy, and fear of regret. Anger and pride often drive destructive escalations and irrational price wars, the fear of regret creates roadblocks to strategic experimentation, and the fear of blame prompts erratic, risk-taking approaches that compromise the well-being of the organization. Ways to effectively manage these include:

Implementing Emotional Circuit-Breakers:

When high-stakes competitive confrontations such as bidding wars or price escalations occur, it is important to introduce mandatory cooling-off periods and independent board reviews of current actions. This prevents pride or anger from creating diversions from rational payoff calculations.

Reducing Fear of Regret to Drive Innovation:

Creating experimental portfolios mitigates the individual fear of regret and encourages managers to take measured risks. This can be achieved by establishing strategic experimentation units such as innovation labs or venture funds.

Decoupling Affective Drivers from Strategic Execution:

Rather than responding emotionally to competitive threats, decisions should be based on statistical probabilities. This can be achieved by incorporating objective, third-party evaluations into major strategic initiatives.

FUTURE RESEARCH DIRECTIONS

This SLR provides a complete behavioural understanding of non-Nash equilibrium in managerial decision-making; however, there are some future research opportunities identified based on the results.

Second, future studies should be field-based and longitudinal, include real executives and organizations, and therefore have more external validity to reflect the complexity of real-world strategic environments, which are the subject of much of the current literature but are conducted in the laboratory.

Secondly, the behaviour game theory framework can be extended to new markets and cross-cultural situations. The literature on managerial cognition, risk perception, social preferences, and emotional responses is too focused on developed economies and may vary across institutional and cultural contexts. Theoretical generalizability would be improved by comparative studies of the inter-country and inter-industry levels.

Thirdly, the interaction of behavioural game theory and digital transformation is an issue that needs to be explored further, especially regarding algorithmic pricing, platform competition, and AI-driven decision-making. There is a great need for the study of human behavioural biases interacting with data-driven and automated strategic decision systems, which is a very important but under-researched area.

Fourth, investigation of the organizational design and governance processes, which can minimize or mitigate behavioural biases in strategic decision-making, would be beneficial. Research focusing on incentive design, performance appraisal systems, and debiasing procedures might yield practical knowledge to be used in improving managerial decision quality.

Finally, new research can include dynamic learning models that involve emotion and social considerations and study how learning, affect, and reputation evolve over time in multiple strategic interactions. These integrative approaches would bring behavioural game theory to a higher level of development to include managerial strategy.

CONCLUSION

This chapter examined the causes behind the systematic deviations of real executives in terms of a systematic literature review (SLR) using the approach of behavioural game theory. The review brings together research from fields of behavioural, cognitive, social, emotional, organisational and learning approaches and shows that non-equilibrium behaviour in managerial decision-making is not random or irrational. It is instead an adaptive response to constraints and complications posed by the actual strategic contexts.

Thematic findings suggest that the goal of full equilibrium optimisation is limited by bounded rationality, while beliefs formation and strategy judgment are affected by cognitive biases and asymmetric risk preferences. Furthermore, strategic interaction is restructured in recurring situations by social preferences, the reputation consideration as well as emotional factors. Organizational and institutional structures perpetuate these behavioural patterns and favor defensibility and performance in the short term over theoretical optimal performance. Learning and adaptation processes also show that strategic behaviour doesn't converge to equilibrium but evolves dynamically with time.

These are the dimensions that form the theoretical framework developed in this chapter and how they break down Nash equilibrium through the interaction of several behavioural layers. The focus is not on the failure of equilibrium as a constraint on managerial decision-making but rather on equilibrium behaviour as a natural and situational product of human cognition and organizational realities. Overall, this literature review confirms that it is better to think of NE as a normative rather than descriptive predictor of managerial behaviour.

Behavioural game theory is a more realistic approach and practically applicable view of strategic decision-making in contemporary organizations. Adopting a behavioural approach can enable scholars and practitioners to build more precise models, strategic instruments, and organizational designs that are better suited to how managers think and act in strategic contexts.

REFERENCES

Ahmed, M. O., El-adaway, I. H., Coatney, K. T., & Eid, M. S. (2016). Construction bidding and the winner's curse: Game theory approach. *Journal of Construction Engineering and Management*, *142*(2), 04015076. DOI: 10.1061/(ASCE)CO.1943-7862.0001058

Akçay, E. (2020). Deconstructing evolutionary game theory: Coevolution of social behaviors with their evolutionary setting. *American Naturalist*, *195*(2), 315–330. DOI: 10.1086/706811 PMID: 32017621

Allegretta, R. A., Angioletti, L., & Balconi, M. (2025). Analytic vs. synthetic decision-making: A behavioral and EEG study with real-world decision-making scenarios. *Neurophysiology*, •••, 1–10. DOI: 10.1007/s11062-025-09964-y

Aumann, R. J. (2023). The world of game theory and game theory of the world: A personal journey. *Revue Économique (Paris)*, *74*(4), 655–660. DOI: 10.3917/e.reco.744.0655

Botzen, W. J. W., Thepaut, L. D., & Banerjee, S. (2025). Kahneman's insights for climate risks: Lessons from bounded rationality, heuristics and biases. *Environmental and Resource Economics*, *88*(10), 2663–2688. DOI: 10.1007/s10640-025-00980-4 PMID: 41079046

Cai, X., Gao, B., & Nan, X. (2025). Distributed event-triggered Nash equilibrium seeking algorithm with quantization communication. *International Journal of Control, Automation, and Systems*, *23*(7), 1956–1966. DOI: 10.1007/s12555-023-0689-8

Chang, Y.-C. (2025). Dynamics of a quantum Cournot-Bertrand duopoly model based on bounded rationality and product substitutability. *Quantum Information Processing*, *24*(7), 217. DOI: 10.1007/s11128-025-04810-w

Chattopadhyay, S., Nelson, N., Au, A., Morales, N., Sanchez, C., Pandita, R., & Sarma, A. (2022). Cognitive biases in software development. *Communications of the ACM*, *65*(4), 115–122. DOI: 10.1145/3517217

Davis, I. (2024). Rational representations of uncertainty: A pluralistic approach to bounded rationality. *Synthese*, *203*(5), 142. DOI: 10.1007/s11229-024-04586-z

Deuerlein, J. W., Elhay, S., Piller, O., & Simpson, A. R. (2023). Modelling flow and pressure control in water distribution systems using the Nash equilibrium. *Journal of Water Resources Planning and Management*, *149*(6), 04023019. DOI: 10.1061/JWRMD5.WRENG-5889

Duan, X., & Guo, R. (2025). Authentically exotic: Understanding how video games foster cultural adaptation and destination image formation among foreign players. *Journal of Hospitality and Tourism Technology*, •••, 1–22. DOI: 10.1108/JHTT-01-2025-0007

Dusi, G. (2024). Reliabilist epistemology meets bounded rationality. *Synthese*, *203*(4), 115. DOI: 10.1007/s11229-024-04525-y

Fares, A., Elazouni, A., & Al-Alawi, M. (2025). Using game theory to negotiate win–win payment terms between contractors and subcontractors. *Journal of Construction Engineering and Management*, *151*(5), 04025023. DOI: 10.1061/JCEMD4.COENG-15140

Hédoin, C. (2015). Accounting for constitutive rules in game theory. *Journal of Economic Methodology*, *22*(4), 439–461. DOI: 10.1080/1350178X.2015.1024874

Keskin, K. (2025). A game theory approach to football predictions. *Public Choice*, •••, 1–21. DOI: 10.1007/s11127-025-01317-x

Khalil, E. L. (2022). The information inelasticity of habits: Kahneman's bounded rationality or Simon's procedural rationality? *Synthese*, *200*(4), 343. DOI: 10.1007/s11229-022-03815-7

Kole, E., Noordegraaf-Eelens, L., & Vringer, B. (2025). Cognitive biases in consumer sentiment: The peak-end rule and herding. *Empirical Economics*, *69*(4), 2141–2211. DOI: 10.1007/s00181-025-02797-y

Lawyer, C., Davani, H. T., & Goharian, E. (2024). Coalitional game theory for stormwater management and green infrastructure practices. *Journal of Water Resources Planning and Management*, *150*(1), 04023070. DOI: 10.1061/JWRMD5.WRENG-5979

Li, K., & Cheung, S. O. (2019). Unveiling cognitive biases in construction project dispute resolution through the lenses of third-party neutrals. *Journal of Construction Engineering and Management*, *145*(11), 04019070. DOI: 10.1061/(ASCE)CO.1943-7862.0001707

Linsbichler, A. (2023). An ultra-refined grammar for interactions: Thoughts on Robert Aumann's philosophy of game theory. *Revue Économique (Paris)*, *74*(4), 635–650. DOI: 10.3917/e.reco.744.0635

Luque-Cerpa, A., & Gutiérrez-Naranjo, M. Á. (2025). A membrane computing approach to the generalized Nash equilibrium. *Natural Computing*, *24*(2), 321–336. DOI: 10.1007/s11047-025-10014-z

Máté, D., Kiss, J. T., & Csernoch, M. (2025). Cognitive biases in user experience and spreadsheet programming. *Education and Information Technologies*, *30*(11), 14821–14851. DOI: 10.1007/s10639-025-13392-0

Matusitz, J. (2009). A postmodern theory of cyberterrorism: Game theory. *Information Security Journal: A Global Perspective*. DOI: 10.1080/19393550903200474

McColl-Kennedy, J. R., Zaki, M., Andreassen, T. W., Coote, L. V., Brea, E., Willer, F., & Andrade, J. (2025). Digital twins: A game changer in customer experience. *Journal of Service Management*, •••, 1–31. DOI: 10.1108/JOSM-12-2024-0540

Nie, J., Ranestad, K., & Tang, X. (2025). Algebraic degrees of generalized Nash equilibrium problems. *Science China. Mathematics*, *68*(7), 1747–1776. DOI: 10.1007/s11425-023-2305-y

Oren, S. (2022). Economics and computation meet cognitive biases. *ACM SIGecom Exchanges*, *20*(1), 67–69. DOI: 10.1145/3572885.3572892

Orlob, G. T. (1992). Water-quality modelling for decision making. *Journal of Water Resources Planning and Management*, *118*(3), 295–307. DOI: 10.1061/(ASCE)0733-9496(1992)118:3(295)

Petracca, E., & Grayot, J. (2023a). Correction to: How can embodied cognition naturalize bounded rationality? *Synthese*, *201*(5), 170. DOI: 10.1007/s11229-023-04152-z

Petracca, E., & Grayot, J. (2023b). How can embodied cognition naturalize bounded rationality? *Synthese*, *201*(4), 115. DOI: 10.1007/s11229-023-04124-3

Pignot, E., Joullié, J.-E., & Gould, A. M. (2025). Ethical design: A post-Lacanian ethnography of a serious healthcare game. *Journal of Organizational Ethnography*, *15*(1), 1–24. DOI: 10.1108/JOE-06-2025-0084

Rao, K. S. M. (2024). Julia Robinson and game theory. *Resonance*, *29*(6), 745. DOI: 10.1007/s12045-024-0745-6

Shen, L. Y., Bao, H. J., Wu, Y. Z., & Lu, W. S. (2007). Using bargaining-game theory for negotiating concession period for BOT-type contract. *Journal of Construction Engineering and Management*, *133*(5), 385–392. DOI: 10.1061/(ASCE)0733-9364(2007)133:5(385)

Sorin, S. (2023). Aumann and game theory. *Revue Économique (Paris)*, *74*(4), 511–528. DOI: 10.3917/e.reco.744.0511

Sumar, S., & Martin, A. K. (2024). Dog as man's best friend? Not according to cognitive biases in episodic memory. *Current Psychology (New Brunswick, N.J.)*, *43*(38), 30306–30310. DOI: 10.1007/s12144-024-06625-x

Sun, P., & Parilina, E. (2025). Hybrid altruistic-Nash equilibrium: Existence and characterization. *International Journal of Game Theory*, *54*(1), 5. DOI: 10.1007/s00182-025-00926-6

Tan, S. (2025). A distributed Nesterov's approach for fast Nash equilibrium seeking in noncooperative games. *Journal of Systems Science and Complexity*, *38*(5), 1987–2006. DOI: 10.1007/s11424-025-4353-7

Thiedmann, P., Dejardin, F., Reiter, L., & Tran, U. S. (2025). Brief online socio-cognitive mindfulness interventions neither improve socio-cognitive mindfulness nor cognitive biases. *Mindfulness*, *16*(6), 1555–1568. DOI: 10.1007/s12671-025-02575-y

Torres-Vila, L. M. (2024). Strategic ejaculate allocation in the mostly monandrous moth *Lobesia botrana*. *Behavioral Ecology and Sociobiology*, *78*(8), 92. DOI: 10.1007/s00265-024-03507-x

Ushakov, V. N., Tarasyev, A. M., & Ershov, A. A. (2024). A supplement to Krasovskii's unification method in differential game theory. *Doklady Mathematics*, *110*(2), 386–392. DOI: 10.1134/S1064562424601604

Wang, Y., Yang, Y., & Deng, X. (2025a). Bounded rationality quantum duopoly games with asymmetric information. *Quantum Information Processing*, *24*(6), 188. DOI: 10.1007/s11128-025-04811-9

Wang, Z., Zhang, C., & Tan, Z. (2025b). Inefficiency of multiplicative approximate Nash equilibrium for scheduling games. *Journal of Combinatorial Optimization*, *49*(3), 38. DOI: 10.1007/s10878-025-01274-7

Xiao, J., Xiao, H., & Li, C. (2024). The complexity of the APP competition model with bounded rationality in platform ecosystem. *Electronic Commerce Research*, •••, 1–27. DOI: 10.1007/s10660-024-09868-9

Zhang, Y., Lian, B., & Lewis, F. L. (2025). Distributed global Nash equilibrium of interactive adversarial graphical games. *Journal of Systems Science and Complexity*, *38*(2), 613–632. DOI: 10.1007/s11424-025-4542-4

KEY TERMS AND DEFINITIONS

Behavioural Game Theory: An extension of classical game theory that incorporates psychological and behavioural insights to explain strategic decision-making under realistic assumptions of bounded rationality, cognitive biases, and social preferences.

Bounded Rationality: A concept describing the cognitive limitations of decision-makers, including restricted information access, limited processing capacity, and time constraints, which prevent them from achieving fully optimal equilibrium strategies.

Cognitive Biases: Systematic patterns of deviation from rational judgment in human thinking, including overconfidence, anchoring, availability bias, and confirmation bias, which distort managerial beliefs and strategic choices.

Loss Aversion: A behavioural tendency wherein individuals experience losses more acutely than equivalent gains, leading to asymmetric risk preferences and conservative or delayed strategic actions in managerial contexts.

Nash Equilibrium: A solution concept in game theory in which no player can benefit by unilaterally changing their strategy, given the strategies of all other players. It serves as the standard benchmark for rational strategic behaviour.

Reference Dependence: A behavioural phenomenon in which outcomes are evaluated relative to a reference point rather than in absolute terms, influencing risk-taking and strategic behaviour in managerial decision-making.

Reinforcement Learning: A learning mechanism through which managers adjust their strategic choices based on past outcomes, gradually adapting behaviour through feedback rather than computing equilibrium strategies analytically.

Social Preferences: Preferences that extend beyond self-interest to include concerns for fairness, reciprocity, trust, and reputation, which influence strategic decisions especially in repeated interactions and negotiation contexts.

Strategic Uncertainty: The inability of managers to fully anticipate the strategies and reactions of competitors, which limits higher-order reasoning and contributes to equilibrium deviation in strategic settings.

Systematic Literature Review: A rigorous, reproducible methodology for identifying, screening, and synthesising existing research on a defined topic, following structured protocols such as the PRISMA framework to ensure transparency and reliability.

Chapter 5

Anticipatory Governance in the Digital Age:
Building Resilient Public Institutions for Uncertain Futures

Varanasi Rahul
http://orcid.org/0000-0003-2407-7654
Acharya Institute of Graduate Studies, India

ABSTRACT

This chapter examines the emerging concept of anticipatory governance as a transformative approach to public management in the digital age. As governments face increasing uncertainty driven by technological disruption, climate risks, global health crises, and geopolitical instability, traditional reactive governance models are proving insufficient. The chapter explores how anticipatory governance integrates strategic foresight, digital intelligence, resilience theory, and public value principles to strengthen the capacity of public institutions to anticipate and manage complex future challenges. It proposes a Digital Anticipatory Governance Framework (DAGF) that combines foresight infrastructure, data-driven intelligence systems, adaptive policy mechanisms, collaborative governance networks, and ethical safeguards. The chapter also discusses global practices, institutional implications, and the risks associated with algorithmic governance and digital divides.

INTRODUCTION

Public institutions are required to adopt a new and different approach in today's governance system context, which is no longer confined to crisis response, but also has to shift from traditional administrative governance to a complex gover-

DOI: 10.4018/979-8-3373-9765-8.ch005

nance system. Anticipatory government's concept is rooted in the idea that it is a necessary transition in public governance in the digital era. It suggests that some new and emerging core competencies are required in the capacity of governments to manage uncertainty, to anticipate future risks and to shape the future society wants to have, and that these core competencies must be combined and applied to strategic foresight, digital technologies, institutional flexibility and approaches to public value. The chapter calls for a governance that is more proactive, rather than merely responding to crises, in order to increase resilience, innovate and achieve sustainable and inclusive development.

This chapter is an overview of the development of public governance and the growing importance of anticipatory governance in the context of complex policy issues. The chapter aims to: (1) gain insight into the evolving context of governance in this technologically driven uncertain and interdependent world; (2) reflect on conceptual and theoretical foundations of anticipatory governance; (3) explore opportunities, challenges and institutional implications of anticipatory governance; (4) offer a blueprint for the future of public governance – the Digital Anticipatory Governance Framework (DAGF); (5) review the field and implications of anticipatory governance in the digital age; and (6) discuss future research directions and trends in anticipation of the development of anticipatory governance in the digital world.

While strategic foresight, adaptive governance, institutional resilience, digital government and public value research are the current areas of the literature, there is a lack of integration. While important in their own right, these viewpoints tend to be treated as distinct and not sufficiently understood how digital intelligence and foresight can be translated into policy action that is adaptive, resilient, collaborative and democratically legitimate in the future. Specifically, very little has been paid attention to the institutional arrangements between early detection, policy experimentation, organizational learning, ethical oversight and public value creation. This chapter aims to fill this gap by crafting the Digital Anticipatory Governance Framework as a composite governance system that enables sensing emerging change, understanding future risks, experimenting with policy interventions, learning from practice, and adapting public action in a context of uncertainty.

BACKGROUND

Research Gap and Theoretical Contribution

Past studies on anticipatory governance have contributed to important learnings about strategic foresight, new technology governance, policy experimentation, institutional readiness and institutional resilience. But this is knowledge spread out amongst a number of theoretical traditions. Strategic foresight research is mainly focused on the study of alternative futures, long term trends and weak signals. Adaptive governance is about experimentation, flexibility, feedback and institutional learning. Institutional resilience investigations are related to the ability of the government to withstand shocks, reorganize, recover, and remain in the ability to provide essential services. Data infrastructure, AI and algorithmic decision making, and public value theory of digital platforms are the key areas of digital governance scholarship, while digital governance is evaluated in terms of legitimacy, equity, participation, trust and societal benefits.

Although both of these perspectives are valid, there is surprisingly little literature that addresses how these can be integrated into an institutional framework that is digitally activated anticipatory governance. Foresight is seen as a special planning process, digitalization as a process of modernizing administration and public value as a normative objective, and resilience as a competence in crisis-management. The interplay between these elements throughout the entire policy process has been thus neglected.

This chapter fills this gap with the introduction of the concept of Digital Anticipatory Governance Framework. The framework makes a significant contribution to the existing body of scholarship in three important ways. Firstly, it brings together strategic foresight, digital intelligence, adaptive policy making, joint governance, institutional resilience and democratic safeguards in one governance framework. Second, it recognizes that anticipatory governance is not a one-time forecasting exercise, but an institutional process. The cycle comprises of sensing, interpretation, deliberation, experimentation, implementation, monitoring, learning and adaptation. Third, it introduces an evaluative dimension, that is in line with conditions of implementation, institutional risks and performance indicators, that can be used as the basis for governments to assess anticipatory governance systems.

The DAGF makes a theoretical and practical contribution. Theoretically it is known as the interaction between foresight, digital capacity, institutional adaptability, resilience and public value. The implications for practice are that the institutional models provided offer governments an institutional blueprint to build institutions of the future that remain transparent, accountable, inclusive and democratic.

The Changing Landscape of Public Governance

The world is experiencing deep change, with fast technological change, a changing climate, geopolitical strife, and shifting expectations of society. Public administration models are of traditional nature, which were shaped in a context of relative stability, hierarchical controls and incremental policy changes, but no longer seem to be well-equipped for addressing the complexity and speed of today's challenges.

Governance in today's world is affected by intertwined and global systems where an economic shock in one country can be followed by a technological shock in another country, a climate crisis in yet another country, and a public health emergency in another country.

These conditions have changed the setting of public institutions and set the stage for new ways of doing business. Governments are now faced with complex policy challenges involving multiple actors, uncertain policy outcomes and rapidly changing policy variables as opposed to predictable problems having clear solutions. It is now being described by scholars and international organizations as a "context of systemic uncertainty and complexity" where traditional governance structures are often inadequate to foresee risks and opportunities that are emerging (OECD, 2024).

Governments will need to learn new governance skills, because they need to be ready to address urgent crises as well as long-term shifts in the society. The need is to transcend reactive crisis management and come up with proactive and future-oriented policy-making. The idea of anticipatory governance has thus become a major approach for helping governments to manage future uncertainty – and to ensure institutional sustainability and democratic accountability (Stephens et al., 2025).

Limitations of Traditional Public Administration

Historically, the traditional public administration systems have focused on stability, predictability and bureaucratic efficiency. The models were created in a time when policy environments were fairly consistent, and governments had a hierarchical decision making system to regulate public affairs. Administrative processes usually had a planning horizon of several years, were defined in terms of hierarchical structures and were organized in a standard way.

These have helped in establishing strong state institutions but are now inadequate in the twenty first century. Modern governance challenges like climate change, digital disruption, pandemic flu and transnational security issues often have nonlinear dynamics and fast-changing conditions. All of this cannot be solved with a set of non-negotiable policies or deliberative procedures.

In addition, traditional governance systems tend to be policy-oriented with short-term timeframes that are based on electoral calendars or political pressures. This orientation can also result in governments' inability to tackle longer-term issues which necessitate long-term strategic planning and inter-sectoral cooperation. This can make it difficult for public institutions to foresee future risks and disruption (Hansen et al., 2022).

The Emergence of Anticipatory Governance

Anticipatory governance has become a key concept in the research of public administration and public policy in recent years. The essence of anticipatory governance is the capacity of governments to systematically explore, anticipate, and prepare for future developments, using foresight methodologies, data-driven insights and adaptive policy frameworks. A key difference between anticipatory systems and response to crises is that anticipatory systems seek to identify weak signals, emerging trends, and to formulate and move towards proactive strategies that increase societal resilience.

It takes into account the fact that uncertainty is a part of life for governance in the modern era, and therefore, the policy should have mechanisms for learning, experimentation and adaptation. Anticipatory governance can be understood as encompassing multiple elements such as strategic foresight, scenario planning, risk assessment, and adaptive policy design. Such tools help policy makers visualize several potential futures and develop policies that are robust in the face of uncertainty (Chenok, 2025).

Importantly, anticipatory governance is not only about predicting the future but about enhancing the capacities of institutions to respond to and to adapt to uncertainty. Incorporating foresight functions into governance processes enables public institutions to anticipate and plan for enduring solutions to complex challenges and to create policies that are effective in a variety of future scenarios (El-Ghalayini, 2025).

Digital Transformation and Public Governance

While anticipatory governance is becoming more popular, governments are investing in digital transformation globally. Technologies like artificial intelligence (AI), big data analytics, cloud computing, and digital platforms are changing the face of public institutions. These technologies provide governments with the capability to gather, manage and process huge volumes of data, in order to provide opportunities for evidence-based policy making and public service.

Digital technologies can improve governments' anticipatory capacities by facilitating advanced types of anticipatory analysis and real-time monitoring. For instance, AI-driven data analysis can help uncover trends and patterns in economic activity, public health indicators, or environmental conditions, which can help policymakers anticipate potential problems before they become crises. In a similar manner, digital platforms can serve as tools to enhance public services by integrating information from various sources, allowing the delivery of more efficient citizen–public service interactions, and enabling more responsive and personalized public services (Joshi et al., 2025).

Balancing Innovation, Ethics, and Democratic Legitimacy

Digital technologies are important resources for anticipatory governance, but they need to be managed in public institutions carefully. AI and predictive analytics can introduce ethical questions in the realm of policy development, such as transparency, fairness, and accountability. The algorithms employed in public decision-making can inadvertently exacerbate or just be outcomes of social inequalities, or they can lack democratic control of their processes.

Also, anticipatory governance needs to be based on principles of public value creation and societal resilience. The purpose of anticipatory systems is to do more than just increase administrative efficiency; it's to increase the ability of governments to safeguard citizens, create sustainable growth, and advance democratic institutions. These goals can only be accomplished through a balanced mix of technology innovation and ethical governance and citizen engagement (Esposito et al., 2025).

Building Resilient Public Institutions

This is a central concept of governance today, and resilience is at its heart. Public administration's view of resilience is their ability to withstand shocks, respond to new situations and continue to deliver vital services in times of crisis. Natural and human-caused disasters such as financial crises, climate change disasters and pandemics have become more common worldwide and urgently call for resilient governance systems to be put in place.

For the anticipatory approach, the governments have an opportunity to inform and plan infrastructure with the help of climate projections and to develop disaster management policies in advance for dealing with climate risks. Similarly, digital EWS can support public health response, such as responding to disease outbreaks and initiating rapid responses. The examples demonstrate the potential of anticipatory governance to build the resilience of public institutions and their ability to address complex challenges (Johnston, 2025).

Toward an Integrated Framework for Anticipatory Digital Governance

The strategic foresight infrastructure provides governments with information on trends, weak signals and what might happen in the future. Digital intelligence systems provide businesses with the resources, tools and data to monitor and predict in real-time. Policy mechanisms that are adaptive allow governments to change and refine policies in light of their experiences. Collaborative governance networks help to integrate scientific, private sector, civil society, international and government expertise. Ethical and democratic protections contribute to the transparency, accountability, inclusion of anticipatory systems and adherence to public values. These systems are key to solving the multifaceted issues of today's global governance (Sarewitz, 2011).

Conceptual Review Methodology

The chapter follows an integrative conceptual review approach for developing the Digital Anticipatory Governance Framework. This method was chosen as the study sought to synthesize theory from multiple research traditions and not to use statistics to merge results of similar empirical research. It synthesizes the literature on anticipatory governance, strategic foresight, adaptive governance, institutional resilience, digital government, algorithmic governance, collaborative governance and public value.

Structured searches were conducted on literature using combinations of the following terms: anticipatory governance, anticipatory government, strategic foresight in government, anticipatory governance in government, adaptive governance, institutional resilience, digital government, anticipatory public value, anticipatory public value-oriented governance, anticipatory innovation governance and algorithmic governance. Peer reviewed journal articles, scholarly books, book chapters and authoritative institutional publications were prioritized. Theoretical bases were built using seminal works and recent research was selected to reflect advances of artificial intelligence, digital transformation, data governance and public-sector innovation.

Thematic synthesis was used to analyze the literature selected. The first phase determined that there was a set of recurring governance capacities, such as foresight, early-warning, data-integration, policy-experimentation, institutional-learning, collaboration, resilience, transparency, public-participation, and ethical oversight. The second stage grouped these capabilities according to their dominant theoretical foundations. The third step involved exploring the complementary, conflict, overlap and gap elements of the theoretical approaches. The final stage involved the re-expression of the recurring themes in the five dimensions of DAGF.

A dimension was added to the framework if it met three criteria: it was supported across more than one body of literature; it served a different institutional purpose; and it helped to turn information about the future into legitimate policy action. The product is conceptual and theory building in nature. It provides orientation to future empirical verification by conducting comparative case studies, institutional evaluations, interviews, surveys, and longitudinal studies.

MAIN FOCUS OF THE CHAPTER

Governance Conditions Requiring Anticipatory Capacity

The Changing Landscape of Public Governance

Governance is changing and requires a change in the way policies are designed, implemented and evaluated by the public institutions. Governments don't work in silos anymore but in a cascading network of global interconnections and unpredictability among economic, environmental, technological and social developments. This increasing level of adaptability, resilience and anticipation in public governance is required to manage new risks and new opportunities that are emerging (OECD, 2022).

Complexity and Interdependence

Traditional policy design is based on models that have linear relationships between policy interventions and outcomes and stable relationships. But such models are not enough when dealing with complex adaptive systems that have feedback mechanisms, nonlinearities and emergent behavior. Governance systems need to therefore become more flexible and adaptable and enable policy makers to effectively respond to the changing circumstances (Guston, 2014).

Adaptive governance processes are based on learning, experimentation, and progressive policy development. Governments should not only have long-term fixed plans but also have mechanisms for policy changes due to new information and changing circumstances. Feedback loops are crucial for enhancing decision making and for governance systems to be effective and responsive to new challenges.

Technological Acceleration

AI systems can analyze large amounts of data in real-time to uncover trends, patterns, and risks that might otherwise go unnoticed, allowing governments to proactively address potential crises before they become uncontrollable. Predictive modelling has become common in the public health surveillance, disaster risk management, economic forecasting and urban planning fields. For instance, predictive analytics can be used to predict disease outbreaks, map possible disaster-prone areas, or track economic signs of financial instability (Spitz, 2025).

The use of digital technologies in governance processes also brings a lot of challenges and risks. Algorithmic decision making systems can be biased, may perpetuate inequality or deliver discriminatory results, and may be based on data that is biased. Algorithmic decision making systems can be biased, may reinforce social inequalities or they can yield discriminatory results, and may be trained on biased data. Moreover, the growing dependence on sophisticated digital systems can cause problems of transparency and accountability: although citizens and policy makers can have more or less access to algorithmic processes, they are often not fully comprehensible (Roy, 2024).

Crisis as a Permanent Condition

The public health systems and global supply chains and economic governance were identified as weak due to the COVID-19 pandemic, for instance. Likewise, the significance of digital security has been emphasized due to the increase of threats faced in the area of critical infrastructure and the continuity of the Nation. The need for resilient governance systems that can effectively respond to environmental shocks has been further emphasized by climate related disasters like floods, wild fires and extreme weather events.

The experiences have made academics and policy makers recognize that there are "normal" and "crisis" governments, yet they are not mutually exclusive. We are in a time of uncertainty and need to accept that there will be disruptions – we need to plan for that in governance. This also moves the emphasis from the crisis response to strategies for resilience building (Redman et al., 2025).

These three conditions (systemic interdependence, technological acceleration and recurring crises) are examples of why anticipatory governance is not about prediction. Governments need to have skills in forecasting risks, in analyzing information and data, in the coordination of inter-institutional actions, in policy changes, in keeping services running, and in safeguarding democratic values. Anticipatory capacity is based on the mixture of informational competence, technological competence, organizational competence, collaborative competence and normative competence.

Conceptual Foundations of Anticipatory Governance

Nowadays, anticipatory governance has become a crucial instrument of public administration to face uncertainties, complexity and speediness of the society. Anticipatory governance differs from traditional governance approaches, which are mostly reactive, based on trying to solve problems, by prioritizing proactive governance approaches and preparing for emerging risks and opportunities before they manifest themselves. This concept is not only based on one theory, but on a multi-disciplinary perspective and approach, integrating a range of theories, such as strategic foresight, complexity science, digital governance theory, and resilience studies (Mokdad, 2025).

Strategic Foresight

The techniques used for the detection of weak signals of change are generally horizon scanning, scenario analysis, trend mapping and Delphi forecasting, which are used to examine the evolution of the technological, economic, environmental and social factors over time. These potential trajectories can be leveraged to guide policy design to meet future conditions. "Strategic foresight" then becomes a way to shift policy-making from a reactive to a proactive model, moving from a reactive approach to events to proactively foreseeing and adapting to them (Webb (2019).

A key advantage of a strategic approach to foresight is that it extends the policy horizon, taking it beyond the political cycle. Elections and the everyday demands of politics can constrain governments from meeting the needs of long term issues like climate change, demographic change or technological change. The foresight methodologies enable policy makers to consider the impact of their decisions now, and the sustainable societal consequences (Evans, 2025).

The Concept of Adaptive Governance and Complexity Science

Compliance mechanisms are not for policymers, as they are inflexible, based on the rule of law, and are averse to experimentation and learning, complexity theory suggests. Experimental and pilot policy programmers or policy cycles can be introduced to allow institutional experimentation and refinement of policy options based on actual policy outcomes. Policy programmers can also be experimental, pilot programmers or be a series of adaptations and learning cycles of policy—development is not just based on the results observed in practice.

In addition, complexity science highlights a need for feedback mechanisms, allowing policy makers to monitor the effect of their policy and make a change in strategies if needed. Oszlak (2024), continuous evaluation and learning processes are crucial to make governance processes adaptive to changes in circumstances and/or new threats.

Digital Governance and Algorithmic Authority

One of the conceptual frameworks that emerged from the fast-growing digital technologies and their influence on the theory of governance is digital governance. Digital governance is the research on the change in the role and function of public institutions in relation to citizens' roles as a result of the use of data infrastructure, AI systems and digital platforms.

With data-driven governance, governments have the capacity to collect and process vast quantities of data and to learn about society and policy outcomes.

Using advanced analytics and machine learning algorithms, policymakers can identify trends in economic activity, environmental shifts, public health metrics and citizen behavior. The following capabilities greatly improve the capabilities of governments to forecast possible risks and create more evidence-based policies (Battistella et al., 2022).

Educational governance also has important questions of algorithmic authority and accountability. Important questions of algorithmic authority and accountability arise in educational governance. With the growing role of automated systems in decision-making processes, issues have emerged regarding the possibility of algorithmic bias, transparency and concentration of power in the governance systems based on data. Thus, it is an integral part of the challenges of contemporary public administration to ensure that digital governance systems are based on ethical and democratic principles (Mišić, 2021).

Resilience Theory and Institutional Capacity

The resilience theory is all about creating governance systems that are efficient but also flexible and robust. Institutions need to be able to adapt and reorganize as they encounter unexpected challenges. To achieve this, investments need to be made in institutional capacity, infrastructure, and collaborative networks to ensure efficient crisis response and recovery (Jin, 2024).

Anticipatory governance plays a part in resilience by allowing governments to learn the vulnerabilities before they become a crisis and create strategies to manage potential risks. Policymakers can use scenario planning, risk assessment, and early-warning systems to understand the potential impacts of various disruptions on public systems, and to create policies that strengthen the resilience of public institutions (Ahern, 2025).

Anticipatory Governance as a Governance Philosophy

The general conceptual framework of anticipatory governance is provided by the above-mentioned conceptual traditions. However, they are not automatically linked to an institutional model that is integrated. Although Foresight can identify a potential disrupter, it is not possible to say that the government institutions are capable of responding to the disrupter. The predictive intelligence possible with digital technologies can be achieved, but not with guarantees of fairness and transparency. Flexibility of policy experimentation could be improved using adaptive policy experimentation, but at the same time it could create unequal policy outcomes across jurisdictions. Resilience measures can help to ensure continuity but also help strengthen current institutional arrangements. A theoretical synthesis to explain the interactions between these perspectives, and how their limitations can be balanced, is therefore required.

Digital Transformation as an Enabler of Anticipation

One of the most important initiatives for innovation in modern public governance is digital transformation. Improvements in data infrastructure, artificial intelligence, digital platforms are changing the way governments are gathering data, interpreting new data patterns and deciding on policy interventions. The digital technologies offer powerful tools that can be used to identify early signs of change, prepare for a range of potential futures, and involve citizens on a more participatory basis in the policy making process, as part of the concept of anticipatory governance.

Early Warning Systems Based on data

Digital technologies, for instance, can be used to support public health surveillance systems and track disease outbreaks and epidemiological trends across geographic areas. These systems use hospital and laboratory health information along with population-level health indicators to detect early warning signals of spread of infectious diseases. In times of global health crisis, these can facilitate the government to take preventive measures and to use medical resources efficiently (Heo et al., 2021).

Early warning systems, in conjunction with predictive analytics, can help to create a set of scenarios and test the resilience of policy responses to various scenarios. These systems can be used to simulate the impact of policies on different shocks, disruptions or other scenarios, thereby strengthening policy design (Roth et al., 2025). Digital technologies are helping to enhance the ability of governments to anticipate and act on complex governance challenges, through the combination of real-time monitoring and scenario-based analysis.

AI and Predictive Policymaking

Within social policy, AI can be used to predict areas of interest where poverty, unemployment, or social unrest is likely to occur, based on demographic and economic patterns. These insights can help governments to implement specific policy measures which will deal with social issues in the most effective ways before they turn larger social problems (Hanisch et al., 2023).

Predictive policymaking must be accompanied by robust and powerful ethical principles and measures of accountability to respond to these concerns. Governments should ensure transparency in decisions made by algorithms, establish data protection measures, and put in place monitoring systems enabling independent review of AI systems. The governance of responsible AI is therefore crucial to sustain democratic legitimacy and yet maximize the advantages of predictive technologies (Guston, 2010).

Digital Platforms and Citizen Engagement

Digital transformation also supports new participatory governance and engagement with citizens beyond improving analytical capabilities. Governments have innovative tools available on the digital platform to collect public feedback, solicit policy suggestions and promote co-creation of solutions. These platforms offer increased opportunities for citizens to be involved in the policymaking processes and to provide valuable input that can enhance the quality and legitimacy of public decision-making.

Theoretical Framework

This chapter introduces an integrated theoretical framework based on four complementary theories: adaptive governance theory, institutional resilience theory, digital state theory and public value theory, which will help to understand how government can be effective in anticipating and responding to new challenges in today's more complex and uncertain context. All these theoretical pillars offer a unique perspective on the ways in which contemporary governance systems can better prepare themselves to anticipate change, cope with crises, and contribute to long-term societal good.

Adaptive Governance Theory

The adaptive governance theory has developed into a key perspective for analyzing how institutions can effectively create, operate and evolve in complex and dynamic policy environments. The traditional approach to governance is typically based on fixed policy frameworks and administrative structures, which are appropriate for relatively stable situations. Yet, the institutions needed to deal with uncertainty and ever-changing realities are needed in the current context of governance challenges, including global health emergencies, technological disruptions, and economic volatility and climate change.

The collaborative networks are another important aspect of adaptive governance. There are frequently a number of stakeholders in complex societal problems, such as government institutions, researchers, private institutions and civil society organizations. Adaptive governance, then, encourages decision-making that is decentralized, and fosters collaboration and knowledge-sharing across institutional boundaries.

These networks help governments to have more varied views, combine expertise and better address new issues.

Institutional Resilience Theory

In adaptive governance, flexibility and learning are central, whereas, in institutional resilience the emphasis is on the ability of the public institutional structures to resist disruption and carry out their core functions during crisis. In the world of recurring crises on a global scale, like financial crisis, pandemic, cyber crisis and climate change crisis, resilience is becoming an important theme in public governance.

Resilient institutions are those that are able to withstand shocks, adapt when they are disrupted and provide essential public services without significant system failure. This is particularly true for complex governance environments in which a crisis may rapidly be transmitted from one sector to another, from one institution to another.

The philosophy of resilience highlights the need for governments to establish relevant institutions that can also anticipate the risks they will face in the future and take steps to make them more resilient at the time of a disruptive event.

Digital State Theory

Digital transformation has profoundly influenced the governance systems of today. The concept of digital transformation has transformed the ways in which people govern today. Digital state theory is concerned with the effect of digital technologies such as AI, big data analysis, cloud computing and digital platforms on the nature of the relationship between governments, citizens, and the policy process.

According to digital state theory, as digital infrastructure has evolved over time, data has become an important governance resource. Today's governance that is carried out in data ecosystems, meaning that data is collected and utilized by various actors including the citizens, private and non-governmental bodies, public institutions etc. These data ecosystems can support government in real-time tracking of social, economic and environmental transformation, and will bring clarity to the data throughout the entire process up to anticipatory policy making.

Public Value Theory

Technological innovation and institutional resilience need to be the two cornerstones of anticipatory governance, but ultimately governance systems need to be evaluated by the measure of added public value. In the theory of public value, it is very significant question whether governance action is beneficial for the well-being of the society and whether it is democratic or not.

Public value theory centers on an action of the government that leads to a result that benefits society as a whole, not just the government or its political or institutional interests. These benefits may include improved public services, increased social equity, sustainable environment, and increased civic involvement.

Public value theory emphasizes the need to consider the societal values and public expectations when designing future-oriented governance strategies, in the context of anticipatory governance. It is important to get systems in place that are deeply rooted in digital technologies and predictive analytics, but respect citizens' rights, are transparent, and promote citizen inclusion.

Critical Synthesis of the Theoretical Perspectives

Institutional Resilience Theory which allows the ability to withstand, continue key operations, reorganize and rebuild after an event. It acknowledges that anticipation can not prevent all crises, and that governance systems need to be redundant, robust, contingency, and have recovery capacity. Public value theory uses the following set of value justifications to assess the results of the policies: (legitimate, equitable, transparent, inclusive and socially beneficial).

Theories may be represented as a relational sequence as institutions. This is done by incorporating the use of digital elements in relation to change. Strategic foresight aids in understanding the meaning of new developments. Adaptive governance transforms the knowledge into policy action, in an experimental and revisionist way. Institutional resilience helps to maintain continuity during risks when they eventuate. The entire procedure is assessed in terms of its public value theory (PVT) to determine whether it has a positive impact on society and democratic legitimacy.

SOLUTIONS AND RECOMMENDATIOS

Framework Development Logic

The five dimensions of the DAGF were synthesized from the thematic and theoretical analyses. Strategic foresight infrastructure is the ability to look at the possible futures in a systematic manner. Digital intelligence systems: information and technology required to monitor changing conditions. Adaptive policy mechanisms are institutional capabilities that are able to translate data into action that may be revised. Collaborative governance networks are the fragmented knowledge and connections to address inter-sectoral problems. Ethical and democratic safeguards are the normative and accountability mechanisms which are needed for legitimacy. (Table 1)

Table 1. Derivation and rationale of the five DAGF dimensions

DAGF dimension	Principal theoretical basis	Institutional function	Reason for inclusion	Risk if absent
Strategic foresight infrastructure	Strategic foresight and anticipatory governance	Identifies weak signals, emerging trends, and alternative futures	Provides long-term orientation	Government remains reactive and short-term focused
Digital intelligence systems	Digital state and digital governance theory	Integrates data, monitoring, modelling, and predictive analysis	Provides timely evidence for anticipation	Decisions depend on fragmented or delayed information
Adaptive policy mechanisms	Adaptive governance and complexity theory	Supports experimentation, pilots, flexible regulation, and policy revision	Converts intelligence into action	Policies remain rigid when conditions change
Collaborative governance networks	Collaborative and network governance	Combines governmental, academic, private-sector, civil-society, and citizen knowledge	Addresses interconnected and cross-sector problems	Institutional silos and knowledge gaps persist
Ethical and democratic safeguards	Public value and responsible digital governance	Protects fairness, transparency, rights, participation, and accountability	Maintains legitimacy and public trust	Digital anticipation may become opaque, discriminatory, or intrusive

Source: Author's own compilation.

Proposed Model: the Digital Anticipatory Governance Framework (DAGF)

In this chapter, building on the work done in previous chapters, a framework, Digital Anticipatory Governance Framework (DAGF) is introduced, which seeks to improve the government's ability to anticipate future challenges and deal with uncertainty. The framework, in particular, integrates key concepts in adaptive governance, resilience theory and digital governance theory, public value theory, to develop a comprehensive framework for future-oriented public management.

The five dimensions of the Digital Anticipatory Governance Framework are interwoven: strategic foresight infrastructure, digital intelligence systems, adaptive policy mechanisms, collaborative governance networks and ethical and democratic safeguards. As one, they enable governments to foresee, influence and stay democratic in the digital age. These components enhance institutional resilience and the ability to anticipate, which enables public institutions to function well in a complex and uncertain governance context.

Strategic Foresight Infrastructure

The first strand in the Digital Anticipatory Governance Framework is to establish strategic foresight infrastructure in government institutions. The systematic exploration of possible developments for the future in order to inform present-day policymaking is strategic foresight. The focus of foresight processes is not on predicting one future scenario but on exploring several different scenarios and analysing the implications for governance systems.

Public institutions with foresight units or public strategic planning offices can be established to institutionalize foresight. The purpose of these units is to conduct the horizon scanning process, identify future trends and evaluate potential future risks that may impact long-term societal development. The inclusion of foresight activities in policies will help governments make decisions on a time horizon greater than that of short-term political cycles.

The results of foresight processes must be connected to the digital intelligence systems and must be based on timely and integrated evidence regarding the scenarios and possible risks.

Digital Intelligence Systems

The second aspect of the framework is on the advancement of digital intelligence systems, which can aid anticipatory policymaking. Governments now have a much greater capacity to collect, manipulate and analyse vast quantities of data as a result of advances in digital technologies. Governments have the potential to leverage data from a variety of sources that can be collected and accessed in one place, to deliver timely information about social, economic and ecological change.

Digital intelligence systems are typically based on a multi-agency, multi-institution and multi-source data integration platform. These sorts of platforms enable the policy-maker to dissect complicated information sets and come to a decision trends that could signal dangers or opportunities. An example is an economic dashboard which can track economic indicators, and a climate monitoring system which can track real time climate changes.

Digital intelligence is a value that must be institutionalized, by having adaptive mechanisms in government, which first analyze, then experiment, and then change policy.

Adaptive Policy Mechanisms

While the insights gained from digital intelligence and foresight are valuable, anticipatory governance requires policy mechanisms to be able to respond to changing conditions. In this third dimension of the framework, adaptive policy processes allow for a change in policy based on new information and/or a change in policy context.

Adaptive policy makes acknowledges that there are sometimes uncertainty and unpredictability in the solution of complex problems in society. Governments can develop policy with scope for change, instead of just policy frameworks. The clauses allow the rules to be amended as needed and/or the procedure to be changed without significantly altering the law.

Collaborative Governance Networks

Collaborative governance networks are a key component of the fourth dimension of the Digital Anticipatory Governance Framework. Problems of modern governance are not usually straightforward and are not always confined to one policy field. No single actor at a single level of governance can solve the challenges of developing solutions to complex problems such as climate change, digital transformation, public health, etc.

Collaborative governance networks are a network of multi-organizational partnerships comprising public institutions, academic researchers, civil society organizations, private actors and international organizations that are brought together to address complex issues. This is a way that these alliances can help the government gain insight or expertise that it may lack in-house, share resources, and develop new solutions that may not exist in the framework of traditional government lines.

Ethical and Democratic Safeguards

The fourth pillar of the Digital Anticipatory Governance Framework is about ethical and democratic protection of anticipatory governance systems. Digital technologies and predictive analytics are powerful tools for policymaking but must be employed around democratic norms and within public trust.

Governance transparency as an important protection is the usage of algorithmic governance systems for decision making. Citizens need to be made aware of the work of data-driven systems and how policies are created by these systems. Good governance is essential for citizens to hold their governments to account and to observe them, a key to democratic legitimacy.

Another vital protection is by means of algorithmic audits and oversight mechanisms. Independent audits can evaluate automated decision-making systems to ensure they are fair and unbiased. These evaluations can be used to identify the potential bias in algorithms and guarantee that digital governance systems are ethical.

Democratic accountability also is assured through participatory oversight mechanisms. Governance processes and decisions should be open to citizens, civil society organizations and independent regulatory bodies for review and input. These can be used to improve democratic oversight and make sure anticipatory governance systems are value-reflecting via public consultations, citizen assemblies, and digital participation platforms.

Ethical protection is present in all dimensions of DAGF and guarantees future-oriented governance to be accountable to citizens and connected to public value.

Operational Cycle of the DAGF

The DAGF is not a quid dam institution based system of pillars but a process of governance. May be expressed in terms of 8 interrelated stages:

Interpret – Decide – Experiment – Do – Check – Learn – Adapt

Governments use horizon scanning, real-time data, expert views and forecasts to look for emerging developments during the sensing phase. The process of interpretation involves examining the meaning, probability, occurrence and possible consequences of such occurrences. Deliberation is a process in which various groups of government, academics, citizens, civil society and the private sector discuss and consider policy options and the impacts on public values.

Protection for ethics and democracy is present all throughout the cycle. They want transparency on how data and assumptions are being used, opportunities to engage with the public, avenues to challenge and consider human and automated decisions, and clear accountability for human and automated decisions. The cycle is thus of the future intelligence, institutional learning and democratic control.

Global and Comparative Perspectives

Anticipatory governance does not work in the same way in all countries. Governments have a range of institutional models due to the varying priorities of their political and administrative, technological and policy agendas. The common goal of anticipatory governance, to be prepared for emerging risks and future uncertainties, is the same, but how this is achieved, is quite different in each national context. Hence, it is helpful to examine international experiences and learn about the possibilities of institutionalizing anticipatory governance in various forms of governance.

Common Characteristics of Successful Anticipatory Governance Models

Comparative studies show that there are a number of common features to the successful anticipatory governance system, although there are variations in institutional design and technological approaches. These are the qualities that enable some governance arrangements to be more effective in tackling complex issues and problems.

Long-term political commitment is one of the key factors. Capacity building of institutions, technology infrastructure and strategic planning are all investments required and on-going in anticipation governance. Political will and political stability is crucial for creating robust anticipatory governance systems in the government and can be supported by strong and stable political commitment to foresight programmers and digital transformation.

Cross-sector collaboration is also a key quality. To achieve effective anticipatory governance, cooperation is necessary between government agencies, academics, the private sector and civil society groups. The collaboration enables the governments to incorporate various skills and viewpoints in their policy-making. To overcome complex governance problems, it is necessary to go beyond the boundaries of the socio-isolated, bureaucratic solutions.

Thirdly, data integration capability is important. It is important to be able to collect, collate and analyse information from a variety of resources to be able to anticipate governance. Governments need to create integrated data infrastructure for interagency information sharing and to provide the basis for more sophisticated analytical use. Integrated data platforms support policy makers to monitor trends and to identify early warning signs of potential risks.

The Need for Cooperation on a Worldwide Level

Many of the governance issues at present are worldwide in nature and anticipatory governance programmers are usually at the national level. Issues such as climate change, epidemics, cyber security threats, economic volatility, do not recognize the borders of the nation and require international cooperation. In this respect, anticipatory governance needs more and more transnational governance and international cooperation.

International organizations and multilateral institutions play very important role as facilitators in this cooperation. They offer opportunities for sharing knowledge, coordinating policies and establishing common governance systems. Global governance networks offer other countries the possibility to share their best practice and lessons learned from anticipatory governance efforts.

Illustrative Governance Applications

Climate-Risk Governance

The planning for long-term climate risks in the field of infrastructure investments, disaster planning, water management, agriculture and urban planning provide illustrations of the importance of long-term climate-risk planning. Climate scenarios are a tool that can help governments to learn more about areas of vulnerability and to test policy vulnerabilities. The implementation needs to involve various national agencies and local governments, scientists, communities and infrastructure providers as partners in order to be effective.

Regulatory Sandboxes

Regulatory sandboxes are environments where new technologies or business models are tested within a controlled environment and are subject to public scrutiny. They capture the adaptive policy aspect of the DAGF since they enable regulators to learn before imposing permanent rules. They need well-defined entry conditions, consumer protection and well-defined assessment and processes for capturing lessons in broader regulation.

Digital Twin and Urban Simulation

Digital twins can simulate the scenarios of transportation, energy, infrastructure, environment and disasters. Tools can help policy makers with decision making on interventions before they become physical elements. Their products are dependent on the assumptions used in the model, data quality, model representation, and the use of the technical tools. They should, therefore, complement rather than call into question political judgment and public discussion.

Cybersecurity Governance

Cybersecurity also provides an example of the importance of being warned in time, coordinated institutionally, made redundant and with contingency plans, and worked together internationally. It also proves that there is a need for resilience in anticipatory governance as not all threats can be anticipated and prevented. The key challenges are being ready to identify risks and to keep critical services operating in the event of a disruption to the digital system.

Challenges and Risks

Anticipatory governance has great potential to help to strengthen public institutions and enhance future orientation in policymaking, but there are also some substantial challenges in implementing anticipatory governance. Several political, technological, institutional and ethical issues may impede the process of implementing such reforms in the government's efforts to institutionalize anticipatory systems. If anticipatory governance is to have a positive impact on resilient and democratic public management without introducing new governance risks, these challenges need to be addressed.

The Short-Sightedness and Paralysis of Politics

One of the most continuous challenges to anticipatory governance is political short-termism. Elections can occur on a relatively short time frame, as they do in a democracy, and it is in such a political context that politicians look to policies that can yield fast and tangible results. Long-term strategic planning is a key element of anticipatory governance and sometimes may be overlooked because of the potential for long-term gains that are not within the span of a political term.

Insufficient Resources, Budget Constraints

Another major challenge is the financial and resource requirements for enhancing capacities in anticipatory governance. Investment in foresight units, foresight digital infrastructure and foresight funding are substantial investments. Governments may find themselves in a fiscal squeeze and unable to invest in such programs in the long term.

The Lack of Information Inequalities and Gaps

With the growing use of digital technologies in anticipatory governance systems, digital divides and social inequality are issues of concern. Digital infrastructure, technological literacy, and quality internet access is limited and/or not equally accessed by social groups and regions. If not designed inclusively, digital governance actions can lead to unintentional reinforcement of inequalities in society.

Ethical Considerations and Bias in Algorithms

More and more governments are using AI and predictive analysis in their decision-making processes, raising concerns about algorithmic bias and responsible governance. Machine learning systems are often based on historical data which contains social biases. Unless these biases are explicitly managed, algorithms could yield unequal results or perpetuate inequities.

Innovation and a Balance of Innovation and Democratic Accountability

The question of technology and democracy is one of the most fundamental challenges of anticipatory governance. Digital technologies and predictive analytics provide great opportunities to enhance policy development and predict society problems. However, with the increasing adoption of automated systems and data-informed decision-making, there has been a worry about the centralization of power in governmental organizations and technology vendors.

Governance Fragmentation

A lack of integrated mandates, data systems, administrative silos, and competition between public agencies can make anticipatory governance difficult. A department may develop information that is not available or usable to another department. If this is to be implemented effectively, these interoperability, common standards, coordinating authority and cross-agency accountability must be maintained.

Bureaucratic Resistance

Public officials might object to anticipatory reform when they see experimentation or data sharing or automation as a threat to a powerful authority, routine, professional expertise, or job security. Punishment for failed pilots when learning has occurred is common in most accountability arrangements, and this risk of failure must also deter pilot projects.

Politicization of Foresight

There is no such thing as apolitical foresight. Governments can make decisions based on scenarios which support their agenda, even if they have less to gain from them than from scenarios that don't. Choosing scenarios with transparency, multiple involvement, independent experts and the public of the assumptions can curb the potential for anticipatory to be used as a political excuse.

Anticipatory Surveillance

It may feel like the norm to gather too much personal data if it's done with predictive analytics and constant monitoring. Goals of risk prevention should not take precedence over privacy, due process, freedom or equality. Anticipatory monitoring should be subject to data minimization, necessity, proportionality, time limits, human oversight and independent oversight.

Model Error and Hubris

Predictive systems can generate false positives, false negatives, model drift or false confidence. The social and political dynamics in complex systems cannot be perfectly forecasted. Digital tools, therefore, should be used to assist in the judgment, and not give the false impression that it is certain. Governments need to convey uncertainty and have contingency plans.

The principal implementation barriers and the corresponding institutional safeguards are summarized in Table 2.

Table 2. Key challenges and mitigation measures in DAGF implementation

Challenge	Likely consequence	Suggested mitigation
Political short-termism	Weak commitment to long-term investments and preparedness	Statutory foresight requirements, long-term policy reviews, and cross-party support
Bureaucratic resistance	Limited experimentation and slow institutional change	Leadership commitment, training, incentives, and protected pilot environments
Governance fragmentation	Poor coordination and weak data sharing	Cross-agency bodies, shared standards, and interoperable systems
Unequal state capacity	Partial or uneven implementation	Phased implementation and capacity-sensitive design
Digital divide	Exclusion of less-connected and vulnerable groups	Digital-inclusion programs and alternative offline participation
Algorithmic bias	Unfair or discriminatory decisions	Independent audits, representative data, explainability, and human oversight
Vendor dependence	Lock-in, weak transparency, and data-sovereignty risks	Open standards, contractual safeguards, and internal technical capacity
Anticipatory surveillance	Privacy violations and declining public trust	Data minimization, proportionality, legal oversight, and appeal mechanisms
Model error	False confidence and unsuitable policy intervention	Uncertainty disclosure, scenario ranges, validation, and contingency planning

Source: Author's own compilation.

Evaluating Digital Anticipatory Governance

The performance of anticipatory governance should not be assessed solely through technological sophistication or predictive accuracy. A system may produce accurate forecasts yet fail to influence policy, exclude marginalized communities, undermine privacy, or lack public legitimacy. Evaluation must therefore examine institutional capacity, policy responsiveness, resilience, ethical governance, participation, and public value.

Table 3 provides a multidimensional approach for evaluating DAGF performance beyond predictive accuracy and technological sophistication.

Table 3. Performance evaluation framework for the DAGF

Evaluation dimension	Illustrative indicators	Possible evidence source
Foresight capacity	Frequency and quality of horizon scanning, scenarios, and long-term reviews	Foresight reports and strategic plans
Detection capability	Speed, relevance, and coverage of emerging-risk alerts	Early-warning records and incident reports
Digital maturity	Data quality, interoperability, cybersecurity, and timeliness	Technology assessments and data audits
Adaptive capacity	Use of pilots, sandboxes, policy reviews, and evidence-based modifications	Policy documents and evaluation reports
Institutional learning	Use of lessons, cross-agency learning, and retention of institutional knowledge	After-action reviews and learning records
Resilience	Continuity of essential services, recovery time, and contingency readiness	Crisis-performance and continuity reports
Collaboration	Stakeholder diversity, participation quality, and information sharing	Consultation records and network assessments
Ethical governance	Algorithmic audits, privacy safeguards, explainability, and appeal mechanisms	Ethics audits and compliance reports
Democratic legitimacy	Public trust, transparency, fairness, and citizen participation	Surveys and consultation reports
Public value	Equity, inclusion, service quality, sustainability, and societal outcomes	Impact assessments and public-value evaluations

Source: Author's own compilation.

FUTURE RESEARCH DIRECTIONS

The relationships outlined in the DAGF need to be tested in the future with empirical evidence. Comparative case studies can consider the similarities and differences in the functioning of the five dimensions in different political systems, administrative traditions, policy sectors and governments. There must be a special emphasis on institutional contexts where the outcomes of the foresight are implemented in terms of budget distribution, rules and legislation, delivery of public goods and services and crisis preparedness decisions.

One of the other important areas of research is related to Artificial Intelligence Systems management. Algorithmic transparency, explanatory power, auditing, human control, model uncertainty, data quality and accountability should be examined when using predictive systems to provide information for public decisions. The effects of anticipatory technologies on privacy, equality, procedural fairness, and distribution of public benefits and risks should also be studied.

There is a need to conduct further research on citizen participation. Moving forward, there is a need to better understand how digital participation platforms affect inclusion, and how well they promote the participation of already-involved and technologically savvy groups. In addition, study of citizen assemblies, participatory foresight, indigenous knowledge, local expertise and community-based monitoring in the process of developing alternative futures could be explored.

The political economy of anticipatory governance policies needs to be further explored, including issues of vendor dependency, data sovereignty, public procurement, institutional power, bureaucratic resistance and the electoral cycle. These factors could impact whether foresight and digital intelligence is translated into policy action.

Finally, the DAGF should be applied in designated policy sectors such as the climate adaptation sector, public health, urban planning, cyber security, migration, social protection, education and infrastructure. Research in the respective sectors would help elucidate the framework and which dimensions would turn out to be most crucial in different circumstances.

CONCLUSION

Anticipatory governance is a transition from the mainly reactive public administration to institutions that are able to foresee change, plan for uncertainty, learn from evidence, and chart future desirable societies. This change is becoming more and more vital, as governments have to function in an environment of technology change, interwoven systems, frequent crises, environmental challenges, and expectations that have evolved rapidly.

Chapter identified an important gap in the literature as a gap in the literature. The strategic foresight, adaptive governance, institutional resilience, digital governance, public value and collaborative governance have been analyzed separately. Each provides valuable input, but they do not come together in establishing the knowledge needed to engage in good and proper policy action in the future. The Digital Anticipatory Governance Framework has been created to tackle this fragmentation.

The DAGF consists of 5 elements, all of which are interdependent: strategic foresight infrastructure, digital intelligence systems, adaptive policy mechanisms, collaborative governance networks, ethical and democratic safeguards. These dimensions are not intended to be a checklist to use alone. In one, they are an institutional system. Foresight is a tool for governments to explore potential futures. Digital Intelligence helps to track the situation and provide evidence in real-time. Adaptive mechanisms convert intelligence into policies that are to be tested and revised. The collaborative networks offer a variety of knowledge and coordinated capacity. Anticipatory practices are ethical, transparent, accountable and fair.

The framework also includes the idea of anticipatory governance as a cyclical process of sensing, interpretation, deliberation, experimentation, implementation, monitoring, learning and adaptation. This is a cyclic logic as opposed to a one-off forecasting and is part of anticipatory governance. It emphasizes that the change of assumptions and policies in an institution is a cyclical process because the new evidence is generated when the policy is changed.

Evaluation of anticipatory governance must not be restricted to predicting or technological advances. It also must be evaluated with regards to institutional learning, adaptability, resilience, public trust, equity, transparency, participation and public value. A technologically advanced system to exclude, obscure or interfere with rights is not 'anticipatory governance'.

The DAGF is a concept that can serve as the basis for future empirical research on DAGF, as well as institutional experimentation. It can be measured at various policy levels and across different governance settings, its size and proposed indicators. It establishes a bridge between the technological capacity and institutional flexibility and democratic legitimacy as a blueprint for governments in becoming more prepared, resilient, inclusive and future-oriented.

REFERENCES

Ahern, D. (2025). *The new anticipatory governance culture for innovation: Regulatory foresight, regulatory experimentation and regulatory learning. arXiv.* https://doi.org//arxiv.2501.05921DOI: 10.48550

Battistella, C., & De Toni, A. F. (2022). Towards a foresight governance system: The case of the port system authority of Trieste. In *2022 7th International Conference on Smart and Sustainable Technologies (SpliTech)* (pp. 1–4). IEEE. https://doi.org/ DOI: 10.23919/SpliTech55088.2022.9854348

Chenok, D. (2025). Envisioning the future of government: How emerging, secure technologies and data flows can enable anticipation and action that improve performance. In *Anticipatory governance: Shaping futures through foresight and innovation* (pp. 221–234). World Scientific., DOI: 10.1142/9789811296000_0014

El-Ghalayini, Y. (2025). Digital transformation: A tool for anticipatory governance. In *Anticipatory governance: Shaping futures through foresight and innovation* (pp. 235–245). World Scientific., DOI: 10.1142/9789811296000_0015

Esposito, M., & Park, J. (2025). Anticipatory capacity through foresight. In *Anticipatory governance: Shaping futures through foresight and innovation* (pp. 39–48). World Scientific., DOI: 10.1142/9789811296000_0003

Evans, A. (2025). Elevating anticipatory analysis in policymaking. In *Anticipatory governance: Shaping futures through foresight and innovation* (pp. 49–67). World Scientific., DOI: 10.1142/9789811296000_0004

Guston, D. H. (2010). The anticipatory governance of emerging technologies. *Applied Science and Convergence Technology*, *19*(6), 432–441. DOI: 10.5757/JKVS.2010.19.6.432

Guston, D. H. (2014). Understanding anticipatory governance. *Social Studies of Science*, *44*(2), 218–242. DOI: 10.1177/0306312713508669 PMID: 24941612

Hanisch, M., Goldsby, C. M., Fabian, N. E., & Oehmichen, J. (2023). Digital governance: A conceptual framework and research agenda. *Journal of Business Research*, *162*, 113777. Advance online publication. DOI: 10.1016/j.jbusres.2023.113777

Hansen, H. K., & Uldam, J. (2022). Assembling transnational policing: Europol's anticipatory governance. *Global Society*, *36*(2), 281–299. DOI: 10.1080/13600826.2021.2021146

Heo, K., & Seo, Y. (2021). Anticipatory governance for newcomers: Lessons learned from the UK, the Netherlands, Finland, and Korea. *European Journal of Futures Research*, *9*(1), 16. Advance online publication. DOI: 10.1186/s40309-021-00179-y

Jin, D. (2024). The challenges and opportunities of public governance in the digital era. *International Journal of Social Sciences and Public Administration*, *2*(3), 472–478. DOI: 10.62051/ijsspa.v2n3.64

Johnston, E. (2025). Anticipatory identity control: Upstream governance on digital platforms. *Dialogues on Digital Society*, *1*(3), 442–446. DOI: 10.1177/29768640251377164

Joshi, A., Goldstein, T., & Moschetta, G. (2025). Anticipatory governance on cybersecurity. In *Anticipatory governance: Shaping futures through foresight and innovation* (pp. 203–219). World Scientific., DOI: 10.1142/9789811296000_0013

Kong, B. (2022). The adjustment logic and reform path of the government governance system and mechanism in the digital age. *Advances in Economics and Management Research*, *1*(2), 16. DOI: 10.56028/aemr.1.2.16

Mišić, J. (2021). Ethics and governance in the digital age. *European View*, *20*(2), 175–181. DOI: 10.1177/17816858211061793

Mokdad, A. A. (2025). Inclusive and intelligent governance. In *Governance in the age of intelligent systems* (pp. 173–238). IGI Global., DOI: 10.4018/979-8-3373-1280-4.ch008

Noack, P. (2025). Technology anticipation and regulation. In *Anticipatory governance: Shaping futures through foresight and innovation* (pp. 191–201). World Scientific., DOI: 10.1142/9789811296000_0012

Organization for Economic Co-operation and Development. (2022). Executive summary. In *OECD public governance reviews*. OECD Publishing., DOI: 10.1787/ccc78971-

Organization for Economic Co-operation and Development. (2022a). *Anticipatory innovation governance*. OECD Publishing., DOI: 10.1787/a20998d5-

Organization for Economic Co-operation and Development. (2023). Emerging technology governance: Towards an anticipatory framework. In Science, O. E. C. D. (Ed.), *Technology and Innovation Outlook*. OECD Publishing., DOI: 10.1787/d67d5380-

Organization for Economic Co-operation and Development. (2024). *Framework for anticipatory governance of emerging technologies. OECD Science, Technology and Industry Policy Papers*. OECD Publishing., DOI: 10.1787/0248ead5-

Oszlak, O. (2024). Gobierno personalizado. [APyS]. *Administración Pública y Sociedad, 17*(17), 65–91. DOI: 10.71047/2524.9568.n17.46560

Redman, A., Balakrishnan, A., & Frank, N. (2025). Unlocking the power of public purpose. In *Anticipatory governance: Shaping futures through foresight and innovation* (pp. 121–134). World Scientific., DOI: 10.1142/9789811296000_0008

Roth, S., & Milojević, I. (2025). Building an architectural framework for anticipatory governance: A case study of the Asian Development Bank. In *Anticipatory governance: Shaping futures through foresight and innovation* (pp. 333–344). World Scientific., DOI: 10.1142/9789811296000_0022

Roy, J. (2024). Digital transformation versus Westminster traditionalism: Mindset, mechanisms and critical enablers of systemic adaptation. *Canadian Public Administration, 67*(4), 481–494. DOI: 10.1111/capa.12598

Sarewitz, D. (2011). Anticipatory governance of emerging technologies. In Marchant, G. E., Allenby, B. R., & Herkert, J. R. (Eds.), *The growing gap between emerging technologies and legal-ethical oversight* (pp. 95–105). Springer., DOI: 10.1007/978-94-007-1356-7_7

Spitz, R. (2025). The AAA framework: Responsible leadership for sustainable futures. In *Anticipatory governance: Shaping futures through foresight and innovation* (pp. 103–120). World Scientific., DOI: 10.1142/9789811296000_0007

Stephens, M., Awamleh, R., & Sicre, F. (2025). Anticipatory—The next form of governance. In *Anticipatory governance: Shaping futures through foresight and innovation* (pp. 3–17). World Scientific., DOI: 10.1142/9789811296000_0001

Webb, J. (2021). Rethinking the governance of technology in the digital age. In Kleinman, D. L., Cloud-Hansen, K., Handelsman, J., & Hurlbut, M. J. (Eds.), *The Oxford handbook of the science of science communication* (pp. 687–701). Oxford University Press., DOI: 10.1093/oxfordhb/9780198800682.013.58

KEY TERMS AND DEFINITIONS

Adaptive Governance: A governance approach that aims to be flexible, learning-oriented, collaborative, and continually adapting policy in response to changing conditions.

Algorithmic Governance: When automated, data-driven systems and algorithms are used to facilitate or shape public decision-making.

Anticipatory Governance: A governance approach that is oriented towards the future and that builds in mechanisms of foresight, strategic planning and adaptive institutions to prepare for emerging risks and opportunities.

Digital Governance: Using digital technologies, data systems, and online platforms to enhance government processes, decision-making, and public service provision.

Institutional Resilience: The ability of public institutions to withstand shocks, adjust to stresses, and continue to provide essential services in uncertain times.

Predictive Analytics: Techniques that apply to data analysis, statistical analysis, and artificial intelligence to anticipate future events, trends or policy results.

Public Value: The values, whether social, economic or democratic, that are produced by the actions and public policies of governments.

Scenario Planning: Strategic foresight approach for decision-making under uncertainty by considering a variety of plausible future scenarios.

Strategic Foresight: Systematic analysis of long-term trends, emerging issues and alternative futures to guide policy decisions in the present.

Systems Thinking: Analytical method whereby relationships between the inter-connected parts of a system are considered and how they affect the system as a whole.

Chapter 6
Anticipatory Governance Strategic Foresight and Government Preparedness for Emerging Risks:
A Forward-Looking Analytical Framework for Managing Uncertainty and Complexity

Alberto Merced Castro Valencia
http://orcid.org/0000-0001-8160-9077
Instituto Tecnológico José Mario Molina Pasquel y Henríquez, Tecnológico Nacional de México, Mexico

Alejandra Medina Lozano
Instituto Tecnológico José Mario Molina Pasquel y Henríquez, Tecnológico Nacional de México, Mexico

ABSTRACT

This chapter analyses anticipatory governance as a public policy approach to strengthen state capacity in addressing emerging risks under conditions of high uncertainty. Drawing on a theoretical, comparative, and applied review, it examines how strategic foresight can be systematically integrated into the policy cycle, including formulation, implementation, and evaluation. The analysis identifies institutional mechanisms aimed at reducing systemic vulnerabilities in key domains

DOI: 10.4018/979-8-3373-9765-8.ch006

such as public health, cybersecurity, energy transition, and artificial intelligence. It argues that effective anticipation depends less on precise forecasting and more on adaptive decision-making architectures, inter-institutional coordination, and continuous learning processes. The chapter also compares international experiences from Finland, Singapore, the United Kingdom, and the United States to extract lessons on analytical capacity, political leadership, regulatory quality, and democratic legitimacy.

INTRODUCTION

Over the last two decades, governments have confronted a convergence of health, climate, technological, financial and geopolitical disruptions that interact in mutually reinforcing ways. These dynamics have been characterized through the language of risk society, volatility and, more recently, polycrisis, where shocks rarely occur in isolation and tend to cascade across systems (Beck, 1992; Taleb, 2007; World Economic Forum, 2024). In this context, public policy based on linear projection, sectoral silos and ex post reaction appears increasingly insufficient, although the extent of its inadequacy varies across policy domains.

Pandemic experience, cyber incidents against critical infrastructure, energy price instability and rapid advances in general-purpose technologies indicate that governments may benefit from permanent anticipatory capabilities rather than occasional emergency plans. Anticipatory governance has emerged as a field that integrates foresight, systemic risk analysis, adaptive policy design and institutional preparedness. Its central contribution is not to promise certainty but to improve the quality of present decisions across multiple plausible futures (Fuerth & Faber, 2012; OECD, 2019, 2020).

Anticipatory governance matters for functional, fiscal and democratic reasons. Functionally, it may help institutions detect weak signals, assess nonlinear threats and organize scalable responses before crisis conditions materialize. Fiscally, it can improve priority setting by shifting resources from costly emergency reaction toward prevention, which under certain conditions reduces public spending volatility. Democratically, it may strengthen institutional credibility by demonstrating that public authorities can learn, adapt and act responsibly under uncertainty (Acemoglu & Robinson, 2012; Boin et al., 2016; Boston, 2017). The magnitude of these effects, however, remains an empirical question requiring more systematic comparative evidence.

Anticipatory governance should not be interpreted as a purely technocratic exercise. Strategic foresight creates public value mainly when linked to political deliberation, distributive choices and accountability mechanisms. The key challenge is therefore not prediction accuracy, but decision quality under uncertainty, intertemporal trade-offs and unequal exposure to risk across social groups and territories (Marchau et al., 2019; Poli, 2017).

When properly institutionalized, strategic foresight functions as a cognitive infrastructure for the state, connecting trend analysis, scenario development, vulnerability mapping and policy stress testing. Where institutionalization is partial, foresight outputs are likely to remain symbolic. Empirical evidence suggests that alignment between national planning, sector regulation, fiscal strategy and crisis management depends on implementation conditions unevenly distributed across administrations (European Commission, 2020; Habegger, 2010).

Government preparedness translates foresight into operational capacity through strategic reserves, interoperable protocols, simulation exercises, flexible regulatory tools, early warning systems and clear chains of command for emergency activation. Comparative evidence indicates, although not uniformly, that better outcomes tend to emerge where foresight and preparedness are integrated into a single learning cycle with periodic review of assumptions, capabilities and institutional performance (Cabinet Office, 2023; U. S. Government Accountability Office, 2023).

The literature on emerging risk remains fragmented in important ways. Futures studies and institutional implementation research often evolve in parallel, with limited integration; resilience debates frequently emphasize post-crisis recovery rather than ex ante architecture; and empirical analysis faces causal identification challenges because successful prevention implies events that do not fully occur (International Risk Governance Council, 2018; Klinke & Renn, 2002; Walker et al., 2013). These fragmentations frame the analytical contribution of this chapter.

This chapter pursues five specific objectives: (i) define core concepts and theoretical foundations of anticipatory governance; (ii) compare international models of foresight institutionalization through a structured comparative analysis; (iii) examine policy instruments for anticipation and preparedness; (iv) evaluate implications for state performance, democratic trust and systemic stability; and (v) propose an operational roadmap for emerging economies operating under constrained resources and high institutional heterogeneity.

BACKGROUND

Theoretical Foundations of Anticipatory Governance

Concept of Anticipatory Governance

Anticipatory governance can be defined as the set of institutional arrangements, knowledge processes and decision mechanisms through which the state identifies emerging risks, explores plausible futures and acts early to reduce harm while preserving strategic public goods. It is a logic of active preparedness rather than rigid planning. The framework combines analytical capacity, organisational coordination and political legitimacy to make uncertainty more governable, without pretending to eliminate it (Fuerth & Faber, 2012; Poli, 2017). The unit of analysis is not a single ministry but the state's cross-system ability to align information, authority and resources across central government, regulators, subnational administrations, scientific communities and private actors.

Historical Evolution

The historical development of anticipatory governance can be summarized in four stages. The first was associated with post-war strategic planning, civil defense and scenario thinking in national security institutions. A second stage incorporated modern risk management approaches in finance, infrastructure, health and environment, emphasizing prevention and regulatory safeguards (Haldane & May, 2011; Klinke & Renn, 2002). A third stage emerged with global disaster risk reduction and climate adaptation agendas, where anticipation became linked to multilateral commitments (Aitsi-Selmi et al., 2015; IPCC, 2023; UNDRR, 2015). A fourth stage, currently unfolding, is defined by technological acceleration, digital interdependence and deep uncertainty, in which anticipatory governance is shifting toward adaptive regulation and continuous learning loops (OECD, 2020; UNESCO, 2021).

Main Theories

Futures Studies and Strategic Foresight

Futures studies argue that the value of anticipation lies not in predicting one correct future but in widening the range of plausible futures that inform present choices. Tools such as horizon scanning, scenario building, backcasting and pathway analysis help policy makers reveal hidden assumptions, test strategic options and avoid overcommitment to linear expectations. In public governance, these tools tend to be useful when they shape actual decision points rather than produce detached reports (Poli, 2017; van der Heijden, 2005). A central insight is epistemic humility: uncertainty is not informational noise that disappears with better data, but a structural feature of complex systems.

Systemic Risk Governance and Resilience

Systemic risk theory emphasizes interdependence, contagion and cascading failure. In tightly coupled systems, localized disruptions can propagate rapidly across finance, energy, transport, health and digital infrastructure. Governance based on isolated sectoral risk management is therefore insufficient. Anticipatory policy must monitor network fragilities, strengthen redundancy and create institutional firebreaks that contain cross-system escalation (Haldane & May, 2011; International Risk Governance Council, 2018). Resilience is not a return to status quo, but the ability to maintain core functions while adapting to changing conditions.

State Capacity and Institutionalism

Institutionalist approaches highlight that anticipation depends on durable administrative capacity: a professional civil service, stable organizations, clear mandates, credible enforcement and interagency cooperation. Where institutions are fragmented or politicized, foresight products rarely influence budget or regulation. Where capacity is stronger, governments are more likely to translate strategic analysis into implementable policy sequences (Acemoglu & Robinson, 2012; North, 1990; Ostrom, 2005). Formal rules alone are insufficient: informal norms, organizational incentives and bureaucratic routines shape whether early warnings are ignored, delayed or transformed into action.

Public Decision Making Under Deep Uncertainty

Under deep uncertainty, policy makers cannot reliably assign probabilities to future states because causal relations are unstable, contested or rapidly evolving. Optimization around a single expected scenario tends to perform poorly. The alternative is robust and adaptive decision design: flexible policy portfolios, trigger-based sequencing, reversible commitments and periodic reassessment of assumptions (Marchau et al., 2019; Walker et al., 2013). This approach is particularly relevant for climate adaptation, AI governance, health preparedness and critical infrastructure planning.

MAIN FOCUS OF THE CHAPTER

Methodology

This chapter adopts a qualitative, theory-driven research design that combines a structured narrative literature review with a comparative institutional analysis of four reference jurisdictions. The methodological choice responds to the conceptual nature of the research questions, which concern how anticipatory governance is institutionalized, what mechanisms link foresight to policy outcomes and which configurations are most transferable to emerging economies. The design follows guidance for interpretive comparative research in public administration (Pollitt & Bouckaert, 2017) and for narrative synthesis in policy studies (Greenhalgh et al., 2018).

Research Design and Analytical Strategy

The study is structured in four sequential stages. A conceptual stage clarifies the constructs of anticipatory governance, strategic foresight and government preparedness. A comparative stage examines institutionalized foresight in four cases purposively selected to maximize variation in political system, administrative tradition and foresight architecture: Finland, Singapore, the United Kingdom and the United States. A synthesis stage extracts cross-case patterns and boundary conditions. An applied stage translates the findings into a roadmap for emerging economies.

Case Selection Criteria

Cases were selected using a most-different-systems logic complemented by analytical relevance. Three criteria were applied: documented institutionalization of foresight in central or parliamentary government structures, with publicly available evidence covering 2010 to 2024; variation in administrative tradition (Nordic-parliamentary, strategic-developmental, Westminster and federal-presidential) sufficient to test the boundaries of foresight transferability; and availability of independent evaluation sources (national audit bodies, OECD reviews and peer-reviewed comparative studies) to triangulate institutional self-descriptions.

Sources and Data Corpus

The evidence base comprises three layers. The first is peer-reviewed academic literature on foresight, anticipatory governance and risk governance, identified through structured searches in Scopus and Web of Science using the descriptors anticipatory governance, strategic foresight, government preparedness, systemic risk, deep uncertainty and adaptive policy, limited to publications between 2000 and 2024. The second comprises official documents and reports from the OECD, European Commission, United Nations, World Bank, IPCC, UNDRR, UNESCO and national risk authorities. The third consists of independent evaluations by national audit institutions and academic comparative reviews used to qualify official narratives.

Analytical Procedure

Documents were coded using a four-dimensional analytical grid: (a) institutional location of foresight capacity, (b) legal and procedural formalization, (c) coordination density across ministries and levels of government and (d) translation mechanisms from foresight outputs to budget, regulation and operations. For each case, evidence was triangulated across academic, official and audit sources. Divergent findings were retained rather than reconciled, on the assumption that contested evidence is itself analytically informative. Cross-case comparison followed a structured-focused logic.

Scope, Limitations and Reflexivity

Three limitations should be acknowledged. First, the comparative scope is restricted to four cases and does not constitute a statistical sample; conclusions should be read as conditional regularities rather than universal claims. Second, the analysis relies on documentary evidence rather than primary interviews, which limits access to informal decision processes. Third, attribution of policy outcomes to foresight practices is inherently difficult because successful prevention is observable only as counterfactual (Marchau et al., 2019; Walker et al., 2013). These limitations are mitigated through source triangulation and explicit identification of contested claims.

International Models of Government Strategic Foresight

This section presents a structured comparative analysis of four institutional models, organized around the four-dimensional analytical grid: institutional location, formalization, coordination density and translation mechanisms. The discussion interprets the conditions under which each model appears to produce policy effects and identifies boundary conditions that constrain transferability.

Nordic-European Model

In several Nordic countries and within the European Union, long-term strategic thinking has been institutionalized through periodic foresight reports, dedicated units linked to the center of government and formal channels connecting executive analysis to legislative deliberation. Finland is frequently cited for integrating futures analysis into parliamentary processes, which appears to reduce, although not eliminate, discontinuity between electoral cycles and long-horizon priorities (Boston, 2017; European Commission, 2023).

At the supranational level, European strategic foresight reports have informed agendas on open strategic autonomy, green transition, industrial policy and digital sovereignty. The model's principal strength is coordination across policy domains and governance levels. Its main observed limitation is the difficulty of translating broad strategic narratives into operational instruments, budgetary commitments and measurable implementation outcomes. Independent evaluations have repeatedly noted gaps between analytical ambition and downstream policy uptake (European Commission, 2023), which qualifies more optimistic accounts in secondary literature.

Anglo-Saxon Model

The Anglo-Saxon model combines national risk assessment, public audit and mission-oriented preparedness. In the United Kingdom, the National Risk Register has become a public reference for high-impact risks. In the United States, periodic high-risk assessments by the Government Accountability Office create institutional pressure to address persistent vulnerabilities (Cabinet Office, 2023; U. S. Government Accountability Office, 2023). The model is comparatively strong in transparency, independent review and accountability architecture, but can face fragmentation across agencies and political cycles. The 2020 pandemic experience in both jurisdictions illustrated that the existence of risk registers does not, by itself, guarantee operational readiness.

Asian Model

Asian experiences, particularly Singapore, illustrate a strategic-state approach in which foresight is closely integrated with executive planning and capability development. Institutional routines include horizon scanning, interagency scenario exercises and stress testing in health security, food systems, digital governance and infrastructure continuity (Habegger, 2010; OECD, 2019). The model's strength lies in coherence between strategic analysis and implementation authority. Its transferability is conditional on political and institutional context: in pluralist settings, similar effectiveness is likely to require additional emphasis on transparency, oversight and participatory legitimacy.

Comparative Synthesis: Institutional and Regulatory Differences

Comparative analysis across the four cases suggests that four variables systematically shape foresight effectiveness. The organizational location of anticipatory capacity matters: central-of-government placement tends to outperform sectoral dispersion in coordination terms but may sacrifice domain depth.

The degree of legal formalization matters: statutory mandates appear to protect foresight from political cycles but require accompanying implementation rules. The density of coordination mechanisms matters: regular interagency routines outperform episodic high-level committees. The quality of data infrastructure conditions the realism of scenario analysis and the speed of early warning translation.

No single institutional template emerges as universally optimal. Effective systems combine common design principles with contextual adaptation, avoiding both rigid overregulation and discretionary governance without evaluation. Policy transfer appears to work best when countries adapt design principles to administrative reality rather than copy institutional forms without implementation support.

Government Policies and Institutional Design for Emerging Risks

Normative Architecture and Multilevel Coordination

Future-oriented policy requires a normative architecture that links long-term planning, medium-term budgeting, sector regulation and crisis protocols. Without these links, foresight outputs tend to remain disconnected from decision authority. Several governments have therefore introduced legal and administrative requirements for periodic risk review, preparedness auditing and cross-ministerial coordination around systemic vulnerabilities (Cabinet Office, 2023; OECD, 2020). Multilevel coordination is particularly relevant in decentralized systems, where risks such as extreme weather, pandemics, cyber incidents or supply disruption require interoperable action across national, regional and local authorities.

Instruments for Anticipation and Preparedness

Widely used instruments include horizon scanning, scenario construction, policy stress tests, simulation exercises, war gaming, contingency budgeting and trigger-based activation protocols. Their effectiveness tends to depend on combined and repeated use rather than isolated application; they must be embedded in budgeting, regulation and operational planning to influence real allocation choices. Recent literature also emphasizes the value of challenge teams and red teaming to reduce groupthink. Structured dissent, premortem analysis and explicit alternative hypotheses can improve institutional sensitivity to low-probability, high-impact threats (Kahneman, 2011; Tetlock & Gardner, 2015).

Early Warning Systems, Data and Public Intelligence

Contemporary anticipation depends on interoperable data systems, analytic capability and ethical governance of digital tools. Real-time monitoring can improve early detection, but also creates risks of opacity, algorithmic bias and overreliance on automated outputs. Effective policy combines advanced analytics with human oversight, transparent governance standards and independent auditing in high-stakes decisions (OECD, 2023; UNESCO, 2021). Institutional performance is determined less by data volume than by the ability to convert data into action, which requires analytic units with decision relevance, secure interagency data-sharing protocols and clear procedures for translating warning signals into policy triggers.

Comparative Legislation in Cyber, Biosecurity and Climate Risks

Comparative regulatory trajectories are uneven. Cyber governance has advanced through incident reporting obligations, critical infrastructure requirements and coordinated response frameworks. Biosecurity governance expanded after the pandemic through stronger surveillance mandates and reserve capacity planning. Climate regulation shows substantial progress in standard setting, although significant implementation gaps remain across territories and sectors (IPCC, 2023; UNDRR, 2015). A central challenge is the avoidance of regulatory islands. Cross-sectoral compatibility is increasingly a precondition for anticipatory effectiveness rather than an optional refinement.

Anticipatory Governance, State Capacity and Development

Impact on Public Performance and Regulatory Quality

Anticipatory capacity appears to shape public performance through three channels: preventive allocation of resources, lower coordination costs during disruption and faster institutional learning following shocks. These channels can improve regulatory quality by increasing predictability, reducing response latency and preserving service continuity under stress (OECD, 2023; World Bank, 2022). Gains are conditional on baseline administrative capability. Governments with weak implementation systems may produce sophisticated foresight analyses without corresponding policy execution; capability building must therefore emphasize operational integration rather than analytical sophistication alone.

Impact on Institutional Trust and Democratic Legitimacy

Public trust tends to increase when governments communicate risk transparently, justify preventive action and report performance honestly. Conversely, chronic improvisation, fragmented messaging and opaque decision processes can undermine legitimacy. Anticipatory governance contributes to democratic quality when it combines technical rigour with public reasoning and accountability (Boin et al., 2016; United Nations, 2021). Legitimacy also depends on fairness: if anticipatory policy protects aggregate stability while leaving vulnerable populations exposed, trust is likely to erode. Equity-sensitive preparedness is therefore not only normatively desirable but institutionally strategic.

Anticipation and Systemic Stability

In complex systems, stability is achieved not by eliminating disturbance but by preventing cascade escalation and preserving critical functions. Anticipatory governance can support this objective by identifying failure points, building redundancy and designing adaptive pathways for continuity (Haldane & May, 2011; Walker et al., 2013). At the macro institutional level, future-oriented policy may operate as a form of public insurance against strategic uncertainty, with effects that vary with administrative capability, political continuity and the credibility of preparedness commitments.

International Case Studies and Analytical Comparison

Finland and Singapore: Institutionalizing Long-Term Vision

Finland has developed a sustained tradition of linking foresight to parliamentary deliberation and strategic governance, which appears to support continuity across administrations. Singapore illustrates a high-integration model in which foresight is closely connected to executive implementation, allowing relatively rapid policy recalibration in key sectors. Despite major differences in political system, both cases suggest the importance of explicit mandates, technical professionalism and routine scenario updating (Boston, 2017; Habegger, 2010). The common analytical lesson is that anticipation becomes effective when routinised in governance architecture rather than treated as exceptional expertise, and that foresight effectiveness depends less on methodological sophistication than on whether the political system delegates implementation authority to actors who can convert analysis into decision.

United Kingdom and United States: Risk Assessment and Accountability

The United Kingdom has consolidated public risk communication and whole-of-government preparedness through recurrent publication of national risk priorities. The United States has relied on independent auditing and high-risk monitoring to identify structural federal vulnerabilities (Cabinet Office, 2023; U. S. Government Accountability Office, 2023). These cases underscore the analytical value of transparency and independent oversight, but also illustrate limits sometimes underplayed: accountability architecture cannot substitute for political coordination capacity. The cumulative GAO record documents persistent vulnerabilities that remain unresolved despite repeated diagnostic reporting, which suggests diagnostic clarity is necessary but not sufficient for effective anticipation.

Analytical Comparison Across the Four Cases

Reading the four cases against the analytical grid yields three patterns. First, integration between foresight and budget authority appears more consequential than the technical refinement of foresight methods: Finland and Singapore both link foresight to allocation cycles, while the United Kingdom and United States rely on diagnostic transparency that influences but does not directly govern allocation. Second, formalization matters but interacts with administrative culture; statutory mandates produce different effects in centralized versus federal systems. Third, the audit-and-transparency model generates strong external accountability but tends to underperform in operational continuity unless paired with implementation mandates. These patterns are propositions requiring additional comparative testing.

Lessons for Emerging Economies

Three practical lessons follow from the comparative analysis. First, it is preferable to begin with a core low-cost capability: a small foresight node at the centre of government, basic cross-agency protocols and strategic risk maps in critical sectors. Second, anticipation should be connected to budget and regulation at an early stage; otherwise foresight tends to remain performative. Third, prioritisation should focus on high-systemic-exposure sectors such as health, energy, water, logistics and digital public infrastructure. Governments should establish a minimum operational capability first, generate visible early results and only then scale toward more complex architecture. Incremental institutionalisation can outperform ambitious but fragile reforms that exceed administrative absorption capacity.

Contemporary Challenges for Future-Oriented Policy

Cognitive Biases and Political Short-Termism

Public decision making is affected by availability bias, overconfidence and present bias. Political cycles can amplify these tendencies by privileging visible short-term outputs over preventive investments whose benefits are diffuse and delayed. As a result, governments may systematically underinvest in preparedness despite plausibly high social returns (Kahneman, 2011; Tversky & Kahneman, 1974). Addressing this challenge requires institutions that protect long-term priorities: mandatory periodic risk reviews, multi-year preparedness indicators and policy commitments that outlive electoral turnover. These mechanisms do not remove politics; they structure political choice around explicit intertemporal trade-offs.

Technical and Organizational Capacity Gaps

Many administrations lack specialized personnel in systemic risk analysis, scenario modelling and adaptive policy design. Data systems are often fragmented across agencies, limiting integrated diagnosis. Staffing instability and weak knowledge retention further reduce preparedness quality. Closing these gaps requires sustained investment in civil service capability, digital interoperability and collaborative networks with universities, research centers and specialized private actors under clear public governance standards. Capacity policy must emphasize retention and organizational memory, not only short-term training.

Governance of Emerging Technologies

Artificial intelligence, advanced automation and biotechnology create simultaneous opportunities and risks. Potential gains in productivity and service delivery coexist with concerns about bias, opacity, concentration of power and security vulnerabilities. Future-oriented policy must combine innovation promotion with proportional precaution, ex ante assessment and ex post auditing in critical applications (OECD, 2023; UNESCO, 2021). Adaptive regulation is central: legal frameworks should allow iterative updating based on evidence while preserving rights, safety and transparency. Both regulatory lag and blanket prohibition can generate high social costs.

International Cooperation and Transboundary Governance

Many emerging risks are intrinsically transnational: pandemics, cyber threats, climate shocks, supply disruptions and financial contagion. No state can effectively manage these risks alone. International cooperation on standards, data exchange and preventive financing is therefore a structural component of anticipatory governance (United Nations, 2021; World Economic Forum, 2024). The policy challenge is to align domestic preparedness with international coordination while preserving national implementation capacity. Cooperation is most effective when global commitments are translated into concrete institutional reforms at home.

SOLUTIONS AND RECOMMENDATIONS

Applied Discussion and Public Policy Design

Causal Mechanisms Between Anticipation and Public Outcomes

The relationship between anticipatory governance and improved public outcomes can be understood through four causal mechanisms: earlier risk detection, ex ante coordination among institutions, preventive resource allocation and iterative learning under changing conditions. Together, these mechanisms tend to reduce response delay, improve policy robustness and limit cumulative losses, although the strength of each mechanism varies with institutional context. Mechanisms do not activate automatically: their effectiveness depends on political leadership, administrative incentives and decision processes that can absorb and act on uncertain information.

Political Economy of Future-Oriented Reform

Reforms for anticipation face distributive and organizational resistance. Preventive investment has diffuse long-term benefits, while administrative and fiscal costs are immediate and visible. Successful reform strategies combine near-term demonstrable gains with gradual institutional change, building coalitions across finance ministries, planning bodies, sector agencies and subnational governments (Mazzucato, 2021; OECD, 2020). Accountability architecture is equally important: if policy systems recognize only visible crisis response and ignore prevention success, institutions remain biased toward reaction.

Priority Sector Agenda: Health, Energy, Climate and Cybersecurity

In health policy, priority actions include integrated surveillance, laboratory resilience and flexible logistics for critical supplies. In energy, governments should strengthen supply security analysis, grid modernization and contingency planning. In climate policy, adaptation requires risk-informed infrastructure and territorial vulnerability management. In cybersecurity, robust governance includes incident reporting, coordinated response architecture and baseline digital hygiene across public administration. A coherent sector agenda requires common risk governance standards and comparable metrics to support cross-sector prioritization.

Roadmap for Emerging Economies

A practical roadmap can be structured in five phases: (1) institutional diagnostics of anticipatory capacity; (2) creation of a central foresight node with convening authority; (3) integration of scenarios into budget and regulatory design; (4) routine simulations and trigger-based operational protocols; and (5) independent evaluation with iterative adjustment. The roadmap follows from the comparative analysis: each phase corresponds to a configuration the four cases suggest is associated with foresight effectiveness. The governing principle is sequential scaling from a minimum viable capability to more advanced architecture.

Methodological Framework for Building Anticipatory Capacity

Analytical, Organizational and Political Dimensions

Operationalizing anticipatory governance benefits from distinguishing three interdependent dimensions. The analytical dimension includes horizon scanning, uncertainty mapping, scenario analysis and vulnerability assessment. The organizational dimension covers interagency protocols, data-sharing routines, specialized units and implementation pathways. The political dimension concerns priority setting, coalition management, legitimacy and accountability for intertemporal choices. This framework helps avoid two common errors: reducing anticipation to technical forecasting detached from decision authority and treating foresight as a one-off report rather than a recurrent public capability (Fuerth & Faber, 2012; Marchau et al., 2019; OECD, 2019).

A practical way to integrate these dimensions is through a five-step anticipatory value chain: exploration, prioritization, design, implementation and learning. Exploration identifies weak signals and emerging vulnerabilities. Prioritization selects strategic risks using impact, exposure and feasibility criteria. Design builds robust policy portfolios with triggers and fallback options. Implementation activates regulatory, fiscal and operational instruments. Learning updates assumptions and capacities on the basis of evidence from simulations and real events.

Institutional Maturity Diagnostics

Building anticipatory capacity requires realistic baseline diagnosis. A five-level maturity scale is useful: Level 1 (incipient) is dominated by ad hoc reaction; Level 2 (basic) includes sectoral risk lists with weak coordination; Level 3 (intermediate) adds recurrent foresight activities and simulation practice; Level 4 (advanced) integrates anticipation into budget, regulation and performance systems; Level 5 (transformational) features continuous learning, adaptive governance and robust multilevel coordination. The scale should be interpreted as an analytical heuristic, since most administrations exhibit different maturity levels across functional domains. Diagnostics should not rely solely on internal self-assessment: independent review, cross-agency peer assessment and external audit improve reliability (Cabinet Office, 2023; U. S. Government Accountability Office, 2023). Decision traceability is critical: evaluators should document how foresight evidence changed concrete choices in investment, regulation, procurement, staffing and coordination.

Indicators of Anticipatory Performance

Measurement in anticipatory governance is methodologically challenging because success often appears as avoided damage. Indicator systems should combine input, process, output and intermediate outcome measures. Input includes preventive budget shares, specialized staffing and data infrastructure coverage. Process indicators include the frequency and quality of scenario exercises, interagency response times and protocol compliance. Output indicators capture updated plans, enacted regulations and completed simulations. Intermediate outcomes include reduced operational disruption, faster response activation and improved continuity of critical services (International Organization for Standardization, 2018; International Risk Governance Council, 2018). Equity-sensitive indicators are indispensable: aggregate preparedness gains can mask persistent vulnerability in low-income groups, remote territories and digitally excluded populations.

Evaluation Strategies and Institutional Learning

Evaluation should be designed as continuous learning rather than terminal compliance review. A robust architecture combines ex ante foresight-informed evaluation, formative monitoring during implementation and ex post review focused on institutional lessons. This triad allows governments to adjust policy while it is still being executed (Marchau et al., 2019; Walker et al., 2013). After-action reviews following simulations and real disruptions are particularly valuable, but findings must be translated into time-bound improvement plans with clear responsibilities and budget implications. Peer learning across countries and subnational governments can accelerate adaptation and lower design costs (OECD, 2020; UNDRR, 2015), although transfer should be selective and context aware.

Integrating Strategic Foresight into the Public Policy Cycle

Public Agenda Setting and Strategic Prioritization

The first policy-cycle stage is the determination of which risks demand active intervention and which require only monitoring. In resource-constrained environments, prioritization cannot be based on media salience alone; it should combine projected impact, systemic exposure, social vulnerability and intervention feasibility. Strategic foresight contributes by widening the horizon of policy attention and revealing interdependencies often obscured by short-term political pressures (European Commission, 2020; OECD, 2019). Future-oriented agendas require institutional devices that preserve strategic continuity across electoral cycles: mandatory risk assessments, periodic reporting to legislatures and preparedness targets linked to interministerial commitments. Participatory processes can further enhance quality by incorporating local knowledge and social priorities.

Policy Formulation and Adaptive Regulatory Design

Once strategic risks are prioritized, formulation must convert scenarios into implementable policy instruments. Rather than rigid rules optimized for a single expected future, adaptive regulation uses review clauses, trigger thresholds and staged commitments (Marchau et al., 2019; Walker et al., 2013). Adaptive design is particularly relevant in fast-evolving technology domains. Regulatory sandboxes, dynamic standards and periodic compliance audits can support experimentation while protecting rights and safety (OECD, 2023; UNESCO, 2021). These tools require supervisory capability and cross-agency coordination to avoid regulatory arbitrage. Formulation quality also depends on assumption governance: challenge mechanisms, independent technical review and structured dissent reduce overconfidence (Kahneman, 2011; Tetlock & Gardner, 2015).

Budgeting, Public Investment and Preventive Finance

Without budget alignment, foresight tends to remain rhetorical. Integration requires the translation of risk analysis into fiscal priorities, contingency reserves and resilience-oriented investment standards, including stress testing of public finance, evaluating exposure of critical infrastructure portfolios and embedding uncertainty assumptions in medium-term expenditure frameworks (OECD, 2020; World Bank, 2022). In infrastructure policy, governments should assess life-cycle vulnerability to climate, cyber and supply disruptions rather than focus solely on up-front construction cost. Financial instruments such as contingency funds, contingent credit lines and risk-transfer mechanisms can complement ordinary budget tools and improve fiscal agility during severe shocks.

Implementation, Coordination and Adaptive Management

Implementation is the stage at which many anticipatory strategies fail. Technically strong plans can collapse if operational roles are unclear, information flows are delayed or subnational capability is weak. Effective governance requires an explicit coordination architecture: lead authority, execution responsibilities, activation criteria and communication protocols (Cabinet Office, 2023; U. S. Government Accountability Office, 2023). Adaptive management depends on real-time monitoring and decision processes that update interventions as evidence evolves, requiring interoperable systems, analytical staffing and leadership willing to revise assumptions. In high-volatility contexts, shorter feedback cycles outperform rigid annual planning routines.

Evaluation, Accountability and Democratic Learning

The final policy-cycle stage determines whether anticipation becomes a durable state capability. Public preparedness dashboards with periodic updates can strengthen transparency, legislative oversight and social accountability. Prevention accountability has distinctive features: success often consists of disruptions that do not occur, so communication strategies must translate technical preparedness gains into understandable public outcomes. Meaningful accountability requires institutional consequence: evaluation results should trigger regulatory updates, budget reallocation, capability reform and scenario revision. Democratic learning is strengthened when governments communicate uncertainty honestly, explain decision criteria and report both achievements and limitations.

Territorial Governance and Multilevel Coordination for Emerging Risks

Territorial Scale of Risk and Institutional Heterogeneity

Emerging risks are territorially uneven. The same hazard can generate very different impacts depending on urban density, infrastructure quality, socio-economic vulnerability, ecological conditions and local administrative capacity. Anticipatory governance cannot therefore be designed exclusively by central institutions; it requires territorial diagnostics and place-sensitive policy adaptation. Institutional heterogeneity across territories is often substantial: some local governments have mature data systems, stable teams and interagency routines; others operate with high staff turnover, weak connectivity and limited technical capacity (UNDRR, 2015; World Bank, 2022). Risk boundaries also rarely match administrative borders.

Vertical Coordination: Centre of Government and Subnational Authorities

Vertical coordination works best when functions are clearly distributed across levels. Central government typically provides strategic direction, standards and financing instruments; subnational governments contribute contextual knowledge, frontline implementation and proximity to communities. Preparedness compacts between levels of government can be useful, including capability targets, simulation requirements, data interoperability standards and conditional financing based on implementation milestones. Permanent coordination forums are preferable to ad hoc crisis meetings (Cabinet Office, 2023; OECD, 2020).

Horizontal Coordination and Interjurisdictional Networks

Horizontal coordination among jurisdictions is essential where risks affect shared systems such as transport corridors, electricity grids, health networks and watersheds. Without cooperative rules, local incentives may produce fragmented responses that increase collective vulnerability. Interjurisdictional governance mechanisms should define mutual assistance protocols, activation criteria, cost-sharing arrangements and dispute-resolution pathways. Regional consortia, shared monitoring hubs and common operating standards can improve efficiency, although asymmetries in capability can create unequal burden sharing. A mature networked approach treats territorial preparedness as a joint public good.

Critical Infrastructure and Territorial Public-Private Governance

Critical infrastructure in energy, telecommunications, transport and logistics is frequently owned or operated by private actors. Anticipatory governance therefore requires institutionalised public-private coordination, including secure information sharing, continuity planning, joint simulations and aligned cybersecurity standards. Public authorities must balance market incentives with public-interest obligations. In highly concentrated sectors, dependence on a small number of operators can amplify systemic risk (Haldane & May, 2011; International Risk Governance Council, 2018). Community organisations and local civil society are also critical territorial partners.

Human Capacity, Organizational Culture and Leadership for Anticipation

Professional Profiles and Strategic Competencies

Anticipatory governance ultimately depends on people and organizations capable of interpreting ambiguous signals, coordinating across silos and making decisions under pressure. The creation of foresight offices is insufficient without professional competencies that bridge analytics, institutional design and public management. Key competencies include systems thinking, scenario modelling, risk communication, adaptive policy design and interagency negotiation. Because no single discipline covers all these domains, governments need multidisciplinary teams and continuous professional development pathways. Cross-functional mobility can further improve anticipatory capacity.

Bureaucratic Incentives and a Learning Culture

Even with technical talent, anticipation tends to fail when bureaucratic incentives reward procedural compliance but penalize early warning and experimentation. Institutional design should incorporate preparedness indicators into performance management for senior and middle leadership. Learning culture requires tolerance for adaptive adjustment: not all preventive interventions will perform as expected, and if every deviation is treated as political failure, organizations tend to hide mistakes rather than correct them (Boin et al., 2016; OECD, 2023). Learning systems are more durable when they combine internal reflection with external scrutiny and peer review.

Political Leadership and Long-Term Strategic Direction

Political leadership is indispensable in anticipatory governance because it sets priorities, legitimises preventive investment and arbitrates short-term versus long-term distributional trade-offs. Without high-level political sponsorship, technical foresight units often remain peripheral to budget and regulatory decisions. Future-oriented leadership combines continuity across electoral transitions, transparent communication of uncertainty and coalition building across ministries, legislatures and territorial authorities. Institutionalization is essential: durable mandates and governance rules must sustain anticipatory capacity beyond individual officeholders (Acemoglu & Robinson, 2012; Boston, 2017).

Public Communication, Trust and Risk Literacy

Preparedness improves when citizens understand risk conditions, trust public institutions and participate in preventive action. Effective communication translates technical uncertainty into clear, actionable guidance without alarmism or false certainty. Consistency across agencies is crucial. Trust is built before crises: transparent data practices, clear explanation of decision criteria and visible accountability for mistakes strengthen institutional legitimacy over time (Cabinet Office, 2023; United Nations, 2021). Risk literacy initiatives in schools, communities and professional training programmes can widen societal preparedness and reduce dependence on last-minute emergency messaging.

Preventive Financing, Fiscal Resilience and the Political Economy of the Long Term

From Reactive Logic to Risk-Informed Budgeting

Most budget systems are designed for routine service delivery rather than strategic uncertainty management. As a result, preventive spending is often crowded out by immediate demands. The transition to risk-informed budgeting means incorporating exposure, vulnerability and preparedness criteria into annual and medium-term allocation decisions. This shift does not imply the sacrifice of present social needs for abstract future goals; it recognizes that unmanaged shocks tend to harm vulnerable populations disproportionately. Preventive investment is therefore both a resilience strategy and an intertemporal equity policy. Budget tagging for resilience-related programmes can improve transparency.

Contingency Funds and Stabilization Instruments

Contingency funds are key tools for reducing budget rigidity during severe disruptions. To be effective, they require clear activation rules, transparent governance and replenishment mechanisms. Governments can complement domestic buffers with contingent credit lines, insurance mechanisms and risk-transfer instruments. These tools do not replace core state capacity, but they can reduce fiscal volatility and protect essential social expenditure during high-impact events (World Bank, 2022). Optimal instrument design depends on national risk profiles, debt sustainability and financial market depth.

Economic Evaluation of Prevention Under Uncertainty

Economic assessment of prevention is methodologically difficult because benefits often materialize as avoided losses over long horizons. Standard cost-benefit approaches may underestimate preventive value when they rely on narrow assumptions or short time windows. Complementary methods based on robustness analysis, scenario comparison and flexibility valuation provide a better fit for deep uncertainty contexts (Marchau et al., 2019; Walker et al., 2013). Distributional analysis is equally important: a policy can be efficient in aggregating while imposing disproportionate burdens on specific sectors or territories.

Political Economy of Long-Term Coalitions

The major barrier to preventive financing is often political rather than technical. Long-term benefits are diffuse and uncertain from an electoral perspective, while short-term fiscal costs are immediate and visible. Comparative evidence suggests three effective tactics: generating early demonstrable wins, institutionalizing multi-year commitments, and aligning incentives among finance authorities, sector ministries and subnational governments (Mazzucato, 2021; OECD, 2020). Preventive policy must also be framed in everyday welfare terms: service continuity, income stability and social protection reliability.

Prospective Scenarios for the Next Decade and Policy Implications

Scenario 1: Coordinated Adaptation and Incremental Resilience

Governments institutionalize baseline anticipatory capabilities without disruptive state transformation. Foresight units become routine at the center of government, interoperability improves gradually and simulation-based learning becomes more common in key sectors. Policy implications include prioritizing high-return institutional upgrades: recurring exercises, risk map updates, interoperable communication protocols and preparedness dashboards. Territorial capability gaps remain the key risk. This pathway is plausible for many middle-income countries because it does not require immediate structural overhaul but may be insufficient under severe systemic shocks.

Scenario 2: Accelerated Technological Disruption and Regulatory Gaps

Innovation in AI, biotechnology and autonomous systems advances faster than public oversight. Risks include cyber fragility, algorithmic discrimination, misinformation amplification and concentration of technological power. Policy response requires adaptive regulation with frequent review cycles, algorithmic auditing in critical domains, minimum transparency standards and strategic talent investment inside public institutions (OECD, 2023; UNESCO, 2021). International coordination on technical norms is becoming increasingly important. The political danger is delayed response followed by over-corrective regulation that suppresses innovation without resolving core safety and accountability risks.

Scenario 3: Geoeconomic Polycrisis and Persistent Fiscal Stress

Geopolitical fragmentation, climate disruption, supply-chain instability and financial volatility interact as a prolonged polycrisis. Governments face simultaneous pressure on social protection, infrastructure investment and debt sustainability. Future-oriented policy must protect critical preparedness cores even under austerity: early warning systems, continuity protocols for essential services and minimum strategic reserves. Prioritization should focus on high-multiplier capabilities that prevent cascade escalation (World Bank, 2022; World Economic Forum, 2024). A central analytical lesson is that fiscal resilience and prevention appear to be complementary rather than competing objectives.

Scenario 4: Renewal of a Future-Oriented State Compact

This more ambitious scenario involves a renewed compact among state, society and market around long-term risk governance. Reforms strengthen technical capability, territorial coordination, participatory legitimacy and accountability for preparedness outcomes. Policy implications include civil service incentive reform, multi-year preparedness commitments, risk-informed budgeting, stronger international cooperation and broad social risk literacy. The pathway is politically demanding but offers higher robustness under volatility. Its feasibility depends on reform coalitions that can convert long-term strategic benefits into tangible near-term improvements.

Cross-Scenario Robust Strategy

Because no single scenario is likely to remain stable over time, governments should build robust policy cores that perform reasonably well across diverse futures. Such a core includes interoperable data governance, clear coordination protocols, baseline preventive finance, independent evaluation and transparent risk communication. Around this core, modular adaptive layers can be activated as conditions evolve: intensified technology oversight, expanded resilience investment, targeted territorial support or deeper international collaboration. The main contribution of anticipatory governance is therefore not deterministic foresight, but the design of resilient decision systems that remain functional under uncertainty, surprise and structural change.

FUTURE RESEARCH DIRECTIONS

Future research should advance along six interlocking agendas derived from the analytical gaps identified in the comparative analysis. Conceptually, scholars should refine definitions, boundaries and overlaps among foresight, resilience, risk governance and innovation systems, and examine how anticipatory governance operates across local, regional, national and transnational levels, including the tensions between centralization and decentralization, and how values, power and ethics shape which futures are imagined, prioritized or excluded.

On institutional capacity and design, research should develop indicators and assessment tools for institutional anticipatory capacity, compare institutional models (foresight units, innovation labs, risk observatories, policy labs, futures councils) across political-administrative cultures, examine how budgeting, regulation, procurement, evaluation and audit can systematically integrate future-oriented analysis, and study how institutions learn from near misses, weak signals and past crises.

On methods, tools and data, scholarship should combine scenarios, horizon scanning, Delphi and participatory methods with big data, AI and early-warning analytics, develop decision-support approaches tailored to public-sector constraints, model how climate, health, technological, financial and geopolitical risks interact, and explore the role of digital twins, simulation environments and shared data platforms in anticipatory policy design.

On participation, democracy and legitimacy, research should examine participatory foresight formats (citizens' assemblies, living labs, territorial dialogues) and their impact on trust and legitimacy, explore whose futures are represented or marginalized, and investigate how narratives and storytelling influence political feasibility and public support.

On policy impact and evaluation, longitudinal and quasi-experimental studies are needed to test whether anticipatory practices improve crisis preparedness, addressing the counterfactual problem identified earlier. Comparative work should examine anticipatory arrangements across countries, policy domains and levels of development, and study scaling pathways from successful pilots to mainstream bureaucratic routines.

On leadership, culture and skills, research should identify the skills public servants, politicians and intermediaries require (futures literacy, systems thinking, sensemaking), explore leadership practices that enable experimentation and tolerate ambiguity, and study how to shift from reactive, compliance-driven cultures to learning-oriented ones.

CONCLUSION

Anticipatory governance is a strategic requirement for states operating in environments defined by complexity, interdependence and deep uncertainty. Its primary contribution is not to provide total control over the future, but to improve present decision quality across multiple plausible trajectories. Governments that institutionalize foresight, preparedness and adaptive learning appear, based on the comparative evidence reviewed here, to be better positioned to protect critical functions, reduce avoidable losses and sustain legitimacy during disruption. The strength of this association varies with administrative capability and political continuity and should be interpreted as a conditional regularity rather than a universal claim.

The comparative analysis of Finland, Singapore, the United Kingdom and the United States supports five concrete policy implications. First, foresight is most consequential when structurally connected to budget authority, since methodological refinement alone does not generate allocative effects. Second, statutory mandates protect anticipatory capacity from electoral discontinuity but require accompanying implementation rules to avoid becoming purely procedural. Third, transparency and independent audit are necessary for accountability but cannot substitute for political coordination capacity. Fourth, decentralized systems require formal preparedness compacts that convert general responsibilities into verifiable commitments between levels of government. Fifth, emerging economies should sequence reform from a minimum viable foresight node toward more complex architecture, generating early demonstrable wins to build durable reform coalitions.

For emerging economies, the most realistic strategy is sequential capacity building: start with core functions, generate early demonstrable outcomes and scale based on iterative evaluation. This approach avoids both inertia and overextension and enables progress under administrative and fiscal constraints. Future-oriented governance should be designed as a practical state capability, not as an abstract planning ideal.

Anticipatory governance also implies a renewed relationship between state, science and society. Anticipation should not technocratize politics; it should democratize preparedness by making uncertainty, trade-offs and strategic priorities visible to citizens. In a world of systemic risk, resilient public institutions depend on this combination of analytical rigor, political responsibility and social legitimacy.

From an implementation perspective, anticipatory governance must be managed as an integrated public management system rather than a stand-alone policy programme, linking leadership mandates, staffing plans, interoperable data protocols, budgeting rules, independent oversight and citizen communication into a coherent architecture with clear sequencing. Governments that focus only on one component tend to produce symbolic compliance rather than resilient performance. Effective systems combine long-term vision with short-term responsiveness: they preserve strategic direction through periodic foresight cycles while delivering tangible near-term improvements in service continuity, risk communication and crisis readiness. Ultimately, the transition toward future-oriented public policy is not a technical luxury; it is a core requirement for democratic resilience in the twenty-first century.

REFERENCES

Acemoglu, D., & Robinson, J. A. (2012). *Why nations fail: The origins of power, prosperity, and poverty.* Crown.

Aitsi-Selmi, A., Egawa, S., Sasaki, H., Wannous, C., & Murray, V. (2015). The Sendai framework for disaster risk reduction: Renewing the global commitment to people's resilience, health, and wellbeing. *International Journal of Disaster Risk Science*, *6*(2), 164–176. DOI: 10.1007/s13753-015-0050-9

Beck, U. (1992). Risk society: Towards a new modernity. *Sage (Atlanta, Ga.).*

Boin, A., 't Hart, P., Stern, E., & Sundelius, B. (2016). *The politics of crisis management: Public leadership under pressure* (2nd ed.). Cambridge University Press. DOI: 10.1017/9781316339756

Boston, J. (2017). *Governing for the future: Designing democratic institutions for a better tomorrow*. Emerald.

Cabinet Office. (2023). *National risk register 2023.* UK Government.

European Commission. (2020). *2020 strategic foresight report: Charting the course towards a more resilient Europe*. European Union.

European Commission. (2023). *2023 strategic foresight report: Sustainability and wellbeing at the heart of Europe's open strategic autonomy*. European Union.

Fuerth, L. S., & Faber, E. M. H. (2012). *Anticipatory governance: Practical upgrades*. National Defense University Press.

Greenhalgh, T., Thorne, S., & Malterud, K. (2018). Time to challenge the spurious hierarchy of systematic over narrative reviews? *European Journal of Clinical Investigation*, *48*(6), e12931. DOI: 10.1111/eci.12931 PMID: 29578574

Habegger, B. (2010). Strategic foresight in public policy: Reviewing the experiences of the UK, Singapore, and the Netherlands. *Futures*, *42*(1), 49–58. DOI: 10.1016/j.futures.2009.08.002

Haldane, A. G., & May, R. M. (2011). Systemic risk in banking ecosystems. *Nature*, *469*(7330), 351–355. DOI: 10.1038/nature09659 PMID: 21248842

Intergovernmental Panel on Climate Change. (2023). *Climate change 2023: Synthesis report. Contribution of Working Groups I, II and III to the Sixth Assessment Report of the Intergovernmental Panel on Climate Change*. IPCC. DOI: 10.59327/IPCC/AR6-9789291691647

International Organization for Standardization. (2018). *ISO 31000: Risk management—Guidelines*. ISO.

International Risk Governance Council. (2018). *Guidelines for the governance of systemic risks*. IRGC.

Kahneman, D. (2011). *Thinking, fast and slow*. Farrar, Straus and Giroux.

Klinke, A., & Renn, O. (2002). A new approach to risk evaluation and management: Risk-based, precaution-based, and discourse-based strategies. *Risk Analysis*, *22*(6), 1071–1094. DOI: 10.1111/1539-6924.00274 PMID: 12530780

Marchau, V. A. W. J., Walker, W. E., Bloemen, P. J. T. M., & Popper, S. W. (Eds.). (2019). *Decision making under deep uncertainty: From theory to practice*. Springer. DOI: 10.1007/978-3-030-05252-2

Mazzucato, M. (2021). *Mission economy: A moonshot guide to changing capitalism*. Harper Business.

North, D. C. (1990). *Institutions, institutional change and economic performance*. Cambridge University Press. DOI: 10.1017/CBO9780511808678

OECD. (2019). *Strategic foresight for better policies: Building effective governance in the face of uncertain futures*. OECD Publishing.

OECD. (2020). *A systemic resilience approach to dealing with Covid-19 and future shocks*. OECD Publishing.

OECD. (2023). *Government at a glance 2023*. OECD Publishing.

Ostrom, E. (2005). *Understanding institutional diversity*. Princeton University Press.

Poli, R. (2017). *Introduction to anticipation studies*. Springer. DOI: 10.1007/978-3-319-63023-6

Pollitt, C., & Bouckaert, G. (2017). *Public management reform: A comparative analysis—Into the age of austerity* (4th ed.). Oxford University Press.

Taleb, N. N. (2007). *The black swan: The impact of the highly improbable*. Random House.

Tetlock, P. E., & Gardner, D. (2015). *Superforecasting: The art and science of prediction*. Crown.

Tversky, A., & Kahneman, D. (1974). Judgment under uncertainty: Heuristics and biases. *Science*, *185*(4157), 1124–1131. DOI: 10.1126/science.185.4157.1124 PMID: 17835457

U.S. Government Accountability Office. (2023). *High-risk series: Efforts made to achieve progress need to be maintained and expanded to fully address all areas*. GAO.

UNDRR. (2015). *Sendai framework for disaster risk reduction 2015–2030*. United Nations Office for Disaster Risk Reduction.

UNESCO. (2021). *Recommendation on the ethics of artificial intelligence*. UNESCO.

United Nations. (2021). *Our common agenda: Report of the Secretary-General*. United Nations.

Van der Heijden, K. (2005). *Scenarios: The art of strategic conversation* (2nd ed.). Wiley.

Walker, W. E., Haasnoot, M., & Kwakkel, J. H. (2013). Adapt or perish: A review of planning approaches for adaptation under deep uncertainty. *Sustainability (Basel)*, *5*(3), 955–979. DOI: 10.3390/su5030955

World Bank. (2022). *World development report 2022: Finance for an equitable recovery*. World Bank.

World Economic Forum. (2024). *The global risks report 2024 (19th ed.)*. World Economic Forum.

KEY TERMS AND DEFINITIONS

Adaptive Governance: A governance mode emphasizing flexibility, iterative learning, experimentation and responsiveness to evolving conditions, enabling institutions to adjust policies as new information emerges.

Anticipatory Governance: A governance approach equipping institutions to systematically anticipate, prepare for and shape emerging futures through foresight, early warning, adaptive planning and continuous learning.

Emerging Risks: New, evolving or previously unrecognized threats characterized by high uncertainty, systemic interdependencies and potentially large impacts, often arising from technological, environmental, geopolitical or socio-economic change.

Future-Oriented Policy: Policy design and implementation that explicitly incorporates long-term implications, alternative futures and intergenerational considerations, with the aim of enhancing resilience, sustainability and societal well-being.

Futures Literacy: Competency enabling individuals and institutions to understand, imagine and use the future for decision making, enhancing creativity, sensemaking and the ability to navigate uncertainty.

Government Preparedness: The capacity of public institutions to detect, assess and respond to emerging risks before they escalate, combining anticipatory planning, resource readiness, interagency coordination and adaptive response mechanisms.

Horizon Scanning: A systematic process for detecting early signs of change, weak signals and emerging issues across domains, used to inform foresight, risk assessment and strategic planning.

Institutional Capacity for Anticipation: The set of organizational capabilities—skills, structures, processes, data systems and cultures—enabling governments to sense weak signals, interpret change and integrate future-oriented insights into policy and operations.

Risk Interdependency: The condition in which risks are linked across sectors, systems or scales, such that disruptions in one domain can cascade into others, requiring integrated and cross-sectoral anticipatory approaches.

Strategic Foresight: A structured set of methods—such as horizon scanning, scenarios and Delphi—used to explore plausible futures, identify emerging risks and opportunities and inform strategic choices under uncertainty.

Chapter 7
Digital Financial Inclusion as Anticipatory Governance:
Public Value, Resilience, and Equity

Shishir Negi
http://orcid.org/0009-0001-8493-1034
Graphic Era University, India

Nidhi Tyagi
http://orcid.org/0000-0002-3996-7644
Graphic Era (Deemed to be) University, India

ABSTRACT

Governments now rely on digital finance to deliver welfare, raise revenue, and move money at a speed and scale beyond the reach of older administrative systems. This chapter treats such systems as a mode of anticipatory governance rather than as technical plumbing. By allowing states to act earlier, faster, and across whole populations, they redistribute risk, alter who becomes visible to the state, and determine who is left out. Drawing together public value theory, scholarship on anticipatory and robust governance, and critical work on datafication, the chapter assembles an integrated lens that reads digital financial infrastructure as a governance choice rather than a neutral upgrade. That lens is then tested against four well-documented cases: Brazil's Pix, Kenya's M-Pesa, India's Aadhaar-enabled benefit transfers and Unified Payments Interface, and Nigeria's 2023 currency redesign. Considered

DOI: 10.4018/979-8-3373-9765-8.ch007

together, the cases demonstrate that one class of technology can either generate or erode public value, according to how authentication, redress, and accountability are designed.

INTRODUCTION

A welfare payment that once moved through clerks, registers, and cash counters can now travel as data between a citizen's identity record, a bank, and a government ledger, often within seconds. The change is usually described as an efficiency gain, but it is also a change in governance. When a state chooses a digital financial channel for a pension, food ration, or fuel subsidy, it is deciding how risk will be allocated, how legitimacy will be established, and how the relationship between citizen and state will work in practice. Those choices are rarely discussed in these terms. They are more often presented as ordinary modernization.

This chapter examines digital financial inclusion as a governance issue rather than simply as a matter of service delivery. Much policy and scholarly discussion still evaluates digital finance through accounts opened, transactions processed, or other measures of uptake. Those measures are useful, but they do not settle the larger question. Payment platforms, benefit-transfer systems, and identity-linked financial services now form part of the infrastructure through which states reach citizens. They influence who can establish an official identity, who can receive an entitlement, and who can be left outside an administrative system. Digital finance therefore belongs to the wider problem of how governments anticipate and manage uncertain futures.

The chapter treats digital financial infrastructure as one expression of anticipatory governance. States build these systems to act earlier: to identify need before it becomes a crisis, move relief during a shock without relying on physical cash, and administer programmes at a scale that manual systems cannot easily match. The pandemic made the difference visible. Governments with functioning digital payment rails could move emergency transfers within days, while others faced much longer delays. Early action, however, is not automatically beneficial. A system capable of reaching a remote household can also deny a payment automatically when an identity check fails. The same administrative capacity can therefore expand access or make exclusion faster and harder to contest.

Three questions guide the analysis. How does digital finance contribute to anticipatory governance and institutional resilience, and when does that same capacity turn into a source of fragility? What does it do to public value and to the relationship between citizens and the state, particularly for people who sit at the margins of administrative visibility? And which governance choices decide whether these systems end up strengthening inclusion and trust, rather than gradually wearing them down? The questions are normative as well as empirical because the evidence does not point in a single direction, even within the same country or programme.

The comparison uses cases with substantial documentation and contested records. Brazil's Pix shows a central bank building an instant-payment system as public infrastructure. Kenya's M-Pesa represents a market-led mobile-money service that became national infrastructure and generated a major dispute over its poverty effects. India's combination of biometric identity, direct benefit transfers, and the Unified Payments Interface represents an unusually extensive attempt to organize finance as public infrastructure, alongside serious, documented exclusion problems. Nigeria's 2023 currency redesign shows the consequences of pushing a population toward cashless transactions faster than institutions and users can absorb. The cases are used to test the framework, not to present any one of them as a model.

The chapter is organized in five stages. It first sets out the conceptual foundations, bringing anticipatory governance, public value, and resilience and robustness into conversation with critical work on datafication and the digital welfare state. It then considers digital finance as public infrastructure and relates it to the platform-state and digital-public-infrastructure debates. The next section examines exclusion, surveillance, risk redistribution, and the limits of inclusion as a development paradigm. The four cases are then compared, followed by design principles and a future research agenda. The conclusion returns to the broader question of how digital finance is changing the state's capacity to act.

A brief standpoint is useful. Although the cases are located in the Global South, the chapter does not treat the South as a testing ground from which lessons move only toward Northern policy settings. India's payment architecture and Brazil's Pix, for example, have themselves become reference points for other governments. The cases are connected instead by a shared governance problem: building high-stakes public infrastructure in conditions marked by inequality, administrative pressure, and rapid technological change. Those conditions are no longer confined to any particular region.

The chapter makes three contributions. It brings anticipatory governance, public value theory, and robustness scholarship into one analytical frame, so a single design decision can be examined for its timing, its public purpose, and the institutional capacity it draws on. The four-country comparison also suggests that how benefits and harms end up distributed tracks governance arrangements more closely than it tracks technological capability. And by identifying exclusion by design, the redistribution of risk, and weakened accountability as recurring problems in authentication-dependent welfare systems, the chapter extends public value failure theory into that domain and turns the findings into practical design principles.

BACKGROUND

Reading digital finance as governance rather than gadgetry calls for three bodies of theory to be brought into conversation. One concerns anticipation and the state's attempt to act upon the future. A second concerns public value and the conditions under which public action creates or destroys it. A third concerns resilience and robustness, the capacity of institutions to keep functioning when conditions grow turbulent. Each carries a critical shadow supplied by scholars who study how data systems sort and govern people. This section assembles an integrated lens rather than surveying the fields exhaustively.

The Anticipatory Turn in Public Management

Anticipatory governance describes a change in how states relate to time. Instead of reacting to events once they have occurred, governments seek the capacity to sense, prepare for, and shape what lies ahead. The most frequently cited formulation belongs to Guston (2014), who characterized anticipatory governance as a society's broad capacity to draw on many kinds of input so that emerging, knowledge-intensive technologies can be guided while guidance remains feasible. His account emerged from work on nanotechnology and stressed three capacities that must be developed in concert: foresight, engagement, and integration. Prediction is not the aim; the aim is institutional readiness, so that a society keeps its ability to steer before its options narrow.

A second, more administrative strand treats anticipatory governance as a practical response to executive institutions facing problems that move faster than established procedures. Fuerth and Faber (2012) describe anticipatory governance in this sense as an effort to equip government to work with increasing speed and complexity. This strand is less concerned with prediction than with building institutions that can prepare, test, adapt, and respond before a problem becomes unmanageable.

Digital Finance Gives the Anticipatory Ambition a Concrete Form

A direct benefit transfer scheme lets a government identify eligible households in advance and pay them automatically once a trigger fires, whether a price shock, a failed harvest, or a pandemic. An instant payment platform lets a state disburse the moment a decision is taken, collapsing the interval between intention and effect. Early-warning and targeting models, increasingly trained on the very transaction data these systems generate, promise to spot distress before it becomes catastrophe. Each of these is anticipation in action. The complication is that anticipation embedded in infrastructure also hardens specific judgements about who counts as legitimate, and it does so at a speed and scale that makes errors hard to detect and harder still to undo.

Public Value and Its Failures

If anticipation captures the temporal ambition of digital governance, public value supplies the yardstick for judging its results. Moore (1995) recast the work of public managers as the creation of public value, akin to but distinct from the private creation of shareholder value, and situated that work within a strategic triangle binding a substantive account of the value being produced, the legitimacy and support needed to pursue it, and the operational capacity to deliver it. The framework earns its place here by refusing to let efficiency stand alone. A digital benefit system that lowers costs while corroding legitimacy, or that serves many while deserting a vulnerable few, has not straightforwardly created public value; it has traded one corner of the triangle for another.

Bozeman (2002, 2007) gave the concept a sharper critical edge through his theory of public value failure, the circumstances in which neither markets nor governments supply the goods and outcomes a society holds to be valuable. His criteria include the collapse of mechanisms for articulating and aggregating public values, the imposition of short time horizons on problems that require long ones, and, most pertinently for this chapter, threats to the subsistence of human beings whose basic provision is withheld. These criteria map almost directly onto the diagnostic categories applied below. An authentication failure that denies someone the food ration to which they are legally entitled is no mere glitch to be engineered away; because it reaches subsistence, it is a public value failure of the gravest kind, and the framework names it as such.

Later scholarship carried public value into the conditions of networked and digital governance. Benington and Moore (2011) collected theoretical and applied treatments that extended the concept well beyond its origins, while Bryson et al. (2014) argued for a public value governance paradigm reaching past both traditional public administration and new public management. Their work provides the bridge by which public value can speak to the platform state, foregrounding legitimacy, equity, and the lived experience of citizens rather than transactions tallied in the aggregate. Within this lineage, public value is gauged not only by what a system does for the many, but by what it does to the few who slip through it.

Resilience, Robustness, and Turbulence

The third strand addresses how institutions withstand stress, the explicit theme of the volume this chapter joins. Ansell and Trondal (2018) separated resilience, the capacity to spring back to a prior state, from robustness, the capacity to sustain function and purpose through flexibility, redundancy, and a repertoire of responses that can be redeployed as conditions shift. The distinction does more than split hairs. A digital payment system that merely restores its previous configuration after a shock is resilient; a system that can keep reaching citizens through several alternative channels when one fails and can revise its rules when reality diverges from its assumptions, is robust. Of the two, robustness is the more demanding property and the more valuable.

Ansell et al. (2021, 2023, 2024) extended this line into a wider theory of robust governance for a turbulent age. They define turbulence as conditions in which events, demands, and support interact and shift in highly variable, inconsistent, and unpredictable ways, and they contend that public institutions increasingly confront problems of this sort. Their remedy is not a return to stability, which turbulence forecloses, but governance able to absorb surprise while still pursuing public purposes. Set beside the data-science perspective of MacArthur et al. (2022), who hold that resilient government now turns on reforming how the state handles data, this literature supplies the chapter's operational vocabulary. The question to put to any digital financial system, then, is not whether it functions in calm conditions but whether it continues to create public value in abnormal ones, which is to say, when it matters most.

The Critical Shadow: Datafication and the Digital Welfare State

Each of these constructive frameworks has a critical counterpart, which the chapter treats as integral rather than opposed. Zuboff (2019) coined surveillance capitalism to describe an economic logic that claims human experience as raw material for data extraction and behavioural prediction. Whatever one concludes about the full thesis, the mechanism she identifies, the conversion of ordinary activity into data assets, is precisely what large-scale digital finance enables, and states are not exempt from the temptation. Through close study of automated systems in the United States, Eubanks (2018) documented how high-technology tools profile, police, and punish poor people, often despite their designers' contrary intentions. Her cases are Northern, yet her finding travels: automation tends to reserve its harshest treatment for those least able to contest it.

The starkest statement of the stakes came from Alston (2019), reporting to the United Nations as Special Rapporteur on extreme poverty and human rights. He cautioned that states risk drifting into what he termed a digital welfare dystopia, where digitization serves to shrink rather than realize social protection, and where the customary expectation that the state answers to the individual is reversed, so that the individual must repeatedly demonstrate their entitlement to an automated state. His report named India's identity system directly, then covering well over a billion people, and cast the matter as one of human rights rather than administration.

Taylor (2017) supplied the concept that ties these critiques to the constructive frameworks above, proposing data justice as a means of connecting digital rights and freedoms globally, organized around concerns about visibility, the freedom to engage or refrain from engaging with technology, and protection from discrimination. Her grounding of data justice in a capabilities approach links directly to Sen (1999), whose understanding of development as the expansion of substantive freedoms supplies the chapter's deepest normative anchor. In Sen's spirit, financial inclusion is valuable to the extent that it enlarges what people can do and to be, not like a figure standing on their own.

Two additional areas of scholarship have developed quickly enough to sit alongside these strands. One concerns the governance of artificial intelligence in public administration. Margetts and Dorobantu (2019) argue that AI may improve state capacity while also creating new questions about accountability, transparency, and institutional control. OECD (2025) similarly treats AI governance as a problem of institutional design rather than technological adoption alone. The other concerns digital public infrastructure. The United Nations Development Programme (2024) frames DPI around safe and inclusive shared digital systems, while the World Bank (2023) documents the expanding role of digital technologies in public and private activity. Together, these sources help place digital finance within a wider infrastructure debate.

An Integrated Lens

Taken together, these strands form the chapter's analytical lens. Digital financial infrastructure can be understood as an anticipatory instrument because it allows governments to act before or during a shock; as a public-value arrangement because its effects must be judged in terms of legitimacy, equity, and collective benefit; and as a robustness problem because failures in one part of the system can expose users when alternatives are absent. Datafication provides the critical counterweight. The same infrastructure that makes a state more capable can also increase surveillance, automate exclusion, or shift risks onto citizens.

Brazil, Kenya, India, and Nigeria were selected on three grounds. Each has a substantial documentary record, allowing the chapter to compare claims with evidence. Each also represents a distinct way of organizing digital financial infrastructure: state-led, market-led, or integrated, with Nigeria providing a case of rapid transition and weak sequencing. Finally, the cases expose different combinations of benefit and harm, which makes them useful for testing the framework rather than merely illustrating it.

MAIN FOCUS OF THE CHAPTER

Digital Finance as Public Infrastructure

The institutional novelty of digital finance is best captured by the phrase the platform states. O'Reilly (2011) popularized the idea of government as a platform, by analogy with technology platforms that supply a stable core of shared services on which others build. In this vision the state need not deliver every service itself; it provides dependable rails, an identity layer, a payments layer, a data-exchange layer, and lets a broader ecosystem of public agencies, private firms, and civil society build applications atop them. The appeal is plain, since a government running good rails can enable far more activity than one attempting to operate every service end to end. The risk, less remarked at first, is equally plain: rails are infrastructure, and whoever controls infrastructure wields a quiet and durable form of power.

This platform idea connects to a deeper argument about state capacity. Kattel and Mazzucato (2018) held that public organizations need dynamic capabilities, the ability to sense, seize, and reconfigure in pursuit of public missions, rather than a narrow competence in administering fixed procedures. Mazzucato and Kattel (2020) pressed the point during the pandemic, naming the capacity to govern data and digital platforms, together with the capacity to adapt and learn, as central to a capable modern state. Margetts and Dorobantu (2019) argued that artificial intelligence and data could be bent to public benefit if governments reimagined how they work, while flagging the governance conditions that would be required. Read alongside the older account of digital-era governance by Dunleavy et al. (2008), this body of work establishes that building digital financial infrastructure is no mere procurement decision but an act of state-building, bringing with it every question of power, accountability, and distribution that state-building entails.

Over the past decade these ideas crystallized into a development paradigm now widely termed digital public infrastructure, or DPI. The canonical claim holds that a handful of foundational digital systems, typically a digital identity layer, a real-time payments layer, and a consent-based data-exchange layer, can act as shared public goods on which an economy and a state may build. India's combination of Aadhaar, the Unified Payments Interface, and associated data systems became the most cited template, and during India's 2023 presidency of the G20 the grouping settled on a definition of DPI as shared digital systems built to be secure and interoperable on open standards, designed for universal access, and treating governance and community as integral rather than incidental. Analysts have noted both the promise and the ambiguity of the term. Work from Bandura et al. (2024) and other observers has stressed that the definition leaves the most consequential questions unsettled: who governs the rails, on what terms private actors may build on them, how rights are safeguarded, and what redress exists when the system errs. DPI specifies architecture without settling the politics of that architecture.

Three features of digital finance as public infrastructure deserve emphasis for the argument here. Infrastructure is, to begin with, sticky. Once a population's welfare, wages, and identity run through a particular set of rails, switching costs grow enormous, and the choices baked into the original design outlast the moment of design by years. This is why anticipatory thinking matters most at the point of construction, since errors embedded early are governed for a long time. Infrastructure is also relational. A payment rail is less an object than a web of relationships among a citizen, an identity record, a financial institution, a regulator, and frequently a private platform; each relationship carries its own accountability gap, and the gaps compound. Infrastructure is, finally, generative in ways its builders cannot wholly foresee. UPI was built to move money, yet it reshaped commerce, credit, and the surrounding data economy. Generativity is the reward of good infrastructure and the reason its governance cannot be fixed once and then forgotten.

Calling digital finance infrastructure is therefore more than a descriptive choice. It identifies certain systems as foundational and gives them a degree of institutional permanence. Once welfare payments, wages, or everyday transactions depend on a digital rail, changing that rail becomes costly. Infrastructure consequently shapes what governments can do, but it also shapes what citizens must rely on.

Issues, Controversies, and Problems: Risk, Inclusion, and Trust in Platform States

The platform state produces a recurring set of governance problems. These problems are not simply technical faults that better engineering will remove. They arise because governing through shared digital systems concentrates decisions about eligibility, identity, data, and access within infrastructures that ordinary users may have little ability to inspect or challenge.

Exclusion by Design

The first and gravest problem is that systems built to include can also exclude and can do so through the very mechanisms meant to guarantee integrity. Where eligibility for a benefit hinges on successful digital authentication, every point of failure in the chain becomes a potential point of denial. A fingerprint that will not be read because of age or manual labour, a server unreachable from a village, a name spelt differently across two databases, a phone drained of charge or signal: any of these can turn a legitimate claimant into a rejected one. Crucially, the burden of such failures falls on the citizen rather than the system. The person must establish afresh that they are who they claim to be, and failing that, the default is denial. Eubanks (2018) traced this dynamic in wealthy-country welfare automation; Alston (2019) generalized it as the inversion of accountability, whereby the individual must answer to the machine rather than the state answering to the individual. As the cases below show, the harm is not hypothetical, and in its most extreme documented form it has cost life.

The Redistribution of Risk

The second problem is that digital financial systems relocate risk rather than removing it. A government moving from cash to digital transfers cuts certain risks for itself, among them physical leakage and slow disbursement, while often raising others for citizens: the risk that a technical failure severs a household with no margin, that a fraudulent transaction empties an account, or that an abrupt policy change strands those without the means to adapt. Bozeman's (2002) framework of public value failure is exact on this point. When a reform compresses the state's time horizon or imperils the subsistence of the most exposed, an appearance of efficiency conceals a transfer of risk from the strong to the weak. Robustness, in Ansell and Trondal's (2018) sense, is what forestalls this; a robust system keeps fallback channels open and tolerates imperfection so that no single failure becomes a catastrophe for the person at the end of the line, whereas a brittle one optimizes for the common case and abandons the exception.

Surveillance and the Inversion of Accountability

The third problem is that financial infrastructure doubles as surveillance infrastructure. Every digital transaction is a record, and records accumulate into a detailed portrait of a person's movements, associations, and circumstances. In a state's hands that portrait is a potent instrument, serviceable for delivering benefits and equally serviceable for monitoring, profiling, and control. Zuboff (2019) traced the commercial logic of extraction, while Taylor (2017) set out the justice questions that arise once people become legible to data systems they can neither see nor contest. The worry is not that surveillance is invariably malign; it is that the capacity arises by default, the safeguards arrive only through deliberate effort, and those most exposed have the least power to insist on them. A platform state lacking strong data protection, independent oversight, and real limits on secondary use has assembled the machinery of a surveillance state, whatever anyone intended.

The Limits of Inclusion as a Paradigm

The fourth problem is conceptual. Critical work on financial inclusion questions whether greater access necessarily produces greater welfare. Mader (2018) found the evidence for the agenda's central claims weaker than their policy prominence suggested, while his earlier work (Mader, 2015) argued that financialization can create new forms of dependence under the language of empowerment. Gabor and Brooks (2017) described a fintech-development complex in which the digital traces of poor households can become assets for financial actors. Natile (2020), examining mobile money, likewise argued that widening access can coexist with gendered exclusion. These arguments do not establish that digital finance is harmful in itself. They do, however, show why an account-based measure of inclusion cannot be treated as evidence of benefit.

Trust connects these problems. Public value theory treats legitimacy as part of effective public action, not as something that appears after a system has been built. People are more likely to trust a digital financial system when it is reliable, fair, and open to challenge; confidence weakens when decisions appear arbitrary or impossible to contest. A single visible failure can therefore matter beyond the individual case, particularly when it affects someone with few alternatives. The cases that follow show how institutional trust can be strengthened or damaged through design choices.

Comparative Insights from the Global South

Four cases anchor the comparison, chosen for the quality of their documentation, the sharpness of the surrounding debates, and their spread across the design space. Brazil's Pix is a state-built payment utility. Kenya's M-Pesa is a market-built system that became infrastructure. India's architecture is the most ambitious attempt to treat finance, identity, and payments as integrated public infrastructure. Nigeria's currency redesign is a cautionary study in sequencing and pace. A word on the global picture is useful first, since the cases sit within a worldwide shift.

The Global Findex database records the scale of the change. By 2021, 76 per cent of adults worldwide had an account, compared with 51 per cent a decade earlier; in developing economies, the share had risen from 42 to 71 per cent (Demirgüç-Kunt et al., 2022). The gender gap in account ownership in developing economies had also narrowed to about six percentage points, while mobile money accounted for a substantial part of growth in Sub-Saharan Africa. These figures establish the scale of financial inclusion. They do not show whether users can rely on the systems behind the accounts, or whether the systems treat people fairly when something goes wrong.

Brazil: Pix and the Payment System as a Public Good

Brazil provides the clearest example in the comparison of a state building a payment system as public infrastructure instead of leaving the core rail to private providers. Banco Central do Brazil launched Pix in November 2020 as an instant-payment system that operates continuously, settles transactions within seconds, and is managed through the central bank's infrastructure. Individuals generally use it without fees, while participating institutions must provide access under the system's rules. Duarte et al. (2022) describe how the central bank used interoperability and its regulatory position to reduce costs and pursue inclusion as an explicit policy objective.

The results came quickly. The Bank for International Settlements analysis reported that Pix drew in tens of millions of people who had made no electronic transfer in the previous year, bringing them into the digital payment system within months, with adoption climbing steeply thereafter. The underlying logic is worth stating, since it inverts the platform-as-private-rails model. By keeping the core public, free at the point of use for individuals, and interoperable by mandate, Brazil wrote the public value goal into the architecture itself. People were included not because a private provider found them profitable but because the rail was built as a public utility and reaching them was the entire point. Read through the chapter's framework, Pix is a case in which anticipation, public value, and robustness were aligned by design, and in which the central bank's capacity, in Mazzucato and Kattel's (2020) sense, matched its ambition.

Pix also raise governance questions. A dominant national payment system concentrated within a central bank places substantial responsibility for competition, data governance, and accountability in one institution. The same central direction that helped adoption can therefore create a potential concentration-of-power problem. The Brazilian case does not show that public provision is automatically better. It shows that whoever controls the core rail must be answerable for how it is operated.

Kenya: M-Pesa and the Contested Evidence on Poverty

Kenya's M-Pesa is one of the most studied digital financial systems in development research and has generated a major dispute over its effects on poverty. Launched in 2007 as a mobile-money service, it allowed users to store and transfer value through their phones and expanded into national financial infrastructure largely through market growth. Suri and Jack (2016) reported that access to M-Pesa increased per-capita consumption and estimated that about 194,000 households moved above the poverty line, with larger effects for female-headed households. Jack and Suri (2014) linked part of the mechanism to improved risk-sharing: mobile money reduced the transaction costs involved when households sought help from family and friends aftershocks.

The strength of those findings made the later challenge important. Bateman et al. (2019) disputed the Suri and Jack results, pointing to omissions, inconsistencies, and methodological problems and drawing attention to the possibility that digital lending could also increase over-indebtedness. Mader (2018) and Natile (2020) place similar concerns within a wider critique of financial inclusion. The dispute has not produced a simple verdict. For the purposes of this chapter, the important point is that market-led digital finance can produce benefits and harm through the same infrastructure. The balance between them depends partly on credit rules, consumer protection, and competition policy. In Kenya, many of these governances responses developed after the lending market had already expanded.

India: Identity, Transfers, and the Two Faces of Digital Finance

India combines biometric identity, direct benefit transfers, and the Unified Payments Interface in an unusually extensive digital-finance architecture. Aadhaar enrolled more than a billion people, direct transfers linked welfare payments to bank accounts, and UPI, launched by the National Payments Corporation of India in 2016, enabled low-cost instant payments at national scale. UPI's transaction volumes have grown into tens of billions per month. The International Monetary Fund has described UPI as the world's largest retail fast-payment system by transaction volume. Estimates that India accounts for nearly half of global real-time payment transactions, however, come from ACI Worldwide rather than a multilateral institution; that distinction should be retained when the figure is cited.

The strongest evidence for benefits comes from field research rather than promotional claims. In a randomized rollout of biometric smartcards in Andhra Pradesh, Muralidharan et al. (2016) found that payments under rural employment and pension schemes became faster and more predictable, with lower leakage and no reduction in access, and that the system was cost-effective. Barnwal (2024), studying direct transfers for cooking-fuel subsidies, found evidence that the reform reduced diversion of subsidized fuel into illicit markets. These findings show that digital transfers can produce public-value gains under institutional conditions.

The scale of the government's savings claims needs more careful treatment. The Government of India has cited cumulative savings of about 3.5 lakh crore rupees from direct benefit transfers over fifteen years, based on reduced leakage. Such figures are advocacy estimates, not peer-reviewed findings. An earlier related claim was also criticized for misreading a World Bank figure that referred to expenditure rather than savings. The appropriate response is to attribute the savings claim clearly and distinguish it from evidence produced through independent evaluation. That distinction is central to the public-value argument because policy claims are themselves part of how public value is communicated.

The Indian record also contains serious exclusion problems. Khera (2017, 2019) argued from field evidence that linking welfare entitlements to biometric authentication created additional points of failure for poor households and that some reported savings could reflect denied entitlements rather than reduced fraud. Drèze et al. (2017), studying food security in Jharkhand, found that compulsory linkage of the public distribution system to digital authentication coincided with reduced receipt of entitlements during the transition. Civil-society investigations and reporting have also linked several starvation deaths to ration-card cancellations or repeated authentication failures. Government officials disputed causal claims in some cases. The chapter therefore treats these deaths as serious, documented findings from civil-society and journalistic sources rather than as judicially settled determinations. The distinction matters because the argument concerns the governance consequences of exclusion, not the assignment of legal responsibility for individual deaths.

Taken together, the Indian evidence shows why the chapter treats governance as decisive. The same broad architecture has been associated with measured reductions in leakage and with documented cases of denied subsistence. The difference lies in design and institutional response: whether authentication is a hard gate, whether fallback routes and human discretion remain available, whether redress can be reached by someone with little power, and whether exclusions are monitored as closely as successful transactions. Anticipatory governance that ignores these conditions protect administrative convenience more readily than citizen security.

Nigeria: When Pace Outruns Readiness

Nigeria's 2023 currency redesign shows what happens when a state drives a population toward digital and cashless transactions faster than its institutions and its people can absorb. In late 2022 the Central Bank of Nigeria announced a redesign of high-value naira notes with a compressed deadline for exchanging old notes, a step officially justified by aims that included curbing illicit cash and hastening a cashless economy. Its execution coincided with severe cash scarcity in the run-up to the February 2023 general election, producing queues, protests, and litigation by state governors against the federal government. Analysis by Monye (2024) found that the policy largely missed its objectives and that the digital alternative was not ready to absorb the displaced demand, observing that the central bank's own digital currency had achieved negligible uptake relative to the cash it was meant to supplement.

The distributional problem is central. Many Nigerian adults remained outside formal banking, and physical cash was therefore a dependable means of daily exchange for people who could not easily substitute digital payments. Moving toward cash lessness before inclusive and robust digital rails were available shifted risk toward groups with the fewest alternatives, including people in the informal sector and rural areas. The case fits the framework closely: the state had an anticipatory ambition, but the system lacked adequate fallback capacity and the public-value calculation failed to account for the costs imposed on those least able to adapt. Nigeria's experience was not simply a failure of digital finance; it was a failure to sequence institutional change with the capacity of the people expected to use it.

Three Models of Governing Digital Finance

Across the four cases, three governance models come into view, and naming them clarifies what is at stake. The first is the public-utility model, exemplified by Brazil, in which the state builds and runs the core rail itself as a public good, mandates interoperability, and writes the inclusion objective into the architecture. Its strength is that public purpose is designed in rather than wished for; its characteristic risk is the concentration of power and data within a single public institution that must then be held to account.

The second is the market-led model, exemplified by Kenya, in which private providers build systems that grow into national infrastructure while the state mostly permits and lightly regulates. Its strength is speed and innovation; its characteristic risk is that the public interest hangs on regulation that often arrives only after harm such as over-indebtedness has already set in.

The third is the integrated public-infrastructure model, exemplified by India, in which the state weave's identity, benefits, and payments into a single architecture treated as foundational. Its strength is reach and the ability to act at scale; its characteristic risk is that integration can also propagate failure. An error in the identity layer, for example, can become a denial of subsistence in the welfare layer. Nigeria is less a fourth model than an example of mis-sequencing, where the ambition of an integrated digital future outran the inclusive and robust rails needed to support it. These models are not fixed outcomes. Public systems can still exclude, market-led systems can be regulated effectively, and integrated systems can include fallback and redress. The typology matters because each arrangement concentrates power and risk differently and therefore requires a different form of accountability.

Table 1. Comparative governance across the four cases

Case	Primary builder	Documented outcome	Governance risk / lesson
Brazil (Pix)	Central bank / public infrastructure	Rapid expansion of instant payments and broad access	Concentration of power and data; accountability must match public control
Kenya (M-Pesa)	Private providers / market-led	Measured gains in payments and risk-sharing; poverty effects remain contested	Consumer protection, credit, and competition rules matter
India	Integrated public infrastructure	Reduced leakage in some programmes; very large payment ecosystem	Authentication failures can turn technical problems into welfare exclusion
Nigeria	State-led rapid transition	Cash scarcity and disruption during the 2023 redesign	Digital transition requires sequencing and funded fallback channels

Source. Author's synthesis from the case evidence discussed in the chapter.

Reading the Cases Together

The four cases do not support a simple ranking. Brazil shows how a state can build payment infrastructure around a public purpose. Kenya shows that market-led systems can generate measurable gains while also creating harms that require regulation, and that the evidence of benefit remains contested. India shows both the gains from digital transfers and the serious consequences that can follow when authentication becomes an unforgiving gate. Nigeria shows how the speed of transition can turn a defensible objective into a regressive shock. Across the cases, the distribution of benefit and harm is more closely related to governance choices than to the mere presence of digital infrastructure. Fallback channels, accessible redress, independent oversight, honest measurement, and attention to the least-served user all affect the outcome. This comparison provides the basis for the recommendations that follow.

SOLUTIONS AND RECOMMENDATIONS

The comparison suggests that digital-finance governance cannot be left until after the infrastructure is in place. Decisions about authentication, data, redress, and fallback are made early and become difficult to change once people depend on the system. The recommendations below are therefore design principles for public managers, regulators, and elected officials. They ask decision-makers to consider failure conditions and vulnerable users at the design stage, consistent with the anticipatory-governance approach developed in the chapter.

Each recommendation is linked to one or more elements of the chapter's framework—anticipatory governance, public value, robustness, and data justice—so that the relationship between the diagnosis and the proposed response is visible.

Design Authentication as a Soft Check Rather Than a Hard Gate (Public Value and Data Justice)

Authentication failures should trigger an alternative route, not an automatic loss of entitlement. A robust system can provide a secondary biometric, an offline process, human review, or temporary payment while the problem is resolved. Khera (2017) and Drèze et al. (2017) document the consequences of hard-gate approaches in India. The basic principle is straightforward: a person should not lose legal entitlement because a machine cannot authenticate them. The entitlement belongs to the claimant; the authentication mechanism is only a means of verifying it.

Build Fallback Channels and Keep Them Funded (Robustness)

Robustness, in the sense used by Ansell and Trondal (2018) and Ansell et al. (2024), requires alternative routes to remain available when the primary channel fails. Cash, manual processing, and assisted access should therefore continue alongside digital channels until the evidence shows that they can safely be reduced. Nigeria's 2023 crisis illustrates the danger of withdrawing the fallback too early. Keeping alternative channels available is not a sign that digital reform is unfinished. It is part of making the system dependable for people who have the fewest alternatives.

Make Redress Accessible to the powerless (Public Value)

A right without an effective remedy is difficult to exercise. Digital financial systems that condition access to public goods on their own correct operation need grievance and appeal routes that can be used by people with limited literacy, no lawyer, and little political influence. Alston (2019) emphasizes the accountability problem created when responsibility for an administrative error is shifted onto the individual. Practical safeguards include accessible complaints procedures, independent appeal, published error rates, and rules that resolve uncertain cases in the claimant's favor.

Govern Data as a Public Trust Rather Than a Free Resource (Data Justice)

Financial infrastructure is also a source of surveillance capacity. Transaction records can reveal movements, relationships, and circumstances, creating possibilities for both service delivery and monitoring. Zuboff (2019) describes the commercial logic of data extraction, while Taylor (2017) connects digital rights to questions of justice. The policy implication is not that digital finance should be abandoned. It is that data collection, retention, secondary use, and sharing should be limited by law, oversight, and meaningful consent. Data minimization and purpose limitation are practical ways of treating financial data as a public responsibility rather than an unrestricted resource.

Measure Honestly and Publish What Fails (Public Value)

Digital-finance programmes are often promoted through aggregate figures, but those figures can conceal exclusion and error. The chapter's comparison shows why savings estimates and market share claims should be separated from peer-reviewed findings. Governments should publish denial and error rates alongside accounts opened and transactions processed, and major claims should be subject to independent evaluation. Muralidharan et al. (2016) and Barnwal (2024) illustrate the value of evidence that can be examined independently. A public-value approach requires governments to report where systems fail as well as where they succeed.

Sequence Transitions to the Pace of Inclusion Rather Than the Ambition of Planners (Anticipatory Governance)

Nigeria, compared with Brazil, shows why the speed of digital transition should follow the readiness of the least-served users rather than the timetable of planners. A transition can reach broad coverage while retaining an alternative channel; withdrawing the alternative to force adoption creates a different set of risks. Anticipatory governance should therefore include the pace of adoption as part of its planning, with particular attention to people who have limited connectivity, documentation, literacy, or access to formal banking.

Keep the Rails Accountable, Whoever Holds Them (Public Value and Robustness)

Brazil's public-utility model and Kenya's market-led model both concentrate power, but in different institutions: the central bank in one case and dominant private providers in the other. The accountability principle is the same. Whoever controls foundational financial infrastructure exercises public power and should be subject to transparency, competition policy, independent regulation, and democratic oversight proportionate to that power. A platform state needs accountability arrangements that match the reach of its infrastructure.

Together, these principles describe a form of digital government that can anticipate problems without becoming coercive, improve efficiency without becoming brittle, and pursue inclusion without treating access as the final measure. None is particularly novel, and several governments already use parts of this approach. The difficulty is institutional: safeguards cost money, slow some processes, and constrain the discretion that comes with centralized systems. Those costs are easier to accept at the design stage than after a failure has damaged trust or denied an entitlement.

FUTURE RESEARCH DIRECTIONS

Several questions remain open. One concerns measurement. There is no widely accepted method for quantifying exclusion in digital benefit systems, so inclusion is measured much more precisely than wrongful denial or authentication failure. Research that develops comparable measures of exclusion error, failed authentication, and denied entitlement would make it possible to assess public value more honestly and to test some of the claims made in support of digital reform.

A second concerns unresolved empirical disputes. The disagreement over M-Pesa's poverty effects between Suri and Jack (2016) and Bateman et al. (2019) illustrates a broader problem: evidence on digital financial inclusion is more contested than its policy prominence suggests. Replication, longer panels, and attention to over-indebtedness and distributional effects would help move the debate beyond average effects. Similar work is needed on India's benefit-transfer systems, where causal studies sit alongside advocacy estimates that have been challenged.

A third concerns comparative governance. The chapter distinguishes state-led, market-led, and integrated models, but systematic comparison is still limited. Future studies could examine how data-protection regimes, grievance systems, and oversight institutions relate to the distribution of benefits and harms. Ansell et al. (2024) provides one possible framework for this work, while digital finance offers a useful set of cases in which governance arrangements can be compared.

A fourth concerns the next technological layer. AI is increasingly being considered for targeting, fraud detection, and credit allocation, which adds another layer of accountability and exclusion risk. Eubanks (2018) shows how automated systems can reproduce disadvantage when people have little ability to challenge decisions. Research should therefore examine these applications before they become embedded in essential financial services. This is consistent with the anticipatory-governance approach because it treats foreseeable risks as design questions rather than problems to document only after harm occurs.

A fifth concerns the wider technological and regulatory horizon. The chapter has not examined AI governance in public financial systems in detail, central bank digital currencies, cybersecurity as financial rails become high-value targets, or cross-border payment systems as instant-payment networks begin to interconnect. These topics extend the framework developed here and would benefit from further study using the same concerns with anticipation, public value, robustness, and data justice.

CONCLUSION

Digital financial infrastructure is changing how states govern. It gives governments the ability to act earlier and at greater scale, and in some settings that capacity has produced real gains. Brazil's Pix brought large numbers of users into an instant-payment system designed as public infrastructure. India's transfer and payment systems operate at a scale that older arrangements could not easily match, while research has documented reductions in leakage in some programmes. The promise of digital finance is therefore not imaginary: these systems can help governments reach people more quickly.

The same capacity can also produce exclusion, surveillance, and shifts of risk onto people with few alternatives. The cases examined here include denied entitlements, cash shortages, and serious concerns about the consequences of authentication failures. The central difference is institutional. Governance choices about authentication, fallback, redress, data, measurement, sequencing, and accountability determine how the infrastructure behaves when ordinary transactions fail or when users do not fit the assumptions built into the system.

The chapter has therefore used four connected lenses: anticipatory governance, public value, robustness, and data justice. Each captures a different problem. Anticipatory governance is concerned with whether the state prepares for future conditions. Public value is concerned with whether the results are socially legitimate and broadly beneficial. Robustness turns on whether the system keeps functioning once conditions change, and data justice turns on who becomes visible, how people are represented, and who bears the consequences of data use. Together, the four give a fuller basis for evaluating digital financial infrastructure than any one of them would alone.

The future-oriented state imagined by this volume is not necessarily the state with the most powerful digital rails. It is the state that can explain how those rails will work, provide alternatives when they fail, and remain answerable to the people who depend on them. Inclusion should be treated as an obligation to be maintained, not merely as a number to be reported.

The chapter's central claim is that inclusion depends on governance as much as on technology. Digital finance gives public institutions considerable capacity, but the effects of that capacity depend on how systems are designed and overseen. In Sen's (1999) terms, such choices can enlarge human freedom or restrict it for people with the fewest alternatives. Good governance therefore requires deliberate attention to vulnerable users, willingness to maintain fallback arrangements, and mechanisms through which people can challenge decisions that affect them.

Stated plainly, the chapter's theoretical contribution is to bring anticipatory governance, public value theory, robustness scholarship, and data justice into one diagnostic framework for digital financial infrastructure. The comparison suggests that this combined lens helps explain differences in outcomes that technology alone cannot account for: governance choices shape who benefits, who bears the risk, and how accountable the resulting systems remain.

AI DISCLOSURE

Generative AI tools were used to assist with structural editing, language refinement, and readability during revision. The author reviewed the revised manuscript and remains responsible for its arguments, evidence, citations, references, and final wording.

REFERENCES

Alston, P. (2019). *Report of the Special Rapporteur on extreme poverty and human rights: Digital welfare states and human rights (United Nations Document A/74/493).* United Nations General Assembly. https://undocs.org/A/74/493

Ansell, C., Sørensen, E., & Torfing, J. (2021). The COVID-19 pandemic as a game changer for public administration and leadership? The need for robust governance responses to turbulent problems. *Public Management Review*, *23*(7), 949–960. DOI: 10.1080/14719037.2020.1820272

Ansell, C., Sørensen, E., & Torfing, J. (2023). Public administration and politics meet turbulence: The search for robust governance responses. *Public Administration*, *101*(1), 3–22. DOI: 10.1111/padm.12874

Ansell, C., Sørensen, E., Torfing, J., & Trondal, J. (2024). *Robust governance in turbulent times*. Cambridge University Press., DOI: 10.1017/9781009433006

Ansell, C., & Trondal, J. (2018). Governing turbulence: An organizational-institutional agenda. *Perspectives on Public Management and Governance*, *1*(1), 43–57. DOI: 10.1093/ppmgov/gvx013

Bandura, R., McLean, M., & Smutny, C. (2024, August 26). *Approaches to digital public infrastructure in the Global South.* Center for Strategic and International Studies. https://www.csis.org/analysis/approaches-digital-public-infrastructure-global-south

Barnwal, P. (2024). Curbing leakage in public programs: Evidence from India's Direct Benefit Transfer policy. *The American Economic Review*, *114*(12), 3812–3846. DOI: 10.1257/aer.20161864

Bateman, M., Duvendack, M., & Loubere, N. (2019). Is fintech the new panacea for poverty alleviation and local development? Contesting Suri and Jack's M-Pesa findings published in Science. *Review of African Political Economy*, *46*(161), 480–495. DOI: 10.1080/03056244.2019.1614552

Benington, J., & Moore, M. H. (Eds.). (2011). *Public value: Theory and practice.* Palgrave Macmillan. DOI: 10.1007/978-0-230-36431-8

Bozeman, B. (2002). Public-value failure: When efficient markets may not do. *Public Administration Review*, *62*(2), 145–161. DOI: 10.1111/0033-3352.00165

Bozeman, B. (2007). *Public values and public interest: Counterbalancing economic individualism.* Georgetown University Press.

Bryson, J. M., Crosby, B. C., & Bloomberg, L. (2014). Public value governance: Moving beyond traditional public administration and the new public management. *Public Administration Review, 74*(4), 445–456. DOI: 10.1111/puar.12238

Demirgüç-Kunt, A., Klapper, L., Singer, D., & Ansar, S. (2022). *The Global Findex Database 2021: Financial inclusion, digital payments, and resilience in the age of COVID-19.* World Bank. DOI: 10.1596/978-1-4648-1897-4

Drèze, J., Khalid, N., Khera, R., & Somanchi, A. (2017). Aadhaar and food security in Jharkhand: Pain without gain? *Economic and Political Weekly, 52*(50), 50–59.

Duarte, A., Frost, J., Gambacorta, L., Koo Wilkens, P., & Shin, H. S. (2022). Central banks, the monetary system and public payment infrastructures: Lessons from Brazil's Pix. *Bank for International Settlements Bulletin No. 52.* Bank for International Settlements. https://www.bis.org/publ/bisbull52.htm

Dunleavy, P., Margetts, H., Bastow, S., & Tinkler, J. (2008). *Digital era governance: IT corporations, the state and e-government.* Oxford University Press.

Eubanks, V. (2018). *Automating inequality: How high-tech tools profile, police, and punish the poor.* St. Martin's Press.

Fuerth, L. S., & Faber, E. M. H. (2012). *Anticipatory governance practical upgrades: Equipping the executive branch to cope with increasing speed and complexity of major challenges.* National Defense University Press.

Gabor, D., & Brooks, S. (2017). The digital revolution in financial inclusion: International development in the fintech era. *New Political Economy, 22*(4), 423–436. DOI: 10.1080/13563467.2017.1259298

Guston, D. H. (2014). Understanding anticipatory governance. *Social Studies of Science, 44*(2), 218–242. DOI: 10.1177/0306312713508669 PMID: 24941612

Jack, W., & Suri, T. (2014). Risk sharing and transaction costs: Evidence from Kenya's mobile money revolution. *The American Economic Review, 104*(1), 183–223. DOI: 10.1257/aer.104.1.183

Kattel, R., & Mazzucato, M. (2018). Mission-oriented innovation policy and dynamic capabilities in the public sector. *Industrial and Corporate Change, 27*(5), 787–801. DOI: 10.1093/icc/dty032

Khera, R. (2017). Impact of Aadhaar in welfare programmes (Social Science Research Network Working Paper No. 3045235). *Social Science Research Network.* DOI: 10.2139/ssrn.3045235

Khera, R. (2019). Aadhaar failures: A tragedy of errors. *Economic and Political Weekly*, *54*(14), 10–13.

MacArthur, B. D., Dorobantu, C. L., & Margetts, H. Z. (2022). Resilient government requires data science reform. *Nature Human Behaviour*, *6*(8), 1035–1037. DOI: 10.1038/s41562-022-01423-6 PMID: 35941235

Mader, P. (2015). *The political economy of microfinance: Financializing poverty*. Palgrave Macmillan. DOI: 10.1057/9781137364210

Mader, P. (2018). Contesting financial inclusion. *Development and Change*, *49*(2), 461–483. DOI: 10.1111/dech.12368

Margetts, H., & Dorobantu, C. (2019). Rethink government with AI. *Nature*, *568*(7751), 163–165. DOI: 10.1038/d41586-019-01099-5 PMID: 30967667

Mazzucato, M., & Kattel, R. (2020). COVID-19 and public-sector capacity. *Oxford Review of Economic Policy*, *36*(Suppl. 1), S256–S269. DOI: 10.1093/oxrep/graa031 PMID: 40504220

Monye, E. (2024, January 18). *Why Nigeria's controversial naira redesign policy hasn't met its objectives*. Carnegie Endowment for International Peace. https://carnegieendowment.org/research/2024/01/why-nigerias-controversial-naira-redesign-policy-hasnt-met-its-objectives?lang=en

Moore, M. H. (1995). *Creating public value: Strategic management in government*. Harvard University Press.

Muralidharan, K., Niehaus, P., & Sukhtankar, S. (2016). Building state capacity: Evidence from biometric smartcards in India. *The American Economic Review*, *106*(10), 2895–2929. DOI: 10.1257/aer.20141346

Natile, S. (2020). *The exclusionary politics of digital financial inclusion: Mobile money, gendered walls*. Routledge. DOI: 10.4324/9780367179618

O'Reilly, T. (2011). Government as a platform. *Innovations: Technology, Governance, Globalization*, *6*(1), 13–40. DOI: 10.1162/INOV_a_00056

OECD. (2025). *Governing with artificial intelligence*. OECD Publishing., DOI: 10.1787/795de142-

Sen, A. (1999). *Development as freedom*. Oxford University Press.

Suri, T., & Jack, W. (2016). The long-run poverty and gender impacts of mobile money. *Science*, *354*(6317), 1288–1292. DOI: 10.1126/science.aah5309 PMID: 27940873

Taylor, L. (2017). What is data justice? The case for connecting digital rights and freedoms globally. *Big Data & Society*, *4*(2), 1–14. DOI: 10.1177/2053951717736335

United Nations Development Programme. (2024). *Universal DPI safeguards framework: A guide to building safe and inclusive DPI for societies*. https://www.undp.org/press-releases/un-releases-universal-dpi-safeguards-framework-promote-safe-and-inclusive-digital-public-infrastructure

World Bank. (2023). *Digital progress and trends report 2023*. World Bank. https://www.worldbank.org/en/publication/digital-progress-and-trends-report

Zuboff, S. (2019). *The age of surveillance capitalism: The fight for a human future at the new frontier of power*. PublicAffairs.

KEY TERMS AND DEFINITIONS

Anticipatory Governance: A mode of governing in which institutions build the capacity to sense, prepare for, and shape emerging risks and opportunities before their options narrow, through foresight, engagement, and assessment integrated into the development of technologies and policies.

Data Justice: A normative framework concerned with fairness in how people are made visible, represented, and treated through their data, connecting digital rights and freedoms to broader questions of equity and capability.

Datafication: The conversion of human activity, including financial transactions, into data that can be stored, analyzed, and acted upon, creating capacities for both service delivery and surveillance.

Digital Financial Inclusion: The provision of access to and use of formal financial services, such as payments, savings, and transfers, through digital channels, especially for populations previously underserved by conventional banking, where access does not by itself guarantee benefit.

Digital Public Infrastructure (DPI): A set of shared, interoperable digital systems, typically a digital identity layer, a real-time payments layer, and a data-exchange layer, intended to function as public goods on which states, markets, and citizens build services.

Platform State: A model of government that provides foundational digital rails and shared services on which a wider ecosystem of public and private actors builds, concentrating infrastructural power in whoever controls the core rails.

Public Value Failure: A situation in which neither markets nor governments provide goods and outcomes a society holds to be valuable, including failures to articulate value honestly, short time horizons, and threats to subsistence.

Public Value: The value created by public action, judged not only by efficiency but by a combination of substantive worth, legitimacy and support, and operational capacity, and attentive to how a system treats those with the least power.

Risk Redistribution: The process by which digital reform reduces certain risks for the state while transferring others onto citizens, often shifting the burden of technical failure or sudden policy change onto the most vulnerable users.

Robustness: The capacity of an institution or system to maintain its function and purpose under turbulence through flexibility, redundancy, and a repertoire of redeployable responses, distinguished from resilience understood narrowly as bouncing back to a prior state.

Chapter 8
Digital Transformation and Social Policy Effectiveness in Digital Government:
Institutional Perspectives From Bulgaria

Venelin Terziev
http://orcid.org/0000-0003-1115-8877
Black Sea Institute, Bourgas, Bulgaria

Marin Georgiev
http://orcid.org/0000-0002-4530-6471
Vitalis Ruse, Ruse, Bulgaria

ABSTRACT

This chapter examines digital government's role in enhancing social policy effectiveness by focusing on Bulgaria's social assistance system. Integrating theoretical and empirical analysis, the study explores how technologies like artificial intelligence, big data, and blockchain improve governance and service delivery. Using a systemic approach, the research demonstrates that digital transformation strengthens coordination and accessibility to foster resilient and inclusive welfare systems. Despite progress, the digital divide and limited administrative capacity remain barriers. The study conceptualizes social effectiveness within digital welfare and provides strategic recommendations for modernizing public management in an uncertain future.

DOI: 10.4018/979-8-3373-9765-8.ch008

INTRODUCTION

Social policy represents one of the fundamental pillars of modern states, playing a crucial role in regulating social relations and ensuring the well-being and security of citizens. It encompasses a comprehensive set of principles, mechanisms, and instruments aimed at reducing social inequalities, preventing social exclusion, and fostering sustainable societal development. In the context of globalization, demographic transformations, and dynamic economic processes, the importance of social policy has significantly increased, positioning it as a strategic tool for achieving social cohesion and economic stability (Esping-Andersen, 1990; Midgley, 1995).

In contemporary academic discourse, social policy is understood as a system of purposeful actions undertaken by the state and society to regulate relationships among different social groups and to ensure equitable access to fundamental social rights and services (Titmuss, 1974). Its multidimensional nature spans areas such as social assistance, social security, employment, healthcare, education, and housing policy, necessitating an interdisciplinary approach to both research and implementation.

In recent years, the rapid advancement of digital technologies has profoundly transformed the functioning of welfare systems worldwide. Governments are increasingly adopting digital tools and data-driven approaches to enhance the efficiency, accessibility, and transparency of social services. The concept of digital transformation refers not only to the introduction of information and communication technologies (ICT) but also to the restructuring of institutional processes and governance models to support more responsive and citizen-centered service delivery (Dunleavy et al., 2006; Margetts & Dunleavy, 2013). This transformation has been further accelerated by the COVID-19 pandemic, which highlighted the necessity of resilient and technology-enabled social protection systems (World Bank, 2022).

Within the European context, digitalization has become a strategic priority for modernizing welfare states. Initiatives such as the European Pillar of Social Rights, the Digital Europe Programme, and the Digital Economy and Society Index (DESI) emphasize the integration of digital technologies into social policy to improve coordination among institutions and enhance access to services (European Commission, 2023, 2024). These developments underline the growing interdependence between social policy effectiveness and digital governance.

The concept of social effectiveness constitutes a central analytical dimension in evaluating social policies. Moving beyond the traditional understanding of economic efficiency, based on cost-benefit ratios, social effectiveness encompasses qualitative and quantitative outcomes related to the satisfaction of human needs, improvement of quality of life, and strengthening of social cohesion (Terziev, 2019). In the digital era, this concept is increasingly linked to the capacity of welfare systems to utilize technological innovations to deliver inclusive and evidence-based policies.

Bulgaria provides a compelling case for examining the intersection between social policy effectiveness and digital transformation. Since the transition to a market economy and subsequent accession to the European Union, the country has undertaken significant reforms aimed at aligning its social protection system with European standards. These reforms include the modernization of institutional structures, the expansion of community-based social services, and the gradual introduction of electronic governance and integrated information systems. Despite this progress, challenges remain, including regional disparities, limited administrative capacity, and the digital divide affecting vulnerable populations.

The primary aim of this chapter is to analyze contemporary approaches to social policy and assess their effectiveness in Bulgaria, with particular emphasis on the role of digital transformation within the welfare system. The study adopts a systemic and interdisciplinary perspective, enabling a comprehensive understanding of the interactions between social, economic, and technological processes.

To achieve this aim, the following research objectives are formulated:

- To examine the theoretical and conceptual foundations of social policy in the context of digital transformation;
- To analyze the concept and indicators of social effectiveness in digitally enabled welfare systems;
- To evaluate the institutional framework of the social assistance system in Bulgaria;
- To identify the role of digital technologies in enhancing the effectiveness and accessibility of social services;
- To propose strategic recommendations for the modernization of welfare systems in line with European and global trends.

The methodological framework of the study combines qualitative and analytical approaches, including systemic analysis, comparative methods, interdisciplinary research, and the examination of legislative documents, policy strategies, and statistical data. This methodological diversity ensures a high level of scientific validity and reliability of the findings.

The scientific contribution of the chapter lies in integrating the concept of social effectiveness with the processes of digital transformation in welfare systems. Furthermore, the study offers a comprehensive institutional analysis of the Bulgarian social assistance system and formulates evidence-based policy recommendations for its modernization. The practical significance of the research is reflected in its potential to support policymakers, practitioners, and scholars in designing more efficient, inclusive, and sustainable social policies.

The chapter is structured into several logically interconnected sections. Following the introduction, the theoretical foundations of social policy and digital welfare transformation are presented. Subsequent sections analyze social effectiveness as a criterion for policy evaluation, examine the institutional framework of social assistance in Bulgaria, and discuss the implications of digitalization for social policy development. The chapter concludes with key findings and strategic recommendations.

This research positions the Bulgarian experience within the broader global discourse on resilient public management by illustrating how institutional adaptation and technological integration contribute to the creation of public value. The analysis emphasizes that digital transformation represents a strategic shift toward anticipatory governance, enabling welfare systems to remain robust and responsive in an era of global uncertainty and rapid socio-economic change. Through this lens, the Bulgarian case serves as a relevant example of how emerging digital models can be leveraged to build more resilient and inclusive public institutions, providing insights applicable to both national and international contexts.

BACKGROUND

Theoretical Foundations Of Social Policy And Digital Transformation Of Welfare Systems

Social policy constitutes a fundamental component of public governance, encompassing a comprehensive system of principles, institutions, and policy instruments aimed at ensuring social protection, promoting equity, and enhancing the overall well-being of citizens. Traditionally, it has been conceptualized as a set of deliberate interventions undertaken by the state to address social risks such as unemployment, poverty, disability, illness, and old age. These interventions play a pivotal role in maintaining social cohesion and supporting sustainable economic development, reflecting the broader societal commitment to solidarity and social justice (Titmuss, 1974).

The evolution of social policy is closely intertwined with the historical development of the welfare state. Early forms of social protection were predominantly based on charitable initiatives and mutual aid mechanisms; however, the socio-economic transformations associated with industrialization and urbanization necessitated the establishment of institutionalized systems of social security. The Bismarckian model of social insurance and the Beveridgean universalist approach laid the foundations of modern welfare states, each embodying distinct principles of redistribution and solidarity (Briggs, 1961). Esping-Andersen's (1990) influential typology of welfare regimes, including liberal, conservative-corporatist, and social democratic, continues to provide an essential analytical framework for understanding variations in social policy across countries. In contemporary contexts, particularly within post-socialist societies such as Bulgaria, welfare systems often display hybrid characteristics shaped by historical legacies, institutional transformations, and processes of European integration.

In recent decades, the conceptualization of social policy has undergone a significant paradigm shift from compensatory and redistributive approaches toward the notion of social investment. This perspective emphasizes the development of human capital through education, employment, and lifelong learning as key drivers of long-term social and economic prosperity. By framing social policy as a productive factor rather than merely a redistributive mechanism, the social investment paradigm highlights its strategic role in fostering sustainable development and societal resilience (Hemerijck, 2013).

Parallel to these theoretical developments, the rapid advancement of information and communication technologies has profoundly transformed the functioning of welfare systems worldwide. Digital transformation has emerged as a central element in the modernization of public administration and social service delivery. In this context, digital transformation should not be understood solely as the digitization of existing administrative procedures but rather as a comprehensive restructuring of institutional processes, governance models, and interactions between stakeholders. In the framework of resilient public management, digital transformation serves as a critical enabler of institutional adaptability. By integrating real-time data and automated processes, welfare systems transition from static bureaucratic structures into dynamic networks capable of maintaining social stability during periods of volatility. The concept of Digital-Era Governance underscores the potential of digital technologies to reintegrate public services, promote needs-based holism, and enhance the efficiency and responsiveness of governmental institutions (Dunleavy et al., 2006; Margetts & Dunleavy, 2013).

The integration of digital technologies into welfare systems has enabled the development of more accessible, transparent, and citizen-centered social services. E-government platforms facilitate online access to social assistance, while integrated information systems enhance coordination among institutions and support evidence-based policymaking. Moreover, the use of big data analytics and artificial intelligence provides opportunities for predictive and personalized service delivery, thereby improving the targeting and effectiveness of social interventions. These technological advancements contribute to the emergence of what is increasingly referred to as "digital welfare states", characterized by enhanced administrative capacity and improved service quality (Organisation for Economic Co-operation and Development [OECD], 2023).

Despite these benefits, the digital transformation of welfare systems also presents significant challenges, particularly in relation to the digital divide. Unequal access to digital infrastructure and disparities in digital literacy may limit the ability of vulnerable populations to benefit from technologically mediated services, potentially exacerbating existing social inequalities. Consequently, ensuring digital inclusion has become a critical prerequisite for maximizing the social effectiveness of digital welfare systems (United Nations, 2022).

Within the European Union, digitalization is recognized as a strategic priority for the modernization of welfare states. Policy initiatives such as the European Pillar of Social Rights and the Digital Economy and Society Index (DESI) provide a comprehensive framework for integrating digital technologies into social policy and for assessing the progress of member states in this domain (European Commission, 2023, 2024). These initiatives emphasize the importance of interoperability, transparency, and citizen-centered service delivery as essential components of effective and sustainable social systems.

The concept of social effectiveness occupies a central position in the evaluation of social policies, extending beyond traditional notions of economic efficiency based on cost-benefit considerations. Social effectiveness encompasses the broader societal outcomes of policy interventions, including improvements in quality of life, social cohesion, equity, and institutional trust (Terziev, 2019). In the context of digital transformation, this concept is increasingly associated with the capacity of welfare systems to leverage technological innovations to enhance accessibility, reduce administrative burdens, and support evidence-based decision-making.

Various analytical models have been developed to assess the effectiveness of social policies within digitally enabled welfare systems. Approaches such as cost-benefit analysis, cost-effectiveness analysis, the logic model, and the Social Return on Investment (SROI) framework provide valuable tools for evaluating both the economic and social impacts of policy interventions (Nicholls et al., 2012). These models enable a comprehensive understanding of how digital innovations contribute to improved policy outcomes and long-term societal benefits.

Bulgaria offers a particularly relevant context for examining the interaction between social policy effectiveness and digital transformation. Since its transition to a market economy and subsequent accession to the European Union, the country has undertaken substantial reforms aimed at modernizing its social protection system and aligning it with European standards. These reforms include the expansion of community-based social services, the development of e-government initiatives, and the implementation of integrated information systems designed to enhance administrative coordination and service accessibility. Nevertheless, challenges persist, including regional disparities in digital infrastructure, limited digital literacy among vulnerable groups, and the need for strengthened institutional cooperation.

In summary, the theoretical foundations of social policy and the ongoing processes of digital transformation are deeply interconnected. The integration of technological innovations into welfare systems not only enhances administrative efficiency but also contributes to the broader objectives of social inclusion and sustainable development. Understanding this interrelationship is essential for assessing the effectiveness of contemporary social policies and for formulating strategic recommendations aimed at the modernization of welfare systems in Bulgaria and beyond.

Institutional Framework and Digitalization of Social Assistance in Bulgaria

The social assistance system in Bulgaria represents a complex network of institutions, legislative mechanisms, and policy instruments aimed at ensuring social protection and supporting vulnerable groups within society. As a fundamental component of the national social policy framework, this system seeks to guarantee a minimum standard of living, prevent social exclusion, and promote the social integration of individuals and families in need. Its development has been strongly influenced by the country's socio-economic transformation following the transition to a market economy and its subsequent accession to the European Union, which necessitated the alignment of national policies with European standards and best practices (Terziev et al., 2025).

The institutional architecture of social assistance in Bulgaria is characterized by a multi-level governance structure involving central government institutions, regional and local authorities, and non-governmental organizations. At the core of this framework stands the Ministry of Labour and Social Policy (MLSP), which is responsible for the formulation and implementation of national social policies, the development of strategic documents, and the coordination of institutional activities within the social sector. The ministry plays a pivotal role in ensuring compliance with European policy frameworks, including the European Pillar of Social Rights, and in guiding the modernization of social protection mechanisms.

The Agency for Social Assistance (ASA) serves as the principal executive body responsible for administering social benefits and services. Through its territorial directorates, the agency conducts needs assessments, determines eligibility for social support, and coordinates the provision of community-based services. Complementing its activities, the Employment Agency implements active labour market policies designed to enhance employability and facilitate the social integration of unemployed individuals. The National Social Security Institute (NSSI) administers the public social insurance system, including pensions and various social benefits, thereby contributing to the overall coherence of social protection.

Local authorities also play a crucial role in the planning and delivery of social services, particularly in the context of decentralization reforms that have enabled municipalities to tailor services to the specific needs of their communities. In addition, non-governmental organizations and social enterprises contribute significantly to the diversification and innovation of social service provision, often addressing the needs of specific vulnerable groups and fostering community engagement.

The legislative framework governing social assistance in Bulgaria is comprehensive and reflects the country's commitment to ensuring social protection and inclusion. Key legal instruments include the Social Assistance Act, the Social Services Act, the Employment Promotion Act, the Child Protection Act, and the Social Security Code. These regulatory frameworks establish the principles, conditions, and procedures for the provision of social support and ensure the harmonization of national legislation with European standards.

In recent years, the Bulgarian social assistance system has undergone significant transformation driven by the increasing integration of digital technologies. Digitalization has emerged as a central element in enhancing the efficiency, transparency, and accessibility of social services. The development of e-government initiatives has enabled citizens to access information and submit applications for social benefits electronically, thereby reducing administrative burdens and processing times (Margetts & Dunleavy, 2013). Integrated information systems facilitate data exchange among institutions, improving coordination and enabling more effective monitoring and evaluation of social programs (Vassil, 2016). Furthermore, the integration of these systems is a prerequisite for institutional resilience, as it allows for a rapid administrative response during socio-economic shocks. By ensuring seamless data flow between the Ministry of Labour and Social Policy, the Agency for Social Assistance, and local authorities, the system can more effectively target resources and maintain continuity of support in volatile environments.

The introduction of digital platforms has also supported the transition from institutional to community-based care, particularly within the process of deinstitutionalization. Digital tools enable better case management, individualized service planning, and real-time communication among stakeholders, contributing to more responsive and person-centered service delivery. Furthermore, the use of digital technologies enhances transparency and accountability, strengthening public trust in social institutions.

Despite these advancements, several challenges continue to affect the digital transformation of social assistance in Bulgaria. Regional disparities in digital infrastructure and access to high-speed internet create unequal opportunities for citizens to benefit from online services (European Commission, 2024; Organization for Economic Co-operation and Development [OECD], 2021). Additionally, limited digital literacy among vulnerable populations, including elderly individuals and persons with disabilities, may hinder the effective utilization of digital platforms. Institutional fragmentation and the need for greater interoperability among information systems also remain significant obstacles to the full realization of a digitally integrated welfare system.

Addressing these challenges requires a comprehensive and strategic approach that combines technological innovation with capacity building and policy coordination. Investments in digital infrastructure, training programs for social workers, and initiatives aimed at enhancing digital inclusion are essential for maximizing the benefits of digital transformation. Moreover, the adoption of data-driven and evidence-based policymaking can significantly improve the effectiveness and sustainability of social interventions (Terziev, 2019). The systematic analysis of these social processes and their academic conceptualization further underscores the necessity of integrating innovative strategies with educational perspectives (Georgiev & Simeonov, 2025).

Bulgaria's experience illustrates both the opportunities and the complexities associated with the transition toward a digitally enabled welfare state. The ongoing modernization of institutional structures and service delivery mechanisms demonstrates the potential of digital technologies to enhance social policy effectiveness, while also highlighting the importance of ensuring inclusiveness and equity in the digital era (European Commission, 2021).

MAIN FOCUS OF THE CHAPTER

Social Effectiveness in Digitally Enabled Welfare Systems

Social effectiveness occupies a central position in the evaluation of contemporary social policies, serving as a multidimensional criterion that reflects the extent to which welfare systems achieve socially significant outcomes. Unlike traditional notions of economic efficiency, which primarily emphasize the relationship between costs and outputs, social effectiveness encompasses broader qualitative and quantitative dimensions, including improvements in quality of life, social inclusion, equity, and institutional trust. This broader understanding allows for a more comprehensive assessment of the societal impact of policy interventions and aligns with the evolving objectives of modern welfare states.

The integration of digital technologies into welfare systems has significantly reshaped the conceptualization and measurement of social effectiveness. Digital transformation enhances the capacity of public institutions to deliver services more efficiently, transparently, and responsively, thereby strengthening the overall performance of social policies. Through the use of e-government platforms, integrated information systems, and data-driven decision-making processes, digitally enabled welfare systems are better equipped to address the complex and dynamic needs of contemporary societies.

One of the most significant contributions of digitalization to social effectiveness is the improvement of accessibility to social services. Online application systems and digital communication channels reduce administrative barriers and enable beneficiaries to access support regardless of geographical location. This is particularly important for individuals living in remote or underserved regions, where traditional service delivery mechanisms may be limited. Furthermore, digital platforms facilitate faster processing of applications and more efficient allocation of resources, thereby enhancing the timeliness and adequacy of social assistance.

Another critical dimension of social effectiveness in the digital era is transparency and accountability. The implementation of digital information systems allows for improved monitoring and evaluation of social programs, enabling policymakers to track outcomes in real time and to identify areas requiring intervention. Enhanced data availability supports evidence-based policymaking and fosters greater public trust in social institutions. In this context, digital technologies contribute not only to administrative efficiency but also to the legitimacy and credibility of welfare systems.

Digital transformation also strengthens institutional coordination, a key determinant of social policy effectiveness. Integrated databases and interoperable information systems facilitate collaboration among various stakeholders, including social assistance agencies, employment services, healthcare providers, and local authorities. Such coordination ensures a more holistic approach to addressing social risks and enables the delivery of personalized and needs-based services. Consequently, beneficiaries receive more comprehensive support, which enhances the overall impact of social interventions.

Despite these advantages, the relationship between digitalization and social effectiveness is not without challenges. The digital divide remains a significant barrier, potentially exacerbating existing social inequalities if vulnerable groups lack access to digital infrastructure or the necessary skills to utilize online services. Elderly individuals, persons with disabilities, and residents of rural areas may face difficulties in engaging with digital platforms, thereby limiting the inclusiveness of digitally enabled welfare systems. Addressing these disparities requires targeted policies aimed at promoting digital literacy, expanding infrastructure, and ensuring the accessibility of digital services.

The evaluation of social effectiveness in digitally transformed welfare systems necessitates the use of comprehensive analytical frameworks. Traditional methods such as cost-benefit analysis and cost-effectiveness analysis remain relevant but must be complemented by approaches that capture the broader social value generated by digital innovations. The Logic Model, which links inputs, activities, outputs, outcomes, and impacts, provides a structured framework for understanding the causal relationships underlying policy interventions. Similarly, the Social Return on Investment (SROI) methodology enables the quantification of social value, incorporating economic, social, and environmental dimensions of policy outcomes.

In addition to these models, contemporary research increasingly emphasizes the importance of performance indicators tailored to digitally enabled welfare systems. Quantitative indicators may include processing times for applications, coverage rates of digital services, reductions in administrative costs, and improvements in employment or poverty levels. Qualitative indicators, such as beneficiary satisfaction, perceived accessibility, and institutional trust, provide valuable insights into the experiential aspects of social policy effectiveness. Together, these indicators enable a holistic assessment of the impact of digital transformation on welfare systems.

The Bulgarian context offers a compelling illustration of the opportunities and challenges associated with enhancing social effectiveness through digitalization. In recent years, the country has undertaken significant efforts to modernize its social assistance system by introducing electronic services, developing integrated information systems, and aligning national policies with European digital and social agendas. These initiatives have contributed to improved administrative efficiency and greater accessibility of services. However, persistent regional disparities in digital infrastructure and varying levels of digital literacy among the population continue to pose challenges to the full realization of social effectiveness.

From a strategic perspective, the successful enhancement of social effectiveness in digitally enabled welfare systems requires a comprehensive and integrated approach. Policymakers must ensure not only the technological modernization of social services but also the development of supportive institutional and regulatory frameworks. Investments in human capital, particularly in the training of social workers and public administrators, are essential for maximizing the benefits of digital transformation. Moreover, the adoption of inclusive design principles and user-centered approaches can help ensure that digital services are accessible to all segments of society.

Social effectiveness in the context of digitally enabled welfare systems represents a dynamic and multifaceted concept that reflects the evolving nature of social policy in the digital age. The integration of digital technologies offers significant opportunities for enhancing the accessibility, transparency, and coordination of social services, thereby strengthening their overall impact on societal well-being. At the same time, addressing the challenges associated with digital inequality and institutional capacity remains essential for ensuring that the benefits of digital transformation are equitably distributed. The Bulgarian experience demonstrates the potential of digitalization to support more effective and inclusive social policies, while also highlighting the importance of strategic planning and continuous evaluation in the pursuit of sustainable welfare systems.

Conceptual Framework of Social Effectiveness in Digitally Enabled Welfare Systems

The concept of social effectiveness has emerged as a central analytical dimension in the evaluation of contemporary social policies, particularly in the context of the ongoing digital transformation of welfare systems. While traditional assessments of policy performance have largely focused on economic efficiency, emphasizing cost-benefit relationships and resource optimization, social effectiveness encompasses a broader set of societal outcomes related to equity, accessibility, inclusion, and improvements in quality of life.

Social effectiveness refers to the extent to which social policies achieve their intended social objectives and contribute to the well-being of individuals and communities. It integrates both quantitative and qualitative dimensions, including the adequacy of social protection, the accessibility of services, the degree of social inclusion, and the level of public trust in institutions. In this sense, social effectiveness represents a multidimensional construct that reflects the societal value generated by policy interventions beyond purely economic considerations (Terziev, 2019; Hemerijck, 2013).

In the digital era, the assessment of social effectiveness requires the incorporation of technological and institutional factors that influence the design and delivery of social services. Digital transformation has fundamentally reshaped welfare systems by enabling more efficient administrative processes, enhancing transparency, and facilitating data-driven decision-making. The integration of e-government platforms, interoperable information systems, and advanced analytical tools allows for more responsive and citizen-centered service provision, thereby strengthening the overall effectiveness of social policies (Dunleavy et al., 2006; Margetts & Dunleavy, 2013).

A key dimension of social effectiveness in digitally enabled welfare systems is accessibility. Digital technologies reduce geographical and administrative barriers, allowing beneficiaries to access social services more easily and efficiently. Online application systems, electronic communication channels, and integrated service platforms contribute to expanding the reach of social protection, particularly for individuals residing in remote or underserved areas.

Another important dimension is efficiency, which reflects the capacity of digital systems to streamline administrative procedures and optimize resource allocation. Automation and data integration reduce processing times and administrative costs, enabling public institutions to deliver services more effectively. However, efficiency must be balanced with considerations of equity to ensure that technological advancements do not inadvertently exclude vulnerable populations.

Transparency and accountability also constitute essential components of social effectiveness. Digital information systems facilitate real-time monitoring and evaluation of social programs, enhancing institutional oversight and reducing opportunities for fraud and mismanagement. Increased transparency strengthens public trust in social institutions, which is a critical factor for the legitimacy and sustainability of welfare systems.

Furthermore, social inclusion represents a fundamental dimension of social effectiveness. While digital transformation offers significant opportunities for expanding access to services, it may also exacerbate existing inequalities if disparities in digital skills and infrastructure are not adequately addressed. Ensuring digital inclusion through targeted policies, digital literacy programs, and accessible service design is therefore essential for maximizing the societal benefits of digital welfare systems (Van Dijk, 2020).

Institutional coordination is another key determinant of social effectiveness. The interoperability of information systems among social assistance agencies, employment services, healthcare providers, and local authorities enables a holistic approach to addressing complex social needs. Such coordination facilitates the delivery of integrated and personalized services, enhancing the overall impact of social policy interventions.

In addition to these dimensions, social effectiveness is closely linked to the long-term sustainability of welfare systems. Digitally enabled governance supports evidence-based policymaking and strategic planning, allowing governments to anticipate social risks and allocate resources more effectively. This forward-looking approach contributes to the resilience and adaptability of welfare systems in the face of demographic, economic, and technological changes.

From a methodological perspective, the evaluation of social effectiveness in digital welfare systems can be supported by various analytical frameworks, including cost-benefit analysis, cost-effectiveness analysis, the logic model, and the Social Return on Investment (SROI) approach (Nicholls et al., 2012).

The conceptualization of social effectiveness is particularly relevant given the ongoing modernization of the social assistance system and the increasing integration of digital technologies. National reforms aimed at enhancing e-government services and institutional interoperability have created new opportunities for improving the accessibility and quality of social services. Nevertheless, challenges such as regional disparities in digital infrastructure, limited digital literacy among vulnerable groups, and the need for strengthened institutional coordination continue to influence the overall effectiveness of social policies.

The conceptual framework of social effectiveness in digitally enabled welfare systems encompasses multiple interrelated dimensions, including accessibility, efficiency, transparency, social inclusion, institutional coordination, and sustainability. This multidimensional perspective provides a comprehensive foundation for analyzing the impact of digital transformation on social policy and serves as a basis for the development of the conceptual model presented in the subsequent section.

Conceptual Model of Social Effectiveness in Digital Welfare Systems

To integrate the theoretical insights and empirical observations presented in this chapter, a conceptual model of social effectiveness in digitally enabled welfare systems is proposed. Rather than being limited to a purely visual representation, the model is articulated through a narrative framework that captures the dynamic and interrelated processes shaping the effectiveness of contemporary social policies in the digital era.

The conceptual model is grounded in a systemic perspective, emphasizing the sequential and mutually reinforcing relationships between technological, institutional, and societal dimensions. It illustrates how digital transformation acts as a catalyst that influences not only administrative efficiency but also broader social outcomes, ultimately contributing to sustainable welfare development.

The first component of the model concerns the inputs, which represent the foundational conditions necessary for the successful digital transformation of welfare systems. These inputs include the availability of robust digital infrastructure, such as broadband connectivity and secure information systems, as well as an enabling legislative and regulatory framework that supports the digitalization of public services. Equally important are institutional capacity and human resources, particularly the competencies of social workers and public administrators in utilizing digital tools. Financial investments, often supported by European funding mechanisms, and effective data governance and cybersecurity measures further strengthen the foundation upon which digital welfare systems are built.

Building upon these inputs, the model highlights a set of processes that translate foundational resources into operational practices. These processes encompass the implementation of e-government services, the integration and interoperability of information systems across institutions, and the adoption of data-driven decision-making mechanisms. Inter-institutional coordination plays a critical role in ensuring that social services are delivered in a coherent and holistic manner, while user-centered service design ensures that digital platforms remain accessible and responsive to the needs of beneficiaries. Together, these processes represent the operational core of digitally enabled welfare systems.

The immediate results of these processes are reflected in the outputs of the model. Digital transformation leads to measurable improvements in administrative efficiency, such as reduced processing times for social assistance applications and an increased number of beneficiaries served. It also enhances transparency and accountability by enabling better monitoring and evaluation of social programs. Furthermore, the expansion of online social services increases the availability and convenience of welfare support, thereby improving the overall performance of social policy implementation.

Beyond these direct outputs, the model emphasizes a set of outcomes that capture the broader societal effects of digital transformation. These outcomes include improved accessibility to social services, greater social inclusion of vulnerable populations, increased beneficiary satisfaction, and strengthened institutional trust. By facilitating more equitable and responsive, and anticipatory service delivery, digitally enabled welfare systems contribute to the enhancement of social policy effectiveness and the promotion of inclusive governance.

The model culminates in a series of long-term impacts, which represent the ultimate objectives of digital transformation within welfare systems. These impacts encompass the strengthening of social cohesion and equity, the development of sustainable and resilient welfare systems, and the improvement of overall quality of life. Additionally, the alignment of national social policies with European and global frameworks - such as the European Pillar of Social Rights and the United Nations Sustainable Development Goals - underscores the strategic significance of digital transformation in achieving broader societal progress.

An important feature of the proposed conceptual model is the presence of feedback mechanisms that connect outcomes and impacts back to the earlier stages of the system. Continuous monitoring and evaluation, supported by digital technologies, enable policymakers to refine institutional processes and resource allocation. This iterative dynamic ensures the adaptability and long-term sustainability of welfare systems in an ever-evolving technological and social environment.

The conceptual model provides a comprehensive analytical framework for understanding how digital transformation can enhance the effectiveness of social policy. While significant progress has been made in the development of e-government services and integrated information systems, the model also highlights the importance of addressing challenges such as regional disparities in digital infrastructure, limited digital literacy among vulnerable groups, and the need for stronger institutional coordination. By situating the Bulgarian experience within this broader conceptual framework, the study offers valuable insights for policymakers and researchers seeking to promote inclusive and sustainable digital welfare systems.

The proposed conceptual model contributes to the academic discourse by offering a holistic and integrative perspective on social effectiveness in the digital age. It bridges the gap between technological innovation and social policy outcomes, providing a structured framework that can be applied in both national and comparative research contexts. The narrative representation of the model enhances its accessibility and applicability, making it a valuable tool for guiding future research and policy development .

Figure 1 illustrates the sequential relationship between digital transformation and social policy effectiveness, progressing from foundational inputs and institutional processes to measurable outputs, societal outcomes, and long-term impacts. The model emphasizes the systemic and integrated nature of digitally enabled welfare systems and their capacity to maintain institutional resilience through continuous feedback loops.

Figure 1. Conceptual model of social effectiveness in digital welfare systems

Source: Developed by the author

Comparative Analysis of Digital Welfare Systems in the European Union

The digital transformation of welfare systems has become a defining feature of social policy development across the European Union. As member states strive to modernize public administration and enhance the effectiveness of social protection, digital technologies play a crucial role in improving accessibility, efficiency, and institutional coordination. A comparative analysis of digital welfare systems provides valuable insights into best practices and policy innovations, enabling the identification of transferable lessons for countries such as Bulgaria.

European countries exhibit varying levels of digital maturity, shaped by differences in institutional capacity, technological infrastructure, and policy priorities. Indicators such as the Digital Economy and Society Index (DESI) and the United Nations E-Government Development Index (EGDI) offer comprehensive frameworks for assessing national progress in digital governance. These indices evaluate dimensions including connectivity, digital public services, human capital, and the integration of digital technologies, thereby facilitating cross-country comparisons.

Among EU member states, Estonia is widely recognized as a global leader in digital governance. Its e-government ecosystem is built upon a highly interoperable infrastructure that enables seamless data exchange among public institutions. The X-Road platform allows citizens to access a wide range of social services online, including social benefits, healthcare, and employment support. This integrated approach significantly reduces administrative burdens and enhances transparency, serving as a benchmark for other countries seeking to modernize their welfare systems.

Finland represents another exemplary model, characterized by a strong emphasis on user-centered digital services and social inclusion. The Finnish welfare system integrates digital platforms with proactive social policies, enabling early identification of social risks and personalized service delivery. High levels of digital literacy and institutional trust further contribute to the effectiveness of these initiatives.

In the Netherlands, digital transformation is closely linked to data-driven governance and inter-institutional collaboration. The Dutch system emphasizes the use of integrated databases to improve the targeting of social benefits and to support evidence-based policymaking. However, the country's experience also highlights the importance of ethical considerations and data protection, particularly in light of the well-known childcare benefits scandal, which underscored the risks associated with algorithmic decision-making.

Germany, while possessing a robust social protection system, has adopted a more gradual approach to digitalization due to its federal administrative structure. Nevertheless, significant progress has been achieved through initiatives aimed at enhancing interoperability and expanding online access to social services. Germany's experience demonstrates that institutional complexity can influence the pace of digital transformation, emphasizing the need for coordinated governance mechanisms.

In comparison to these countries, Bulgaria has made notable progress in the digitalization of its social assistance system, particularly through the development of e-government services and integrated information systems. However, the country continues to face challenges related to digital infrastructure, regional disparities, and varying levels of digital literacy. According to recent DESI assessments, Bulgaria ranks below the EU average in several dimensions of digital development, indicating the need for continued investment and policy reform. Bridging the gap between Bulgaria and the EU digital leaders is not merely a matter of infrastructure, but a strategic necessity for building a resilient public administration capable of maintaining social protection standards during cross-border crises.

The comparative perspective reveals several key factors that contribute to the successful digital transformation of welfare systems. First, institutional interoperability is essential for ensuring seamless coordination among public agencies. Second, user-centered service design enhances accessibility and satisfaction among beneficiaries. Third, digital literacy and public trust play a critical role in facilitating the adoption of digital services. Fourth, robust data protection and ethical governance frameworks are necessary to safeguard citizens' rights and maintain institutional legitimacy.

These findings offer valuable lessons for Bulgaria and other countries undergoing similar transitions. By adopting best practices from leading EU member states, policymakers can strengthen the effectiveness and inclusiveness of national welfare systems. At the same time, the comparative analysis underscores the importance of adapting international experiences to the specific socio-economic and institutional contexts of individual countries.

The comparative analysis of digital welfare systems within the European Union highlights both the diversity of national approaches and the common strategic objectives guiding their development. The experiences of Estonia, Finland, the Netherlands, and Germany demonstrate that successful digital transformation requires a holistic and integrated approach that combines technological innovation with institutional reform and social inclusion. For Bulgaria, leveraging these lessons can significantly enhance the effectiveness and sustainability of its welfare system in the digital age.

SOLUTIONS AND RECOMMENDATIONS

The analysis presented in this chapter highlights the growing interdependence between social policy effectiveness and the digital transformation of welfare systems. The integration of digital technologies into social assistance mechanisms has not only enhanced administrative efficiency but has also reshaped the conceptual and operational foundations of contemporary welfare states. In this context, digitalization emerges as a strategic enabler of more inclusive, transparent, and responsive social policies.

The findings underscore that the effectiveness of social policy can no longer be assessed solely through traditional economic indicators. Instead, it requires a multidimensional perspective that incorporates accessibility, equity, institutional coordination, and user satisfaction. Digital transformation contributes significantly to these dimensions by facilitating faster service delivery, improving data management, and enabling evidence-based decision-making. The Bulgarian case illustrates how the modernization of institutional structures and the implementation of electronic services can strengthen the capacity of welfare systems to respond to complex social needs.

One of the central insights of the study is the role of integrated governance in enhancing social policy outcomes. The interoperability of information systems among institutions such as the Ministry of Labour and Social Policy, the Agency for Social Assistance, the National Social Security Institute, and the Employment Agency enables a more holistic and coordinated approach to social protection. This integration reduces administrative fragmentation and supports the development of personalized and needs-based services, thereby increasing the overall social effectiveness of policy interventions.

At the same time, the analysis reveals that digital transformation is not merely a technological process but also an institutional and societal one. Successful implementation depends on the alignment of legal frameworks, organizational capacities, and human resources. The transition toward digitally enabled welfare systems necessitates significant investments in administrative capacity, including the training of social workers and public officials to effectively utilize digital tools. Without such investments, the potential benefits of digitalization may remain underutilized.

Another critical issue highlighted in the discussion is the persistence of the digital divide, which poses a significant challenge to the inclusiveness of digital welfare systems. Vulnerable groups - such as elderly individuals, persons with disabilities, residents of rural areas, and those with limited digital skills - may encounter barriers in accessing online services. Consequently, digital transformation must be accompanied by targeted measures aimed at promoting digital inclusion, including the development of accessible user interfaces, community-based support services, and digital literacy programs.

From a policy perspective, several strategic implications emerge. First, governments should prioritize the development of interoperable and integrated information systems that enable seamless data exchange among institutions. Such systems are essential for improving coordination, reducing duplication of efforts, and enhancing the accuracy of beneficiary targeting. Second, the adoption of data-driven and evidence-based policymaking should be encouraged, as the availability of real-time data allows for more effective monitoring and evaluation of social programs.

Third, policymakers should ensure that digital transformation is guided by principles of inclusiveness and equity. This involves addressing infrastructural disparities, particularly in rural and remote areas, and ensuring that digital services are accessible to individuals with diverse needs. The incorporation of universal design principles and multilingual interfaces can further enhance accessibility and user engagement.

Fourth, the establishment of robust data protection and cybersecurity frameworks is essential for maintaining public trust in digital welfare systems. As social assistance programs increasingly rely on the collection and processing of personal data, safeguarding privacy and ensuring compliance with regulations such as the General Data Protection Regulation (GDPR) becomes a critical component of effective governance.

Fifth, fostering cross-sectoral collaboration and stakeholder engagement is vital for the successful implementation of digital welfare reforms. Partnerships between public institutions, private sector actors, academic organizations, and civil society can facilitate innovation and support the co-creation of user-centered social services. Such collaborative approaches contribute to the sustainability and adaptability of welfare systems in a rapidly changing technological environment, thereby serving as a cornerstone of resilient public management in times of crisis.

In addition to these strategic considerations, the study highlights the importance of aligning national policies with broader European and global frameworks. Initiatives such as the European Pillar of Social Rights, the Digital Europe Programme, and the United Nations Sustainable Development Goals (SDGs) provide valuable guidance for the modernization of welfare systems. By aligning national reforms with these frameworks, countries can enhance policy coherence and benefit from shared knowledge and resources.

The Bulgarian experience offers valuable lessons for other countries undergoing similar transitions. While significant progress has been achieved in the digitalization of social services, continued efforts are required to strengthen institutional capacity, improve interoperability, and ensure equitable access to digital technologies. The findings of this chapter therefore contribute not only to the academic discourse on social policy and digital governance but also to the practical development of more effective and inclusive welfare systems.

The discussion emphasizes that digital transformation represents a powerful catalyst for enhancing effectiveness of social policy. However, its success depends on a comprehensive and integrated approach that combines technological innovation with institutional reform and social inclusion. By adopting such an approach, policymakers can ensure that digital welfare systems contribute meaningfully to social cohesion, sustainable development, and the overall well-being of citizens.

FUTURE RESEARCH DIRECTIONS

Technological Innovations in Welfare Systems: Artificial Intelligence, Big Data, and Blockchain

The rapid advancement of digital technologies has significantly reshaped the landscape of welfare systems, enabling governments to enhance the efficiency, responsiveness, and inclusiveness of social policies. Among the most transformative innovations are artificial intelligence (AI), big data analytics, and blockchain technology. These technological developments are redefining the ways in which social services are designed, delivered, and evaluated, contributing to the emergence of more adaptive and data-driven welfare states.

Artificial intelligence has become an increasingly important tool in public administration, offering new opportunities for predictive analytics, automation, and personalized service delivery. In the context of welfare systems, AI can be utilized to identify individuals at risk of social exclusion, forecast unemployment trends, and optimize the allocation of social benefits. Machine learning algorithms enable the analysis of large datasets to detect patterns and support evidence-based decision-making, thereby improving the targeting and effectiveness of social interventions. For example, several European countries have implemented AI-driven systems to streamline eligibility assessments and enhance case management processes. These applications not only reduce administrative burdens but also facilitate more proactive and preventive social policies. This transition toward anticipatory governance, powered by AI, allows welfare systems to identify and mitigate social risks before they escalate into systemic crises.

Big data analytics further complements the capabilities of artificial intelligence by enabling the processing and interpretation of vast amounts of information generated by public institutions. Welfare systems produce extensive administrative data related to employment, health, education, and social assistance. When effectively integrated and analyzed, these datasets can provide valuable insights into social needs and policy outcomes. Big data supports real-time monitoring and evaluation of social programs, allowing policymakers to assess their impact and adjust interventions accordingly. Moreover, data-driven approaches enhance transparency and accountability by enabling more accurate reporting and performance measurement.

Blockchain technology represents another promising innovation with the potential to transform welfare systems. Characterized by its decentralized and immutable ledger, blockchain enhances the security and transparency of transactions, making it particularly suitable for the administration of social benefits. By ensuring the integrity of beneficiary records and reducing the risk of fraud, blockchain can strengthen public trust in social institutions. Additionally, smart contracts can automate the disbursement of social payments based on predefined eligibility criteria, thereby increasing efficiency and reducing administrative costs. Although the adoption of blockchain in the social sector is still at an early stage, pilot projects in several countries demonstrate its potential to improve governance and service delivery.

Despite the significant opportunities offered by these technological innovations, their implementation in welfare systems also raises important ethical, legal, and social considerations. One of the primary concerns relates to algorithmic bias, which may arise when AI systems are trained on incomplete or unrepresentative datasets. Such biases can lead to discriminatory outcomes, particularly for vulnerable groups, thereby undermining the principles of equity and social justice. Ensuring fairness and transparency in algorithmic decision-making is therefore essential for maintaining the legitimacy of digital welfare systems.

Another critical issue involves data protection and privacy. The extensive use of personal data in AI and big data applications necessitates robust regulatory frameworks to safeguard citizens' rights. In the European context, the General Data Protection Regulation (GDPR) provides a comprehensive legal framework for ensuring the ethical and secure processing of personal information. Compliance with these regulations is fundamental for building public trust and ensuring the sustainable adoption of digital technologies in welfare systems.

From an organizational perspective, the successful integration of technological innovations requires substantial investments in digital infrastructure and human capital. Public institutions must develop the necessary technical expertise and institutional capacity to effectively manage and utilize advanced technologies. Training programs for social workers and public administrators are essential for facilitating this transition and for ensuring that technological tools complement, rather than replace, human-centered approaches to social service delivery.

In the Bulgarian context, the adoption of artificial intelligence, big data, and blockchain technologies is gradually emerging as part of broader efforts to modernize public administration and enhance the effectiveness of social policies. While significant progress has been achieved in the digitalization of administrative services, the implementation of advanced technologies remains at an early stage. Nevertheless, ongoing national and European initiatives provide a strong foundation for future development, offering opportunities to leverage technological innovation in support of more inclusive and efficient welfare systems.

Digital Inclusion and Digital Divide: Challenges for Vulnerable Groups

The digital transformation of welfare systems has created unprecedented opportunities for improving the accessibility, efficiency, and responsiveness of social services. However, alongside these benefits, it has also introduced new forms of inequality associated with disparities in access to digital technologies and the skills required to use them effectively. The concepts of digital inclusion and the digital divide have therefore become central to contemporary discussions on the modernization of social policy.

Digital inclusion refers to the ability of all individuals and communities to access and effectively use information and communication technologies (ICT) for participation in social, economic, and civic life. In contrast, the digital divide encompasses the gaps that exist between individuals and groups in terms of access to digital infrastructure, digital literacy, and the capacity to benefit from digital services (Van Dijk, 2020). These disparities can significantly influence the effectiveness of digitally enabled welfare systems, potentially reinforcing existing social inequalities if not adequately addressed.

The digital divide is a multidimensional phenomenon that manifests across several interconnected levels. The first-level digital divide relates to physical access to digital infrastructure, such as broadband internet and digital devices. The second-level digital divide concerns differences in digital skills and competencies required to navigate online environments. The third-level digital divide involves disparities in the outcomes derived from the use of digital technologies, including the ability to leverage digital services for improving socio-economic conditions. Understanding these dimensions is essential for designing inclusive digital welfare policies.

Vulnerable groups are disproportionately affected by digital inequalities. Older adults often face barriers related to limited digital literacy, reduced confidence in using technology, and physical impairments that hinder interaction with digital interfaces. Persons with disabilities may encounter accessibility challenges if digital platforms are not designed according to universal design principles. Unemployed individuals and those with low levels of education may lack both the financial resources and the skills necessary to engage with digital services. Additionally, residents of rural and remote areas frequently experience limited connectivity, while ethnic minorities and migrants may face linguistic and cultural barriers that restrict their access to digital welfare services.

Within the European Union, digital inclusion has become a strategic priority, reflected in policy initiatives such as the European Pillar of Social Rights, the Digital Europe Programme, and the European Skills Agenda. These frameworks emphasize the importance of equitable access to digital technologies and the development of digital competencies as essential components of social cohesion and sustainable development (European Commission, 2023, 2024). Furthermore, the United Nations E-Government Survey highlights the role of inclusive digital governance in achieving the Sustainable Development Goals, particularly those related to reducing inequalities and promoting inclusive institutions (United Nations, 2022).

Significant progress has been made in expanding digital public services; however, challenges related to digital inclusion persist. According to recent European assessments, Bulgaria continues to rank below the EU average in terms of digital skills and connectivity. Regional disparities between urban and rural areas, combined with socio-economic inequalities, contribute to uneven access to digital welfare services. These challenges underscore the necessity of targeted policy interventions aimed at bridging the digital divide.

Addressing digital inequalities requires a comprehensive and multidimensional policy approach. Infrastructure development is a fundamental prerequisite, ensuring universal access to high-speed internet and affordable digital devices. Equally important is the promotion of digital literacy, which can be achieved through educational programs, community training initiatives, and lifelong learning opportunities. Special attention should be given to the training of social workers, who play a critical role in supporting beneficiaries in navigating digital platforms.

Another essential aspect of digital inclusion is the adoption of universal design and accessibility standards. Digital welfare platforms should be designed to accommodate the diverse needs of users, including those with disabilities or limited digital experience. Features such as simplified interfaces, multilingual support, and alternative communication channels can significantly enhance usability and accessibility. Additionally, maintaining hybrid service delivery models, which combine digital and traditional face-to-face interactions, ensures that individuals who are unable or unwilling to use digital technologies are not excluded from social support.

From a governance perspective, fostering institutional collaboration and stakeholder engagement is crucial for promoting digital inclusion. Partnerships between public institutions, non-governmental organizations, educational institutions, and the private sector can facilitate the development of innovative solutions tailored to the needs of vulnerable populations. Community-based initiatives, such as digital support centers and mobile service units, have proven effective in enhancing access to digital welfare services.

While digital transformation offers significant potential for enhancing the effectiveness of welfare systems, its success ultimately depends on the extent to which it promotes social inclusion. Bridging the digital divide is therefore not only a technological challenge but also a social and policy imperative. The Bulgarian experience demonstrates that targeted and coordinated policy efforts can significantly enhance digital inclusion, thereby maximizing the societal benefits of digital transformation.

CONCLUSION

Digital transformation of welfare systems represents one of the most significant developments in contemporary social policy, reshaping the ways in which social services are designed, delivered, and evaluated. This chapter has explored the interrelationship between social policy effectiveness and digitalization, emphasizing how technological innovations can enhance the accessibility, transparency, and responsiveness of social assistance systems. By integrating theoretical perspectives with an empirical analysis of the Bulgarian context, the study contributes to a deeper understanding of the opportunities and challenges associated with the transition toward digitally enabled welfare states.

The analysis began with an examination of the theoretical foundations of social policy, highlighting its evolution from traditional redistributive approaches to more comprehensive social investment strategies. This conceptual shift reflects the growing recognition of social policy as a productive factor that supports sustainable development and social cohesion. The incorporation of digital transformation into this framework further expands the analytical scope of social policy, positioning technology as a key driver of institutional modernization and policy innovation.

A central focus of the chapter was the concept of social effectiveness, understood as a multidimensional criterion encompassing improvements in quality of life, social inclusion, equity, and institutional trust. The findings demonstrate that digital technologies significantly enhance social effectiveness by streamlining administrative processes, enabling data-driven decision-making, and facilitating better coordination among institutions. The use of integrated information systems and e-government platforms allows for more efficient service delivery and more accurate targeting of beneficiaries, thereby increasing the overall impact of social interventions.

The empirical analysis of the Bulgarian social assistance system illustrates both the progress achieved and the challenges that remain in the process of digital transformation. Institutional reforms and the introduction of electronic services have contributed to improved accessibility and efficiency. However, persistent issues such as regional disparities in digital infrastructure, limited digital literacy among vulnerable populations, and the need for greater interoperability among information systems continue to hinder the full realization of a digitally integrated welfare system. These findings underscore the importance of adopting a comprehensive and inclusive approach to digitalization that addresses technological, institutional, and social dimensions.

From a policy perspective, the chapter highlights several strategic implications. First, the development of interoperable and integrated digital infrastructures is essential for enhancing institutional coordination and reducing administrative fragmentation. Second, investments in human capital, particularly in the training of social workers and public administrators, are crucial for maximizing the benefits of digital transformation. Third, ensuring digital inclusion through improved infrastructure and digital literacy initiatives is necessary to prevent the exacerbation of existing social inequalities. Fourth, the establishment of robust data protection and cybersecurity frameworks is fundamental for maintaining public trust in digital welfare systems. Finally, aligning national reforms with European and global policy frameworks, such as the European Pillar of Social Rights and the United Nations Sustainable Development Goals, can strengthen policy coherence and support sustainable development.

The scientific contributions of this chapter are multifaceted. The study advances the conceptualization of social effectiveness by integrating it with the processes of digital transformation in welfare systems. It also provides a comprehensive institutional analysis of the Bulgarian social assistance system, offering insights that are relevant for both national and international audiences. Furthermore, the chapter proposes a set of evidence-based policy recommendations that can inform the modernization of welfare systems in other countries undergoing similar transitions.

Despite its contributions, the study is subject to several limitations. The analysis is primarily based on qualitative and institutional data, which may limit the generalizability of the findings. Future research could benefit from incorporating quantitative methodologies, such as econometric analyses or large-scale surveys, to provide a more robust assessment of the impact of digital transformation on social policy outcomes. Additionally, comparative studies across different national contexts would enhance the understanding of how varying institutional and socio-economic conditions influence the effectiveness of digital welfare systems.

Looking ahead, the continued evolution of digital technologies, including artificial intelligence, big data analytics, and blockchain, offers significant potential for further enhancing the effectiveness and sustainability of social policies. However, the successful integration of these technologies will depend on the ability of policymakers to balance innovation with ethical considerations, data protection, and social inclusion. As welfare systems continue to adapt to the demands of the digital age, ongoing research and interdisciplinary collaboration will be essential for ensuring that technological advancements translate into tangible social benefits.

Digital transformation serves as a powerful catalyst for the modernization of welfare systems and the enhancement of social policy effectiveness. The Bulgarian experience demonstrates that, while significant progress has been achieved, sustained efforts are required to address remaining challenges and to ensure that the benefits of digitalization are equitably distributed. By adopting a strategic and inclusive approach, policymakers can harness the potential of digital technologies to create more resilient, efficient, and socially responsive welfare systems, ensuring that the Bulgarian welfare state remains a robust pillar of stability in an increasingly volatile digital age (Terziev, 2019).

REFERENCES

Briggs, A. (1961). The welfare state in historical perspective. *Archives Européennes de Sociologie*, *2*(2), 221–258. DOI: 10.1017/S0003975600000412

Dunleavy, P., Margetts, H., Bastow, S., & Tinkler, J. (2006). *Digital era governance: IT corporations, the state, and e-government*. Oxford University Press. DOI: 10.1093/acprof:oso/9780199296194.001.0001

Esping-Andersen, G. (1990). *The three worlds of welfare capitalism*. Princeton University Press.

European Commission. (2021). *Proposal for a regulation laying down harmonised rules on artificial intelligence (Artificial Intelligence Act)*. Publications Office of the European Union.

European Commission. (2023). *European pillar of social rights: Social scoreboard*. Publications Office of the European Union.

European Commission. (2024). *Digital economy and society index (DESI) 2024*. Publications Office of the European Union.

Georgiev, M., & Simeonov, S. (2025). Research of social processes in the works of Venelin Terziev. In *Innovation and sustainability in digital era: The role of economics and business strategies with education perspectives* (pp. 425–435). Peter Lang.

Hemerijck, A. (2013). *Changing welfare states*. Oxford University Press.

Margetts, H., & Dunleavy, P. (2013). The second wave of digital-era governance. *Philosophical Transactions of the Royal Society A: Mathematical, Physical and Engineering Sciences, 371*(1987), 20120382. https://doi.org/DOI: 10.1098/rsta.20120382

Midgley, J. (1995). *Social development: The developmental perspective in social welfare*. Sage Publications.

Nicholls, J., Lawlor, E., Neitzert, E., & Goodspeed, T. (2012). *A guide to social return on investment (SROI)*. The SROI Network.

Organisation for Economic Co-operation and Development [OECD]. (2021). *Bridging the digital divide: Inclusive growth in the digital era*. OECD Publishing.

Organisation for Economic Co-operation and Development [OECD]. (2023). *Digital government index 2023: Results and key findings*. OECD Publishing.

Terziev, V. (2019). Social efficiency as a measure of social activities. *IJASOS – International E-Journal of Advances in Social Sciences, 5*(14), 656–662. https://doi.org/DOI: 10.18769/ijasos.592076

Terziev, V., Georgiev, M., & Simeonov, S. (2025). *Transformation and change of the social and educational system*. gabriell-e-lit.

Titmuss, R. M. (1974). *Social policy: An introduction*. George Allen & Unwin.

United Nations. (2022). *United Nations e-government survey 2022: The future of digital government*. United Nations.

Van Dijk, J. (2020). *The digital divide*. Polity Press.

Vassil, K. (2016). Estonian e-government ecosystem: Foundations, applications, and outcomes. *World Development, 84*, 1–15. DOI: 10.1016/j.worlddev.2015.06.001

World Bank. (2022). *Social protection and jobs responses to COVID-19: A real-time review of country measures*. World Bank.

KEY TERMS AND DEFINITIONS

Agency For Social Assistance (ASA): The principal executive body in Bulgaria responsible for administering social benefits, conducting needs assessments, and coordinating community-based services.

Artificial Intelligence (AI): Advanced machine learning algorithms and predictive analytics used in public administration to automate eligibility assessments and identify individuals at risk of social exclusion.

Digital Divide: The multidimensional gap between different social groups regarding their physical access to digital infrastructure, level of digital literacy, and ability to benefit from online services.

Digital Inclusion: The strategic process of ensuring that all individuals, particularly vulnerable groups, have the necessary resources and skills to access and effectively use information and communication technologies.

Digital Transformation: The comprehensive restructuring of institutional processes, governance models, and service delivery through the integration of information and communication technologies to support citizen-centered outcomes.

Digital Welfare State: A modernized model of the welfare state characterized by the use of e-government platforms, integrated information systems, and data-driven approaches to enhance social protection.

Institutional Interoperability: The capacity of different governmental information systems and agencies to exchange data seamlessly and coordinate their activities to provide holistic social services.

Social Effectiveness: A multidimensional evaluation criterion that measures the success of social policies based on qualitative and quantitative outcomes such as quality of life, equity, and social cohesion.

Social Investment Paradigm: A policy framework that focuses on developing human capital through education and employment as a productive factor for long-term economic and social prosperity.

Systemic Approach: A research and management perspective that views the welfare system as a complex network of interrelated social, economic, and technological processes requiring integrated coordination.

Chapter 9
From E-Services to Anticipatory Governance:
Cambodia's Digital Government Pathways for Resilient, Trustworthy, and AI-Enabled Public Management

Sovanna Huot
http://orcid.org/0009-0006-8335-442X
Department of Political Science, University of Delhi, New Delhi, India

Sovannaroth Chheang
http://orcid.org/0009-0007-3382-7169
Department of Education, Sovanna Elton Foreign Language School (SELS), Phnom Penh, Cambodia

ABSTRACT

This chapter explores issues in Cambodia's fragmented e-services and proposes frameworks for resilient, trusted digital governance. It argues that resilient public service ecosystems rely on digital government as a governance change framework and filling governance gaps. Using insights from complex systems, digital governance, AI in public administration, and trust, it presents a six-block framework. The chapter also builds a Cambodia-focused framework based on five core capability areas: digital infrastructure and platforms, interoperability and data stewardship, anticipatory capacity, ethical AI governance, and trust-building networks. The five core capability areas are complemented by five primary enablers: leadership, legal frameworks, sustainable financing, digital skills, and standards and interoperability.

DOI: 10.4018/979-8-3373-9765-8.ch009

The policy road map includes these capabilities in five pillars. In the Global South, it provides an ethical, feasible digital governance model that focuses on public value and enhances digital governance.

INTRODUCTION

Twenty years ago, digital government was viewed as transforming a specific state function. Today, it is considered a fundamental aspect of state functioning. Margetts and Dunleavy (2013) highlight that new digital technologies influence how government activities are managed. The integration of information processing, complexity management, and citizen relations governance shapes modern public administration. Janssen and Van Der Voort (2016) argue that digital government entails more than just automating tasks; it signifies a complete overhaul of institutional structures and processes, including coordination, decision-making, and accountability. According to Cordella and Bonina (2012), digital structures embody the values and beliefs that guide government-citizen relations and the state's public values. Digital government serves as a tool for the state to navigate an increasingly volatile environment marked by unpredictable risks and threats, as well as a more demanding and frustrated citizenry. From Meijer and Bolívar's (2016) perspective, the digital order entails reconfiguring information structures and problem definitions. In contrast, Klievink et al. (2012) argue that digital systems and infrastructures create new relationships that enhance the state's resilience and adaptability.

The Cambodian government's Digital Economy and Society Policy 2021-2035 and Digital Government Policy 2022-2035 aim to position the country globally by leveraging technology for infrastructure, data protection, trust, and growth. Digital services improve public services and transparency through data networks, centres, and digital IDs. While expanding citizen services, public management stays resilient when services are robust and adaptable. The government strives to build resilience via data management and decision-making, integrating foresight, early warning, and anticipatory governance to foster a learning, adaptive system. Cambodia sees links among data governance, interoperability, platforms, cybersecurity, and data-centricity (Royal Government of Cambodia, 2022). Capacity building in data governance focuses on stewardship and data security (OECD Korea Policy Centre, 2023). Divides, data literacy, and privacy concerns accompany rapid digital adoption. As Huot (2026) observed, platform infrastructures may enhance state capacity and may serve a governance function; without governance, platforms are likely to be used for state-level surveillance (Van Zoonen, 2016). Trust and legitimacy are the pillars of developing digital government in the country and of fairness, reliability, and accountability. Trust is predicated on the quality of services and on the justice of legal processes (Bouckaert & Van de Walle, 2003). Digital government reforms strengthen legitimacy by expanding services and deepening civic engagement (Dunlop & Radaelli, 2018). This is part of a trust–technology paradox. Digital innovations build trust, yet skepticism about privacy and the politicization of digital tools remains, especially in Cambodia's regulatory environment (Prasodjo, 2026).

Key challenges remain despite progress. Digital government emphasizes efficiency but often neglects people-centered design and views transformation as only technical. Limited complexity science use hampers pandemic and cyber threat responses, while absent foresight tools weaken resilience. Trust relies on fairness, quality, and transparency, but privacy risks may worsen inequalities. In Cambodia, inconsistent standards and poor interoperability fragment digital services. Crippling limitations on systems increase structural problems. Some assessments indicate that Cambodia requires not only physical systems but also the infrastructural skills in data management, data protection and safety, legal analysis, and change management (OECD Korea Policy Centre, 2023). Digital Government documents point to leadership and teamwork, but there are gaps in incentives and skills. Janssen et al. (2012) say that using advanced analytics or AI without sufficient safeguards creates gaps. Coupled with Cybersecurity and AI threats, the situation has worsened. The Policy identifies safe, secure, and reliable infrastructure and security management, paired with a recovery plan, as the basis for reliable digital services (Royal Government of Cambodia, 2022). Even with these measures, trust will not be achieved. It is said that the 'resilience traps' are strong, increasing systems' reliance amid a lack of security, governance, and accountability (Raieste et al., 2024). This is an even bigger challenge for Cambodia, given the rapid growth of digital technologies and uneven institutional preparedness.

This research aims to examine the capabilities and boundaries of Cambodia's digital government transformation within a resilience-based governance framework. This research focuses on the public interoperability, digital governance, anticipatory, and resilient dimensions of Cambodia's digital governance. Among other things, this research considers gaps in digital literacy, access, and privacy, as well as the fragmented nature of services and weak response and resolution frameworks, and integrates the adaptive, resilient, and sustainable dimensions of Cambodia's digital governance.

This research offers a framework integrating digital governance, resilient communities, anticipatory governance, and trust-based AI, emphasizing security, interoperability, and legitimacy. Unlike typical evaluations based on online services, it assesses access, inclusion, and trust. The policy guides Cambodia from fragmented e-services to a resilient, inclusive digital state. The framework highlights digital government's role in building trust, ensuring service continuity, advancing data governance, and strengthening cyber resilience, expanding Cambodia's digital dialogue beyond technology to encompass resilience, legitimacy, and public value. In Cambodia, data issues, digital literacy, and access hinder the adoption of Digital Identity and E-services. Addressing these is key to improving governance and resilience. Without systems rooted in resilience, anticipation, and legitimacy, Cambodia's digital transformation risks remaining fragmented.

This chapter develops an adaptable Cambodia framework and expands digital government research through resilience, anticipatory governance, trustworthy AI, cybersecurity, and public value. It shifts the focus from e-service maturity to resilient public management and provides policymakers with phased reforms, governance areas, and metrics for trust, equity, continuity, and cyber-resilience. Centered on Cambodia's digital governance, it emphasizes global South discussions on building trustworthy, resilient, AI-ready governance in lower-middle-income countries. A Cambodia-focused framework is built on five core capabilities: digital infrastructure, interoperability, anticipatory capacity, ethical AI governance, and trust networks. These are supported by five enablers: leadership, legal frameworks, financing, digital skills, and standards. The policy roadmap integrates these into five implementation pillars.

BACKGROUND

Theoretical and Conceptual Framework: Resilience, Anticipation, and Digital Public Value

Resilient Public Management in Complex Adaptive Systems

Rather than being equated with (or synonymous with) stability or continuity, resilience in public management is more often now referred to as a composite capability that combines robustness, adaptability, and learning. Comfort et al. (2010) suggest that resilient public organizations can absorb disturbances, sustain core functions, and reorganize structures to ensure they continue to perform under different conditions. According to Duit (2016), resilient governance is characterized by the ability to adapt institutional design and policy tools in response to emerging information and threats. Contemporary views see public sector organizations as complex adaptive systems in which resilience involves planning, foresight, flexible adaptation to shocks, and learning after crises.

Complexity scholars argue that linear planning fails in unpredictable systems with many actors, feedback loops, and non-linear dynamics, making outcomes hard to predict. Traditional plan—implement—evaluate cycles create fragile strategies by assuming stability. Complexity management favors adaptive approaches. The resilience literature presents a contradiction: some emphasize robustness to prevent reliability issues arising from centralization, while others warn that it can cause inflexibility and vulnerability. Resilient systems balance stability, adaptation, and learning. Management, viewed as organizational learning, occurs through networks. Digital management systems can be resilient or fragile, based on security and governance.

Digital Government Models: From E-Government to the Digital State

Citing an evolution in digital government models, Heeks (2005) noted that they progressed from information-only portals to integrated service delivery frameworks and, finally, to intelligent, data-driven service delivery systems. Initially, digital government models focused on the existence and availability of basic government services; later models began to address the political and organizational complexities. Current digitalization, according to Dunleavy (2006), is the reintegration and complete redesign of government services, rather than a simple increase in the number of government websites. In addition, Klievink et al. (2012) argued that digitization had shifted toward platform government, in which shared resources such as digital identities and data layers enable and guide government service delivery with a high degree of coordination and innovation, thus giving rise to smart, or algorithmic, states. Dunleavy (2006), Heeks (2005), Ubaldi (2013), and Wirtz et al. (2019) mentioned that these smart states would have advanced data analytics embedded in government services.

There are also critiques of digital government models; for instance, stage models create a narrow, technology-dominated, more deterministic, and less contested view of the digital government system (Janssen & Van Der Voort, 2016). Cordella and Bonina (2012) also argue that measuring the number of e-services or the degree of integration increases the risk of losing sight of the core processes, accountability levels, and performance of the digital government system. The study of data platforms suggests that centralized control in digital government systems may aid innovation; however, it raises concerns about vendor lock-in, data monopolies, and decision-making (Dunleavy, 2006; Jonathan et al., 2024). Understanding the difference between digital government systems providing e-services and those offering integrated, effective, and accountable services is crucial. Transitioning from e-government to the digital state requires new interfaces and governance. In Cambodia, where e-services are rapidly expanding but data governance and interoperability are weak, this distinction is particularly important.

Anticipatory Governance and Strategic Foresight

Anticipatory governance examines the methods by which nations transition from reacting to crises to engaging more proactively with uncertainty. According to Boyd et al. (2015), the resilience of institutions derives from the ability to work with multiple future scenarios and to identify weak signals to alter their approach to problems of an opportunity or threat nature that are not yet fully formed. In its 2021 report, the OECD situates anticipatory governance within the policy, regulatory, and budgetary dimensions of governance and defines strategic foresight as the systematic investigation of alternative future scenarios to inform and guide decision-making. Along similar lines, Tõnurist and Hanson (2020) argue that innovation governance as a whole requires a variety of structures and processes that incorporate foresight into routine decision-making, and is not limited to so-called "future labs". Foresight is more likely to affect an organization's policy context when it is linked to budgetary and other resource-related cycles. According to the (OECD, 2021, 2025), scenario-based analyses and early warning systems have been used by some ministries to guide budgetary, regulatory, and investment decisions. Components like scenario analyses, early warning systems, and risk foresight are key to an organization's policy and budget decisions.

The literature addresses shortcomings as well. Habegger (2010) describes how foresight exercises become more workshops and less participatory; OECD (2021) describes how anticipatory capacity is often hoarded by units in isolation, with very little influence on the bureaucracy in which they exist, creating "foresight islands." For this chapter, digital government and foresight communities must be developed in parallel, with little coupling between strategic foresight and digital and data governance (Tõnurist & Hanson, 2020). This chapter argues that anticipatory governance and digital government are interdependent. In Cambodia, this involves integrating planning and budgeting for anticipatory capacities with digital governance, and designing resilient digital platforms and data governance.

Algorithmic and AI-Enabled Public Management

AI and public administration literature identify considerable possibilities and challenges. Mehr and Ash (2017) claim that AI would assist governments in managing information, automating procedures, detecting fraud, and enhancing predictive policy analysis. Wirtz et al. (2019) describe how public organizations are using AI in conversational agents, document processing, predictive maintenance, and support for judgment. In their global study, Young et al. (2019) show that AI helps with the timing of service delivery, the detection of fraud, and the implementation of focused interventions. Nevertheless, the critical literature identifies problems with bias in algorithms. For example, in the work of Janssen and Kuk (2016), AI in public management systems reflects biases in social issues and stems from a biased training set. Wirtz et al. (2019) also examine the challenges public organizations face with the "black box" of AI systems in support of judgment, and how the absence of limits on the use of AI in public management creates systems that are opaque, biased, and unresponsive.

An appropriate response is emerging, with increasing calls for 'bounded' AI within the public sector. Scholars support human-in-the-loop systems where algorithms assist but do not replace human judgment in high-stakes decisions (Janssen & Kuk, 2016). They emphasize the need for audit trails, impact assessments, and explainability tools so citizens can understand, challenge, and contest algorithm-influenced decisions. Young et al. (2019) further state that public value alignment requires agencies to have the capacity to scrutinize vendor systems and possess the necessary expertise in data science, ethics, law, and procurement. Public administration that uses AI and algorithms will not be seen as an autonomous, intelligent state. Instead, emphasis is on governance frameworks for fraud detection, service triage, and demand forecasting that ensure transparency, human oversight, and avenues for contesting AI decisions.

Trust, Legitimacy, and Democratic Resilience in Digital States

Trust and legitimacy form the core of the democratic resilience of digital states. The digital transformation alters the structures of trust and legitimacy. Bouckaert and Van de Walle (2003) consider trust to be a function of service performance and fairness. Dunlop and Radaelli (2018) argue that digital government enhances the legitimacy of government by offering more convenient, reliable services and by improving transparency, participation, and complaint resolution. Access to open data and digital participation are important factors in reinforcing perceptions of competence, integrity, and, in turn, legitimacy (Prasodjo, 2026). However, several issues arise. Van Zoonen (2016) cites privacy and data protection in the face of state and legal protection as worrisome. According to Prasodjo (2026), digital transformation can produce greater inequality in access to services. Finally, the digital ecosystem of the modern world can be used to post false information and to undermine public trust in institutions, thereby creating a new environment of crisis governance (Raieste et al., 2024).

This mixture of opportunities and threats has consisted of a "trust-technology paradox." Governments create digital systems as infrastructure to build trust among citizens through faster, more transparent services. Citizens are likely to use digital systems, share data, and accept AI-supported services, based on existing trust levels, provided that reasonable safeguards for their rights and privacy are in place (Prasodjo, 2026). In digital states, the resilience of democracy depends on the relationship between service design (user-centered services, secure identity, open data, safe data) and government services (accountability, participation, and complaint filing).

A Cambodia-Adapted Integrative Model

This chapter proposes an integrative model for Cambodia's digital government. Resilience research highlights that adaptable, learning-oriented public management can be sustained through flexible systems. Digital government transformation requires system-wide changes like interconnected infrastructure, shared platforms, and data-driven approaches, moving beyond isolated portals. Anticipatory governance uses digital tools and data for planning through strategic foresight and early warning systems. Emphasizing human accountability and transparency, constrained AI helps with triage, prediction, and anomaly detection. Democratic resilience in the digital space relies on accountability, inclusion, participation, and transparency to build trust.

Using the information presented in this chapter, the conceptualization of Cambodia's digital public management system resilience is considered as a result of the interaction of five capability domains:

- Reliable, secure, robust, and scalable digital systems and services infrastructure and platforms
- Interoperability and data stewardship
- Anticipatory capability
- Tethered and ethical artificial intelligence governance
- Collaborative and trust-building networks

The capabilities of this framework-digital infrastructure, interoperability, anticipatory capacity, ethical AI governance, and collaborative networks-yield three outcomes: resilient public management, enhanced public value, and fortified trust. It helps assess gaps in Cambodia's digital government and the pathways from fragmented e-services to resilient, trustworthy governance, as illustrated in Figure 1.

Figure 1. Cambodia-adapted integrative model for digital public management system resilience.

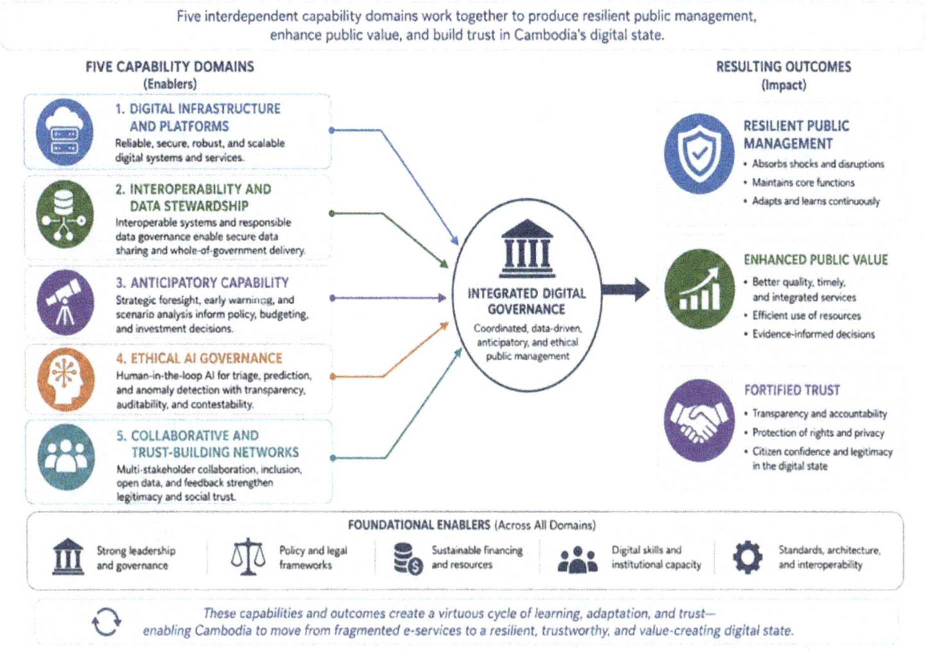

Source: Authors' synthesis based on Comfort et al. (2010), Duit (2016), Janssen and Van Der Voort (2016), Tõnurist and Hanson (2020), OECD (2019, 2021, 2025), and Cambodia's Digital Government Policy 2022–2035.

Methodology and Evidence Strategy

Chapter Design

This chapter offers a policy-centered analysis rooted in Cambodia's context and comparative studies of digital government, resilience, and anticipatory governance. Instead of relying on a single empirical study, it constructs a Cambodia-centric, resilient digital government framework drawing on multiple sources. The main evidence is ERIA's review of Cambodia's digital policies, including the Digital Economy and Society Policy Framework 2021–2035 and the Cambodia Digital Government Policy 2022–2035, reflecting ICT reforms over two decades. The chapter uses conceptual clarification, document analysis, and case studies to design an evidence-based pathway with high potential and low risk for Cambodia. It adopts an interpretive and normative stance, employing frameworks such as the OECD Digital Government Policy and data models to evaluate Cambodia's resilience and advanced digital government, treating these as heuristic tools rather than definitive measures. Given Cambodia's status as a lower-middle-income, post-conflict country, its opportunities and constraints are compared with ASEAN and the Global South to identify governance gaps.

Evidence Sources

This chapter consists of four main categories of evidence: academic literature, global policy frameworks, comparative regional analyses, and policy and practice documents from Cambodia. Scholarship on digital government, resilience, and anticipatory governance provides mental models. Works on complex adaptive systems explain the interplay of robustness, flexibility, and learning of public organizations in the face of uncertainty (Comfort et al., 2010; Duit, 2016). From early e-government models to platform architectures and the development of data-driven states, there is much to draw on to understand the current state of digitalization in Cambodia (Klievink et al., 2012). Anticipatory governance, strategic foresight, and the work of the OECD provide frameworks for understanding how early-warning, scenario, and stress-test methodologies are incorporated into the policy and budget process (OECD, 2021; Tõnurist & Hanson, 2020). The studies on the governance of AI and algorithms provide a balanced view of the opportunities and challenges AI presents for the field of public management (Janssen & Kuk, 2016; Young et al., 2019). The studies on trust, legitimacy, and digital participation provide a framework for analyzing the interaction between digital government and trust and democratic participation (Bouckaert & Van de Walle, 2003).

Second, the assessment of Cambodia's institutional arrangements is derived from international policy frameworks and reviews. The OECD Digital Government Policy Framework and the models of data-driven public sectors and data governance provide analytical lenses for assessing Cambodia's "digital by design," platform government, and data-centric government (OECD Korea Policy Centre, 2023). The OECD's work on the development of anticipatory capability and strategic foresight provides examples of flexible systems and foresight tools from other countries, as well as frameworks for assessing Cambodia's current institutional arrangements (OECD, 2025).

Third, comparative studies of ASEAN and the Global South do offer some regional reference frameworks. Southeast Asian studies on the region's governance deficits highlight implementation challenges in interoperability, standards, and capacities that are also relevant to Cambodia (Rahmansya et al., 2025). ASEAN-level instruments, such as the ASEAN Digital Masterplan 2025, help clarify Cambodia's goals and potential avenues for regional cooperation in cross-border data, cybersecurity, and digital identity (ASEAN, 2021). The Global South debates on digitalization and resilience frameworks also offer insights into the sequencing of reforms, with varying degrees of feasibility, given limited resources, donor dependency, and capacity levels (RIS, 2023).

Fourth, Cambodia-specific policy and practice patterns are the primary focus of the evidence base. The Cambodia Digital Government Policy 2022–2035 and the Digital Economy and Society Policy Framework 2021–2035 are analyzed in detail with respect to their goals, visions, and strategies, as well as their institutional and implementation priorities (Royal Government of Cambodia, 2022). ERIA's chapter on digital government and trade is cited to delineate the trajectory of digital government policies and diagnose the focus of digital government initiatives to date (Soeng & Kao, 2024). Korean Policy Center capacity-building surveys for Cambodia are also cited to provide insights into perceptions of gaps in data governance, interoperability, and skills among Cambodian policymakers and their international counterparts (OECD Korea Policy Centre, 2023).

To systematically manage and analyze this diverse corpus, all key policy documents, scholarly articles, and regional reports were added to NVivo as primary sources. NVivo was included in this research because it helps researchers manage and analyze qualitative data, including policy and evaluation documents (Lumivero, 2026, April 8). In this chapter, NVivo was used to encode the information against the set categories of the theory (for example, "resilience," "interoperability," "data governance," "anticipatory capacity," "trust and legitimacy," "AI use and safeguard," etc.) and to identify gaps, patterns, and discrepancies across different documents.

The evidence categories are presented and described in Table 1 along with the primary sources and the analytical framework.

Table 1. Evidence-based and analytical roles

Evidence category	Primary analytical contribution
Resilience and complexity scholarship	Clarifies resilience as robustness, adaptability, and learning; justifies focus on adaptive management loops
Digital government and platform state literature	Provides models and critiques of e-government–to–digital-state trajectories; highlights the role of interoperability and platforms
Anticipatory governance and foresight	Frames early-warning, scenario planning, and stress-testing as core governance capabilities linked to planning and budgeting
AI and algorithmic governance	Identifies bounded AI use cases and governance risks (bias, opacity, accountability); informs "ethical AI" pillar
Trust, legitimacy, and digital participation	Elaborates the link between digital government, trust, and legitimacy; surfaces the trust–technology paradox and digital exclusion risks

continued on following page

Table 1. Continued

Evidence category	Primary analytical contribution
International frameworks and capacity reviews	Offers benchmarks and conceptual tools for data-driven, user-driven digital government; contextualizes Cambodia in ASEAN
Cambodia policy and practice documents	Grounds analysis in Cambodian institutional dynamics, priorities, and implementation pathways; informs trajectory mapping.

Source: Authors' own synthesis based on the literature review, international digital government frameworks, and Cambodia-specific policy and practice documents analyzed in this chapter.

Analytical Strategy

This analytical strategy combined NVivo-supported qualitative content analysis with conceptual mapping and comparative interpretation. The first step involved importing texts into NVivo for analysis. The texts included the Cambodia Digital Government Policy, the Digital Economy and Society Policy Framework, ERIA's Cambodia chapter, the OECD capacity building materials, and select ASEAN & Global South reports. Based on the theoretical literature (Flick, 2018), an initial coding framework was established. The key parent nodes included resilience, digital infrastructure, interoperability, data governance, anticipatory capacity, AI and algorithms, trust and legitimacy, cybersecurity, and digital skills and leadership. During the coding process, the node names were made more context-specific. The policy texts from Cambodia (Royal Government of Cambodia, 2022) provided examples for node naming. These included priority actions on data governance, central coordination arrangements, and public-private partnerships.

Using NVivo, text coded for "resilience," "interoperability," and "data governance" was analyzed to identify explicit or implicit linkages between Cambodia's policy documents and digital infrastructures and resilient goals. Matrix coding queries examined the frequency and contexts where the terms "trust," "citizen-centered services," and "cybersecurity" occurred alongside "digital government" in Cambodian and ASEAN documents. This made it possible to identify the "resilience leverage points": groupings of data stewardship, cross-government cooperation, cybersecurity, and the skills and trust needed to support all of these, identified in the global discourse and Cambodian policy, and seen as critically important. The next step was to reconstruct Cambodia's digital government trajectory and place it on the digital government continuum. From data provided by ERIA on national policy and other documents, the first step was to identify the order of Cambodia's first ICT master plans, e-commerce law, the Digital Economy and Society Policy Framework, and the Digital Government Policy and its strategic goals, along with the ten strategies, and the 83 priority actions (Royal Government of Cambodia,

2022; Soeng & Kao, 2024). From there, the digital government literature was used to describe Cambodia's progress along the continuum from digitization and integration to Platform Government and the earliest forms of "Intelligent" capabilities (Klievink et al., 2012).

The third step employed a phased approach and governance design by reviewing Cambodian policies on data governance, open data, cybersecurity, the OECD framework (digital by design, data-driven public sector, government as a platform), and anticipatory governance principles (foresight, early warning, stress testing). It established four phases: consolidating e-services and data governance; building interoperability and platforms; developing anticipatory capacity and AI pilots; and scaling with adaptive capacity. These flexible stages support capability development given limited resources.

Ethics, Rights, and Public Value Lens

An ethics, rights, and public value lens focused on privacy, data protection, consent, non-discrimination, inclusion, and accountability. NVivo nodes highlighted references in Cambodian documents to data governance, open data, cybersecurity, feedback, grievance redress, and confidence-building with citizens (Royal Government of Cambodia, 2022) and were compared to the normative frameworks of digital rights and public value, which highlight privacy, protection of due process, and transparency as core values, and the measurement of digital government (Cordella & Bonina, 2012; Van Zoonen, 2016).

User experience was assessed through both ethical and performance indicators. Segments in Khmer policy texts that focused on user-centered design, minimizing red tape, "no wrong door" policies, and inclusivity in digital services were coded and linked to the trust and legitimacy literature (Bouckaert & Van de Walle, 2003). This coding enabled the chapter to analyze whether the proposed reforms were assessed through the prism of efficiency, equity, voice, and contestability. While developing the implementation roadmap, the proposed actions (e.g., expanding digital identity, adopting AI-based triage, or data centralization) were evaluated through this ethical lens. The inquiry was not whether the proposed actions would enhance resilience and performance, but whether they would do so in a manner that upheld privacy, diminished exclusion, and either increased public trust or, at the very least, did not diminish it.

Limitations

This chapter's methodology has limitations, as it primarily focuses on policy documents and secondary literature rather than direct or quantitative evidence.

NVivo aided content analysis, but is insufficient for evaluating services, citizen engagement, or organizational studies. The analysis of Cambodia's digital government resilience is preliminary and needs further testing, as it depends on sector readiness and may not reflect local nuances. Future research should examine specific sectors to refine the framework. The current digital services analysis is limited, with sparse data and only a narrow view of resilience, relying on existing methodologies such as rankings. Therefore, this chapter identifies these gaps but does not conduct a resilience assessment.

Lastly, the policy environment is changeable. The Digital Government Policy 2022–2035 and related strategies are in flux, and new regulations, systems, and trial runs are likely to emerge in the coming years (OECD Korea Policy Centre, 2023; Royal Government of Cambodia, 2022). The integrative model and implementation roadmap developed in this context should therefore be considered a temporally limited analytical construct that will likely be adjusted as Cambodia's digital governance architecture matures, and new information comes to light.

MAIN FOCUS OF THE CHAPTER

Findings and Discussion

High-volume, citizen-facing services, such as customs, trade, and other registration and payment services, are the focus of Cambodia's first wave of digital government. ERIA assessed the advancement of digital public services in Cambodia, noting that the Cambodian authorities have made electronic customs declarations and other border procedures available, thereby minimizing the need for in-person contact and lengthy border-related trade psychology procedures (Soeng & Kao, 2024). The World Bank also supports the view that, despite uneven coverage, successive ICT policies and e-government programs have been geared toward providing "one-stop" online transactions for firms and citizens (World Bank, 2020). These initiatives boost resilience by processing high-volume transactions online, reducing the fragility and vulnerability of in-person, paper-based services to crises such as pandemics or floods.

Access to digital services varies across sectors and groups. ERIA notes disparities between online trade and social services (Soeng & Kao, 2024). Scholars initially saw digital services as supporting economic transactions and urban users (Heeks, 2005). Cambodia invests in platforms such as the Ministry of Interior's online complaints portal. Despite progress, surveys show low trust and usage; less than half of Cambodians are comfortable with online government services (Ramekh, 2024, March 16). Cambodia seeks to boost accessibility, inclusion, and integration of services through diverse design approaches, focusing on accessible, low-resource digitization, assisted access, and outreach. It advances e-Government but faces interoperability issues. The Digital Government Policy aims to build cloud data centers, improve connectivity, and expand CamDX, inspired by Estonia's X-Road, for secure data exchange. ASEAN countries struggle with fragmented e-Government due to poor data protocols, but Cambodia's CamDX aims to unify regional data. The OECD (2025) warns that without frameworks, ministries might refuse to participate, risking vendor lock-in. Cambodia needs transparent governance, incentives, and measures to avoid silos and ensure seamless inter-system e-Government. E-Government is adopting real-time data, with early efforts in performance management and learning systems.

The Digital Government Policy aims to establish a national infrastructure database, develop more advanced statistics, and enhance data analysis in the design of policies and services (Royal Government of Cambodia, 2022). ERIA's trade-focused chapter notes that digital customs and trade systems generate extensive operational data, yet they are not adequately integrated with other performance and risk management systems (Soeng & Kao, 2024). Resilience literature suggests that planning that incorporates dashboards, KPIs, and other performance indicators becomes resilient when it identifies not only throughput and efficiency, but also continuity, recovery time, error rate, citizen satisfaction, and equity of access (Janssen et al., 2012). Most performance systems worldwide focus on what is easily measurable, leading to 'metric gaming' and an emphasis on quantitative measures of public value at the expense of qualitative dimensions (Muller, 2018). The connection between data, budgeting, and program changes remains unclear. The OECD (2025) analyses suggest that, with the right data, budgeting can be an iterative process in which service and risk performance guide adjustments to resources and policies. Cambodian policy documents are vague on data governance and lack links between digital service data and fiscal decisions. Examples include public health and economic tracking; ASEAN, including Cambodia, used digital tools during COVID-19 for aid and food security. Anticipatory governance connects early warning to planning, but Cambodia hasn't fully adopted it. Building crisis-response capacity is vital, with resilience research emphasizing after-action reviews to improve systems (Comfort et al., 2010; Duit, 2016).

As of now, there are still not many explicit references to AI in digital government policy in Cambodia; however, as in many other countries, Regional and Global trends provide examples of likely scenarios and governance challenges. Evidence from many countries shows that AI and advanced analytics are being used in public agencies for case triaging, identifying fraud and anomalies, risk rating, and demand forecasting (Young et al., 2019). In Cambodia, similar issues could arise in tax, customs, social protection, and complaint systems. Limited governance in implementation poses significant risks. On the one hand, the algorithmic governance systems of Janssen and Kuk (2016) could amplify bias if designed with poor data and even less margin for bias, while the systems remain unexplainable to users and the entities that supervise them. On the other hand, Wirtz et al. (2019) show that the use of AI in public services raises questions about accountability and due process, particularly the risk of adverse effects on individuals from automated systems that operate in a nontrans parent manner. In Cambodia, where the governance structures for data protection and AI are in their infancy, the unregulated, early use of AI would likely erode trust in digital governance and lead to a widespread perception of arbitrary governance (Chheang & Huot, 2026).

Evidence supports a "bounded and accountable" AI model for public management, stressing human controls, documentation, audits, impact assessments, and ethics in data science and law. Trust is key to Cambodia's digital government, which seeks to improve the quality of life and confidence. Yet surveys show that only about 47% trust online transactions, with even fewer feeling safe, underscoring how crucial trust is to the acceptance of digital channels and data sharing. Citizen experience relies on responsiveness and feedback channels for trust. The new online complaint system shows a commitment to transparency by centralizing submissions. To improve, it should be assessed for transparency, responsiveness, resolution time, fairness, and citizen feedback. Unresponsive systems harm trust. Equity issues and digital divides, especially between rural and urban areas and small and large enterprises, affect the experience, as studies from the World Bank and ERIA in Cambodia reveal. (Soeng & Kao, 2024; World Bank, 2020).

Research has shown that cybersecurity is crucial to developing a trustworthy and resilient digital government in Cambodia. As part of the Digital Government Policy, a national cybersecurity framework is a must. Secure digital platforms and safeguarding national information infrastructure and data are also part of this Policy. This includes implementing primary and disaster-recovery data centers (Royal Government of Cambodia, 2022). The OECD capacity-building initiative also supports cybersecurity and stress management in the context of digital government (OECD Korea Policy Centre, 2023). In the public domain, there is a noticeable denial of actual and formal practice. Trust in Cambodia's digital government is undermined by the management of personal data, the opacity surrounding data breaches, and the lack of legislation on personal data protection (Ramekh, 2024, March 16).

More generally, there are also interconnections between cybersecurity and democratic resilience. With the rapid development of digital environments for citizen feedback and interaction, as well as for service delivery, cyber-attacks and disinformation can undermine the legitimacy of institutions. Association of Southeast Asian Nations (ASEAN) regional analyses of the impacts of COVID-19 and food security show that governments must defend citizens' trust in times of crisis by strengthening systems, combating disinformation, and maintaining credible public communication (ASEAN, 2021). In Cambodia, technical cybersecurity solutions, guidelines for transparent incident reporting, data and cybersecurity communication, and actions against disinformation and to promote media literacy are needed. Table 2 summarizes key domains, trends, and implications for resilience-focused digital governance.

Table 2. Cambodia's digital government pathways and resilience implications

Thematic domain	Observed pattern in Cambodia	Implications for resilient, anticipatory digital governance
Service delivery resilience	Expansion of online customs, trade, and selected citizen-facing services; new digital complaint portal; uneven uptake and trust.	Reduces queue fragility but must be complemented by inclusive design, assisted access, and trust-building measures
Interoperability and coordination	Development of CamDX and national data centers; recognition of need for shared platforms; persistent organizational silos.	Platform logic offers potential gains but requires strict data governance rules, incentives, and clear institutional ownership.
Data-driven performance	Policy emphasis on data-centric government; limited integration of service data into budgeting and program adjustment.	Dashboards and KPIs must track resilience and equity and be linked to resource allocation to avoid symbolic "data-ism."
Anticipatory capacity	Strong climate early-warning systems and sectoral risk monitoring; limited integration into whole-of-government foresight.	Existing systems provide a foundation but need to be embedded in planning and budgeting as routine, cross-sector anticipatory practices.
AI-enabled use and safeguards	Nascent policy references, likely future use in triage and fraud detection, and limited legal and institutional safeguards.	AI should be introduced as bounded pilots with human oversight, explainability, auditability, and appeal mechanisms.
Trust, inclusion, cybersecurity	Explicit goal of building confidence; low reported trust in e-government; evolving cybersecurity and data-protection frameworks.	Trust and democratic resilience require strong cybersecurity, transparent communication, effective grievance systems, and measures to mitigate digital divides.

Source: Authors' own synthesis based on the Cambodia-focused evidence and resilience implications analyzed in this chapter.

Policy and Implementation Roadmap for Cambodia

The policy roadmap for Cambodia consists of six mutually reinforcing pillars. Each of them translates possible options into governance priorities. According to the OECD's digital government principles, these pillars prioritize institutional capabilities over fragmented solutions (OECD, 2019, 2021). They engage with the strategic priorities set out in Cambodia's Digital Government Policy for 2022–2035. Among them are the construction of a secure, data-centric government and the provision of services that strengthen citizens' trust (Royal Government of Cambodia, 2022).

Pillar 1 focuses on creating an infrastructure for digital interoperability. The construction of national data centers, an upgraded government network, and the Cambodia Data Exchange (CamDX) show that Cambodia is moving towards the "government as a platform" model (Royal Government of Cambodia, 2022). According to the OECD's approach to digital government, shared platforms and services are the basis for collaboration among multiple government agencies to reduce duplication and increase government resilience (OECD, 2021). For Cambodia, this means consolidating and standardizing infrastructure and service layers while ensuring their safety, governance, transparency, and elasticity over time.

With Pillar 2, there is an emphasis placed on anticipatory governance capacity. The OECD defines anticipatory governance as the "systematic embedding and application of strategic foresight throughout the entire governance architecture" (OECD, 2021). Building such capacity in Cambodia requires strengthening foresight and risk analysis functions in central agencies (e.g., in the Ministry of Economy and Finance or a digital government steering committee), integrating scenario analysis and policy cycle early warning indicators, and connecting climate, disasters, and other sectoral early warning systems to national planning and budgeting systems (OECD, 2025; UNDP, 2022). This pillar thus comprises far more than the technical tools, including mandates, competencies, institutional frameworks, and iterative processes for future-oriented decision-making.

Pillar 3 focuses on ethical and accountable AI governance. The global trend of AI use in public administration has called for governance frameworks that incorporate fairness, transparency, and accountability (Janssen & Kuk, 2016; Wirtz et al., 2019). In public-sector AI governance, the design and implementation of a risk-based approach to classifying AI systems, as well as bias audits, explainability frameworks, and high standards of human oversight, particularly for high-risk systems, are vital (Essert Inc., 2025). For Cambodia, this pillar focuses on establishing standards and, in due course, regulations for AI in public services to require accountability, bias audits, and documented decisions, as well as the provision of appeal mechanisms and a minimum level of capability for internal reviews in key ministries.

Pillar 4 focuses on trust and citizen-centered service design. The literature from the OECD and the World Bank shows that, for trust to be built and for digital government to deliver value to the public, services must be user-driven, inclusive, and transparent (Bouckaert & Van de Walle, 2003). Cambodia's Digital Government Policy mentions user-centric principles and the objective of building citizens' trust in using digital services (Royal Government of Cambodia, 2022). The implementation of this pillar entails service charters, information on rights and service standards and are made available to the public, an integrated grievance system (which includes the new online complaint system), and design that actively and meaningfully includes the targeted users of the service to co create and test the service, taking into account barriers created by the level of language and digital literacy, and disabilities.

Pillar 5 focuses on Cybersecurity and Continuity. The current view of resilience acknowledges that digital disruptions to public services must be addressed in business continuity plans, including cybersecurity (Chheang & Huot, 2026). Cambodia's framework already mandates the development of national cybersecurity and data recovery services (Royal Government of Cambodia, 2022). This pillar operationalizes policies by creating cyber-resilient services that protect systems, assets, and personnel via formal audits of resilience architecture and security guarantees with providers.

In Pillar 6, we see capability building and change management. Across the evidence on foresight and digital government, European and digital transformation programs show that skills, leadership, and organizational culture are key to successful transformations (OECD Korea Policy Centre, 2023). In Cambodia, some capacity-building initiatives focus on digital skills and data governance for certain government agencies (Phin & Huot, 2026). This pillar advocates a systematic approach by training civil servants in digital skills, data stewardship, cybersecurity, and policy foresight, plus incentivizing cross-agency collaboration at strategic levels.

These pillars work in tandem, not in isolation; their collective impact provides an environment in which digital government fosters resilience and public trust. Given resource and capacity constraints, a phased approach is necessary to implement these pillars. While some Cambodian policies break the digital government roadmap into three short (2022–2025), mid- (2026–2030), and long- (2031–2035) term periods (Royal Government of Cambodia, 2022; Soeng & Kao, 2024), the proposed phases work in the confines of these periods but take a dependency approach to capabilities.

In Phase 1, e-services will be integrated and basic data governance frameworks established. The focus will be on consolidating existing online services and stabilizing services that prioritize high-impact, high-volume transactions (e.g., customs, licensing, taxation, key citizen registrations), as well as integrating core service offerings online. The usability, accessibility, and security of online service offerings will be enhanced (Soeng & Kao, 2024). Foundational data governance will include establishing roles and units for data governance, protecting and sharing data, and establishing initial data governance within ministries and basic data catalogs. This foundational data governance will be established in accordance with the OECD's recommendations for the data-driven public sector (OECD, 2019).

In Phase 2, the frameworks will focus on data interoperability, service integration, and the establishment of shared platforms. Phase 1 will be the foundation for this Phase. The core data exchange layer (CamDX) will be built upon, and its use will be prioritized in selected ministries. This will be guided by common data standards and APIs (Royal Government of Cambodia, 2022). Reduced redundancy and integrated service user journeys will be emphasized through shared digital identity, authentication, and payment services. Focused on life events (e.g., starting a business, birth registration, land transactions), these will minimize citizens' need to navigate multiple portals.

In Phase 3, anticipatory governance tools and AI use cases are introduced in a more circumscribed manner. Following the establishment of the core infrastructure and governance systems in Cambodia, participatory strategic foresight and early warning systems would be formally instituted within the central ministries (OECD, 2021). Such systems would integrate with Cambodia's planning and budgeting. Stress tests for system resilience would be routinely included in these processes. AI would pilot in low- to moderate-risk cases like triaging non-emergency services, detecting anomalies in tax and customs, and assessing capacity, all under strict oversight, risk assessment, and governance frameworks (Essert Inc., 2025; Young et al., 2019).

In Phase 4, governance frameworks and risk assessments would become formal, integrated into standard procedures and training for public servants. Instead of central units, these would be embedded across all line ministries and agencies. Data generated from digital government services would be routinely used to adjust government programs and services and to make budgeting decisions (OECD, 2025). Mechanisms for collecting public feedback on government services, such as complaints and satisfaction surveys, would be analyzed regularly, and findings would be used to enhance services. The alignment of the frameworks with specific implementation phases is depicted in Table 3.

Table 3. Alignment of pillars and implementation phases

Pillar/Phase	Phase 1: Consolidate & govern data	Phase 2: Interoperate & integrate	Phase 3: Anticipate & pilot AI	Phase 4: Scale & institutionalize
Interoperable infrastructure	Stabilize key e-services; basic security; initial data policies	Expand CamDX; enforce standards; roll out shared components	Stress-test platforms; enhance redundancy	Continuous improvement; lifecycle management
Anticipatory capacity	Identify risk domains; map existing early-warning systems	Link sectoral data to central monitoring	Establish foresight units; integrate scenarios into plans	Embed foresight across sectors; routinize stress-testing
Ethical AI governance	Develop initial guidelines and risk taxonomy	Build internal literacy; data quality improvements	Pilot bounded AI use cases with audits and appeals	Codify standards; expand only proven, well-governed use cases

continued on following page

Table 3. Continued

Pillar/Phase	Phase 1: Consolidate & govern data	Phase 2: Interoperate & integrate	Phase 3: Anticipate & pilot AI	Phase 4: Scale & institutionalize
Trust & citizen-centered design	Service charters; accessibility baselines; maintain multi-channel access	Integrate services around life events; simplify journeys	Use feedback and data to refine services; co-design pilots	Institutionalize participatory design and grievance responsiveness
Cybersecurity & continuity	Define critical systems; basic incident response plans	Strengthen monitoring and audits; vendor security clauses	Regular stress tests and exercises align with AI risk controls	Mature SOC-like capabilities; transparent incident reporting
Capability & change management	Core digital literacy and data-stewardship training	Cross-agency teams; change-management support	Specialized skills in foresight, data science, and AI ethics	Leadership development; continuous learning culture

Source: Authors' own synthesis based on the proposed policy pillars and phased implementation roadmap developed in this chapter.

A digital government roadmap with built-in resilience likely needs a monitoring and evaluation (M&E) system that incorporates resilience, trust, and equity, rather than one that restricts its scope to measuring output volumes or cost reductions. Work conducted by the OECD on data-driven public sectors has shown that metrics should align with policy objectives. It should focus on learning, rather than primarily on behavioral control (OECD, 2019). In Cambodia, three groups of metrics are particularly important. First, resilience metrics encompass both continuity and recovery. These include metrics such as the number or percentage of critical services maintained during operational disruptions, the average recovery time for digital incidents, the uptime of key platforms, and the error or failure rates for high-volume transactions (Comfort et al., 2010). As for early warning systems, the lead time and alerts for an event, as well as the coverage of the at-risk population, may serve as proxies for anticipatory capacity.

Second, trust metrics should be defined and constructed based on citizens' perceptions and experiences. These perceptions can be captured by the digital services satisfaction, fairness, transparency, and data protection surveys. Moreover, trust can be further assessed and measured by evaluating operational indicators such as the number of complaints, the complaint resolution rate, and the average time to resolve complaints. In Cambodia, trust in e-governance institutions is at an all-time low (Huot & Chheang, 2026). Thus, monitoring the evolution of the identified metrics may be key to evaluating whether the digital governance initiative has a positive impact on trust in public institutions. Lastly, equity metrics should be used to assess the beneficiaries of e-governance initiatives.

According to Raihan et al. (2025), recent research on digital equity governance suggests that success should be measured by how well underserved groups can both access and use services. This is a more equitable approach than merely counting how many services have been digitized. For Cambodia, measures of success should include how many services can be accessed via mobile or low-bandwidth internet; how services are utilized, especially when this data is segmented by socio-economic status, gender, and geography; and how many digital services have assisted access points located in rural and underserved communities (Soeng & Kao, 2024; World Bank, 2020). The equitable effects of digital services would be best measured through a combination of advanced analytics, qualitative surveys, and feedback via augmented portal analytics.

SOLUTIONS AND RECOMMENDATIONS

In the context of Cambodia's digital government transformation, the focus should be on resilient, anticipatory, inclusive, and trusted digital governance. The first recommendation is to make interoperability, data governance, and cybersecurity the primary infrastructure of the public sector. Cambodia has taken some steps with digital policy, national digital data systems, and the CamDX platform. With the addition of institutional mandates and data standards, secure data-sharing protocols, and improved coordination of ministries and agencies, these digital systems will have a greater impact. A whole-of-government approach should be adopted to address fragmentation, minimize service duplication, and ensure that the provision of digital services remains business as usual, even in times of crisis.

Second, Cambodia should embed anticipatory governance into its digital public management systems. Digital transformation must not only improve service delivery but also strengthen the state's ability to detect emerging risks and adapt policy responses. Integrating early-warning tools, risk mapping, and stress testing into planning, budgeting, and policymaking will support this shift. Connecting health, climate, disaster, economic, and other monitoring systems within national planning can help make foresight-based governance a standard practice rather than an exception.

Third, we must proceed with caution, limits, and accountability in applying artificial intelligence to public administration. Anomaly detection and service demand forecasting are examples of low- to moderate-risk AI applications that Cambodia may consider. These, along with administrative triage and fraud-risk identification, should be undertaken only in the presence of protections that include human oversight, explainability, and documentation, as well as audit and bias-review trails and appeal mechanisms. To the extent AI is introduced, it should be an adjunct to decision-making to enhance accountability. This becomes critical in areas that impact citizens' rights and welfare, as well as public access to government services and trust in government.

Fourth, digital government reform must prioritize citizen-centred and inclusive design. Services should be organized around real-life events and user journeys, not administrative convenience, and supported by a "no wrong door" approach that allows access through digital, assisted, or in-person channels. This is especially important for rural, low-income, elderly, and disabled citizens, as well as those with limited digital skills. Inclusive digital services should incorporate user testing with affected communities, clear service commitments, transparent information on personal data processing, and multilingual, accessible platforms.

Fifth, strengthening trust-building mechanisms is crucial for improving Cambodia's digital governance. Fair, secure, and responsive systems encourage widespread public use. Cambodia should therefore enhance processes for grievance handling, complaint resolution, public feedback, and assurances on privacy and data protection. Digital complaint platforms should register complaints, provide timely responses, track resolutions, and use the data to improve services. Transparent reporting and communication about security incidents are also essential to prevent misinformation and maintain institutional integrity.

Finally, Cambodia must invest in strengthening institutional capacity and change management. Digital transformation requires not only new systems but also skilled personnel with competencies in data governance, digital service design, and cross-departmental collaboration. Training should therefore emphasize governance capabilities, supported by digital tools to manage organizational change. Without strong political commitment and corresponding legal and governance reforms, digital initiatives will remain short-lived and deliver limited public value.

FUTURE RESEARCH DIRECTIONS

Future studies should focus on empirically assessing the resilience of Cambodia's digital government system. This may include assessing service continuity, recovery time after disruptions, readiness for cyberattacks, platform availability, complaint resolution rates, and digital systems' ability to maintain public service delivery amid disruptions. Another important direction is the study of citizens' trust in digital governance. Future research should focus on citizens' perceptions of digital identity and online public services; data and trust; the roles of governance and cybersecurity; and AI-enabled services in Public Administration. Special focus should be placed on the rural-urban divide, the digitally included and excluded, micro and medium enterprises, and service- and system-user-adjacent vulnerable communities. Surveys, interviews, and service-user studies, in a mixed-method approach, are critical to the study of digital governance.

Future research should assess Cambodia's preparedness for AI-enabled public service management, examining its legal, ethical, and technical readiness, as well as the safeguards needed to prevent algorithmic bias. Priority areas include taxation, customs, social protection, education, health, and complaint-handling services. Studies should focus on bias, accountability, and transparency in AI-supported functions, as well as on oversight mechanisms and citizens' rights to contest automated decisions.

Research involving other ASEAN and Global South countries would be valuable. Cross-country comparisons could situate Cambodia's digital government reforms alongside those facing similar challenges in interoperability, cybersecurity, data governance, the digital divide, and uneven institutional capacities. Such work could also underscore the importance of sequencing reforms and balancing the expansion of shared services with the regulation of data flows and the protection of digital sovereignty. Future research should examine the political economy of digital government in Cambodia, particularly as the state increasingly relies on cloud services, cross-border digital infrastructures, and Shared Services. These developments raise new challenges related to data control, accountability, vendor lock-in, and national sovereignty. Understanding these dynamics will be essential for designing governance innovations.

CONCLUSION

This chapter has focused on why resilient digital government is more than expanded e-services or automated public administration. In the case of Cambodia, digital transformation is the state's governance capacity for anticipation, flexibility, and the adaptive provision of and learning from the disruption of critical public services. While digital governance can aid in the transformation, it must be embedded in strong governance, ethical frameworks, institutional capacity, and citizen engagement.

The analysis shows that Cambodia is moving from fragmented digital services toward a more integrated—and potentially anticipatory—digital government model. Yet major challenges persist in public trust, digital inclusion, and core governance capacities. If these issues remain unresolved, digital initiatives may deepen fragmentation and exacerbate social exclusion, ultimately weakening confidence in public institutions. Therefore, Cambodia's digital transformation should be assessed by its ability to protect citizens' rights, reduce inequalities, and strengthen legitimacy, rather than by the sheer number of online platforms or services offered.

This chapter's main contribution is to create a Cambodia-specific resilient, AI-enabled digital governance model with five capability domains, a phased policy roadmap, and a monitoring framework. It is practically relevant, helping policymakers build digital systems and govern them through trust, cybersecurity, oversight, participation, and learning. Amid rapid digitalization and limited legal security and trust, especially in Cambodia and similar countries, this chapter offers a valuable, adapted framework for resilient digital governance. This framework covers digital governance aspects, emphasizing secure, adaptable roles that build citizen trust. It advocates a phased transition from fragmentation to resilience and inclusivity. Ultimately, Cambodia's digital governance depends on technology and effective public systems to ensure a safe, adaptable, and accountable digital transformation.

REFERENCES

ASEAN. (2021). *ASEAN Digital Masterplan 2025*. ASEAN Secretariat. https://asean.org/wp-content/uploads/2021/08/ASEAN-Digital-Masterplan-2025.pdf

Bouckaert, G., & Van de Walle, S. (2003). Comparing measures of citizen trust and user satisfaction as indicators of 'good governance': Difficulties in linking trust and satisfaction indicators. *International Review of Administrative Sciences*, *69*(3), 329–343. DOI: 10.1177/0020852303693003

Boyd, E., Nykvist, B., Borgström, S., & Stacewicz, I. A. (2015). Anticipatory governance for social-ecological resilience. *Ambio*, *44*(S1, Suppl 1), 149–161. DOI: 10.1007/s13280-014-0604-x PMID: 25576289

Chheang, S., & Huot, S. (2026). Safeguarding digital classrooms: Cybersecurity implications of AI-driven tools in Cambodian education. [JEILT]. *Journal of Education Innovation & Language Teaching*, *2*(1), 24–46. DOI: 10.63381/jeilt.v2i1.86

Comfort, L. K., Boin, A., & Demchak, C. C. (2010). *Designing resilience: Preparing for extreme events*. University of Pittsburgh Pre. DOI: 10.2307/j.ctt5hjq0c

Cordella, A., & Bonina, C. M. (2012). A public value perspective for ICT enabled public sector reforms: A theoretical reflection. *Government Information Quarterly*, *29*(4), 512–520. DOI: 10.1016/j.giq.2012.03.004

Duit, A. (2016). Resilience thinking: Lessons for public administration. *Public Administration*, *94*(2), 364–380. DOI: 10.1111/padm.12182

Dunleavy, P. (2006). *Digital era governance: IT corporations, the state, and e-government*. Oxford University Press. DOI: 10.1093/acprof:oso/9780199296194.001.0001

Dunlop, C. A., & Radaelli, C. M. (2018). The lessons of policy learning: Types, triggers, hindrances and pathologies. *Policy and Politics*, *46*(2), 255–272. DOI: 10.1332/030557318X15230059735521

Essert Inc. (2025). *AI governance in the public sector: Essential frameworks for government agencies*. Essert Inc. https://essert.io/ai-governance-in-the-public-sector

Flick, U. (2018). Doing qualitative data collection–charting the routes. In Flick, U. (Ed.), *The SAGE handbook of qualitative data collection* (pp. 3–16). SAGE Publications., DOI: 10.4135/9781526416070.n1

Habegger, B. (2010). Strategic foresight in public policy: Reviewing the experiences of the UK, Singapore, and the Netherlands. *Futures*, *42*(1), 49–58. DOI: 10.1016/j.futures.2009.08.002

Heeks, R. (2005). *Implementing and managing eGovernment: An international text*. SAGE Publications.

Huot, S. (2026). Digital diplomacy in Cambodia: Embracing artificial intelligence for strategic engagement and national development. In Turan, A., & Ucuzal, H. (Eds.), *Diplomacy in the age of artificial intelligence* (pp. 307–330). IGI Global Scientific Publishing., DOI: 10.4018/979-8-3373-4937-4.ch013

Huot, S., & Chheang, S. (2026). Public security and trust-building in Cambodia: Navigating challenges of the post-truth era for positive developmental progress. In Ağırdil, O., & Ayhan, U. (Eds.), *Navigating public security in the age of post-truth: Challenges and implications* (pp. 245–274). IGI Global Scientific Publishing., DOI: 10.4018/979-8-3373-6786-6.ch009

Janssen, M., Charalabidis, Y., & Zuiderwijk, A. (2012). Benefits, adoption barriers and myths of open data and open government. *Information Systems Management*, *29*(4), 258–268. DOI: 10.1080/10580530.2012.716740

Janssen, M., & Kuk, G. (2016). The challenges and limits of big data algorithms in technocratic governance. *Elsevier*, *33*(3), 371–377. DOI: 10.1016/j.giq.2016.08.011

Janssen, M., & Van Der Voort, H. (2016). Adaptive governance: Towards a stable, accountable and responsive government. *Elsevier*, *33*(1), 1–5. DOI: 10.1016/j.giq.2016.02.003

Jonathan, G. M., Perjons, E., & Rusu, L. (2024). Digital transformation-driven decentralisation of public governance. *Procedia Computer Science*, *239*, 1220–1229. DOI: 10.1016/j.procs.2024.06.290

Klievink, B., Van Stijn, E., Hesketh, D., Aldewereld, H., Overbeek, S., Heijmann, F., & Tan, Y.-H. (2012). Enhancing visibility in international supply chains: The data pipeline concept. [IJEGR]. *International Journal of Electronic Government Research*, *8*(4), 54–64. DOI: 10.4018/jegr.2012100104

Lumivero. (2026, April 8). *Matrix coding query*. NVivo help. https://help-nv.qsrinternational.com/20/win/Content/queries/matrix-coding-query.htm

Margetts, H., & Dunleavy, P. (2013). The second wave of digital-era governance: A quasi-paradigm for government on the Web. *Philosophical Transactions. Series A, Mathematical, Physical, and Engineering Sciences*, *371*(1987), 1–17. DOI: 10.1098/rsta.2012.0382 PMID: 23419851

Mehr, H., & Ash, H. (2017). *Artificial intelligence for citizen services and government.* Ash Center for Democratic Governance and Innovation, Harvard Kennedy School.

Meijer, A., & Bolívar, M. P. R. (2016). Governing the smart city: A review of the literature on smart urban governance. *International Review of Administrative Sciences, 82*(2), 392–408. DOI: 10.1177/0020852314564308

Muller, J. (2018). *The tyranny of metrics.* Princeton University Press.

OECD. (2019). *The path to becoming a data-driven public sector (OECD Digital Government Studies). Organisation for Economic Co-operation and Development (OECD).* Publishing., DOI: 10.1787/059814a7-

OECD. (2021). *21st-century readers: Developing literacy skills in a digital world.* Organisation for Economic Co-operation and Development Publishing., DOI: 10.1787/a83d84cb-

OECD. (2025). *Building anticipatory capacity with strategic foresight in government: Lessons from Lithuania, Italy, and Malta (OECD Public Governance Reviews).* OECD Publishing. DOI: 10.1787/d7eb0bb6-en

OECD Korea Policy Centre. (2023). *Capacity Building Programme Cambodia 2023: Advancing a data-driven government in Cambodia.* Public Governance Programme, OECD Korea Policy Centre. https://www.oecdkorea.org/eng

Phin, K., & Huot, S. (2026). Generative AI and Cambodian curriculum: Risks and rewards for student learning and research integrity [JEILT]. *Journal of Education Innovation & Language Teaching, 2*(1), 47–59. DOI: 10.63381/jeilt.v2i1.87

Prasodjo, T. (2026). Public trust reloaded: The impact of data transparency and digital participation on government legitimacy in the era of open government. *Golden Ratio of Social Science and Education, 6*(1), 53–67. DOI: 10.52970/grsse.v6i1.1894

Rahmansya, J., Mehta, A., & Bautista, M. J. (2025). The digital governance gap in Southeast Asia: A comparative study of Indonesia, India, and the Philippines. *Asian Digital Governance Problems, 2*(1), 1–17. DOI: 10.71435/643063

Raieste, A., Rebane, A., Tapupere, M., & McBride, K. (2024). *Government resilience in the digital age.* Nortal & Oxford Internet Institute.

Raihan, M. M., Subroto, S., Chowdhury, N., Koch, K., Ruttan, E., & Turin, T. C. (2025). Dimensions and barriers for digital (in) equity and digital divide: A systematic integrative review. *Digital Transformation and Society, 4*(2), 111–127. DOI: 10.1108/DTS-04-2024-0054

Ramekh, S. (2024, March 16). *Opinion: Balancing public trust and cybersecurity*. Future Forum. https://www.futureforum.asia/post/opinion-balancing-public-trust-and-cybersecurity

RIS. (2023). *Global South and perspectives on development partnerships*. Research and Information System for Developing Countries. https://www.ris.org.in/en/node/3743

Royal Government of Cambodia. (2022). *Cambodia digital government policy 2022–2035: Establishing digital government to improve the people's quality of life and build trust among the people through better public service provision*. Ministry of Post and Telecommunications. https://mptc.gov.kh/en/2022/04/cambodia-digital-government-policy-2022-2035

Soeng, R., & Kao, T. (2024). Digital government in promoting trade: The case of Cambodia. In L. Chen & F. Kimura (Eds.), *Empowering Online Public Service in Asia: The Digital Frontier* (pp. 269–292). Economic Research Institute for ASEAN and East Asia (ERIA). https://www.eria.org/uploads/10_Chapter-9-The-Case-of-Cambodia.pdf

Tõnurist, P., & Hanson, A. (2020). *Anticipatory innovation governance: Shaping the future through proactive policy making* [OECD Working Papers on Public Governance No. 44]. OECD Publishing., DOI: 10.1787/cce14d80-

Ubaldi, B. (2013). *Open government data: Towards empirical analysis of open government data initiatives* [OECD Working Papers on Public Governance No. 22]. OECD Publishing., DOI: 10.1787/5k46bj4f03s7-

UNDP. (2022). *Digital strategy 2022-2025: Creating a world in which digital is an empowering force for people and planet*. United Nations Development Programme. https://digitalstrategy.undp.org

Van Zoonen, L. (2016). Privacy concerns in smart cities. *Government Information Quarterly*, *33*(3), 472–480. DOI: 10.1016/j.giq.2016.06.004

Wirtz, B. W., Weyerer, J. C., & Geyer, C. (2019). Artificial intelligence and the public sector—Applications and challenges. *International Journal of Public Administration*, *42*(7), 596–615. DOI: 10.1080/01900692.2018.1498103

World Bank. (2020). *Bridging the digital divide: Harnessing data through cloud computing*. World Bank Group. https://blogs.worldbank.org/en/digital-development/bridging-the-digital-divide--harnessing-data-through-cloud-compu?utm_source

Young, M. M., Bullock, J. B., & Lecy, J. D. (2019). Artificial discretion as a tool of governance: A framework for understanding the impact of artificial intelligence on public administration. *Perspectives on Public Management and Governance*, *2*(4), 301–313. DOI: 10.1093/ppmgov/gvz014

KEY TERMS AND DEFINITIONS

Anticipatory Governance: Approach in which government bodies use early warning systems and scenario-based stress testing as aspects of foresight to prepare for multiple possible futures and integrate this preparation into their normal day-to-day planning and budgeting.

Digital Government: The conceptualization of the digital redesign of public government services, beyond a mere online public service.

Interoperability: The ability of different systems and organizations within the government to securely share and reuse data and digital services through common standards, shared platforms, and agreed-upon, assessed procedures.

Public Value: This refers to the positive outcomes that governments create for society, including efficient, fair services, the safeguarding of rights, and responsive government services, ultimately fostering greater trust and legitimacy in government and its services.

Resilience: The ability of public institutions to adjust their strategies and operations under stress, while retaining their essential functions and learning from disruptive events.

Trustworthy AI: The application of artificial intelligence to the management of public affairs in ways that promote transparency, justice, and explainability, while retaining human control over the system and providing accessible mechanisms of appeal.

Chapter 10
Digital Governance in Latin American Public Libraries:
Public Value and Resilient Management

Fabio Moscoso Duran
http://orcid.org/0000-0003-1664-0283
Alcalá University, Spain

Walter Jair Barragan Rodríguez
Malta University, Malta

Daniel Salazar Rodriguez
Universidad Nacional Abierta y a Distancia, Colombia

ABSTRACT

This chapter analyses how public libraries in Latin America can serve as digital governance infrastructures oriented towards creating public value and resilient public management. The central argument is that the digital transformation of libraries should not be limited to the incorporation of online technologies, platforms, or services, but should be evaluated for its capacity to expand effective access, strengthen citizens' capacities, promote institutional trust, and reduce territorial gaps. The chapter proposes the Digital Governance and Public Value Creation Model for Public Libraries, structured into six dimensions: digital governance, technological infrastructure, digital inclusion, public value, organisational capaci-

DOI: 10.4018/979-8-3373-9765-8.ch010

ties, and territorial resilience. The model shows how libraries can mediate between the digital state and citizens through access, training, guidance, participation and territorial adaptation.

INTRODUCTION

Digital transformation has become a priority for public sector modernization, institutional innovation and service improvement in Latin America. Governments have promoted e-government portals, online platforms, digital identity systems, open data, interoperability and mechanisms for citizen participation. These developments mark a shift from face-to-face procedures to more integrated and user-oriented schemes. In this chapter, digital governance is used as a broader analytical concept. While e-government refers mainly to electronic service delivery and administrative procedures, digital governance also includes institutional arrangements, coordination mechanisms, data infrastructures, platforms, citizen capabilities, ethical principles, mediation practices and accountability mechanisms through which digital transformation creates public value. However, digitalization of the State does not by itself guarantee inclusion, trust or public value. Services may be available but inaccessible to people without connectivity, devices, skills, information literacy or confidence. This is especially visible in Latin America, where digital government advances amid inequality, territorial gaps, uneven institutional capacities and varying levels of trust. The problem is not only the absence of digital services, but the difficulty many citizens face in understanding and using them effectively (Espinosa Zárate et al., 2023). The digital divide is therefore technological, educational, informational, administrative, territorial and democratic. When procedures, public aid, educational registration, health appointments or information requests move online, people with fewer access and use capacities may become more vulnerable (Espinosa Zárate et al., 2023). Comparative research across the Americas and the Caribbean shows that inclusion policies are more effective when they combine connectivity, devices and skills while adapting to rural, remote and disadvantaged communities (Robinson et al., 2020).

In this context, public libraries acquire strategic relevance. Their territorial presence, universal access orientation, community legitimacy and pedagogical capacity position them as intermediate institutions between citizens, digital public services and community networks. Their role is not to replace administrative functions, but to provide access, guidance, information literacy, digital mediation, citizen learning and responsible referral. The central argument of this chapter is that Latin American public libraries can be reinterpreted as infrastructures of digital governance and public value creation. This requires moving beyond a narrow view of digital libraries such as online catalogues, e-lending, connectivity or equipment. Digital transformation becomes meaningful when these resources are combined with institutional capacity, professional mediation, territorial alliances, digital ethics, citizen training and evaluation. A digital public library should therefore be assessed not only by technological modernization, but by its capacity to expand rights, strengthen autonomy, improve trust and support community resilience.

The chapter connects five fields: digital government, resilient public management, public libraries, digital inclusion and public value. This integration is necessary because public digitalization is simultaneously technological, institutional, social and territorial. Digital government provides the institutional and technological frame; resilient public management introduces adaptation and continuity; public libraries offer proximity infrastructure; digital inclusion identifies access and capability gaps; and public value assesses social, administrative and community benefits.

The objective is to analyze how public libraries in Latin America can contribute to digital governance, public value creation and resilient public management through access, mediation, information literacy, citizen inclusion and territorial adaptation. The originality of this chapter lies in reframing public libraries as digital governance infrastructures rather than merely as cultural, documentary or access-oriented institutions. The proposed framework integrates digital governance, public value creation and resilient public management into a model adapted to Latin American territorial inequalities. It shows how libraries can mediate between digital public services and citizens' real capabilities, especially where social inequality, institutional fragmentation, uneven connectivity and limited trust restrict effective access.

The chapter is also informed by prior research engagement with the LibrarIN Horizon Europe project, focused on value co-creation, social innovation, participatory management, collaborative innovation and sustainable models for a new generation of libraries. LibrarIN conceptualizes libraries as community hubs and agents of social innovation that respond to societal needs through digital transformation, co-creation spaces, personalized services, partnerships, digital literacy and effective management (LibrarIN, 2025). This provides a conceptual background for viewing public libraries as proximity institutions that generate public value through mediation, collaboration, institutional learning and community engagement.

The chapter proceeds as follows. First, it reviews digital government and public management in Latin America. Second, it conceptualizes public libraries as digital governance infrastructures. Third, it analyses public value creation at the citizen, administrative and territorial-community levels. Fourth, it examines resilience, inclusion and territorial adaptation. Fifth, it presents the proposed model. Finally, it discusses public policy and management implications, future research and conclusions.

BACKGROUND

Latin American Background: Territorial Inequality, Digital Government and Public Libraries

Latin America should not be treated as a homogeneous digital governance space. The region includes countries, metropolitan areas, intermediate cities, rural territories, border zones, indigenous communities and peripheral urban settlements with very different levels of connectivity, institutional capacity, public service provision and library development. These differences shape how citizens experience digital government. For some users, digital public services may represent simplification, autonomy and faster access to public procedures. Others may create new barriers related to connectivity, administrative language, digital literacy, trust, documentation requirements, accessibility, and lack of human accompaniment (ECLAC, 2024; OECD, 2023; OECD, 2024).

This territorial heterogeneity is central to understanding the role of public libraries in digital governance. In large urban areas, libraries may support advanced digital citizenship, open data and complex digital services; in intermediate municipalities, they may assist with administrative procedures, employment, education and social protection; and in rural, peripheral or underserved territories, they may provide basic connectivity, trusted mediation and access to reliable information (IFLA & Technology and Social Change Group, 2019; UNESCO, 2023). Their contribution is therefore not limited to computers or internet access, but to translating digital public services into meaningful and usable opportunities for citizens. This perspective is particularly relevant in Latin America because digital transformation often advances in contexts marked by persistent inequality, institutional fragmentation, uneven administrative capacity and unequal access to digital infrastructure. As a result, the mere availability of digital platforms does not guarantee effective access to rights or the creation of public value. Public libraries can help reduce this gap by combining access, mediation, training, trust-building, and territorial knowledge. Their contribution is therefore not limited to providing computers or internet access; it lies in their ability to translate digital public services into meaningful, usable opportunities for citizens.

Therefore, the proposed model's Latin American relevance does not depend on assuming that all libraries have the same capacities or operate under similar institutional conditions. Rather, it lies in offering a flexible framework for analyzing how different types of libraries, under varying territorial and organizational conditions, can contribute to digital governance, public value creation, and resilient public management. This territorial sensitivity is essential for avoiding universalistic digital transformation models that overlook local inequalities and the uneven distribution of public capabilities across the region.

Digital transformation in Latin America must be understood as an institutional, organizational and social process, not only as technological adoption. Although digitized procedures, portals, interoperability, digital identity and public data have gained prominence, they do not automatically improve the relationship between the State and citizens. Digital government creates public value when it reduces administrative barriers, strengthens institutional capacities, builds trust and contributes to inclusive and resilient public administration. Regional literature shows that Latin American governments have promoted inclusion policies, but digital divides persist and affect low-income populations more intensely as technologies evolve (Bisset Alvarez et al., 2015).

Digital policies often measure success through availability indicators: online procedures, platforms, automated services, databases or registered users. These indicators are necessary but insufficient. A platform may be available yet inaccessible to people with low digital literacy, older adults, rural communities, migrants, people with disabilities or citizens without adequate devices or stable connectivity. The central issue is therefore not only service availability, but effective use. Gil-Garcia et al. (2018) argue that digital government must be analyzed with public administration because technologies reshape decision-making, service delivery, accountability, organizational structures and citizen relations. Digital government is not a technological layer added to the State, but a transformation of coordination, response and value creation capacities. Mergel et al. (2019) also show that digital transformation goes beyond converting analogue procedures into electronic ones: it requires service redesign, new professional competencies and people-centred institutional cultures. This is crucial in Latin America, where procedure digitization may advance faster than administrative redesign and citizen capacity-building.

In Latin America and the Caribbean, digital government advances amid social inequality, territorial gaps and heterogeneous institutional capacities. The OECD/CAF (2023) highlights that digital technologies and data can support inclusive, responsive and resilient services when linked to governance frameworks, institutional capacities and people-centred design. The OECD/IDB Digital Government Index assesses digital design by default, data-driven government, government as a platform, openness, user orientation and proactivity (OECD, 2024). These dimensions show that digital maturity depends on infrastructure, leadership, coordination, data, standards, organizational capabilities and legitimacy.

Latin American digital government faces a structural tension. Modernization agendas seek efficiency, simplification, interoperability, automation and service improvement, while inequality, low connectivity, limited skills, complex administrative language, fragmentation and distrust still restrict citizen use (OECD, 2023;

Figueredo Jr. & Silva, 2026). The analysis must therefore move from digital service supply to real conditions of access and appropriation. Moore (1995) argues that public management should be evaluated by socially valuable and legitimate results. In digital reform, this means improving lives, expanding rights and building trust, not only reducing costs. Cordella and Bonina (2012) add that public sector technologies are valuable only through the institutional purposes, organizational arrangements and social benefits they support.

From this perspective, digital government should be analyzed as a strategy for public value creation. Twizeyimana and Andersson (2019) identify e-government values such as better services, efficiency, transparency, participation, trust, inclusion and welfare. In Latin America, these values matter because digitalization can expand opportunities but also reproduce inequalities if it lacks inclusion, mediation and capacity-building policies. Resilient public management adds that administrations must sustain services, adapt to crises and respond to territorial needs. The COVID-19 pandemic showed that public action depended on institutional capacity, social trust and citizens' ability to access support (Bird et al., 2023). In Latin America, library closures and service interruptions also revealed the need to reinvent services through remote provision, expanded information and community responses (Talavera-Ibarra, 2022).

Public libraries have traditionally supported reading, culture, information and education. In digitalized societies, they can also mediate between State digital services and citizens' real capacities. Public digitalization is experienced through concrete actions: filling in forms, requesting grants, booking appointments, downloading certificates, accessing educational platforms or exercising rights online. When these actions become confusing or intimidating, digital government weakens. Libraries can reduce this distance through connectivity, informational guidance, digital literacy, support in understanding services and responsible referral.

In this sense it is key to mention the Dimensions of Digital Government and the Potential Contribution of Public Libraries. Table 1 shows that public libraries can be complementary infrastructures for access, mediation and learning within digital government. They do not design platforms or manage central systems; they help citizens interact with them more autonomously, in an informed way and safely. This is especially relevant where the gap between digital availability and effective use remains wide. Latin America needs not only more platforms, but stronger capacities to transform digitalization into inclusion, trust, participation, learning and resilience.

Table 1. Dimensions of Digital Government and the Potential Contribution of Public Libraries

Dimension of digital government	*Public management challenge*	*Potential contribution of public libraries*	*Expected public value*
Service digitalization	Prevent online procedures from excluding citizens with low digital autonomy	Basic guidance, access to connectivity and support in the use of digital services	Effective access to public services
Data-driven government	Understand territorial needs and barriers to access	Aggregate identification of citizen demands and local digital divides	Better territorial diagnosis
Interoperability	Coordinate public entities, systems and services	Articulation with educational, cultural, social and administrative networks	More integrated services
User orientation	Design understandable and accessible services	Feedback from users' everyday experience	Improving the citizen experience
Digital inclusion	Reducing gaps in access, use and skills	Digital training, information literacy and support for vulnerable groups	Greater citizen autonomy
Public resilience	Sustaining access, information and support in crisis contexts	Library as a territorial node of reliable information and community accompaniment	Greater institutional and territorial response capacity

Source: Authors' elaboration based on Gil-Garcia et al. (2018), Mergel et al. (2019), OECD/CAF (2023) and OECD & Inter-American Development Bank (2024).

Public Libraries as Digital Governance Infrastructures

Public libraries have traditionally provided access to reading, cultural preservation, knowledge democratization and citizen training. In the State's digital transformation, this definition is insufficient. The contemporary public library can be understood as a proximity infrastructure connecting citizens with information, technologies, digital services, training capacities and community networks. This is especially relevant in Latin America, where digital government advances amid persistent social, territorial and technological gaps. IFLA-UNESCO (2022) defines public libraries as a living force for education, culture, inclusion and information, and as essential institutions for participation, well-being and equitable knowledge access (IFLA & UNESCO, 2022). From a digital government perspective, this role gains an additional dimension. Access to rights, social programs, procedures, education, public information and participation is increasingly mediated by platforms. The library can therefore bridge institutional systems and citizens' effective capacities to understand and use them.

In Latin America, this interpretation has particular significance because public libraries operate in territories where digital transformation coexists with persistent inequality, uneven connectivity, fragmented public services and heterogeneous institutional capacities. In many communities, especially rural, peripheral, low-income, migrant or indigenous territories, the main challenge is not only whether digital public services exist, but whether citizens can understand, trust and use them effectively. Public libraries can therefore act as local mediation infrastructures that connect national digital agendas with everyday citizen needs, translating digital government from a platform-centred policy into a socially accessible and territorially grounded public service experience.

Infrastructure is central to this argument. It is not only buildings, networks or devices, but also a governance architecture that organizes actors, rules, technologies and collaborative practices. This matters in Latin American digital governance, where platforms may depend on open architectures, formal and informal rules, and collaboration between government and civil society (Aguerre & Bonina, 2024). In libraries, infrastructure includes spaces, collections, connectivity, equipment, staff, access standards, training programs, community relations and institutional links.

Libraries can contribute to an inclusive digital future through affordable connectivity, skills development, open resources and collaboration with governments on inclusion strategies (UNESCO, 2025). In Latin America, the challenge is to build the social and institutional capacities that make digitalization useful. Advanced platforms remain exclusive if citizens lack accompaniment, learning and mediation. This aligns with meaningful access to information: access is not only connectivity or availability, but also skills, confidence, relevant content, support and the ability to transform information into learning, participation, rights and well-being (International Federation of Library Associations and Institutions & Technology and Social Change Group, 2019).

Libraries as digital governance infrastructures can also be understood through public policy, public access and digital inclusion. Jaeger et al. (2012) show that the digital divide, literacy and inclusion have shaped library policies and public Internet services. Libraries translate policy goals into accompaniment, training and access. This is especially important when national strategies speak of interoperability, digital identity, open data or automation, while citizens experience them as forms, grants, appointments, certificates, information requests or educational registration.

In terms of governance, public libraries occupy an intermediate position between administration, communities and local actors. They can collaborate with municipal governments, social services, schools, universities, employment agencies, older adults' organizations, migrant associations and digital literacy programs. This makes the library a hub of collaborative governance. It does not replace State platforms but improves the public system's capacity to reach citizens and adapt services to local needs. Library mediation involves guidance, translation of administrative language, access to reliable information, learning support, skill-building and responsible referral.

This role requires limits. Libraries should not become substitute administrative offices or assume legal or technical responsibilities belonging to other entities. Their function should be guidance, literacy, basic accompaniment and referral, protecting users, privacy, staff capacity and the library's educational, cultural and informational mission. Table 2 distinguishes between a digitized library and a library integrated into digital governance. The former offers online catalogues, e-lending, or digital resources; the latter supports citizens in exercising their rights, accessing services, building skills, and participating in public life. Therefore, the library's value lies not only in offering digital resources but also in helping citizens convert those resources into effective access, autonomy, and participation.

Table 2. Functions of public libraries as digital governance infrastructures

Function	*Description*	*Institutional mechanism*	*Expected public value*
Digital access	Provision of connectivity, devices, safe spaces and digital resources	Libraries as public technological access points	Reducing access gaps
Citizen mediation	Support for understanding and using public digital services	Library staff as informational and digital intermediaries	Effective use of public services
Skills training	Development of digital, informational and media skills	Workshops, literacy and lifelong learning programs	Autonomy and digital citizenship
Community engagement	Spaces for deliberation, consultation and community production of knowledge	Library as a civic forum and meeting space	Strengthening participation
Information governance	Guidance on access, evaluation and use of public information	Curation, information literacy and data access	Greater transparency and trust
Institutional articulation	Coordination with governments, schools, universities, social services and community organizations	Local collaboration networks	More integrated and territory-sensitive services
Community resilience	Continuity of information, support and learning in crisis contexts	Library as a territorial support node	Greater capacity for social adaptation

Source: Authors' elaboration based on IFLA & UNESCO (2022), Jaeger et al. (2012), Vera-Baceta and Gómez-Hernández (2021) and UNESCO (2025).

Figure 1 represents the public library as a proximity node within a digital governance ecosystem. Citizens, digital public services, community networks and digital capacities are not isolated elements; they are connected through library mediation. In this relationship, the library facilitates access to digital services, supports learning processes, strengthens trust and links citizens with community and institutional resources. The figure therefore shows that the library's contribution is relational: it connects actors, resources and capacities that would otherwise remain fragmented.

Figure 1. Public libraries as digital governance infrastructures

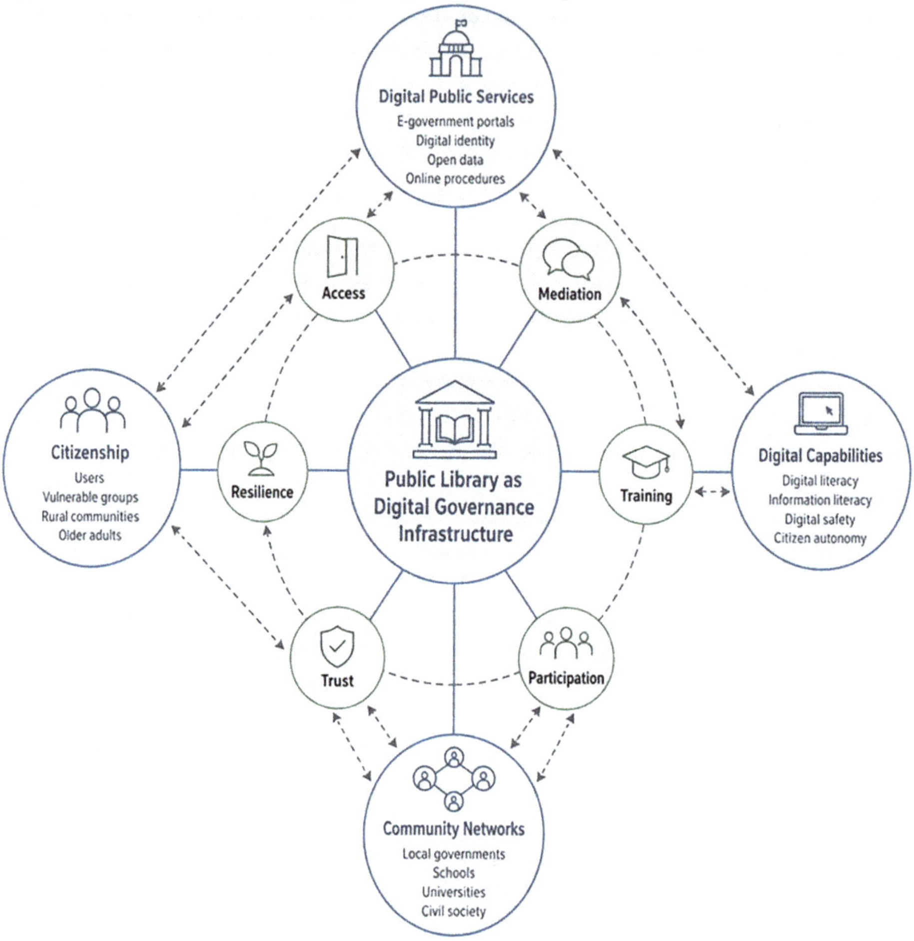

Source: Authors.

Knowledge commons theory also helps frame this role. Hess and Ostrom (2007) argue that knowledge is a shared resource requiring rules, institutions and governance practices for access, equitable use and sustainability. Public libraries can therefore organize access to knowledge and public information on the principles of equity, openness, and community use. Many Latin American libraries face budget constraints, inconsistent connectivity, technological obsolescence, limited specialized staff, weak institutional recognition, and poor integration with digital government policies. Their role as local digital infrastructures is therefore a strategic possibility that requires investment, planning, training and inter-institutional coordination.

The challenge is to move from the library as an isolated cultural facility to the library as a territorial platform for access, mediation, capacities and public value, while protecting open access, privacy, pluralism, informational neutrality, inclusion, cultural diversity and public trust.

MAIN FOCUS OF THE CHAPTER

Creating Public Value in Digital Public Libraries

The digital transformation of public libraries must be evaluated not only by technologies, platforms, catalogues or digital services, but by their capacity to generate public value. Public value refers to social, institutional, democratic and territorial benefits that improve lives, strengthen State legitimacy, expand citizen capacities and support collective well-being. A digital library creates value when it facilitates rights, reduces access barriers, strengthens skills, improves trust and expands participation.

Moore (1995) analyses public management through its capacity to produce socially valuable and legitimate results. This perspective is useful for public libraries because it moves beyond operational indicators towards human development, digital inclusion, informed citizenship and community cohesion. Cordella and Bonina (2012) argue that public sector technologies should be analyzed from public value because they are not inherently valuable; their value depends on purposes, actors, organizational arrangements and social benefits. Thus, a digital public library should be assessed by the public outcomes generated through technological modernization.

Twizeyimana and Andersson (2019) identify public values such as service improvement, efficiency, transparency, participation, trust, inclusion and welfare. These dimensions connect digital government and public libraries. When libraries mediate between citizens and digital services, they facilitate access, reduce transaction costs, promote learning, strengthen community ties and make the State more understandable. In Latin America, this matters because digitalization can deepen inequalities when access depends on connectivity, devices, skills, literacy or capacity to navigate administrative systems.

The first level of value creation concerns citizens. Public libraries expand capacities to access information, use services, develop skills, participate and make informed decisions. They do not replace the State or solve structural inequalities but can reduce concrete barriers that prevent people from benefiting from digitalization.

Access is the most visible dimension. In territories with connectivity gaps, inadequate devices or low digital literacy, libraries can be entry points to the digital ecosystem. Yet access must be meaningful, safe and accompanied. Digital inclusion combines material access, skills, trust, relevant content and the ability to use technologies for specific needs (Jaeger et al., 2012; Real et al., 2014).

Public libraries also generate value by strengthening digital and informational skills. In contexts of misinformation, online procedures and abundant information, citizens need to search, evaluate and use information critically. Libraries are well positioned to offer training programs, workshops, advice and lifelong learning. They also strengthen autonomy: when users learn to complete procedures, request help, access platforms, consult information or protect data, they increase their future capacity to interact with the State. Libraries should therefore accompany users rather than simply do procedures for them. Trust is another outcome: accessible and culturally close library spaces can reduce institutional distance and make digital services less intimidating.

The second level of value creation concerns public administration. Libraries can extend the territorial reach of services, identify recurring obstacles, improve user experience, generate aggregate knowledge about access barriers and strengthen institutional legitimacy. Libraries may observe barriers such as complex forms, technical language, authentication problems, unclear requirements, accessibility gaps or low procedural understanding. If treated in aggregated and privacy-friendly ways, this knowledge can guide clearer and more inclusive services. Libraries can also mediate legitimacy: when the digital State is difficult to use, trust erodes; when proximity institutions help citizens understand and use services, the public experience improves.

At the territorial and community level, digital public libraries contribute to social cohesion, community resilience, lifelong learning, reduction of territorial inequalities and collective capacities. This is crucial in Latin America, where digital divides are spatial and institutional as well as individual.

The public library can function as social infrastructure of proximity. Its value lies in services, bonds, encounters, collective learning and community trust. Literature on libraries and resilience shows contributions to social capital, reliable information and local crisis response capacity (Grace & Sen, 2013; Veil & Bishop, 2014; Vårheim, 2017).

As summarized in Table 3, public value can be organized into three levels: citizenship, public administration and territory-community. This moves evaluation beyond activity indicators. The number of trained users matters, but it is also necessary to know whether users gained autonomy, accessed relevant services, improved participation, reduced exclusion barriers or helped administration identify problems. Evaluation should combine activity, result and impact indicators. From a territorial perspective, libraries can reduce inequalities between connected and disconnected citizens and between territories with different institutional capacities.

Table 3. Levels of public value creation in digital public libraries

Public Value Level	*Primary Beneficiary*	*Value creation mechanisms*	*Expected results*	*Possible indicators*
Value for citizens	Users, households and vulnerable groups	Digital access, mediation, training, information literacy and basic accompaniment	Autonomy, digital inclusion, trust, participation and access to rights	Trained users, accompanied procedures, satisfaction, improvement of skills and effective use of services
Value for public administration	Local governments, public agencies, library systems, and social services	Territorial extension, user feedback, institutional coordination and support for digital services	Improvement of citizen experience, legitimacy, territorial diagnosis and reduction of administrative barriers	Number of partnerships, referrals, recurring demands identified, joint programs, and accessibility improvements
Value for the territory and the community	Local communities, municipalities and social and cultural networks	Spaces for meeting, lifelong learning, reliable information, local memory and crisis response	Social cohesion, community resilience, territorial equity and social capital	Community participation, collaborative activities, territorial coverage, resilience programs and local projects

Source: Authors' elaboration based on Moore (1995), Cordella and Bonina (2012), Jaeger et al. (2012), Twizeyimana and Andersson (2019) and Real et al. (2014).

Figure 2 presents a value-creation chain in which digital resources become public value only when they are mediated by library action. Connectivity, devices, platforms and information resources are enabling conditions, but they do not automatically produce inclusion or autonomy. Library mediation transforms access into learning, trust and citizen capacities; these capacities then allow people to use digital services and information more effectively. The figure therefore links technological resources with social, administrative and territorial outcomes through mediation and capability-building.

Figure 2. Public Value Creation Chain in Digital Public Libraries

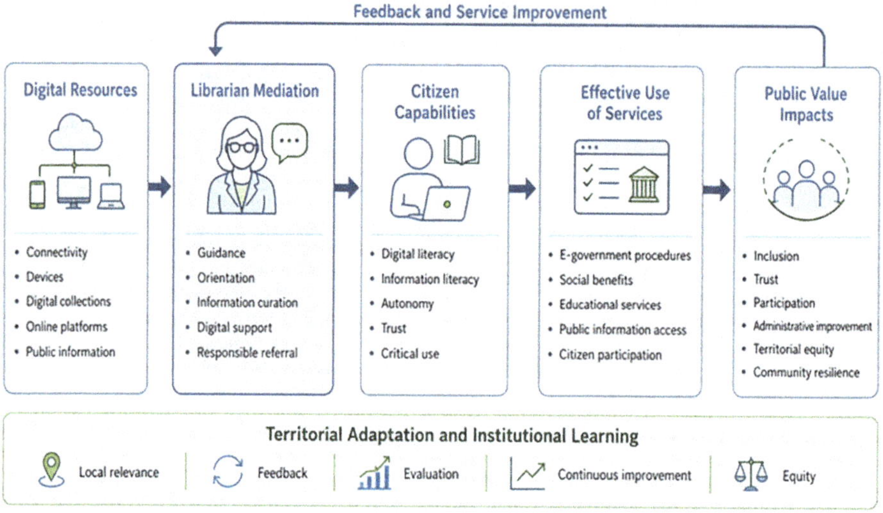

Source: Authors.

Resilience, Inclusion and Territorial Adaptation

The digital transformation of public libraries in Latin America must also be analyzed through resilience, inclusion and territorial adaptation. In territories marked by digital divides, inequality, administrative fragmentation and crisis vulnerability, libraries can serve as proximity infrastructures that sustain information access, learning and community support.

Public resilience is the capacity of institutions, communities and governance systems to anticipate, resist, adapt to and recover from shocks or structural change. In digital governance, resilience depends not only on platforms, data centers or interoperability, but also on intermediate institutions that maintain the State-citizen relationship when access becomes difficult. The OECD/CAF (2023) stresses that digital technologies support responsive and resilient administrations when embedded in governance frameworks, institutional capacities and people-centered design. Public libraries contribute to resilience through territorial proximity, community trust and educational capacity. Proximity places them where digital administration may be distant; trust encourages people to seek guidance; education transforms access into learning and autonomy. Grace and Sen (2013), Veil and Bishop (2014) and Vårheim (2017) link libraries with community resilience, technology assistance, local information, social capital and trust.

This function is not limited to disasters, pandemics or service interruptions. It also appears in ordinary vulnerability: low connectivity, limited public services, difficulties with digital procedures, inadequate devices or distrust. In these contexts, libraries provide stable spaces for information, guidance and learning. Digital inclusion should not be reduced to Internet access. It requires material, cognitive, cultural and administrative conditions to use technologies meaningfully: devices, connectivity, skills, information literacy, trust, security, data protection and relevant services. In Latin America, libraries can play a compensatory role through public access, training and accompaniment.

Digital inclusion is also a condition for exercising rights. When services, education, aid applications, appointments and participation move online, people without sufficient skills are disadvantaged. The digital divide becomes a citizenship gap. Libraries can help bridge formal availability and effective access, but this role requires resources, trained staff, ethical protocols, coordination and recognition within digital inclusion policies.

Territorial adaptation is the third component. Digital transformation is often designed through national strategies, regulations and centralized platforms, but implementation occurs in territories with different capacities, resources, organizational cultures and needs. Digital governance therefore requires mechanisms that adapt policies to large cities, intermediate municipalities, rural areas, peripheries and indigenous territories. Libraries can support territorial adaptation because they know community needs and observe user barriers, including procedural complexity, platform difficulties, administrative language, limited devices, security fears, misinformation or lack of rights knowledge. Managed ethically and in aggregate, this information can inform more territory-sensitive policies.

Not all libraries can play the same role. Urban libraries with strong connectivity and partnerships may develop advanced digital citizenship or open data programs. Rural or peripheral libraries may prioritize basic access, initial literacy, support for essential procedures and connection with services. Both require differentiated strategies and indicators. Resilience, inclusion and territorial adaptation reinforce each other. Digitally inclusive communities are more resilient; territorially adapted administrations are more inclusive; and libraries integrated into governance networks can strengthen both by acting as local nodes of access, learning and coordination. Public libraries can therefore be seen as infrastructures of territorial resilience, not because they assume all response functions, but because they sustain reliable information, learning, orientation, connectivity, community support and meeting spaces.

This role also requires sustainability. Libraries cannot contribute to resilience if they operate precariously. Stable financing, technological maintenance, continuous training, service updating, data protection, accessibility and alliances are essential. Strengthening libraries is therefore part of strengthening the territorial State. In Latin

America, they can help close the gap between centrally designed digital government and diverse citizen realities.

Digital Governance Model and Public Value for Public Libraries

This chapter proposes the Digital Governance and Public Value Creation Model in Public Libraries as a conceptual, multidimensional and policy-oriented heuristic framework for analyzing how Latin American public libraries can support digital governance, public value creation and resilient public management. The model does not seek to predict outcomes statistically or to establish causal effects directly. Rather, it organizes the main institutional, technological, social, organizational and territorial dimensions that explain how public libraries may operate as proximity-based digital governance infrastructures. It assumes that digital transformation should not be assessed solely through technologies, platforms, or digital resources, but through the capacity to articulate governance arrangements, citizen capabilities, human mediation, organizational readiness, territorial adaptation, and public value creation. The model rests on three premises: digital government requires institutions that connect platforms with citizens' effective capacities; public libraries can serve as governance infrastructures because of proximity, access, trust, education and community embeddedness; and public value emerges when digital resources are translated into access, autonomy, administrative improvement, social cohesion, territorial equity and resilience.

The model was developed through conceptual synthesis rather than primary empirical fieldwork. Its construction followed an interpretive and integrative logic based on four sources: academic literature on digital governance, public value, libraries, inclusion, resilience and territorial adaptation; institutional evidence on digital government and territorial gaps in Latin America; library-oriented frameworks on access to information, mediation and meaningful access; and the authors' research engagement with LibrarIN on value co-creation, social innovation and collaborative library services (LibrarIN, 2025). Accordingly, its six dimensions should be understood as analytically grounded propositions rather than statistically validated constructs. Future research should test their empirical relevance through case studies, surveys, interviews, participatory workshops and mixed-method evaluations.

The model was developed through conceptual synthesis rather than primary empirical fieldwork. Its construction followed an interpretive and integrative logic based on four sources: academic literature on digital governance, public value, libraries, inclusion, resilience and territorial adaptation; institutional evidence on digital government and territorial gaps in Latin America; library-oriented frameworks on access to information, mediation and meaningful access; and the authors' research engagement with LibrarIN on value co-creation, social innovation and collaborative library services (LibrarIN, 2025). Accordingly, its six dimensions should be understood as analytically grounded propositions rather than statistically validated constructs. This approach aligns with digital transformation literature, which highlights organizational change, service redesign, professional skills and user orientation (Mergel et al., 2019).

This approach aligns with digital transformation literature, which highlights organizational change, service redesign, professional skills and user orientation (Mergel et al., 2019). It also draws on public value approaches to digital government, where technologies acquire meaning only when they produce socially valuable, legitimate and inclusive results (Cordella & Bonina, 2012; Twizeyimana & Andersson, 2019). The model also adopts public value governance as a collaborative process. Bryson et al. (2014) argue that public value governance articulates actors, capacities, legitimacy, participation and collective outcomes. This helps explain why libraries' contribution depends not only on internal resources, but also on their capacity to connect institutions, interpret needs and facilitate inclusive State-citizen relations.

Based on this methodological construction, the model is organized into six interdependent dimensions. Each dimension represents a necessary and non-substitutable condition in the proposed framework: governance defines institutional integration; infrastructure enables digital access; citizen capabilities make access meaningful; public value links library action to outcomes; organizational capacity sustains implementation; and territorial resilience adapts the model to unequal local contexts. The dimensions should not be read as isolated components, but as mutually reinforcing elements of a governance ecosystem.

The first dimension is digital governance and institutional coordination. It refers to the regulatory frameworks, leadership arrangements, financing mechanisms, partnerships, standards, protocols and evaluation systems that determine whether public libraries are formally integrated into digital government ecosystems. Digital governance is understood here not as the simple adoption of digital tools by public administrations, but as the institutional capacity to coordinate technologies, rules, data, organizations, citizens' capabilities, and accountability mechanisms to create public value. In this sense, the question is not only whether libraries use digital resources, but also whether they are institutionally recognized as actors within digital service ecosystems, inclusion strategies, and territorial governance networks. Without formal recognition, financing and intergovernmental coordination, public libraries may continue providing access, guidance and mediation informally, but their contribution remains fragmented, underfunded and weakly connected to digital transformation policies.

The second dimension is technological infrastructure and interoperability: connectivity, devices, platforms, accessibility, security, data protection and links with public services. Infrastructure enables digital functions but is insufficient without mediation, training and governance.

The third dimension is digital inclusion and citizen capabilities: digital literacy, information literacy, media skills, trust, autonomy and critical information use. Public digitalization generates value only when people can use services effectively, safely and meaningfully.

The fourth dimension is public value creation. For citizens, value means access, autonomy, participation and rights. For administration, it means better user experience, legitimacy, knowledge of barriers and territorial reach. For communities, it means cohesion, social capital, resilience, equity and reliable information.

The fifth dimension is organizational capacity and professional transformation. Libraries need trained staff, flexible routines, leadership, management change, ethical criteria, mediation skills and evaluation capacity. This requires a sustained professional strategy, not only goodwill or isolated training.

The sixth dimension is resilience, sustainability and territorial adaptation. Resilience is understood here not only as the capacity to respond to emergencies, but as a broader governance capacity that combines preparedness, service continuity, institutional learning, adaptation and territorial responsiveness. In the case of public libraries, resilience refers to their ability to maintain access to reliable information, digital support, learning opportunities, community coordination and trusted mediation under both crisis conditions and ordinary situations of vulnerability. This dimension is especially important in Latin America, where public libraries operate within highly unequal territorial contexts marked by uneven connectivity, budget instability, environmental risks, social vulnerability, administrative fragmentation and unequal state presence. From this perspective, a resilient digital public library is not merely a library with technological infrastructure; it is an institution capable of adapting its services, partnerships, professional practices and mediation strategies to diverse and changing community needs while contributing to sustainable public value creation.

Table 4 distinguishes enabling components, mediation mechanisms and expected results. Its value is to avoid reducing digital libraries to technology. Digital transformation requires governance, infrastructure, capabilities, public value, professionalization and resilience; without these dimensions, technology may exist without inclusion, sustainability or evaluation.

Table 4. Dimensions of the digital governance model and public value for public libraries

Dimension	*Guiding question*	*Main components*	*Expected result*
Digital governance and institutional coordination	How is the library integrated into the digital government ecosystem?	Leadership, partnerships, financing, norms, protocols, standards and evaluation	Institutional integration and sustainability
Technology infrastructure and interoperability	What technological conditions allow inclusive digital services?	Connectivity, devices, platforms, accessibility, cybersecurity, data protection and interoperability	Effective and secure digital access
Digital inclusion and citizen skills	How are digital resources transformed into capabilities?	Digital literacy, mediation, information skills, trust and digital citizenship	Autonomy, inclusion and participation
Creating public value	What benefits are generated for citizens, administration and territory?	Access to rights, trust, improvement of services, social cohesion and legitimacy	Citizen, institutional and community value
Organizational capabilities and professional transformation	What skills does the library need to fulfil new functions?	Staff training, change management, mediation, digital ethics and evaluation	Professionalization and institutional innovation
Resilience, sustainability and territorial adaptation	How does the library respond to local crises and needs?	Continuity, flexibility, partnerships, financial sustainability and cultural relevance	Resilient and territorially adapted public management

Source: Authors' elaboration based on Bryson et al. (2014), Cordella and Bonina (2012), Mergel et al. (2019), OECD/CAF (2023) and Twizeyimana and Andersson (2019).

Because resilience and territorial adaptation depend on local institutional and community conditions, the model should be applied with sensitivity to the diversity of public libraries in Latin America. Although public libraries may share a common democratic mission, they differ significantly in resources, institutional dependence, territorial embeddedness, staff profiles, connectivity, community trust and service demands. The following typology illustrates how the model may require differentiated application across library contexts (table 5).

Table 5. Territorial Typology of Public Libraries for Digital Governance Analysis

Type of public library	Likely digital governance priorities	Required capacities	Main risks
Metropolitan or large urban libraries	Advanced digital citizenship, open data, civic innovation, digital learning, access to complex digital public services.	Specialized staff, strong connectivity, institutional partnerships, digital literacy programs, data literacy, innovation-oriented services and evaluation capacity.	Intra-urban inequality, exclusion of vulnerable groups, overemphasis on technology, unequal use among social groups and weak coordination with social policy.
Intermediate municipal libraries	Administrative procedures, education, employment and social protection	Local government coordination, trained staff, municipal integration, service-oriented routines, referral mechanisms and partnerships with schools or local agencies.	Dependence on municipal resources, uneven professionalization, limited budgets, fragmented service provision and weak continuity of digital programs.
Rural or peripheral libraries	Basic connectivity, trusted mediation and essential public services	Stable connectivity, polyvalent staff, community trust, mobile or hybrid services, basic digital equipment and links with regional or national support networks.	Isolation, low funding, technological obsolescence, insufficient infrastructure, limited staff and weak institutional support.
Community or popular libraries	Participation, local memory, informal learning and social cohesion	Community governance, local networks, participatory methods, flexible programming, volunteer support and recognition of local knowledge.	Precarious funding, weak formal recognition, dependence on community labour, limited integration with public policy and lack of stable infrastructure.
Indigenous or intercultural libraries	Intercultural mediation, linguistic relevance and access to rights	Intercultural mediation, multilingual materials, community leadership, culturally relevant digital content, respect for local knowledge systems and participatory governance.	Technological imposition, linguistic exclusion, cultural mismatch, lack of adapted services and insufficient recognition of community knowledge.

Source. Author

This typology does not imply rigid categories. Many Latin American libraries combine characteristics from several types. Its purpose is analytical: to show that the six dimensions of the model should be adapted to territorial context, institutional capacity and community needs. The model should therefore guide differentiated strategies rather than uniform digital transformation policies.

The model's theoretical contribution lies in integrating fields often analyzed separately: digital government, library studies and public value. It places library mediation at the center of digital governance. Its central proposition is that public libraries create public value when technological access is combined with institutional coordination, professional mediation, citizen capability-building and territorial adaptation. The central mechanism is institutional mediation: libraries translate digital resources into meaningful uses through guidance, training, accompaniment, information curation, referral and safe learning spaces. Without mediation, the library is only an access point; with mediation, it becomes a digital citizenship infrastructure.

Public platforms are usually designed through administrative, technical or regulatory logics, while citizens face them with unequal capacities and diverse contexts. Libraries reduce this distance through understandable language, guidance and trust-building. The model proposes a value creation sequence: governance defines roles and resources; infrastructure enables access; mediation transforms access into learning and trust; citizen capacities enable effective use; and effective use generates public value. Evaluation and institutional learning then feed back into the model, making it dynamic rather than linear.

Figure 3 shows the model as a dynamic governance architecture. Digital governance defines the institutional conditions; technological infrastructure enables access; library mediation connects resources with citizen capacities; and these capacities generate public value outcomes. Resilience, sustainability and territorial adaptation operate as cross-cutting dimensions because they influence all stages of the model. The model does not claim that all Latin American libraries already fulfil these functions or can do so without resources. Its purpose is to provide an analytical framework for digital government and resilient public management.

Figure 3. Digital governance model and public value creation in public libraries

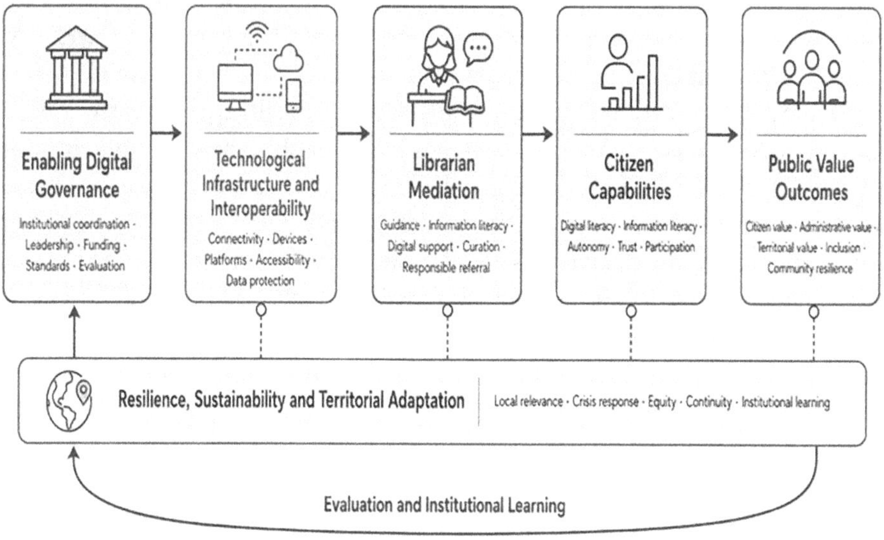

Source: Authors.

The model should not be applied as a uniform recipe. Some libraries can become advanced digital citizenship nodes, while others need basic connectivity, technological updating, staff training or institutional strengthening. It is a flexible tool for diagnosing capacities, identifying gaps, planning interventions and evaluating outcomes.

From a policy perspective, the model can be used as: a diagnostic framework for library digital maturity; a planning tool for inclusion, mediation and professional transformation; an evaluation guide for public value; and a coordination instrument linking libraries with digital government, public innovation and territorial resilience.

Academically, the model connects digital government, public libraries, public value, inclusion and resilient management. These challenges are not only technological, library-related or administrative; they involve governance, inequalities, mediation, trust and territorial adaptation. The model shifts the debate from digital libraries as technological modernization to public libraries as infrastructures for digital governance and public value creation.

SOLUTIONS AND RECOMMENDATIONS

The model has implications for public policy, library management, digital transformation and cooperation in Latin America. If public libraries can function as digital governance and public value infrastructures, they should not be treated only as cultural facilities or peripheral local services. They should be incorporated into digital government, inclusion, public innovation, education, participation and territorial resilience agendas.

First, public libraries should be explicitly incorporated into national and local digital government strategies. Digital policies often focus on platforms, interoperability, data, identity, automation and cybersecurity, while libraries remain in cultural or educational policies. This separation limits their contribution. Integrating libraries into digital agendas would recognize their proximity role, especially where citizens need support to use digital services.

This incorporation must be reflected in plans, budgets, indicators and coordination mechanisms. It requires roles, resources, standards and collaboration channels. The OECD/CAF Digital Government Review (2023) stresses inclusive and responsive services through governance, institutional coordination and people-centered design. Libraries can complement this agenda when they receive formal recognition and support.

Second, library digital transformation should be financed as sustained public policy. Connectivity, devices, maintenance, accessibility, platform updating, security, staff training and assessment require recurring resources. Without them, libraries cannot offer stable access, reliable accompaniment or locally adapted services.

Third, library staff need professional development beyond document management: digital and information literacy, mediation, privacy, accessibility, data protection, public information curation, source evaluation, training design and inter-institutional collaboration. These functions require time, recognition and organizational support.

Staff training matters because mediation is the model's central mechanism. Technology does not make a library inclusive if staff cannot guide diverse users. Clear protocols and referral channels are also needed so staff are not overburdened or asked to assume administrative responsibilities.

Fourth, digital library services should prioritize vulnerable groups: older adults, rural populations, people with disabilities, low-income households, migrants, indigenous communities, young people with low information literacy and users unfamiliar with digital procedures. Libraries can offer differentiated access, training, guidance and accompaniment with privacy, respect and progressive autonomy. This design also requires accessibility: clear language, understandable interfaces, face-to-face support, adapted materials, suitable schedules and programs sensitive to local contexts. In culturally or linguistically diverse territories, libraries can help translate public information socially, without replacing administration.

Fifth, local alliances are essential. Libraries should work with governments, schools, universities, social services, community organizations and employment agencies. These networks expand services, share resources, design relevant programs, avoid duplication and enable responsible referral. Public value governance depends on articulating actors, capacities, legitimacy and collective results (Bryson et al., 2014). Alliances also improve territorial adaptation. Libraries may detect recurring problems with public platforms, forms or language. Through aggregate and ethical feedback, this information can help redesign services, simplify procedures, improve accessibility or reinforce support programs.

Sixth, digital libraries need public value indicators. Evaluation should go beyond users, workshops, devices or connections and measure autonomy, effective service access, skills, trust, participation, vulnerable-group inclusion, coordination and territorial resilience. Technologies should be assessed by their contribution to public purposes, not only efficiency (Cordella & Bonina, 2012). Indicators should combine activity, outcome and impact. Activity indicators measure workshops, users or equipment; outcome indicators assess skills, satisfaction and effective use; impact indicators observe autonomy, participation, trust, inclusion and resilience. This evidence helps justify investment and improve programs.

Table 6 summarizes a roadmap for integrating libraries into digital government strategies. National governments should include libraries in digital, inclusion and connectivity agendas; local governments should recognize them as territorial nodes; library systems should update management, training, evaluation and alliances; and international cooperation should treat libraries as social infrastructure for reducing digital divides. Implementation must be gradual because starting conditions differ. Libraries can contribute to the institutional last mile by making digital government socially accessible and territorially meaningful.

Table 6. Roadmap for integrating public libraries into digital government strategies

Line of action	*Priority action*	*Risk it addresses*	*Expected result*
Institutional recognition	Include public libraries in digital government, digital inclusion and territorial resilience plans	Marginality of libraries in technology policies	Greater institutional coherence and strategic visibility
Sustainable financing	Allocate resources for connectivity, devices, maintenance, accessibility, and staffing	Technological obsolescence and dependence on temporary projects	Sustainable library digital transformation
Professional training	Train staff in digital mediation, privacy, accessibility, information literacy, and responsible referral	Staff overload and low operational capacity	Better citizen support and higher quality of service
Inclusive services	Prioritizing vulnerable groups and territories with greater digital divides	Reproduction of inequalities in access to digital government	Greater equity and effective access to rights and services
Local alliances	Coordinate libraries with governments, schools, universities, social services, employment agencies, and community organizations	Institutional fragmentation and duplication of efforts	More integrated, relevant and territorially adapted services
Value assessment	Measure autonomy, trust, competencies, effective access, participation, inclusion and resilience	Superficial assessment based on activities only	Better decision-making and evidence of public impact
Digital ethics	Establish protocols for privacy, data minimization, informational neutrality, and informed consent	Risks of surveillance, data misuse, or loss of trust	Greater legitimacy, security and citizen trust
Delimitation of functions	Define what the library can do, what it should not assume, and when to refer users to other services	Administrative instrumentalization and confusion of responsibilities	Institutional protection and operational clarity

Source: Authors' elaboration based on Bryson et al. (2014), Cordella and Bonina (2012), IFLA & UNESCO (2022), OECD/CAF (2023) and UNESCO (2025).

Seventh, digital ethics is essential. Integrating libraries into digital government ecosystems creates risks for privacy, data protection, surveillance, dependency, bias and misuse of personal information. Because libraries are trusted spaces for intellectual freedom and equitable information access, mediation programs must include data minimization, confidentiality, informed consent and responsible referral.

Digital ethics also requires neutrality and pluralism. Library staff may help users understand processes, locate information and improve skills, but they should not make decisions for users or assume legal or administrative responsibilities. This boundary protects both users and institutions.

FUTURE RESEARCH AGENDA ON PUBLIC LIBRARIES, DIGITAL GOVERNANCE AND RESILIENT MANAGEMENT

The future research agenda must move from conceptual formulation to empirical, comparative and applicable evidence. Although digital government, inclusion, public value and library studies provide relevant contributions, more research is needed to integrate these fields from a Latin American perspective. Public libraries are not only cultural or educational institutions; they may also support State digital transformation, citizen inclusion and territorial resilience.

The first line of research is to operationalize the model. Its six dimensions should be translated into variables, indicators and evaluation criteria, leading to diagnostic instruments, maturity matrices or public value indices. Measurement should include not only infrastructure and activities, but also mediation, autonomy, trust, vulnerable-group inclusion, alliances and territorial adaptation.

A second line is comparative research across Latin American countries, cities and territories. The region is heterogeneous in institutional development, library systems, digital policies, fiscal capacity, connectivity, regulation and public trust. Comparing large cities, intermediate municipalities, rural areas, peripheries and indigenous territories would identify different digital library models and enabling or limiting factors.

A third line should evaluate the impact of digital inclusion programs. Libraries often provide workshops, advice, Internet access and user support, but effects are not always measured. Research should assess whether these programs improve autonomy, service access, participation, trust and information capacities through mixed quantitative and qualitative methods.

A fourth line should examine rural, peripheral and community libraries as infrastructures of territorial equity. These institutions face connectivity, funding, staffing, distance and sustainability challenges (Real et al., 2014). In Latin America, this is important because public services, institutional capacities and digital opportunities are unevenly distributed.

A fifth line concerns digital ethics, privacy and artificial intelligence. Virtual assistants, chatbots, automated analysis and algorithmic platforms create opportunities and risks. Libraries could support critical literacy on AI, personal data, bias and misinformation, but research must avoid assigning them functions without adequate resources, training or regulation.

A final line should focus on participatory methodologies and service co-creation. Libraries can convene citizens, administration and communities to identify problems, test solutions, improve administrative language and design literacy programs. Co-creation research shows that participation can make services more relevant and legitimate (Voorberg et al., 2015). These lines require case studies, comparative methods, surveys, interviews, focus groups and mixed methods. Participatory action research may be especially useful for designing, implementing and evaluating programs with libraries and communities.

CONCLUSION

This chapter argues that public libraries in Latin America can be reinterpreted as infrastructures for digital governance, public value creation and resilient public management. This shifts the library from a cultural facility or documentary service to a public institution of proximity, mediation, learning, inclusion and territorial articulation. Digital transformation should not be reduced to technologies, catalogues, lending platforms, connectivity or equipment. It becomes meaningful when digital resources are integrated with institutional capacities, human mediation, information literacy, community trust, public coordination and citizen value. A digital public library should therefore be evaluated by its ability to expand rights, reduce gaps, strengthen capacities and improve relations between the State, citizens and territory.

This discussion is especially relevant in Latin America, where digital government advances alongside social, territorial and institutional inequalities. Public platforms, electronic procedures and interoperability do not guarantee inclusion. For many people, digitalization may become a barrier when connectivity, skills, trust, administrative understanding and support are lacking. Public libraries can act as intermediary institutions by translating digital government strategies into concrete citizen experiences. The chapter's main conceptual contribution is the Digital Governance and Public Value Creation Model in Public Libraries. The model organizes digital public libraries around six interdependent dimensions: governance and coordination; technological infrastructure and interoperability; digital inclusion and citizen capacities; public value; organizational capacities and professional transformation; and resilience, sustainability and territorial adaptation.

The model shows that public value is created at three levels. Citizens benefit through access, skills, autonomy, trust and participation. Public administration benefits through territorial reach, improved user experience, barrier identification and legitimacy. Territories and communities benefit when public libraries contribute to cohesion, resilience, lifelong learning, equity and reliable information.

The chapter avoids an idealized view. Latin American public libraries face budget constraints, uneven connectivity, technological obsolescence, limited specialized staff, weak integration with digital government policies and poor impact evaluation. Their role as governance infrastructures requires policy decisions, investment, professionalization, coordination and sustainability. Libraries can guide, train, mediate and refer responsibly, but they should not replace administrative bodies. Their potential lies in combining proximity, trust and pedagogical capacity.

Academically, the chapter connects digital government, public libraries, digital inclusion, public value and resilient management. This integration is necessary because public digitalization is technological, institutional, social, territorial and democratic. Libraries show how digital policies meet citizens' real capacities. The main conclusion is that public libraries can become digital governance and public value infrastructures when institutionally strengthened, sustainably financed, integrated into governance networks, professionalized and evaluated for their contribution to citizens, administration and territory. Under these conditions, they can support more inclusive, adaptive and resilient public management in Latin America.

DISCLOSURE OF DELEGATION TO GENERATIVE AI

The authors declare that generative AI tools were used to support the research and writing process, including literature search support, source systematization, proofreading, editing, translation support, citation auditing, APA style checking, figure drafting, and review of academic writing in English. All AI-assisted outputs were reviewed, verified, and edited by the authors. Human validation included checking factual claims, verifying DOI and URL availability, reviewing the consistency between in-text citations and references, and identifying possible hallucinated or unsupported content. No empirical data were generated, fabricated, modified, or analyzed by AI. The use of AI was conducted under the authors' responsibility for academic integrity and in accordance with publisher disclosure requirements. The GAI tool used was ChatGPT. Responsibility for the final manuscript lies entirely with the authors.

REFERENCES

Aguerre, C., & Bonina, C. (2024). Open government, civic tech and digital platforms in Latin America: A governance study of Montevideo's urban app "Por Mi Barrio". *Information Systems Journal, 34*(4), 1037–1067. DOI: 10.1111/isj.12468

Bird, M. D., Arispe, S., Muñoz, P., & Freier, L. F. (2023). Trust, social protection, and compliance: Moral hazard in Latin America during the COVID-19 pandemic. *Journal of Economic Behavior & Organization, 206*, 279–295. DOI: 10.1016/j.jebo.2022.12.010 PMID: 36570103

Bisset Alvarez, E., Grossi de Carvalho, A. M., & Gregorio Vidotti, S. A. B. (2015). Políticas públicas de inclusión digital: El caso de América Latina y Cuba [Public policies for digital inclusion: The case of Latin America and Cuba]. *Biblios: Journal of Librarianship and Information Science, 58*(58), 42–53. DOI: 10.5195/biblios.2015.203

Bryson, J. M., Crosby, B. C., & Bloomberg, L. L. (2014). Public value governance: Moving beyond traditional public administration and the new public management. *Public Administration Review, 74*(4), 445–456. DOI: 10.1111/puar.12238

Cordella, A., & Bonina, C. M. (2012). A public value perspective for ICT-enabled public sector reforms: A theoretical reflection. *Government Information Quarterly, 29*(4), 512–520. DOI: 10.1016/j.giq.2012.03.004

Economic Commission for Latin America and the Caribbean. (2024, November 8). *eLAC begins a new stage centered on concrete actions and projects, with the approval of the Digital Agenda for Latin America and the Caribbean 2026* [Press release]. United Nations. https://www.cepal.org/en/pressreleases/elac-begins-new-stage-centered-concrete-actions-and-projects-approval-digital-agenda

Espinosa Zárate, Z., Camilli Trujillo, C., & Plaza-de-la-Hoz, J. (2023). Digitalization in vulnerable populations: A systematic review in Latin America. *Social Indicators Research, 170*(3), 1183–1207. DOI: 10.1007/s11205-023-03239-x

Figueredo, E.Jr, & Silva, L. C. S. (2026). Challenges of digital services in public administration in the era of digital transformation: A systematic literature review. *Journal of the Knowledge Economy, 17*(4), 11926–11955. Advance online publication. DOI: 10.1007/s13132-026-03277-z

Gil-Garcia, J. R., Dawes, S. S., & Pardo, T. A. (2018). Digital government and public management research: Finding the crossroads. *Public Management Review, 20*(5), 633–646. DOI: 10.1080/14719037.2017.1327181

Grace, D., & Sen, B. (2013). Community resilience and the role of the public library. *Library Trends*, *61*(3), 513–541. DOI: 10.1353/lib.2013.0008

Hess, C., & Ostrom, E. (Eds.). (2007). *Understanding knowledge as a commons: From theory to practice*. MIT Press.

International Federation of Library Associations and Institutions, & the Technology and Social Change Group. (2019). *Development and access to information 2019*. International Federation of Library Associations and Institutions. https://www.ifla.org/publications/development-and-access-to-information-da2i-report-2019/

International Federation of Library Associations and Institutions, & UNESCO. (2022). *IFLA-UNESCO Public Library Manifesto 2022*. International Federation of Library Associations and Institutions. https://www.ifla.org/public-library-manifesto/

Jaeger, P. T., Bertot, J. C., Thompson, K. M., Katz, S. M., & DeCoster, E. J. (2012). The intersection of public policy and public access: Digital divides, digital literacy, digital inclusion, and public libraries. *Public Library Quarterly*, *31*(1), 1–20. DOI: 10.1080/01616846.2012.654728

Librar, I. N. (2025, June 23). *LibrarIN launches groundbreaking managerial guidelines to boost collaborative innovation in libraries* [Press release]. https://librarin.eu/

Mergel, I., Edelmann, N., & Haug, N. (2019). Defining digital transformation: Results from expert interviews. *Government Information Quarterly*, *36*(4), 101385. Advance online publication. DOI: 10.1016/j.giq.2019.06.002

Moore, M. H. (1995). *Creating public value: Strategic management in government*. Harvard University Press.

Organisation for Economic Co-operation and Development, & CAF Development Bank of Latin America and the Caribbean. (2023). Digital government review of Latin America and the Caribbean: Building inclusive and responsive public services. *OECD Publishing*. DOI: 10.1787/29f32e64-en

Organisation for Economic Co-operation and Development, & Inter-American Development Bank. (2024). 2023 OECD/IDB Digital Government Index of Latin America and the Caribbean: Results and key findings. *OECD Publishing*. DOI: 10.1787/14e1c5e8-en-fr

Real, B., Bertot, J. C., & Jaeger, P. T. (2014). Rural public libraries and digital inclusion: Issues and challenges. *Information Technology and Libraries*, *33*(1), 6–24. DOI: 10.6017/ital.v33i1.5141

Robinson, L., Schulz, J., Dodel, M., Correa, T., Villanueva-Mansilla, E., Leal, S., Magallanes-Blanco, C., Rodriguez-Medina, L., Dunn, H. S., Levine, L., McMahon, R., & Khilnani, A. (2020). Digital inclusion across the Americas and Caribbean. *Social Inclusion (Lisboa)*, *8*(2), 244–259. DOI: 10.17645/si.v8i2.2632

Talavera-Ibarra, A. M. (2022). Trends in Latin America: Libraries' challenges magnified by the COVID-19 pandemic. *Library Trends*, *71*(2), 198–214. DOI: 10.1353/lib.2022.a922375

Twizeyimana, J. D., & Andersson, A. (2019). The public value of e-government: A literature review. *Government Information Quarterly*, *36*(2), 167–178. DOI: 10.1016/j.giq.2019.01.001

UNESCO. (2023). *UNESCO's Communication and Information Sector: Upholding information as a public good, advancing universal access, digital inclusion and freedom of expression.* UNESCO. https://unesdoc.unesco.org/ark:/48223/pf0000387119

UNESCO, & International Federation of Library Associations and Institutions. (2025). *Global network of libraries and local impact: A policy roadmap to build an inclusive digital future.* UNESCO Digital Library. https://unesdoc.unesco.org/ark:/48223/pf0000396214

Vårheim, A. (2017). Public libraries, community resilience, and social capital. *Information Research,* 22(1), Article colis1642. https://informationr.net/ir/22-1/colis/colis1642.html

Veil, S. R., & Bishop, B. W. (2014). Opportunities and challenges for public libraries to enhance community resilience. *Risk Analysis*, *34*(4), 721–734. DOI: 10.1111/risa.12130 PMID: 24164095

Vera-Baceta, M.-Á., & Gómez-Hernández, J.-A. (2021). *"Digital citizenship spaces" in public libraries: A proposal for their integration within the framework of the National Digital Skills Plan.* Anuario ThinkEPI, 15, Article e15b02. DOI: 10.3145/thinkepi.2021.e15b02

Voorberg, W. H., Bekkers, V. J. J. M., & Tummers, L. G. (2015). A systematic review of co-creation and co-production with citizens in public innovation. *Public Management Review*, *17*(9), 1333–1357. DOI: 10.1080/14719037.2014.930505

KEY TERMS AND DEFINITIONS

Citizen Capacities: A set of skills, knowledge and conditions that allow people to access, understand and use public services and digital technologies autonomously, critically and securely.

Digital Citizenship: Ability to participate in public life, access rights, use services, interact with institutions and exercise civic responsibilities through digital environments.

Digital Governance: A set of institutional arrangements, capacities, standards, platforms, data, and coordination mechanisms that enable the public sector to design, deliver, and evaluate digital services oriented towards public value.

Digital Inclusion: Process by which people and communities access digital technologies, information, skills and services in an effective, meaningful and secure way, reducing social, territorial and educational barriers.

Digital Public Libraries: Library institutions that integrate technological resources, digital services, professional mediation, and access to information to expand opportunities for learning, citizen participation, and social inclusion.

Library Mediation: Professional function through which libraries responsibly guide, accompany, train and refer citizens to information, digital resources and public services.

Public Value: Social, institutional, democratic or territorial benefit generated by a public action that improves capacities, trust, access to rights, inclusion, participation and collective well-being.

Territorial Resilience: The capacity of a territory to adapt, respond and recover in the face of crises, inequalities or transformations through institutional, community and social networks.

Compilation of References

Abbas, A. E., Van Velzen, T., Ofe, H., Van De Kaa, G., Zuiderwijk, A., & De Reuver, M. (2024). Beyond control over data: Conceptualizing data sovereignty from a social contract perspective. *Electronic Markets, 34*(1), 20. DOI: 10.1007/s12525-024-00695-2

Acemoglu, D., & Robinson, J. A. (2012). *Why nations fail: The origins of power, prosperity, and poverty.* Crown.

Addo, A. (2022). Orchestrating a digital platform ecosystem to address societal challenges: A robust action perspective. *Journal of Information Technology, 37*(4), 359–386. DOI: 10.1177/02683962221088333

Aguerre, C., & Bonina, C. (2024). Open government, civic tech and digital platforms in Latin America: A governance study of Montevideo's urban app "Por Mi Barrio". *Information Systems Journal, 34*(4), 1037–1067. DOI: 10.1111/isj.12468

Ahern, D. (2025). *The new anticipatory governance culture for innovation: Regulatory foresight, regulatory experimentation and regulatory learning. arXiv.* https://doi.org//arxiv.2501.05921DOI: 10.48550

Ahmed, M. O., El-adaway, I. H., Coatney, K. T., & Eid, M. S. (2016). Construction bidding and the winner's curse: Game theory approach. *Journal of Construction Engineering and Management, 142*(2), 04015076. DOI: 10.1061/(ASCE)CO.1943-7862.0001058

Aitsi-Selmi, A., Egawa, S., Sasaki, H., Wannous, C., & Murray, V. (2015). The Sendai framework for disaster risk reduction: Renewing the global commitment to people's resilience, health, and wellbeing. *International Journal of Disaster Risk Science, 6*(2), 164–176. DOI: 10.1007/s13753-015-0050-9

Akçay, E. (2020). Deconstructing evolutionary game theory: Coevolution of social behaviors with their evolutionary setting. *American Naturalist, 195*(2), 315–330. DOI: 10.1086/706811 PMID: 32017621

Al Mokdad, A. (2025). Inclusive and intelligent governance: Enabling sustainability through policy and technology. In *Social system reforms to achieve global sustainability* (pp. 173–238). IGI Global. DOI: 10.4018/979-8-3373-1280-4.ch008

Allegretta, R. A., Angioletti, L., & Balconi, M. (2025). Analytic vs. synthetic decision-making: A behavioral and EEG study with real-world decision-making scenarios. *Neurophysiology*, •••, 1–10. DOI: 10.1007/s11062-025-09964-y

Alqahtani, A., Yan, J., Vlahu-Gjorgievska, E., & Cao, C. (2025). *Factors influencing citizens' adoption of AI-enabled public services in Saudi Arabia: The role of cybersecurity, privacy, and trust.* DOI: 10.1145/3785153

Alston, P. (2019). *Report of the Special Rapporteur on extreme poverty and human rights: Digital welfare states and human rights (United Nations Document A/74/493).* United Nations General Assembly. https://undocs.org/A/74/493

Anand, S., & Wan Mohamed, W. M. (2025). AI as an autonomous decision-maker in governance: A new era of policy formulation. In *The power of agentic AI: Redefining human life and decision-making in Industry 6.0* (pp. 81–96). Springer Nature Switzerland. DOI: 10.1007/978-3-031-89424-4_6

Andreoni, A., & Roberts, S. (2022). Governing digital platform power for industrial development: Towards an entrepreneurial-regulatory state. *Cambridge Journal of Economics*, *46*(6), 1431–1454. Advance online publication. DOI: 10.1093/cje/beac055

Androutsopoulou, M., Carayannis, E. G., Askounis, D., & Zotas, N. (2025). Leveraging AI for enhanced e-government: Optimizing the use of open governmental data. *Journal of the Knowledge Economy*, *16*(3), 12998–13033. DOI: 10.1007/s13132-024-02317-w

Ansell, C., Sørensen, E., & Torfing, J. (2021). The COVID-19 pandemic as a game changer for public administration and leadership? The need for robust governance responses to turbulent problems. *Public Management Review*, *23*(7), 949–960. DOI: 10.1080/14719037.2020.1820272

Ansell, C., Sørensen, E., & Torfing, J. (2023). Public administration and politics meet turbulence: The search for robust governance responses. *Public Administration*, *101*(1), 3–22. DOI: 10.1111/padm.12874

Ansell, C., Sørensen, E., Torfing, J., & Trondal, J. (2024). *Robust governance in turbulent times*. Cambridge University Press., DOI: 10.1017/9781009433006

Ansell, C., & Trondal, J. (2018). Governing turbulence: An organizational-institutional agenda. *Perspectives on Public Management and Governance*, *1*(1), 43–57. DOI: 10.1093/ppmgov/gvx013

Anubi, O., & Konstantinou, C. (2020). Enhanced resilient state estimation using data-driven auxiliary models. *IEEE Transactions on Industrial Informatics*, *16*(1), 639–647. DOI: 10.1109/TII.2019.2924246

Aragani, V. M., Anumolu, V. R., & Selvakumar, P. (2025). Democratization in the age of algorithms: Navigating opportunities and challenges. In *Democracy and democratization in the age of AI* (pp. 39–56). IGI Global. DOI: 10.4018/979-8-3693-8749-8.ch003

Arsène, S., Mabi, C., & Carey-Libbrecht, L. (2021). Public action through the lens of digital governmentality. *Reseaux (London)*, *225*(1), 9–22. DOI: 10.3917/res.225.0009

ASEAN. (2021). *ASEAN Digital Masterplan 2025*. ASEAN Secretariat. https://asean.org/wp-content/uploads/2021/08/ASEAN-Digital-Masterplan-2025.pdf

Asmawanti-S, D., Afiah, N. N., Ritchi, H., & Suharman, H. (2025). Literature review of government digital services based on public value theory and citizen perspectives. *Cogent Business & Management*, *12*(1), 2518494. DOI: 10.1080/23311975.2025.2518494

Attard, J., Orlandi, F., & Auer, S. (2016). Data driven governments: Creating value through open government data. In *Transactions on Large-Scale Data- and Knowledge-Centered Systems XXVII* (Vol. 9860, pp. 84-110). DOI: 10.1007/978-3-662-53416-8_6

Attard, J., Orlandi, F., Scerri, S., & Auer, S. (2015). A systematic review of open government data initiatives. *Government Information Quarterly*, *32*(4), 399–418. DOI: 10.1016/j.giq.2015.07.006

Aumann, R. J. (2023). The world of game theory and game theory of the world: A personal journey. *Revue Économique (Paris)*, *74*(4), 655–660. DOI: 10.3917/e.reco.744.0655

Azhar, A. (2026). AI in government: Future trends and recommendations. In *Artificial intelligence and government: Examining the roles and uses of AI in enhancing government operations* (pp. 367–393). Springer Nature Switzerland. DOI: 10.1007/978-3-032-12344-2_16

Badawy, W. (2025). Algorithmic sovereignty and democratic resilience: Rethinking AI governance in the age of generative AI. *AI and Ethics*, *5*(5), 4855–4862. DOI: 10.1007/s43681-025-00739-z

Bandura, R., McLean, M., & Smutny, C. (2024, August 26). *Approaches to digital public infrastructure in the Global South.* Center for Strategic and International Studies. https://www.csis.org/analysis/approaches-digital-public-infrastructure-global-south

Barnwal, P. (2024). Curbing leakage in public programs: Evidence from India's Direct Benefit Transfer policy. *The American Economic Review*, *114*(12), 3812–3846. DOI: 10.1257/aer.20161864

Bateman, M., Duvendack, M., & Loubere, N. (2019). Is fintech the new panacea for poverty alleviation and local development? Contesting Suri and Jack's M-Pesa findings published in Science. *Review of African Political Economy*, *46*(161), 480–495. DOI: 10.1080/03056244.2019.1614552

Battistella, C., & De Toni, A. F. (2022). Towards a foresight governance system: The case of the port system authority of Trieste. In *2022 7th International Conference on Smart and Sustainable Technologies (SpliTech)* (pp. 1–4). IEEE. https://doi.org/ DOI: 10.23919/SpliTech55088.2022.9854348

Beck, U. (1992). Risk society: Towards a new modernity. *Sage (Atlanta, Ga.).*

Begany Grace, M., & Gil-Garcia, J. R. (2024). Open government data initiatives as agents of digital transformation in the public sector: Exploring the extent of use among early adopters. *Government Information Quarterly*, *41*(3), 101955. Advance online publication. DOI: 10.1016/j.giq.2024.101955

Belhaj, Y., & Boulahoual, A. (2024). La gouvernance des données au service de la création de valeur publique: Cas du Maroc. *American Scientific Journal*, *3*(23), 635–654. DOI: 10.5281/zenodo.11122145

Benington, J., & Moore, M. H. (Eds.). (2011). *Public value: Theory and practice.* Palgrave Macmillan. DOI: 10.1007/978-0-230-36431-8

Bird, M. D., Arispe, S., Muñoz, P., & Freier, L. F. (2023). Trust, social protection, and compliance: Moral hazard in Latin America during the COVID-19 pandemic. *Journal of Economic Behavior & Organization*, *206*, 279–295. DOI: 10.1016/j.jebo.2022.12.010 PMID: 36570103

Bisset Alvarez, E., Grossi de Carvalho, A. M., & Gregorio Vidotti, S. A. B. (2015). Políticas públicas de inclusión digital: El caso de América Latina y Cuba [Public policies for digital inclusion: The case of Latin America and Cuba]. *Biblios: Journal of Librarianship and Information Science*, *58*(58), 42–53. DOI: 10.5195/biblios.2015.203

Boin, A., 't Hart, P., Stern, E., & Sundelius, B. (2016). *The politics of crisis management: Public leadership under pressure* (2nd ed.). Cambridge University Press. DOI: 10.1017/9781316339756

Bolton, M., & Mintrom, M. (2023). RegTech and creating public value: Opportunities and challenges. *Policy Design and Practice*, *6*(3), 266–282. DOI: 10.1080/25741292.2023.2213059

Boston, J. (2017). *Governing for the future: Designing democratic institutions for a better tomorrow*. Emerald.

Botzen, W. J. W., Thepaut, L. D., & Banerjee, S. (2025). Kahneman's insights for climate risks: Lessons from bounded rationality, heuristics and biases. *Environmental and Resource Economics*, *88*(10), 2663–2688. DOI: 10.1007/s10640-025-00980-4 PMID: 41079046

Bouckaert, G., & Van de Walle, S. (2003). Comparing measures of citizen trust and user satisfaction as indicators of 'good governance': Difficulties in linking trust and satisfaction indicators. *International Review of Administrative Sciences*, *69*(3), 329–343. DOI: 10.1177/0020852303693003

Boullier, D. (2022). *Puissance des plateformes numériques, territoires et souverainetés* (2e éd.) [Research paper]. Sciences Po, Centre d'Études Européennes et de Politique Comparée.

Boyd, E., Nykvist, B., Borgström, S., & Stacewicz, I. A. (2015). Anticipatory governance for social-ecological resilience. *Ambio*, *44*(S1, Suppl 1), 149–161. DOI: 10.1007/s13280-014-0604-x PMID: 25576289

Bozeman, B. (2002). Public-value failure: When efficient markets may not do. *Public Administration Review*, *62*(2), 145–161. DOI: 10.1111/0033-3352.00165

Bozeman, B. (2007). *Public values and public interest: Counterbalancing economic individualism*. Georgetown University Press.

Briggs, A. (1961). The welfare state in historical perspective. *Archives Européennes de Sociologie*, *2*(2), 221–258. DOI: 10.1017/S0003975600000412

Brown, A., Fishenden, J., Thompson, M., & Venters, W. (2017). Appraising the impact and role of platform models and Government as a Platform (GaaP) in UK Government public service reform: Towards a Platform Assessment Framework (PAF). *Government Information Quarterly*, *34*(2), 167–182. Advance online publication. DOI: 10.1016/j.giq.2017.03.003

Bryson, J. M., Crosby, B. C., & Bloomberg, L. (2014). Public value governance: Moving beyond traditional public administration and the new public management. *Public Administration Review*, *74*(4), 445–456. DOI: 10.1111/puar.12238

Buttow, C. V., & Weerts, S. (2022). Public sector information in the European Union policy: The misbalance between economy and individuals. *Big Data & Society*, *9*(2), 20539517221124587. Advance online publication. DOI: 10.1177/20539517221124587

Buyannemekh, B., Picazo-Vela, S., Luna, D., & Luna-Reyes, L. (2024). Understanding value of digital service delivery by governments in Mexico. *Government Information Quarterly*, *41*(2), 101936. DOI: 10.1016/j.giq.2024.101936

Cabinet Office. (2023). *National risk register 2023*. UK Government.

Cai, X., Gao, B., & Nan, X. (2025). Distributed event-triggered Nash equilibrium seeking algorithm with quantization communication. *International Journal of Control, Automation, and Systems*, *23*(7), 1956–1966. DOI: 10.1007/s12555-023-0689-8

Calzati, S., & Van Loenen, B. (2023). A fourth way to the digital transformation: The data republic as a fair data ecosystem. *Data & Policy*, *5*, e21. Advance online publication. DOI: 10.1017/dap.2023.18

Calzati, S., & Van Loenen, B. (2025). The Data Republic: Fostering a sustainable, inclusive and resilient digital transformation for the European Union. *Frontiers in Political Science*, *7*, 1670152. Advance online publication. DOI: 10.3389/fpos.2025.1670152

Cao, J. (2024). The role of digital governance in improving government transparency and citizen engagement. *Applied Mathematics and Nonlinear Sciences*, *9*(1), 20243368. Advance online publication. DOI: 10.2478/amns-2024-3368

Caron, D. J. (2021). *Écosystème de la transformation de l'administration publique vers le numérique*. Presses de l'Université du Québec. https://www.puq.ca/catalogue/livres/ecosysteme-transformation-administration-publique-vers-numerique-3906.html

Carrillo, F. (2026). Artificial intelligence and big data in global politics: How AI and ML influence power, governance, and democracy. In *International relations, misinformation and polarization* (pp. 1–11).

Chandrasekhar, R. (2025). *Sustainable open data ecosystems through data quality, governance, and infrastructure: Unlocking social, political and economic value*. https://hal.science/hal-05328147v1

Chang, Y.-C. (2025). Dynamics of a quantum Cournot-Bertrand duopoly model based on bounded rationality and product substitutability. *Quantum Information Processing*, *24*(7), 217. DOI: 10.1007/s11128-025-04810-w

Chattopadhyay, S., Nelson, N., Au, A., Morales, N., Sanchez, C., Pandita, R., & Sarma, A. (2022). Cognitive biases in software development. *Communications of the ACM*, *65*(4), 115–122. DOI: 10.1145/3517217

Chen, L., Tong, T., Tang, S., & Han, N. (2021). Governance and Design of Digital Platforms: A Review and Future Research Directions on a Meta-Organization. *Journal of Management*, *48*(1), 147–184. DOI: 10.1177/01492063211045023

Chen, L., Yi, J., Li, S., & Tong, T. W. (2022). Platform governance design in platform ecosystems: Implications for complementors' multihoming decision. *Journal of Management*, *48*(3), 630–656. DOI: 10.1177/0149206320988337

Chenok, D. (2025). Envisioning the future of government: How emerging, secure technologies and data flows can enable anticipation and action that improve performance. In *Anticipatory governance: Shaping futures through foresight and innovation* (pp. 221–234). World Scientific., DOI: 10.1142/9789811296000_0014

Chheang, S., & Huot, S. (2026). Safeguarding digital classrooms: Cybersecurity implications of AI-driven tools in Cambodian education. [JEILT]. *Journal of Education Innovation & Language Teaching*, *2*(1), 24–46. DOI: 10.63381/jeilt.v2i1.86

Chowdhury, R. H. (2022). *Digital government initiatives and national resilience: How digital governance frameworks were transformed post-COVID to maintain national services.* World Journal of Advanced Engineering Technology and Sciences., DOI: 10.30574/wjaets.2022.7.1.0098

Comfort, L. K., Boin, A., & Demchak, C. C. (2010). *Designing resilience: Preparing for extreme events.* University of Pittsburgh Pre. DOI: 10.2307/j.ctt5hjq0c

Cordella, A., & Bonina, C. M. (2012). A public value perspective for ICT enabled public sector reforms: A theoretical reflection. *Government Information Quarterly*, *29*(4), 512–520. DOI: 10.1016/j.giq.2012.03.004

Cordella, A., Gualdi, F., & Van de Laar, M. (2024). Digital skills within the public sector: A missing link to achieve the Sustainable Development Goals (SDGs). *Information Polity*, *29*(1), 13–33. Advance online publication. DOI: 10.3233/IP-230008

Cordella, A., & Paletti, A. (2019). Government as a platform, orchestration, and public value creation: The Italian case. *Government Information Quarterly*, *36*(4), 101409. DOI: 10.1016/j.giq.2019.101409

Cristofari, G., & Gerbaudo, P. (2025). Towards an empowered 'Platform State'. *In Proceedings of Digital Government Research.* DOI: 10.59490/dgo.2025.958

Danneels, L., & Viaene, S. (2025). Organizational capabilities for Government as a Platform: The case of engaging the labour market ecosystem. *Information Polity, 30*(3), 180–200. Advance online publication. DOI: 10.1177/15701255251349949

Davies, P., Fritzsche, A., Parry, G., & Wood, Z. (2023). Data, resilience, and identity in the digital age. *Strategic Change, 32*(6), 169–174. Advance online publication. DOI: 10.1002/jsc.2560

Davis, I. (2024). Rational representations of uncertainty: A pluralistic approach to bounded rationality. *Synthese, 203*(5), 142. DOI: 10.1007/s11229-024-04586-z

Demirgüç-Kunt, A., Klapper, L., Singer, D., & Ansar, S. (2022). *The Global Findex Database 2021: Financial inclusion, digital payments, and resilience in the age of COVID-19.* World Bank. DOI: 10.1596/978-1-4648-1897-4

Deuerlein, J. W., Elhay, S., Piller, O., & Simpson, A. R. (2023). Modelling flow and pressure control in water distribution systems using the Nash equilibrium. *Journal of Water Resources Planning and Management, 149*(6), 04023019. DOI: 10.1061/JWRMD5.WRENG-5889

Díaz-Arancibia, J., Hochstetter-Diez, J., Bustamante-Mora, A., Sepúlveda-Cuevas, S., Albayay, I., & Arango-López, J. (2024). Navigating digital transformation and technology adoption: A literature review from small and medium-sized enterprises in developing countries. *Sustainability (Basel), 16*(14), 5946. DOI: 10.3390/su16145946

Dincă, G., Bărbu ă, M., & Dincă, D. (2025). Crisis as a Catalyst: Difference-in-Differences Evidence on Digital Public Service Transformation in the European Union. *Administrative Sciences.* Advance online publication. DOI: 10.3390/admsci15100393

Dmitrieva, N., Minchenko, O., & Rylskikh, E. (2022). Digital platforms as a regulator and the regulated subject, or how platforms change the system of public administration. *Public Administration Issues.* DOI: 10.17323/1999-5431-2022-0-2-60-84

Doré, G. (2023). La privatisation numérique: Déstabilisation et réinvention du service public [Compte rendu]. *RECMA, 370-371*(4), 133–134. DOI: 10.3917/recma.370.0134

Doshi, A. R., & Schmidt, W. (2024). Soft governance across digital platforms using transparency. *Strategy Science, 9*(2), 185–204. DOI: 10.1287/stsc.2023.0006

Drèze, J., Khalid, N., Khera, R., & Somanchi, A. (2017). Aadhaar and food security in Jharkhand: Pain without gain? *Economic and Political Weekly*, *52*(50), 50–59.

Duan, X., & Guo, R. (2025). Authentically exotic: Understanding how video games foster cultural adaptation and destination image formation among foreign players. *Journal of Hospitality and Tourism Technology*, •••, 1–22. DOI: 10.1108/JHTT-01-2025-0007

Duarte, A., Frost, J., Gambacorta, L., Koo Wilkens, P., & Shin, H. S. (2022). Central banks, the monetary system and public payment infrastructures: Lessons from Brazil's Pix. *Bank for International Settlements Bulletin No. 52*. Bank for International Settlements. https://www.bis.org/publ/bisbull52.htm

Duit, A. (2016). Resilience thinking: Lessons for public administration. *Public Administration*, *94*(2), 364–380. DOI: 10.1111/padm.12182

Dunleavy, P., & Margetts, H. (2023). Data science, artificial intelligence and the third wave of digital era governance. *Public Policy and Administration*, *40*(2), 185–214. DOI: 10.1177/09520767231198737

Dunleavy, P., Margetts, H., Bastow, S., & Tinkler, J. (2006). *Digital era governance: IT corporations, the state, and e-government*. Oxford University Press. DOI: 10.1093/acprof:oso/9780199296194.001.0001

Dunleavy, P., Margetts, H., Bastow, S., & Tinkler, J. (2008). *Digital era governance: IT corporations, the state and e-government*. Oxford University Press.

Dunlop, C. A., & Radaelli, C. M. (2018). The lessons of policy learning: Types, triggers, hindrances and pathologies. *Policy and Politics*, *46*(2), 255–272. DOI: 10.1332/030557318X15230059735521

Dusi, G. (2024). Reliabilist epistemology meets bounded rationality. *Synthese*, *203*(4), 115. DOI: 10.1007/s11229-024-04525-y

Economic Commission for Latin America and the Caribbean. (2024, November 8). *eLAC begins a new stage centered on concrete actions and projects, with the approval of the Digital Agenda for Latin America and the Caribbean 2026* [Press release]. United Nations. https://www.cepal.org/en/pressreleases/elac-begins-new-stage-centered-concrete-actions-and-projects-approval-digital-agenda

Egala, S., Alhassan, A.-H. S., & Boakye, J. A. (2025). Unleashing public sector innovation. *In Proceedings of Digital Government Research*. DOI: 10.59490/dgo.2025.976

Esping-Andersen, G. (1990). *The three worlds of welfare capitalism.* Princeton University Press.

Espinosa Zárate, Z., Camilli Trujillo, C., & Plaza-de-la-Hoz, J. (2023). Digitalization in vulnerable populations: A systematic review in Latin America. *Social Indicators Research, 170*(3), 1183–1207. DOI: 10.1007/s11205-023-03239-x

Espinosa, V. I., & Pino, A. (2025). E-Government as a development strategy: The case of Estonia. *International Journal of Public Administration, 48*(2), 86–99. DOI: 10.1080/01900692.2024.2316128

Esposito, P., & Tufo, M. (2024). How to Retrace Public Value Creation in the Era of Digital and Sustainable Transformation? Insights from a Recovery Plan. *Journal of Comprehensive Social Science Research.* DOI: 10.33790/jcssr1100107

Esposito, F. M. (2024). Platforming public administration: An empirical analysis on the institutionalization of digital technologies. *Tecnoscienza — Italian Journal of Science &. Technology Studies, 15*(1), 39–59. DOI: 10.6092/issn.2038-3460/18779

Essert Inc. (2025). *AI governance in the public sector: Essential frameworks for government agencies.* Essert Inc. https://essert.io/ai-governance-in-the-public-sector

Eubanks, V. (2018). *Automating inequality: How high-tech tools profile, police, and punish the poor.* St. Martin's Press.

European Commission. (2020). *2020 strategic foresight report: Charting the course towards a more resilient Europe.* European Union.

European Commission. (2021). *Proposal for a regulation laying down harmonised rules on artificial intelligence (Artificial Intelligence Act).* Publications Office of the European Union.

European Commission. (2023). *2023 strategic foresight report: Sustainability and wellbeing at the heart of Europe's open strategic autonomy.* European Union.

European Commission. (2023). *European pillar of social rights: Social scoreboard.* Publications Office of the European Union.

European Commission. (2024). *Digital economy and society index (DESI) 2024.* Publications Office of the European Union.

Fares, A., Elazouni, A., & Al-Alawi, M. (2025). Using game theory to negotiate win–win payment terms between contractors and subcontractors. *Journal of Construction Engineering and Management, 151*(5), 04025023. DOI: 10.1061/JCEMD4.COENG-15140

Figueredo, E.Jr, & Silva, L. C. S. (2026). Challenges of digital services in public administration in the era of digital transformation: A systematic literature review. *Journal of the Knowledge Economy*, *17*(4), 11926–11955. Advance online publication. DOI: 10.1007/s13132-026-03277-z

Flick, U. (2018). Doing qualitative data collection–charting the routes. In Flick, U. (Ed.), *The SAGE handbook of qualitative data collection* (pp. 3–16). SAGE Publications., DOI: 10.4135/9781526416070.n1

Fornell, C., & Larcker, D. F. (1981). Evaluating structural equation models with unobservable variables and measurement error. *JMR, Journal of Marketing Research*, *18*(1), 39–50. DOI: 10.1177/002224378101800104

Francis-Auton, E., Cheek, C., Austin, E., Ransolin, N., Richardson, L., Safi, M., Hayba, N., Testa, L., Harrison, R., Braithwaite, J., & Clay-Williams, R. (2024). Exploring and understanding the 'experience' in experience-based codesign: A state-of-the-art review. *International Journal of Qualitative Methods*, *23*, 16094069241235563. Advance online publication. DOI: 10.1177/16094069241235563

Frucquet, P., & Carassus, D. (2023). *Territoires numériques: Comment favoriser la (co-)création de valeur publique?* https://univ-pau.hal.science/hal-04362404

Fuerth, L. S., & Faber, E. M. H. (2012). *Anticipatory governance practical upgrades: Equipping the executive branch to cope with increasing speed and complexity of major challenges*. National Defense University Press.

Fuerth, L. S., & Faber, E. M. H. (2012). *Anticipatory governance: Practical upgrades*. National Defense University Press.

Gabor, D., & Brooks, S. (2017). The digital revolution in financial inclusion: International development in the fintech era. *New Political Economy*, *22*(4), 423–436. DOI: 10.1080/13563467.2017.1259298

Georgiev, M., & Simeonov, S. (2025). Research of social processes in the works of Venelin Terziev. In *Innovation and sustainability in digital era: The role of economics and business strategies with education perspectives* (pp. 425–435). Peter Lang.

Gil, L. R. A. (2023). *La gouvernance des données en tant que « biens communs »: étude juridico-stratégique pour une valorisation publique des données informationnelles [Thèse de doctorat]*. https://theses.hal.science/tel-04042474

Gil-Garcia, J. R., Dawes, S. S., & Pardo, T. A. (2018). Digital government and public management research: Finding the crossroads. *Public Management Review*, *20*(5), 633–646. DOI: 10.1080/14719037.2017.1327181

Gomes, P. M., & Cardoso, T. (2025). AI-driven transformation in public governance. In *Public governance practices in the age of AI* (pp. 81–108). IGI Global. DOI: 10.4018/979-8-3693-9286-7.ch005

Grace, D., & Sen, B. (2013). Community resilience and the role of the public library. *Library Trends*, *61*(3), 513–541. DOI: 10.1353/lib.2013.0008

Greenhalgh, T., Thorne, S., & Malterud, K. (2018). Time to challenge the spurious hierarchy of systematic over narrative reviews? *European Journal of Clinical Investigation*, *48*(6), e12931. DOI: 10.1111/eci.12931 PMID: 29578574

Grimmelikhuijsen, S. (2023). Explaining why the computer says no: Algorithmic transparency affects the perceived trustworthiness of automated decision-making. *Public Administration Review*, *83*(2), 241–262. DOI: 10.1111/puar.13483

Gross, N., & Geiger, S. (2023). Choreographing for public value in digital health? *Big Data & Society*, *10*(2), 20539517231220622. Advance online publication. DOI: 10.1177/20539517231220622

Guston, D. H. (2010). The anticipatory governance of emerging technologies. *Applied Science and Convergence Technology*, *19*(6), 432–441. DOI: 10.5757/JKVS.2010.19.6.432

Guston, D. H. (2014). Understanding anticipatory governance. *Social Studies of Science*, *44*(2), 218–242. DOI: 10.1177/0306312713508669 PMID: 24941612

Habegger, B. (2010). Strategic foresight in public policy: Reviewing the experiences of the UK, Singapore, and the Netherlands. *Futures*, *42*(1), 49–58. DOI: 10.1016/j.futures.2009.08.002

Hair, J. F., Hult, G. T. M., Ringle, C. M., & Sarstedt, M. (2022). *A primer on partial least squares structural equation modeling (PLS-SEM)* (3rd ed.). Sage.

Haldane, A. G., & May, R. M. (2011). Systemic risk in banking ecosystems. *Nature*, *469*(7330), 351–355. DOI: 10.1038/nature09659 PMID: 21248842

Hanisch, M., Goldsby, C. M., Fabian, N. E., & Oehmichen, J. (2023). Digital governance: A conceptual framework and research agenda. *Journal of Business Research*, *162*, 113777. Advance online publication. DOI: 10.1016/j.jbusres.2023.113777

Hansen, H. K., & Uldam, J. (2022). Assembling transnational policing: Europol's anticipatory governance. *Global Society*, *36*(2), 281–299. DOI: 10.1080/13600826.2021.2021146

Han, Y., & Xie, L. (2025). Sustainable Governance of Digital Platform Ecosystem: A life cycle perspective through multiple governance parties. *Sustainability (Basel), 17*(8), 3628. Advance online publication. DOI: 10.3390/su17083628

Haug, N., Dan, S., & Mergel, I. (2024). Digitally-induced change in the public sector: A systematic review and research agenda. *Public Management Review, 26*(7), 1963–1987. DOI: 10.1080/14719037.2023.2234917

Hédoin, C. (2015). Accounting for constitutive rules in game theory. *Journal of Economic Methodology, 22*(4), 439–461. DOI: 10.1080/1350178X.2015.1024874

Heeks, R. (2005). *Implementing and managing eGovernment: An international text.* SAGE Publications.

Hein, A., Engert, M., Ryu, S., Schaffer, N., Hermes, S., & Krcmar, H. (2023). Building open government data platform ecosystems: A dynamic development approach that engages users from the start. *Government Information Quarterly, 40*(4), 101878. DOI: 10.1016/j.giq.2023.101878

Hein, A., Schreieck, M., Riasanow, T., Setzke, D. S., Wiesche, M., Böhm, M., & Krcmar, H. (2019). Digital platform ecosystems. *Electronic Markets, 30*(1), 87–98. DOI: 10.1007/s12525-019-00377-4

He, J., He, Y., Hu, J., & Guo, Y. (2025). Intelligent governance: The AI-driven new paradigm of governmental adaptive governance. *Journal of US-China Public Administration, 22*(1), 1–27.

Hemerijck, A. (2013). *Changing welfare states.* Oxford University Press.

Henseler, J., Ringle, C. M., & Sarstedt, M. (2015). A new criterion for assessing discriminant validity in variance-based structural equation modeling. *Journal of the Academy of Marketing Science, 43*(1), 115–135. DOI: 10.1007/s11747-014-0403-8

Heo, K., & Seo, Y. (2021). Anticipatory governance for newcomers: Lessons learned from the UK, the Netherlands, Finland, and Korea. *European Journal of Futures Research, 9*(1), 16. Advance online publication. DOI: 10.1186/s40309-021-00179-y

Hess, C., & Ostrom, E. (Eds.). (2007). *Understanding knowledge as a commons: From theory to practice.* MIT Press.

Hietala, H., & Päivärinta, T. (2025). Governing collective ambidexterity: Antecedents, mechanisms, and outcomes in digital service ecosystems. *Government Information Quarterly, 42*(1), 102001. DOI: 10.1016/j.giq.2024.102001

Hood, C. (1991). A public management for all seasons? *Public Administration, 69*(1), 3–19. DOI: 10.1111/j.1467-9299.1991.tb00779.x

Huot, S. (2026). Digital diplomacy in Cambodia: Embracing artificial intelligence for strategic engagement and national development. In Turan, A., & Ucuzal, H. (Eds.), *Diplomacy in the age of artificial intelligence* (pp. 307–330). IGI Global Scientific Publishing., DOI: 10.4018/979-8-3373-4937-4.ch013

Huot, S., & Chheang, S. (2026). Public security and trust-building in Cambodia: Navigating challenges of the post-truth era for positive developmental progress. In Ağırdil, O., & Ayhan, U. (Eds.), *Navigating public security in the age of post-truth: Challenges and implications* (pp. 245–274). IGI Global Scientific Publishing., DOI: 10.4018/979-8-3373-6786-6.ch009

Iden, J., & Bygstad, B. (2024). Managing digital transformation with sociotechnical systems theory. *European Journal of Information Systems*, *33*(6), 789–807. DOI: 10.1080/0960085X.2024.2347950

Idzi, F., & Gomes, R. (2022). *Digital governance: government strategies that impact public services*. Global Public Policy and Governance., DOI: 10.1007/s43508-022-00055-w

Intergovernmental Panel on Climate Change. (2023). *Climate change 2023: Synthesis report. Contribution of Working Groups I, II and III to the Sixth Assessment Report of the Intergovernmental Panel on Climate Change*. IPCC. DOI: 10.59327/IPCC/AR6-9789291691647

International Federation of Library Associations and Institutions, & the Technology and Social Change Group. (2019). *Development and access to information 2019*. International Federation of Library Associations and Institutions. https://www.ifla.org/publications/development-and-access-to-information-da2i-report-2019/

International Federation of Library Associations and Institutions, & UNESCO. (2022). *IFLA-UNESCO Public Library Manifesto 2022*. International Federation of Library Associations and Institutions. https://www.ifla.org/public-library-manifesto/

International Organization for Standardization. (2018). *ISO 31000: Risk management—Guidelines*. ISO.

International Risk Governance Council. (2018). *Guidelines for the governance of systemic risks*. IRGC.

Jack, W., & Suri, T. (2014). Risk sharing and transaction costs: Evidence from Kenya's mobile money revolution. *The American Economic Review*, *104*(1), 183–223. DOI: 10.1257/aer.104.1.183

Jacob, S., Defacqz, S., & Agossou, N. (2022). *Promesses et défis de la transformation numérique du secteur public*. Chaire de recherche sur l'administration numérique, Université Laval.

Jaeger, P. T., Bertot, J. C., Thompson, K. M., Katz, S. M., & DeCoster, E. J. (2012). The intersection of public policy and public access: Digital divides, digital literacy, digital inclusion, and public libraries. *Public Library Quarterly*, *31*(1), 1–20. DOI: 10.1080/01616846.2012.654728

Janowski, T., Estevez, E., & Baguma, R. (2018). Platform governance for sustainable development: Reshaping citizen-administration relationships in the digital age. *Government Information Quarterly*, *35*(4, Suppl.), S1–S16. DOI: 10.1016/j.giq.2018.09.002

Janssen, M., & Kuk, G. (2016). The challenges and limits of big data algorithms in technocratic governance. *Elsevier*, *33*(3), 371–377. DOI: 10.1016/j.giq.2016.08.011

Janssen, M., & Van Der Voort, H. (2016). Adaptive governance: Towards a stable, accountable and responsive government. *Elsevier*, *33*(1), 1–5. DOI: 10.1016/j.giq.2016.02.003

Janssen, M., Brous, P., Estevez, E., Barbosa, L. S., & Janowski, T. (2020). Data governance: Organizing data for trustworthy Artificial Intelligence. *Government Information Quarterly*, *37*(3), 101493. DOI: 10.1016/j.giq.2020.101493

Janssen, M., Charalabidis, Y., & Zuiderwijk, A. (2012). Benefits, adoption barriers and myths of open data and open government. *Information Systems Management*, *29*(4), 258–268. DOI: 10.1080/10580530.2012.716740

Janssen, M., Konopnicki, D., Snowdon, J., & Ojo, A. (2017). Driving public sector innovation using big and open linked data (BOLD). *Information Systems Frontiers*, *19*(2), 189–195. DOI: 10.1007/s10796-017-9746-2

Jin, D. (2024). The challenges and opportunities of public governance in the digital era. *International Journal of Social Sciences and Public Administration*, *2*(3), 472–478. DOI: 10.62051/ijsspa.v2n3.64

Johnston, E. (2025). Anticipatory identity control: Upstream governance on digital platforms. *Dialogues on Digital Society*, *1*(3), 442–446. DOI: 10.1177/29768640251377164

Jonathan, G. M., Perjons, E., & Rusu, L. (2024). Digital transformation-driven decentralisation of public governance. *Procedia Computer Science*, *239*, 1220–1229. DOI: 10.1016/j.procs.2024.06.290

Jovanovic, M., Sjodin, D., & Parida, V. (2021). Co-evolution of platform architecture, platform services, and platform governance: Expanding the platform value of industrial digital platforms. *ArXiv*, abs/2102.04862. DOI: 10.1016/j.technovation.2020.102218

Kahneman, D. (2011). *Thinking, fast and slow*. Farrar, Straus and Giroux.

Kattel, R., & Mazzucato, M. (2018). Mission-oriented innovation policy and dynamic capabilities in the public sector. *Industrial and Corporate Change*, *27*(5), 787–801. DOI: 10.1093/icc/dty032

Kausche, K., & Weiss, M. (2024). Platform power and regulatory capture in digital governance. *Business and Politics*. Advance online publication. DOI: 10.1017/bap.2024.33

Keskin, K. (2025). A game theory approach to football predictions. *Public Choice*, •••, 1–21. DOI: 10.1007/s11127-025-01317-x

Khalil, E. L. (2022). The information inelasticity of habits: Kahneman's bounded rationality or Simon's procedural rationality? *Synthese*, *200*(4), 343. DOI: 10.1007/s11229-022-03815-7

Khera, R. (2017). Impact of Aadhaar in welfare programmes (Social Science Research Network Working Paper No. 3045235). *Social Science Research Network*. DOI: 10.2139/ssrn.3045235

Khera, R. (2019). Aadhaar failures: A tragedy of errors. *Economic and Political Weekly*, *54*(14), 10–13.

Kim, E. (2026). Institutionalizing predictive AI in public administration: Algorithmic governance and the case of a wildfire forecasting system. *Policy and Internet*, *18*(1), e70029. DOI: 10.1002/poi3.70029

Klievink, B., Van Stijn, E., Hesketh, D., Aldewereld, H., Overbeek, S., Heijmann, F., & Tan, Y.-H. (2012). Enhancing visibility in international supply chains: The data pipeline concept. [IJEGR]. *International Journal of Electronic Government Research*, *8*(4), 54–64. DOI: 10.4018/jegr.2012100104

Kline, R. B. (2023). *Principles and practice of structural equation modeling* (5th ed.). Guilford Press.

Klinke, A., & Renn, O. (2002). A new approach to risk evaluation and management: Risk-based, precaution-based, and discourse-based strategies. *Risk Analysis*, *22*(6), 1071–1094. DOI: 10.1111/1539-6924.00274 PMID: 12530780

Kock, N. (2015). Common method bias in PLS-SEM: A full collinearity assessment approach. *International Journal of e-Collaboration, 11*(4), 1–10. DOI: 10.4018/ijec.2015100101

Kole, E., Noordegraaf-Eelens, L., & Vringer, B. (2025). Cognitive biases in consumer sentiment: The peak-end rule and herding. *Empirical Economics, 69*(4), 2141–2211. DOI: 10.1007/s00181-025-02797-y

Kong, B. (2022). The adjustment logic and reform path of the government governance system and mechanism in the digital age. *Advances in Economics and Management Research, 1*(2), 16. DOI: 10.56028/aemr.1.2.16

Korotun, O., & Veretin, L. (2025). *Theoretical and methodological principles of state regulation of the digitalization of consumer market infrastructure in the context of sustainable development.* Market Infrastructure., DOI: 10.32782/infrastruct85-2

Kud, A. (2021). Decentralized Information Platforms in Public Governance: Reconstruction of the Modern Democracy or Comfort Blinding. *International Journal of Public Administration, 46*(3), 195–221. DOI: 10.1080/01900692.2021.1993905

Lanna, M. (2025). Plateformes et gouvernance des données. *RPN, 1*(1). Advance online publication. DOI: 10.62688/RPN20259194

Lawyer, C., Davani, H. T., & Goharian, E. (2024). Coalitional game theory for stormwater management and green infrastructure practices. *Journal of Water Resources Planning and Management, 150*(1), 04023070. DOI: 10.1061/JWRMD5.WRENG-5979

Lee, J.-Y., Kim, B., & Yoon, S.-H. (2024). A conceptual digital policy framework via mixed-methods approach: Navigating public value for value-driven digital transformation. *Government Information Quarterly, 41*(3), 101961. DOI: 10.1016/j.giq.2024.101961

Lewerenz, S., Moen, A., & Martins, H. (2025). Public value and digital health: The example of guiding values in the national digital health strategy of France. *International Journal of Medical Informatics, 196*, 105794. DOI: 10.1016/j.ijmedinf.2025.105794 PMID: 39862565

Librar, I. N. (2025, June 23). *LibrarIN launches groundbreaking managerial guidelines to boost collaborative innovation in libraries* [Press release]. https://librarin.eu/

Li, K., & Cheung, S. O. (2019). Unveiling cognitive biases in construction project dispute resolution through the lenses of third-party neutrals. *Journal of Construction Engineering and Management, 145*(11), 04019070. DOI: 10.1061/(ASCE)CO.1943-7862.0001707

Linsbichler, A. (2023). An ultra-refined grammar for interactions: Thoughts on Robert Aumann's philosophy of game theory. *Revue Économique (Paris)*, *74*(4), 635–650. DOI: 10.3917/e.reco.744.0635

Lin, Z., & Yaakop, M. R. (2024). Research on digital governance based on Web of Science - A bibliometric analysis. *Frontiers in Political Science*, *6*, 1403404. DOI: 10.3389/fpos.2024.1403404

Liu, C., & Li, Y. (2025). Research on AI-driven public policy decision support systems. In *Proceedings of the 2025 2nd International Conference on Digital Economy and Computer Science* (pp. 777–781). DOI: 10.1145/3785706.3785827

Lumivero. (2026, April 8). *Matrix coding query*. NVivo help. https://help-nv.qsrinternational.com/20/win/Content/queries/matrix-coding-query.htm

Luna, D. E., Picazo-Vela, S., Battulga, B., & Luna-Reyes, L. F. (2024). Creating public value through digital service delivery from a citizen's perspective. *Government Information Quarterly*, *41*(2), 101928. DOI: 10.1016/j.giq.2024.101928

Luna, D., Duarte-Valle, A., Picazo-Vela, S., & Luna-Reyes, L. (2015). Digital governance and public value creation at the state level. *Information Polity*, *20*(2,3), 167–182. DOI: 10.3233/IP-150360

Lu, P., Zhou, L., & Fan, X. (2023). Platform governance and sociological participation. *The Journal of Chinese Sociology*, *10*(1), 3. Advance online publication. DOI: 10.1186/s40711-023-00181-w PMID: 36909780

Luque-Cerpa, A., & Gutiérrez-Naranjo, M. Á. (2025). A membrane computing approach to the generalized Nash equilibrium. *Natural Computing*, *24*(2), 321–336. DOI: 10.1007/s11047-025-10014-z

Ly, B., Ly, R., & Ma, S. (2026). Digital transformation and flexibility in public services: Knowledge, culture and digital infrastructures. *Journal of Innovation & Knowledge*, *13*, 100947. DOI: 10.1016/j.jik.2026.100947

MacArthur, B., Dorobantu, C., & Margetts, H. (2022). Resilient government requires data science reform. *Nature Human Behaviour*, *6*(8), 1035–1037. DOI: 10.1038/s41562-022-01423-6 PMID: 35941235

Mader, P. (2015). *The political economy of microfinance: Financializing poverty*. Palgrave Macmillan. DOI: 10.1057/9781137364210

Mader, P. (2018). Contesting financial inclusion. *Development and Change*, *49*(2), 461–483. DOI: 10.1111/dech.12368

Marchau, V. A. W. J., Walker, W. E., Bloemen, P. J. T. M., & Popper, S. W. (Eds.). (2019). *Decision making under deep uncertainty: From theory to practice*. Springer. DOI: 10.1007/978-3-030-05252-2

Margetts, H., & Dunleavy, P. (2013). The second wave of digital-era governance. *Philosophical Transactions of the Royal Society A: Mathematical, Physical and Engineering Sciences, 371*(1987), 20120382. https://doi.org/DOI: 10.1098/rsta.20120382

Margetts, H., & Dorobantu, C. (2019). Rethink government with AI. *Nature, 568*(7751), 163–165. DOI: 10.1038/d41586-019-01099-5 PMID: 30967667

Margetts, H., & Dunleavy, P. (2013). The second wave of digital-era governance: A quasi-paradigm for government on the Web. *Philosophical Transactions. Series A, Mathematical, Physical, and Engineering Sciences, 371*(1987), 1–17. DOI: 10.1098/rsta.2012.0382 PMID: 23419851

Marty, F. (2020). Accès aux données, coopétition intra-plateforme et concurrence inter-plateformes numériques. *Revue d'Economie Industrielle, 169*, 221–246. DOI: 10.4000/rei.8967

Masoudi, M. (2025). Algorithmic governance, data-driven decision making, and the transformation of democratic accountability in contemporary states. *Advanced Journal of Management. Humanity and Social Science, 2*(1), 10–22.

Máté, D., Kiss, J. T., & Csernoch, M. (2025). Cognitive biases in user experience and spreadsheet programming. *Education and Information Technologies, 30*(11), 14821–14851. DOI: 10.1007/s10639-025-13392-0

Matusitz, J. (2009). A postmodern theory of cyberterrorism: Game theory. *Information Security Journal: A Global Perspective*. DOI: 10.1080/19393550903200474

Mazzucato, M. (2021). *Mission economy: A moonshot guide to changing capitalism*. Harper Business.

Mazzucato, M., & Kattel, R. (2020). COVID-19 and public-sector capacity. *Oxford Review of Economic Policy, 36*(Suppl. 1), S256–S269. DOI: 10.1093/oxrep/graa031 PMID: 40504220

McCarthy, S., Rowan, W., Mahony, C., & Vergne, A. (2023). The dark side of digitalization and social media platform governance: A citizen engagement study. *Internet Research, 33*(6), 2172–2204. DOI: 10.1108/INTR-03-2022-0142

McColl-Kennedy, J. R., Zaki, M., Andreassen, T. W., Coote, L. V., Brea, E., Willer, F., & Andrade, J. (2025). Digital twins: A game changer in customer experience. *Journal of Service Management*, •••, 1–31. DOI: 10.1108/JOSM-12-2024-0540

Mehr, H., & Ash, H. (2017). *Artificial intelligence for citizen services and government.* Ash Center for Democratic Governance and Innovation, Harvard Kennedy School.

Meijer, A., & Bolívar, M. P. R. (2016). Governing the smart city: A review of the literature on smart urban governance. *International Review of Administrative Sciences, 82*(2), 392–408. DOI: 10.1177/0020852314564308

Mergel, I., Edelmann, N., & Haug, N. (2019). Defining digital transformation: Results from expert interviews. *Government Information Quarterly, 36*(4), 101385. DOI: 10.1016/j.giq.2019.06.002

Mericskay, B. (2021). Les effets de l'open data et du big data dans la fabrique des cartes de l'action publique. In Les cartes de l'action publique (pp. 107-128). DOI: 10.4000/books.septentrion.127177

Mersico, L., Aureli, S., & Foschi, E. (2025). *Exploring the role of digital platforms in promoting value co-creation: evidence from the Italian municipal solid waste management system.* Sustainability Accounting, Management and Policy Journal., DOI: 10.1108/SAMPJ-03-2024-0317

Midgley, J. (1995). *Social development: The developmental perspective in social welfare.* Sage Publications.

Mišić, J. (2021). Ethics and governance in the digital age. *European View, 20*(2), 175–181. DOI: 10.1177/17816858211061793

Monye, E. (2024, January 18). *Why Nigeria's controversial naira redesign policy hasn't met its objectives.* Carnegie Endowment for International Peace. https://carnegieendowment.org/research/2024/01/why-nigerias-controversial-naira-redesign-policy-hasnt-met-its-objectives?lang=en

Moon, M. J., Lee, S., Park, S., & Park, I. (2025). The dawn of disruptive technology-driven future government. *Futures for the Public Sector, 141.*

Moore, M. H. (1995). *Creating public value: Strategic management in government.* Harvard University Press.

Muller, J. (2018). *The tyranny of metrics.* Princeton University Press.

Muralidharan, K., Niehaus, P., & Sukhtankar, S. (2016). Building state capacity: Evidence from biometric smartcards in India. *The American Economic Review, 106*(10), 2895–2929. DOI: 10.1257/aer.20141346

Nagaraj, A. (2024). A mapping lens for estimating data value. *Special Issue 4: Democratizing Data.* DOI: 10.1162/99608f92.82f0de5a

Nascimento, P. V. M., de Siqueira, P. B. B., Chrispim, N., Chaves, R. M., Barbosa, C. E., & de Souza, J. M. (2025). The future of AI in government services and global risks: Insights from design fictions. *European Journal of Futures Research, 13*(1), 9. DOI: 10.1186/s40309-025-00253-9

Natile, S. (2020). *The exclusionary politics of digital financial inclusion: Mobile money, gendered walls*. Routledge. DOI: 10.4324/9780367179618

Nicholls, J., Lawlor, E., Neitzert, E., & Goodspeed, T. (2012). *A guide to social return on investment (SROI)*. The SROI Network.

Nicoli, M., & Paltrinieri, L. (2019). Platform cooperatives. *The South Atlantic Quarterly, 118*(4), 801–819. Advance online publication. DOI: 10.1215/00382876-7825624

Nie, J., Ranestad, K., & Tang, X. (2025). Algebraic degrees of generalized Nash equilibrium problems. *Science China. Mathematics, 68*(7), 1747–1776. DOI: 10.1007/s11425-023-2305-y

North, D. C. (1990). *Institutions, institutional change and economic performance*. Cambridge University Press. DOI: 10.1017/CBO9780511808678

O'Reilly, T. (2011). Government as a platform. *Innovations: Technology, Governance, Globalization, 6*(1), 13–40. DOI: 10.1162/INOV_a_00056

OECD Korea Policy Centre. (2023). *Capacity Building Programme Cambodia 2023: Advancing a data-driven government in Cambodia*. Public Governance Programme, OECD Korea Policy Centre. https://www.oecdkorea.org/eng

OECD. (2019). *Strategic foresight for better policies: Building effective governance in the face of uncertain futures*. OECD Publishing.

OECD. (2019). *The path to becoming a data-driven public sector (OECD Digital Government Studies). Organisation for Economic Co-operation and Development (OECD)*. Publishing., DOI: 10.1787/059814a7-

OECD. (2020). *A systemic resilience approach to dealing with Covid-19 and future shocks*. OECD Publishing.

OECD. (2021). *21st-century readers: Developing literacy skills in a digital world*. Organisation for Economic Co-operation and Development Publishing., DOI: 10.1787/a83d84cb-

OECD. (2023). *Government at a glance 2023*. OECD Publishing.

OECD. (2025). *Building anticipatory capacity with strategic foresight in government: Lessons from Lithuania, Italy, and Malta (OECD Public Governance Reviews)*. OECD Publishing. DOI: 10.1787/d7eb0bb6-en

OECD. (2025). *Governing with artificial intelligence*. OECD Publishing., DOI: 10.1787/795de142-

Ooijen, C., Ubaldi, B., & Welby, B. (2019). A data-driven public sector. *OECD Working Papers on Public Governance*. DOI: 10.1787/19934351

Oren, S. (2022). Economics and computation meet cognitive biases. *ACM SIGecom Exchanges*, *20*(1), 67–69. DOI: 10.1145/3572885.3572892

Organisation for Economic Co-operation and Development [OECD]. (2021). *Bridging the digital divide: Inclusive growth in the digital era*. OECD Publishing.

Organisation for Economic Co-operation and Development [OECD]. (2023). *Digital government index 2023: Results and key findings*. OECD Publishing.

Organisation for Economic Co-operation and Development, & CAF Development Bank of Latin America and the Caribbean. (2023). Digital government review of Latin America and the Caribbean: Building inclusive and responsive public services. *OECD Publishing*. DOI: 10.1787/29f32e64-en

Organisation for Economic Co-operation and Development, & Inter-American Development Bank. (2024). 2023 OECD/IDB Digital Government Index of Latin America and the Caribbean: Results and key findings. *OECD Publishing*. DOI: 10.1787/14e1c5e8-en-fr

Organization for Economic Co-operation and Development. (2022). Executive summary. In *OECD public governance reviews*. OECD Publishing., DOI: 10.1787/ccc78971-

Organization for Economic Co-operation and Development. (2022a). *Anticipatory innovation governance*. OECD Publishing., DOI: 10.1787/a20998d5-

Organization for Economic Co-operation and Development. (2023). Emerging technology governance: Towards an anticipatory framework. In Science, O. E. C. D. (Ed.), *Technology and Innovation Outlook*. OECD Publishing., DOI: 10.1787/d67d5380-

Organization for Economic Co-operation and Development. (2024). *Framework for anticipatory governance of emerging technologies. OECD Science, Technology and Industry Policy Papers*. OECD Publishing., DOI: 10.1787/0248ead5-

Orlob, G. T. (1992). Water-quality modelling for decision making. *Journal of Water Resources Planning and Management, 118*(3), 295–307. DOI: 10.1061/(ASCE)0733-9496(1992)118:3(295)

Ostrom, E. (2005). *Understanding institutional diversity*. Princeton University Press.

Oszlak, O. (2024). Gobierno personalizado. [APyS]. *Administración Pública y Sociedad, 17*(17), 65–91. DOI: 10.71047/2524.9568.n17.46560

Panda, M., Hossain, M. M., Puri, R., & Ahmad, A. (2025). Artificial intelligence in action: Shaping the future of public sector. *Digital Policy. Regulation & Governance, 27*(6), 668–686. DOI: 10.1108/DPRG-10-2024-0272

Petracca, E., & Grayot, J. (2023a). Correction to: How can embodied cognition naturalize bounded rationality? *Synthese, 201*(5), 170. DOI: 10.1007/s11229-023-04152-z

Petracca, E., & Grayot, J. (2023b). How can embodied cognition naturalize bounded rationality? *Synthese, 201*(4), 115. DOI: 10.1007/s11229-023-04124-3

Phin, K., & Huot, S. (2026). Generative AI and Cambodian curriculum: Risks and rewards for student learning and research integrity [JEILT]. *Journal of Education Innovation & Language Teaching, 2*(1), 47–59. DOI: 10.63381/jeilt.v2i1.87

Pignot, E., Joullié, J.-E., & Gould, A. M. (2025). Ethical design: A post-Lacanian ethnography of a serious healthcare game. *Journal of Organizational Ethnography, 15*(1), 1–24. DOI: 10.1108/JOE-06-2025-0084

Podsakoff, P. M., MacKenzie, S. B., Lee, J.-Y., & Podsakoff, N. P. (2003). Common method biases in behavioral research: A critical review of the literature and recommended remedies. *The Journal of Applied Psychology, 88*(5), 879–903. DOI: 10.1037/0021-9010.88.5.879 PMID: 14516251

Poli, R. (2017). *Introduction to anticipation studies*. Springer. DOI: 10.1007/978-3-319-63023-6

Pollitt, C., & Bouckaert, G. (2017). *Public management reform: A comparative analysis—Into the age of austerity* (4th ed.). Oxford University Press.

Porcher, S., Cristofini, O., Gimenez, J., & Beuve, J. (2024). Transformation digitale des services publics locaux et valeur publique: Une étude de cas sur la santé et la formation professionnelle en France. *Gestion et management public, 12*(3), 31-47. DOI: 10.3917/gmp.123.0031

Prasodjo, T. (2026). Public trust reloaded: The impact of data transparency and digital participation on government legitimacy in the era of open government. *Golden Ratio of Social Science and Education, 6*(1), 53–67. DOI: 10.52970/grsse.v6i1.1894

Profiroiu, C., Negoi ă, C. I., & Costea, A. V. (2023). Digitalization of public administration in EU member states in times of crisis: The contributions of the national recovery and resilience plans. *International Review of Administrative Sciences*, *90*(2), 336–352. DOI: 10.1177/00208523231177554

Qadri, S. (2025). Artificial intelligence and public administration: Actors, governance, and policies. *Social Science Review Archives*, *3*(4), 3200–3212.

Rahmansya, J., Mehta, A., & Bautista, M. J. (2025). The digital governance gap in Southeast Asia: A comparative study of Indonesia, India, and the Philippines. *Asian Digital Governance Problems*, *2*(1), 1–17. DOI: 10.71435/643063

Raieste, A., Rebane, A., Tapupere, M., & McBride, K. (2024). *Government resilience in the digital age.* Nortal & Oxford Internet Institute.

Raihan, M. M., Subroto, S., Chowdhury, N., Koch, K., Ruttan, E., & Turin, T. C. (2025). Dimensions and barriers for digital (in) equity and digital divide: A systematic integrative review. *Digital Transformation and Society*, *4*(2), 111–127. DOI: 10.1108/DTS-04-2024-0054

Ramekh, S. (2024, March 16). *Opinion: Balancing public trust and cybersecurity.* Future Forum. https://www.futureforum.asia/post/opinion-balancing-public-trust-and-cybersecurity

Rao, K. S. M. (2024). Julia Robinson and game theory. *Resonance*, *29*(6), 745. DOI: 10.1007/s12045-024-0745-6

Real, B., Bertot, J. C., & Jaeger, P. T. (2014). Rural public libraries and digital inclusion: Issues and challenges. *Information Technology and Libraries*, *33*(1), 6–24. DOI: 10.6017/ital.v33i1.5141

RIS. (2023). *Global South and perspectives on development partnerships.* Research and Information System for Developing Countries. https://www.ris.org.in/en/node/3743

Robinson, L., Schulz, J., Dodel, M., Correa, T., Villanueva-Mansilla, E., Leal, S., Magallanes-Blanco, C., Rodriguez-Medina, L., Dunn, H. S., Levine, L., McMahon, R., & Khilnani, A. (2020). Digital inclusion across the Americas and Caribbean. *Social Inclusion (Lisboa)*, *8*(2), 244–259. DOI: 10.17645/si.v8i2.2632

Romanishyn, A., Malytska, O., & Goncharuk, V. (2025). AI-driven disinformation: Policy recommendations for democratic resilience. *Frontiers in Artificial Intelligence*, *8*, 1569115. DOI: 10.3389/frai.2025.1569115 PMID: 40821951

Royal Government of Cambodia. (2022). *Cambodia digital government policy 2022–2035: Establishing digital government to improve the people's quality of life and build trust among the people through better public service provision.* Ministry of Post and Telecommunications. https://mptc.gov.kh/en/2022/04/cambodia-digital-government-policy-2022-2035

Roy, J. (2024). Digital transformation versus Westminster traditionalism: Mindset, mechanisms and critical enablers of systemic adaptation. *Canadian Public Administration, 67*(4), 481–494. DOI: 10.1111/capa.12598

Rozgonyi, K. (2023). Accountability and platforms' governance: The case of online prominence of public service media content. *Internet Policy Review, 12*(4). Advance online publication. DOI: 10.14763/2023.4.1723

Rukanova, B., Van Engelenburg, S., Ubacht, J., Tan, Y.-H., Geurts, M., Sies, M., Molenhuis, M., Slegt, M., & Van Dijk, D. (2023). Public value creation through voluntary business to government information sharing enabled by digital infrastructure innovations. *Government Information Quarterly, 40*(2), 101786. DOI: 10.1016/j.giq.2022.101786

Sadhu, S. K. (2025). Data protection as a public good: leveraging ai/ml for scalable digital resilience. *Journal of Computer Science and Technology Studies.* DOI: 10.32996/jcsts.2025.7.131

Sarewitz, D. (2011). Anticipatory governance of emerging technologies. In Marchant, G. E., Allenby, B. R., & Herkert, J. R. (Eds.), *The growing gap between emerging technologies and legal-ethical oversight* (pp. 95–105). Springer., DOI: 10.1007/978-94-007-1356-7_7

Sarstedt, M., Hair, J. F.Jr, Nitzl, C., Ringle, C. M., & Howard, M. C. (2020). Beyond a tandem analysis of SEM and PROCESS: Use of PLS-SEM for mediation analyses! *International Journal of Market Research, 62*(3), 288–299. DOI: 10.1177/1470785320915686

Sen, A. (1999). *Development as freedom.* Oxford University Press.

Shen, L. Y., Bao, H. J., Wu, Y. Z., & Lu, W. S. (2007). Using bargaining-game theory for negotiating concession period for BOT-type contract. *Journal of Construction Engineering and Management, 133*(5), 385–392. DOI: 10.1061/(ASCE)0733-9364(2007)133:5(385)

Soeng, R., & Kao, T. (2024). Digital government in promoting trade: The case of Cambodia. In L. Chen & F. Kimura (Eds.), *Empowering Online Public Service in Asia: The Digital Frontier* (pp. 269–292). Economic Research Institute for ASEAN and East Asia (ERIA). https://www.eria.org/uploads/10_Chapter-9-The-Case-of-Cambodia.pdf

Sorin, S. (2023). Aumann and game theory. *Revue Économique (Paris), 74*(4), 511–528. DOI: 10.3917/e.reco.744.0511

Sukma, N., & Yamnill, S. (2025). A new public management model for open data collaboration in sustainable digital insurance ecosystems. *Frontiers in Political Science, 7*, 1598403. Advance online publication. DOI: 10.3389/fpos.2025.1598403

Sumar, S., & Martin, A. K. (2024). Dog as man's best friend? Not according to cognitive biases in episodic memory. *Current Psychology (New Brunswick, N.J.), 43*(38), 30306–30310. DOI: 10.1007/s12144-024-06625-x

Sung, W., & Lee, J. (2024). A longitudinal study on the diffusion and the divide in the use of e-government services among vulnerable citizens in Korea. *Government Information Quarterly, 41*(2), 101938. Advance online publication. DOI: 10.1016/j.giq.2024.101938

Sun, P., & Parilina, E. (2025). Hybrid altruistic-Nash equilibrium: Existence and characterization. *International Journal of Game Theory*, *54*(1), 5. DOI: 10.1007/s00182-025-00926-6

Suri, T., & Jack, W. (2016). The long-run poverty and gender impacts of mobile money. *Science*, *354*(6317), 1288–1292. DOI: 10.1126/science.aah5309 PMID: 27940873

Talavera-Ibarra, A. M. (2022). Trends in Latin America: Libraries' challenges magnified by the COVID-19 pandemic. *Library Trends*, *71*(2), 198–214. DOI: 10.1353/lib.2022.a922375

Taleb, N. N. (2007). *The black swan: The impact of the highly improbable*. Random House.

Tang, X., Zena, K., & Fillip. (2025). Communication pathways in multilevel governance: A review of digital innovation and public value. *Review of Communication Research*. DOI: 10.52152/RCR.V13.S9

Tan, S. (2025). A distributed Nesterov's approach for fast Nash equilibrium seeking in noncooperative games. *Journal of Systems Science and Complexity*, *38*(5), 1987–2006. DOI: 10.1007/s11424-025-4353-7

Tariq, M. U. (2024). Integrating ESG Principles Into Corporate Governance for Sustainable Ecosystem Services. In Castanho, R. (Ed.), *ESG and Ecosystem Services for Sustainability* (pp. 89–118). IGI Global., DOI: 10.4018/979-8-3693-3771-4.ch004

Tariq, M. U. (2024). Leveraging artificial intelligence for a sustainable and climate-neutral economy in Asia. In Ordóñez de Pablos, P., Almunawar, M., & Anshari, M. (Eds.), *Strengthening sustainable digitalization of Asian economy and society* (pp. 1–21). IGI Global., DOI: 10.4018/979-8-3693-1942-0.ch001

Tariq, M. U. (2024). Metaverse in business and commerce. In Kumar, J., Arora, M., & Erkol Bayram, G. (Eds.), *Exploring the use of metaverse in business and education* (pp. 47–72). IGI Global., DOI: 10.4018/979-8-3693-5868-9.ch004

Taylor, L. (2017). What is data justice? The case for connecting digital rights and freedoms globally. *Big Data & Society*, *4*(2), 1–14. DOI: 10.1177/2053951717736335

Terziev, V. (2019). Social efficiency as a measure of social activities. *IJASOS – International E-Journal of Advances in Social Sciences, 5*(14), 656–662. https://doi.org/DOI: 10.18769/ijasos.592076

Terziev, V., Georgiev, M., & Simeonov, S. (2025). *Transformation and change of the social and educational system*. gabriell-e-lit.

Tetlock, P. E., & Gardner, D. (2015). *Superforecasting: The art and science of prediction*. Crown.

Thiedmann, P., Dejardin, F., Reiter, L., & Tran, U. S. (2025). Brief online socio-cognitive mindfulness interventions neither improve socio-cognitive mindfulness nor cognitive biases. *Mindfulness*, *16*(6), 1555–1568. DOI: 10.1007/s12671-025-02575-y

Titmuss, R. M. (1974). *Social policy: An introduction*. George Allen & Unwin.

Tonon, C. (2020). La GovTech, nouvelle frontière de la souveraineté numérique. *Institut français des relations internationales (IFRI)*. https://www.ifri.org/sites/default/files/migrated_files/documents/atoms/files/tonon_govtech_nov2020.pdf

Tõnurist, P., & Hanson, A. (2020). *Anticipatory innovation governance: Shaping the future through proactive policy making* [OECD Working Papers on Public Governance No. 44]. OECD Publishing., DOI: 10.1787/cce14d80-

Toots, M., McBride, K., Kalvet, T., & Krimmer, R. (2017). Open data as enabler of public service co-creation: Exploring the drivers and barriers. In 2017 Conference for E-Democracy and Open Government (CeDEM) (pp. 102-112). DOI: 10.1109/CeDEM.2017.12

Törnberg, P. (2023). How platforms govern: Social regulation in digital capitalism. *Big Data & Society*, *10*(1), 20539517231153808. Advance online publication. DOI: 10.1177/20539517231153808

Torres-Vila, L. M. (2024). Strategic ejaculate allocation in the mostly monandrous moth *Lobesia botrana. Behavioral Ecology and Sociobiology*, *78*(8), 92. DOI: 10.1007/s00265-024-03507-x

Trist, E. (1981). *The evolution of socio-technical systems: A conceptual framework and an action research program* (Occasional Paper No. 2). Ontario Quality of Working Life Centre.

Türk, P. (2020). L'État plateforme numérique. *Revue du droit public, 2020*(5), 1189-1212. https://droit.cairn.info/article/RDP_095_1189

Tversky, A., & Kahneman, D. (1974). Judgment under uncertainty: Heuristics and biases. *Science*, *185*(4157), 1124–1131. DOI: 10.1126/science.185.4157.1124 PMID: 17835457

Twizeyimana, J. D., & Andersson, A. (2019). The public value of E-Government — A literature review. *Government Information Quarterly*, *36*(2), 167–178. DOI: 10.1016/j.giq.2019.01.001

U.S. Government Accountability Office. (2023). *High-risk series: Efforts made to achieve progress need to be maintained and expanded to fully address all areas*. GAO.

Ubaldi, B. (2013). *Open government data: Towards empirical analysis of open government data initiatives* [OECD Working Papers on Public Governance No. 22]. OECD Publishing., DOI: 10.1787/5k46bj4f03s7-

UNDP. (2022). *Digital strategy 2022-2025: Creating a world in which digital is an empowering force for people and planet*. United Nations Development Programme. https://digitalstrategy.undp.org

UNDRR. (2015). *Sendai framework for disaster risk reduction 2015–2030*. United Nations Office for Disaster Risk Reduction.

UNESCO, & International Federation of Library Associations and Institutions. (2025). *Global network of libraries and local impact: A policy roadmap to build an inclusive digital future*. UNESCO Digital Library. https://unesdoc.unesco.org/ark:/48223/pf0000396214

UNESCO. (2021). *Recommendation on the ethics of artificial intelligence*. UNESCO.

UNESCO. (2023). *UNESCO's Communication and Information Sector: Upholding information as a public good, advancing universal access, digital inclusion and freedom of expression.* UNESCO. https://unesdoc.unesco.org/ark:/48223/pf0000387119

United Nations Development Programme. (2024). *Universal DPI safeguards framework: A guide to building safe and inclusive DPI for societies.* https://www.undp.org/press-releases/un-releases-universal-dpi-safeguards-framework-promote-safe-and-inclusive-digital-public-infrastructure

United Nations. (2021). *Our common agenda: Report of the Secretary-General.* United Nations.

United Nations. (2022). *United Nations e-government survey 2022: The future of digital government.* United Nations.

Ushakov, V. N., Tarasyev, A. M., & Ershov, A. A. (2024). A supplement to Krasovskii's unification method in differential game theory. *Doklady Mathematics, 110*(2), 386–392. DOI: 10.1134/S1064562424601604

Valle-Cruz, D., & García-Contreras, R. (2023). Towards AI-driven transformation and smart data management: Emerging technological change in the public sector value chain. *Public Policy and Administration, 40*(2), 254–275. DOI: 10.1177/09520767231188401

Van Der Heide, J. (2025). *Data driven & high tech (KB-38) : Digital transformation of the agro-food and life sciences towards a sustainable.* Resilient And Equitable Future State., DOI: 10.18174/693994

Van der Heijden, K. (2005). *Scenarios: The art of strategic conversation* (2nd ed.). Wiley.

Van Dijk, J. (2020). *The digital divide.* Polity Press.

Van Zoonen, L. (2016). Privacy concerns in smart cities. *Government Information Quarterly, 33*(3), 472–480. DOI: 10.1016/j.giq.2016.06.004

Vårheim, A. (2017). Public libraries, community resilience, and social capital. *Information Research,* 22(1), Article colis1642. https://informationr.net/ir/22-1/colis/colis1642.html

Vassil, K. (2016). Estonian e-government ecosystem: Foundations, applications, and outcomes. *World Development, 84,* 1–15. DOI: 10.1016/j.worlddev.2015.06.001

Veil, S. R., & Bishop, B. W. (2014). Opportunities and challenges for public libraries to enhance community resilience. *Risk Analysis, 34*(4), 721–734. DOI: 10.1111/risa.12130 PMID: 24164095

Venkatesh, V., & Bala, H. (2008). Technology Acceptance Model 3 and a research agenda on interventions. *Decision Sciences, 39*(2), 273–315. DOI: 10.1111/j.1540-5915.2008.00192.x

Vera-Baceta, M.-Á., & Gómez-Hernández, J.-A. (2021). *"Digital citizenship spaces" in public libraries: A proposal for their integration within the framework of the National Digital Skills Plan.* Anuario ThinkEPI, 15, Article e15b02. DOI: 10.3145/thinkepi.2021.e15b02

Vestues, K., Mikalsen, M., & Monteiro, E. (2021). Using digital platforms to promote a service-oriented logic in public sector organizations. *A case studies.* 1–10. DOI: 10.24251/HICSS.2021.269

Vial, G. (2019). Understanding digital transformation: A review and a research agenda. *The Journal of Strategic Information Systems, 28*(2), 118–144. DOI: 10.1016/j.jsis.2019.01.003

Villodre, J. (2025). A three-model approach to understand social media-mediated transparency in public administrations. *International Review of Administrative Sciences, 91*(1), 111–129. DOI: 10.1177/00208523241261896

Virtanen, P., & Harri, J. (2023). Public value creation mechanisms in the context of public service logic: An integrated conceptual framework. *International Journal of Public Administration*. Advance online publication. DOI: 10.1080/14719037.2023.2268111

Voorberg, W. H., Bekkers, V. J. J. M., & Tummers, L. G. (2015). A systematic review of co-creation and co-production with citizens in public innovation. *Public Management Review, 17*(9), 1333–1357. DOI: 10.1080/14719037.2014.930505

Walker, W. E., Haasnoot, M., & Kwakkel, J. H. (2013). Adapt or perish: A review of planning approaches for adaptation under deep uncertainty. *Sustainability (Basel), 5*(3), 955–979. DOI: 10.3390/su5030955

Walravens, N., & Ballon, P. (2013). Platform business models for smart cities: From control and value to governance and public value. *IEEE Communications Magazine, 51*(6), 72–79. DOI: 10.1109/MCOM.2013.6525598

Wang, J., Zhou, X., Ma, Y., & Choi, Y. (2025, May 20). Yunning, & Choi, Y. (2025a). Public data elements and enterprise digital transformation: A quasi-natural experiment based on open government data platforms for sustainable urban planning. *Sustainability (Basel), 17*(10), 4676. Advance online publication. DOI: 10.3390/su17104676

Wang, X., Lei, M., Wang, D., & Cao, J. (2025b). Research on dynamic incentive mechanism for co-creation of value in innovation-oriented platform ecosystem considering supervision. *Symmetry*, *17*(11), 1884. Advance online publication. DOI: 10.3390/sym17111884

Wang, Y., Wang, J., Gao, F., & Song, J. (2024). Unveiling value patterns via deep reinforcement learning in heterogeneous data analytics. *Patterns (New York, N.Y.)*, *5*(5), 100965. Advance online publication. DOI: 10.1016/j.patter.2024.100965 PMID: 38800362

Wang, Y., Yang, Y., & Deng, X. (2025a). Bounded rationality quantum duopoly games with asymmetric information. *Quantum Information Processing*, *24*(6), 188. DOI: 10.1007/s11128-025-04811-9

Wang, Z., Zhang, C., & Tan, Z. (2025b). Inefficiency of multiplicative approximate Nash equilibrium for scheduling games. *Journal of Combinatorial Optimization*, *49*(3), 38. DOI: 10.1007/s10878-025-01274-7

Webb, J. (2021). Rethinking the governance of technology in the digital age. In Kleinman, D. L., Cloud-Hansen, K., Handelsman, J., & Hurlbut, M. J. (Eds.), *The Oxford handbook of the science of science communication* (pp. 687–701). Oxford University Press., DOI: 10.1093/oxfordhb/9780198800682.013.58

Weigl, L., Roth, T., Amard, A., & Zavolokina, L. (2024). When public values and user-centricity in e-government collide — A systematic review. *Government Information Quarterly*, *41*(3), 101956. DOI: 10.1016/j.giq.2024.101956

Wirtz, B. W., Langer, P. F., & Schmidt, F. W. (2021). Digital government: Business model development for public value creation - A dynamic capabilities based framework. *Public Administration Quarterly*, *45*(3), 232–255. DOI: 10.37808/paq.45.3.2

Wirtz, B. W., Weyerer, J. C., & Geyer, C. (2019). Artificial intelligence and the public sector—Applications and challenges. *International Journal of Public Administration*, *42*(7), 596–615. DOI: 10.1080/01900692.2018.1498103

Wirtz, B. W., Weyerer, J. C., & Kehl, I. (2022). Governance of artificial intelligence: A risk and guideline-based integrative framework. *Government Information Quarterly*, *39*(4), 101685. DOI: 10.1016/j.giq.2022.101685

World Bank. (2020). *Bridging the digital divide: Harnessing data through cloud computing*. World Bank Group. https://blogs.worldbank.org/en/digital-development/bridging-the-digital-divide--harnessing-data-through-cloud-compu?utm_source

World Bank. (2022). *Social protection and jobs responses to COVID-19: A real-time review of country measures*. World Bank.

World Bank. (2022). *World development report 2022: Finance for an equitable recovery*. World Bank.

World Bank. (2023). *Digital progress and trends report 2023*. World Bank. https://www.worldbank.org/en/publication/digital-progress-and-trends-report

World Economic Forum. (2024). *The global risks report 2024 (19th ed.)*. World Economic Forum.

Xiao, J., Xiao, H., & Li, C. (2024). The complexity of the APP competition model with bounded rationality in platform ecosystem. *Electronic Commerce Research*, •••, 1–27. DOI: 10.1007/s10660-024-09868-9

Yabe, T., Rao, P., Ukkusuri, S., & Cutter, S. (2022). Toward data-driven, dynamical complex systems approaches to disaster resilience. *In Proceedings of the National Academy of Sciences of the United States of America,* 119. DOI: 10.1073/pnas.2111997119

Yannis, C., & Gerasimos, K. (2026). Rule-based AI systems for public governance: A framework for smarter, transparent, and citizen-centered governance. In *Artificial intelligence and government: Examining the roles and uses of AI in enhancing government operations* (pp. 59–87). DOI: 10.1007/978-3-032-12344-2_4

Young, M. M., Bullock, J. B., & Lecy, J. D. (2019). Artificial discretion as a tool of governance: A framework for understanding the impact of artificial intelligence on public administration. *Perspectives on Public Management and Governance*, *2*(4), 301–313. DOI: 10.1093/ppmgov/gvz014

Yukhno, A. (2024). Digital transformation: Exploring big data governance in public administration. *Public Organization Review*, *24*(1), 335–349. DOI: 10.1007/s11115-022-00694-x

Zhalgas, Y. (2025). State creative procurement in the digital age: challenges of transparency and public trust. *Человек и Культура*. DOI: 10.25136/2409-8744.2025.5.75808

Zhang, Y., Lian, B., & Lewis, F. L. (2025). Distributed global Nash equilibrium of interactive adversarial graphical games. *Journal of Systems Science and Complexity*, *38*(2), 613–632. DOI: 10.1007/s11424-025-4542-4

Zhao, B., Cheng, S., Schiff, K. J., & Kim, Y. (2023). Digital transparency and citizen participation: Evidence from the online crowdsourcing platform of the City of Sacramento. *Government Information Quarterly*, *40*(4), 101868. DOI: 10.1016/j.giq.2023.101868

Zhu, X. (2026). Public administration with, of, and through AI: Toward a new paradigm in the era of intelligence. *Journal of Chinese Governance*, *11*(1), 30–57. DOI: 10.1080/23812346.2025.2578589

Zuboff, S. (2019). *The age of surveillance capitalism: The fight for a human future at the new frontier of power*. PublicAffairs.

About the Contributors

Rafael Perez-Uribe is a Doctor in Business Sciences Nebrija University. Diploma of Advanced Studies in Applied Economics, Nebrija University. Master in Organization Management at EAN University. Maître es Sciences Université du Québec a Chicoutimi. Specialist in Evaluation and Construction of Management Indicators for Higher Education, School of Business Administration. Postgraduate studies such as Kenkyusei (Researcher attached) in Total Quality Control and Quality Circles, Fukushima University, Japan. Business Administrator, Jorge Tadeo Lozano University. Former Full professor was assigned to the Research Department and director of the management research group of large, small, and medium-sized companies (G3PYMES-A1 in Minciencias until 2020) of EAN University. At the present time, Minciencias Senior Researcher and independent professor and Consultant in Management Process. Modeling expert. I have participated in the structuring of the following management models that include diagnosis, evaluation, and organizational intervention: MMOM- model of modernization and innovation for the management of organizations-; PENTEX- Pentagon of excellence-; RISE -Innovation route for the business sustainability-; TMN-Trust Methodological Network-; CSM-Corporate Strategic Management-; IMOS-Innovation Model for Organizational Sustainability-; MMAI -Management Model from Artifitial Intelligence-.

Ivan Vargas-Ramirez is a PhD in Management with two Master's degrees, one in Industrial Engineering and another in Government and Public Policy. Postdoctoral visiting researcher specialized in governance models for sustainability. Director of Investproject VR and Associate Researcher at Minciencias (Colombia). Expert in the design, implementation, and evaluation of national and international public plans and policies, with extensive experience in public administration, governance, and evidence-based policymaking in complex socio-economic and environmental contexts.

Maria Ramirez-Garzon is a PhD in Administration, Master's degree in teaching and Specialist in human resources. Experience in Teaching, Research and Business Consulting. Junior Researcher Minciencias. Independent Management Professor. Investproject VR.

Luz Lozano-Correa is a Doctor in Administration, Master in Organizational Management, Master in Science, Specialist in Human Resources Management and Psychologist. Certified Master Coach. Experience as a consultant in national and multinational companies related to corporate human talent management processes oriented towards humanistic and organizational training.; planning, design, development and monitoring of alternative processes of excellence to the organizational value chain, coaching and feedback, Train the trainer, development of management skills, effective management skills, Change Management and strategies, Strengthening of Teamwork and Internalization of Corporate Values and Competencies, experiential education, commercial growth workshops, diagnosis, evaluation and intervention of organizational climate, management and business improvement. University teacher-researcher in undergraduate and postgraduate courses in management areas related to human development and organizational management. National and international speaker on issues of management and strategic processes in organizations and on the development of skills, human talent, coaching-mentoring, emotional intelligence, quality of work life, occupational health, customer service, leadership, development of "human talents"." through entrepreneurship, change management, development of high-performance teams, among others. Speaker at different events on topics related to Human Talent, Coaching and Social Responsibility.

***

Ranjithkumar A is currently serving as an Assistant Professor of Political Science at the School of Law, Vel Tech University, Avadi, Chennai, Tamil Nadu. With a distinguished academic and professional career, he holds a Ph.D. in Politics and International Studies from Pondicherry University, a Master of Population Studies (MPS) from the International Institute for Population Sciences, Mumbai, and an M.A. in Development Administration from Gandhigram Rural Institute – Deemed University. He has also completed a Postgraduate Diploma in Industrial Relations and Labour Law (PGDIR & LL) from Pondicherry University and a B.P.Ed. from Vinayaka Missions University, Salem. Dr. Ranjithkumar has qualified the National Eligibility Test (NET) for Assistant Professor in Human Rights and Duties, Political Science, and Public Administration, conducted by the University Grants Commission (UGC), and was awarded the Dr. S. Radhakrishnan Postdoctoral Fellowship in

Humanities and Social Sciences for the year 2014-15. His professional experience includes roles as an Assistant Professor at DLR Arts and Science College, Arcot, and Gandhigram Rural Institute, as well as research positions at Alagappa University, the National Law School of India University, and the Institute of Grassroots Governance. Dr. Ranjithkumar's research focuses on the Indian Political System, Local Government, Political Thought and Theories, Dalit Studies, and Development Administration. He has published over 35 research papers in leading journals and authored/edited 10 books on topics such as social justice, gender, and caste. He has received an International Travel Grant from the Indian Council of Social Science Research (ICSSR) to participate in the "Democratization and Autocratization: IPSA 75th Anniversary Conference" in Lisbon, Portugal, and Financial Assistance from ICSSR, Hyderabad, for organizing a National Conference on "Empowering Vulnerable Communities: Strategies for Inclusive Social Development." Dr. Ranjithkumar is an active member of professional bodies such as the International Political Science Association (IPSA) and the Indian Political Science Association, and he has organized over 10 international webinars and seminars. His areas of interest include Indian politics, local governance, Dalit studies, gender studies, and human rights.

Walter Barragán Rodríguez is a Grants Finance Executive at the University of Malta, dedicated to strengthening the university's research performance through the strategic and financial facilitation of externally-funded projects. With a career building up to this role for over 10 years, his background includes serving as an Economic Researcher and Consultant for key organizations such as the International Organization for Migration (IOM) and local government entities. Academically, he holds a Master's Degree in Public Administration from Universidad Anáhuac México and a degree in Economics. He has authored publications on socioeconomic impact and regional competitiveness, reinforcing his analytical work in academic administration

Anang Cahyono, S.AP., S.H., M.Si. is a senior lecturer with 15 years of academic experience, currently serving as Dean of the Faculty of Engineering at the University of Tulungagung (2022–2026) and as a member of the Tulungagung Regency Education Council, holding a doctoral degree in Public Administration, actively engaged as a permanent faculty member, an accomplished researcher with an H-index of 9 and 2,450 citations in 2025, a recipient of national research grants from the Indonesian Ministry of Research and Higher Education for seven consecutive years, an author of reference books and intellectual property in governance and digital governance, and a contributor to Scopus-indexed and SINTA 2–accredited journals.

Alberto Merced Castro Valencia is a full-time professor and researcher affiliated with the Department of Business Management Engineering at the Tecnológico Nacional de México/Instituto Tecnológico José Mario Molina Pasquel y Henríquez, Zapopan Academic Unit. He is a member of Mexico's National System of Researchers, where he conducts research in the field of economic and financial sciences, with a focus on public finance, fiscal policy, exchange rates, economic governance, and applied macroeconomic analysis. He has a solid academic and research trajectory, actively contributing to the generation of scientific knowledge through the publication of articles in peer-reviewed and indexed journals, as well as book chapters and research projects with impact on public policy analysis and economic development in Mexico and Latin America. His work is characterized by the use of quantitative and econometric methodologies aimed at supporting decision-making in the public sector. He has participated as a speaker in national and international conferences, notably at the XIV International Conference on Public Finance at Universidad Panamericana, where he received recognition for the quality of his research. He also collaborates in academic networks and inter-institutional projects focused on strengthening applied research and the training of highly qualified human capital. In the teaching domain, he delivers courses in finance, accounting, and research methodology, contributing to the development of professionals with critical thinking, analytical rigor, and ethical commitment. His academic work is distinguished by the integration of scientific research with professional practice, promoting a strategic and innovative perspective in business and public management. Currently, his research lines focus on anticipatory governance, institutional resilience, fiscal sustainability, and the analysis of public policies in contexts of uncertainty, with the aim of contributing to the design of evidence-based solutions for contemporary economic challenges.

Sovannaroth Chheang earned her bachelor's degree in English from Build Bright University, Phnom Penh, Cambodia in 2016, after teaching both part-time and full-time English at the Kindergarten Association. She taught English and was the general assistant at Sovanna Elton Foreign Language School (SELS) in Phnom Penh. She has extensive experiences in classroom administration, language instruction, curriculum designs, and student involvement, complementing the school's foreign language learning objectives. Her academic goals are pursuing a master's degree in English education, related humanities and social sciences, classroom innovation, and research-informed teaching. She combines academic research with practical experiences to improve English education in Cambodia and social science research, including Scopus-indexed publications (Author ID: 60466414900).

Ismail El Bazi holds a Doctorate in Computer Science from Hassan 1er University and an Engineering degree in Computer Engineering from Cadi Ayyad University. After 12 years of professional experience in the field of Software Engineering with International IT companies, he joined the Sultan Moulay Slimane University in 2019 as Associate Professor. His research focuses are Arabic Natural Language Processing, Data Science, and Agentic Intelligence.

Marin Georgiev is an Associate Professor from Georgi Rakovski Military Academy, Sofia, Bulgaria. Ph.D. in Organisation and Management at Vasil Levski National Military University, Veliko Tarnovo, Bulgaria. Assoc. Prof. Georgiev has over 200 scientific papers, articles, and reports in Bulgarian, Russian, and English published in scientific journals and proceedings of international conferences, 2 monographs in Bulgarian, and 1 textbook. There are more than 40 publications in the referenced systems of Web of Science and Scopus. His research interests are in the areas of Economics, Education, and National security.

Sovanna Huot is a PhD candidate in Political Science at the University of Delhi, India. He serves as Vice Principal at a Cambodian Government High School, overseeing academic leadership and school administration. He earned a Master of Education in High School Principalship from the National Institute of Education (NIE) in Phnom Penh in 2022. His research focuses on education governance, digital transformation in education, policy implementation, school leadership, and comparative public policy in developing countries. With teaching and publication experience in political science and education—his work appears in Scopus-indexed publications (Author ID: 59316244400)—his interdisciplinary background makes him well-equipped to edit a volume exploring governance, policy, and education across global, national, and local (glonalcal) contexts.

Youssef Jouali holds a Ph.D. in Economics and Management from the Faculty of Legal, Economic, and Social Sciences in Casablanca. He currently works as a faculty member and researcher at the National School of Business and Management in Béni Mellal (ENCG Béni Mellal), where he teaches courses in taxation, management control, and financial engineering, while also supervising students on their capstone projects. His research focuses primarily on earnings management, artificial intelligence, corporate governance, social and green entrepreneurship, and issues related to sustainable developme

Alejandra Medina Lozano is currently the Director of the Zapopan Academic Unit of the Instituto Tecnológico José Mario Molina Pasquel y Henríquez, where she leads academic, administrative, and institutional strengthening processes aimed at educational quality, research, and engagement with the productive and social environment. She is a professor-researcher and a member of Mexico's National System of Researchers, a distinction that recognizes her trajectory in the generation of scientific knowledge and her contribution to academic development in the country. Her research work has focused on the analysis of relevant issues within the fields of economic-administrative sciences and management, promoting rigorous and applied approaches to address contemporary challenges. She has extensive experience in higher education teaching, human capital development, and participation in research projects, as well as in the publication of articles in peer-reviewed journals and book chapters. Her academic work is characterized by a commitment to excellence, educational innovation, and the strengthening of institutional capacities. In the field of academic management, she has promoted strategic initiatives aimed at academic development, the continuous improvement of educational programmes, and the consolidation of academic research groups, contributing to the positioning of the institution at both regional and national levels. Dr. Medina Lozano is distinguished by her leadership, spirit of service, and commitment to the comprehensive education of students, as well as by her contribution to strengthening the higher education system in Mexico.

Shishir Negi is a Doctoral researcher at Graphic Era (Deemed to be university) with training in sociology and economics. His work engages questions of governance, institutional change, digital transformation, and social inequality in contemporary societies also serving as Research Associate with the Office of the Chief Electoral Officer, Uttarakhand, contributing to election management frameworks, training pedagogy, and capacity building initiatives. Experienced in instructional design, curriculum development, and multi-stakeholder coordination. Adept at translating complex policy research into actionable training materials and governance solutions for government bodies and international organizations.

Abdellah Ousri is an Associate Professor of Economics and Management and a Ph.D. candidate in Management Sciences. His research focuses on financial auditing, artificial intelligence in auditing, organizational governance, and digital transformation. He is also interested in quantitative research methods in management and enhancing the quality of financial reporting.

Varanasi Rahul is an Assistant Professor at Acharya Institute of Graduate Studies, Bangalore, holds three postgraduate degrees (M.Com in Accounting & Taxation, M.Com in Management, and MA in History) and is a semi-qualified Cost Accountant. He has cleared UGC NET in Commerce twice, AP SET in Commerce, History, and Management, and TS SET in Commerce. With 3 years of teaching experience and 6 months at PwC, he is also a freelance archaeologist, epigraphist, and numismatist. He has authored 3 books, published 6 research articles, contributed 9 book chapters, and written 30+ newspaper articles. Rahul has applied for 11 patents, with 1 granted and 09 published.

Rajveer Rawlin holds a PhD and an MBA in Finance and serves as an Associate Professor at CHRIST University. He has tracked capital markets in both the US and India since 1993, specializing in macroeconomic cycles, banking profitability metrics, and econometric investment analysis.

Daniel Salazar Rodríguez is a university faculty member and doctoral candidate affiliated with the Escuela de Ciencias Administrativas, Contables, Económicas y de Negocios (ECACEN) at the Universidad Nacional Abierta y a Distancia (UNAD), Colombia, where he serves as National Director of the Master's Program in Marketing. He holds extensive expertise in strategic marketing, neuromarketing, and business administration, with over 15 years of teaching experience at the undergraduate and graduate levels. His research interests include territorial marketing, consumer behavior, strategic foresight, and digital learning environments. He has led formative research seminars, supervised graduate thesis projects, and coordinated academic programs in marketing and business administration. He also serves as an entrepreneurship project evaluator at Universidad Sergio Arboleda's Center for Innovation, Entrepreneurship, and Business.

Muhammad Usman Tariq is a strategic higher education leader and scholar with more than 18 years of international experience across academia, research, and industry. He holds dual doctorates, a PhD in Artificial Intelligence and a Doctorate in Business Administration and has published extensively as the author of research articles, case studies, book chapters, and academic texts. His contributions also include several patents, reflecting his applied research in technology, business, and education. He is the Founder and CEO of TheCaseHQ.com, a global hub for professional certification programmes, narrative and video case studies, and digital learning innovation. In addition, he serves as President of the Gulf Higher Education Network (Gulf HE), an initiative dedicated to advancing academic practice, faculty development, and institutional collaboration across the region. He is a Principal Fellow of Advance HE (UK), Chartered Fellow of the CIPD (UK), Senior Fellow of SEDA (UK), and a Senior Member of IEEE, reflecting his standing as both an academic innovator and a global professional leader.

Venelin Terziev is a Professor from Angel Kanchev Rousse University – Bulgaria, Vasil Levski National Military University, Veliko Tarnovo, Bulgaria, and University of Telecommunications and Post, Sofia, Bulgaria. D.Sc. in Economics – “Organization and management in the sphere of immaterial production (defence and national security)" at the Vasil Levski National Military University – Veliko Tarnovo, Bulgaria; D.Sc. in Economics – "Finance, currency, credit, and insurance (social security)" at Dimitar Tzenov Academy of Economics – Svishtov, Bulgaria; D.Sc. in Social Activities – "Organization and management of social activities" at Burgas Free University – Burgas, Bulgaria; Ph.D. in Political economy at Chernorisets Hrabar Varna Free University – Bulgaria. Full Member of the Russian Academy of Natural History, Moscow, Russia. Prof. Terziev has over 2000 scientific papers, articles, and reports in Bulgarian, Russian, English, and French published in scientific journals and proceedings of international conferences; 40 monographs in English and Russian; 4 monographs in Bulgarian and 4 textbooks and handbooks.

Nidhi Tyagi is working as an Professor at Graphic Era (Deemed to be University), Dehradun. under the aegis of Department of Humanities & Social Sciences. She was the founder member of Law College of Teerthanker Mahaveer University, Moradabad and rendered her services to the esteemed organization for a period of 10 years. Dr. Nidhi has vast teaching experience of 19 years and has represented the Department in BCI, UGC, NAAC inspections and various administrative and academic activities. Besides, she has been contributing to different domains of Sociology and Indian Society. She has devoted herself to scholastic research and published many outstanding papers in different academic journals. Furthermore, Dr. Nidhi has presented more than 22 papers at national and international conferences.

José Vargas-Hernández, M.B.A.; Ph.D. Member of the National System of Researchers of Mexico and a research professor at Tecnológico Mario Molina Unidad Zapopan formerly at University Center for Economic and Managerial Sciences, University of Guadalajara. Professor Vargas-Hernández has a Ph. D. in Public Administration and a Ph.D. in Organizational Economics. He has undertaken studies in Organisational Behaviour and has a Master of Business Administration, published four books and more than 200 papers in international journals and reviews (some translated to English, French, German, Portuguese, Farsi, Chinese, etc.) and more than 300 essays in national journals and reviews. He has obtained several international Awards and recognition.

Index

A

B

C

D

E

F

G

I

L

M

N

P

R

S

T

W

www.ingramcontent.com/pod-product-compliance
Lightning Source LLC
LaVergne TN
LVHW062029101126
852251LV00005B/61